Michael & hi

Without y
would never have
happened.

Much love
Kay.

Provincial Society and Empire

WORLDS OF THE EAST INDIA COMPANY

ISSN 1752-5667

This series offers high-quality studies of the East India Company, drawn from across a broad chronological, geographical and thematic range. The rich history of the Company has long been of interest to those who engage in the study of Britain's commercial, imperial, maritime and military past, but in recent years it has also attracted considerable attention from those who explore art, cultural and social themes within an historical context. The series will thus provide a forum for scholars from different disciplinary backgrounds, and for those whose have interests in the history of Britain (London and the regions), India, China, Indonesia, as well as the seas and oceans.

The editors welcome submissions from both established scholars and those beginning their career; monographs are particularly encouraged but volumes of essays will also be considered. All submissions will receive rapid, informed attention. They should be sent in the first instance to:

Professor H. V. Bowen, Department of History, Swansea University, Swansea SA2 8PP. Email: h.v.bowen@swansea.ac.uk

Previously published titles are listed at the back of this volume

PROVINCIAL SOCIETY AND EMPIRE

The Cumbrian Counties and the East Indies, 1680–1829

K. J. Saville-Smith

THE BOYDELL PRESS

First published 2018
The Boydell Press, Woodbridge

ISBN 978-1-78327-281-5

The Boydell Press is an imprint of Boydell & Brewer Ltd
PO Box 9, Woodbridge, Suffolk IP12 3DF, UK
and of Boydell & Brewer Inc.
668 Mt Hope Avenue, Rochester, NY 14620–2731, USA
website: www.boydellandbrewer.com

A CIP catalogue record for this title is available from the British Library

The publisher has no responsibility for the continued existence or accuracy of URLs for external or third-party internet websites referred to in this book, and does not guarantee that any content on such websites is, or will remain, accurate or appropriate

This publication is printed on acid-free paper

Typeset by Fakenham Prepress Solutions, Fakenham, Norfolk NR21 8NN

Printed and bound in Great Britain by
TJ International Ltd, Padstow, Cornwall

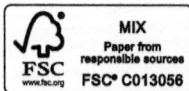

MIX
Paper from
responsible sources
FSC
www.fsc.org   FSC® C013056

CONTENTS

List of Illustrations   vii
Acknowledgements   ix
List of Abbreviations   xi
Glossary   xiii

Chapter 1 The Provincial World and Global Encounters   1
Chapter 2 Cumbrian Contexts, Patterns and Lives   31
Chapter 3 Why Go to the East Indies?   67
Chapter 4 'Passage to India'   97
Chapter 5 Returning and Returns   131
Chapter 6 Conclusion: 'Use of Globes'   167

Appendix A East Indies Enumerated Cumbrian Men   187
Appendix B East Indies Enumerated Cumbrian Women   223
Appendix C East Indies Women, Associated Cumbrian Men and
     Their Children   227
Appendix D Hudleston, Kin Connections and the East Indies   231
Appendix E East Indies connections of the Winders, Stephensons
     and Fawcetts   239
Appendix F East Indies connections of the Braddylls, Wilsons and
     Gales   245
Appendix G Kin Connections of Catherine Holme   249
Appendix H Kin Connections of Thomas Cust   253

Bibliography   257
Index   283

ILLUSTRATIONS

Plates

2.1 Memorial stone of Edward Stephenson before the altar of
Crosthwaite Parish Church, Keswick (Photo by the author)   46

4.1 An Interesting scene on board an East-Indiaman, showing the
Effects of a heavy Lurch, after dinner, circa 1818 (Reproduced by
permission of the National Maritime Museum, Greenwich)   98

5.1 John Bellasis's Randall Lodge, Malabar Hill, Bombay
(Reproduced by permission of the British Library)   155

5.2 John Stables by George Romney (Reproduced by permission
Hulton Archive, Getty Images)   158

5.3 Mrs Stables and her daughters Harriet and Maria, engraved
by J. R. Smith from painting by George Romney   159

5.4 Major Pierson and the Brahman (Reproduced by courtesy of the
Yale Center for British Art, Gift of Mr and Mrs J. Richardson
Dilworth, Yale BA 1938, transfer from the Yale University Art
Gallery)   160

Figures

1.1 Origins of East India Company Chairmen, c. 1700–1829   18

1.2 Origins of East India Company Directors, c. 1700–1829   18

2.1 Number and Moving Average of Appointments/Licences of
Cumbrian Men by Year of Initial Appointment or Licence to the
East Indies, 1680–1829   33

2.2 Rate of Male Appointment and Licences to the East Indies Prior
to 1804   36

2.3 Comparative Social Composition of British-born Bengal Army
Officers and Cumbrian East India Appointees and Licensees   39

2.4 Kin-nodes and Connections through Cumbrian Men Involved in
the East Indies, 1688–1829   43

2.5 Ainslie Kin, the East Indies and the Cumbrian Iron Industry   59

5.1 Average Probate Value (England and Wales) of East Indies
Cumbrian Men and Westmorland and Cumbrian Men with
Probate Dying April 1858–1867   139

Map

2.1 Cumbrian Natal Locations of Enumerated Men Involved in the
     East Indies   38

Tables

2.1 Lysons' Cumberland Gentlemen and Baronets Seats 1816 and
     the East Indies   41
5.1 Probate Values East Indies Cumbrian Men Dying After 1857 in
     England and Wales   137

The author and publishers are grateful to all the institutions and individuals listed for permission to reproduce the materials in which they hold copyright. Every effort has been made to trace the copyright holders; apologies are offered for any omission, and the publishers will be pleased to add any necessary acknowledgement in subsequent editions.

ACKNOWLEDGEMENTS

This book represents many hours alone, but it has never been lonely. The research and writing has thrust me directly into a crush of eighteenth-century Cumbrians. There are many residing in the twenty-first century who accompanied me and contributed to this book. My thanks to Francesca Halfacre of the Cumbria Archive Service; John Creagh who designed the map and the kin-related graphics; and Peter Sowden and Nick Bingham of Boydell & Brewer who guided me through the intricacies of publication while valuing the importance of the narrative.

I owe a profound debt to many at Lancaster University but particularly to Professor Angus Winchester and Dr James Taylor for their critical gaze and shrewd commentary based on deep familiarity with Cumbria and the changing world of British business respectively. Thanks, too, to Professor Clare Anderson (Leicester University) and Dr Deborah Sutton (Lancaster University) for their encouragement and astute observations drawing on their innovative work on global, India and imperial histories.

There is not space to list the many others whose friendship and support have been so important to the completion of this book. I must make special mention of my cousins Michael and Liz Corfe, who, along with extended family and my fictive kin, provided much appreciated hospitality during my periodic research trips to England. My colleague and friend Ruth Fraser generously covered my responsibilities as well as her own when I was immersed in the archives. Immeasurable thanks to Nina Saville-Smith, who helped me decipher eighteenth-century script, and her patient, even enthusiastic, response to being told about one more fragmentary Cumbrian biography. It is impossible to overstate the importance of my partner Bev James's love, confidence, domestic support, and the assistance she gave with typical generosity as well as a critical and intelligent eye.

ABBREVIATIONS

BL	British Library
Bucks.	Buckinghamshire
CAS	Cumbrian Archive Service
Cumb.	Cumberland
CWAAS	Cumberland and Westmorland Antiquarian and Archaeological Society
Eng.	England
HEIC	Honourable East India Company. See East India Company in the glossary
IOR	India Office Records held in the British Library
Lancs.	Lancashire
LAS	Lancashire Archive Service
NUM	Nottingham University Manuscripts Collection
OXDNB	*Oxford Dictionary of National Biography*
PCC PROB	*Prerogative Court of Canterbury and Related Probate Jurisdictions: Will Registers*
PPR National Probate Calendar	Principal Probate Registry, *Calendar of the Grants of Probate and Letters of Administration made in the Probate Registries of the High Court of Justice in England*
Westm.	Westmorland

GLOSSARY

Anglo-Indian	During the long eighteenth century this term was used for individuals defined as a national of the British Isles but who had been born in or lived much of their lives in the East Indies. A term with multiple meanings, by the late nineteenth and twentieth century it was increasingly, but not universally, used to refer to children of fathers from the British Isles with Indian mothers. The latter were also referred to as Eurasian.
batta	Additional allowances over and above salaries and stipends.
budgerow	Large boat used on the Ganges with commodious accommodation providing a luxurious but slow form of travel. Used for goods also. Usually hired for pleasure trips, but owned by wealthy Indians and foreigners.
cadet	East India Company appointees to military service. This term also refers to a younger son but this meaning is rarely used in this book.
cadetship	Entry level for military appointees to the East India Company's military service.
consols	Consolidated annuities. A form of bonds issued by the Bank of England.
Cumbrian	Native of Cumberland or refers to the Cumbrian counties.
Cumbrian counties	Cumberland, Westmorland and Lancashire North of the Sands.
customary tenure	Customary tenantright allows tenants to devise or sell land but required payments to the manor when tenants changed and the lord of the manor changed. There were a variety of other customary dues to which the tenant was liable, but this also gave tenants significant rights including restraining the levels of fines and rents.

East India Company	Joint stock company given royal assent for the monopoly of trade in East Indies until trade was deregulated in 1694. A second joint stock company for East Indies trade was established by act of parliament in 1698. This new company, the English Company Trading to the East Indies, was merged with the old company in 1708 and a trade monopoly re-established. The amalgamated company was formally named the United Company of Merchants of England Trading to the East Indies. Also known as the Honourable East India Company (HEIC) and John Company.
East Indiaman	A ship built for East Indies service contracted by or built by the East India Company.
East Indies	A term of variable meaning and often applied inconsistently in the eighteenth century. In this book, it refers to the areas in which the East India Company operated or sought influence including the Indian sub-continent, South East Asia and parts of China.
firman	An official permission, patent, order, passport or other recognition or proclamation issued by the Mughal emperor.
long eighteenth century	Somewhat variable in definition, in this book it refers to the period from around the Glorious Revolution in 1688 to 1829.
nabob	Anglicisation of nawab, referring to Anglo-Indians who have acquired wealth, influence and power through their activities in the East Indies. A contemporary term.
nabobina	A more recently used term to refer to the wives, and sometimes daughters, of nabobs.
nawab	A title bestowed by Mughal emperors to local Muslim rulers in semi-autonomous states and provincial governors.
pagoda	A unit of currency. The British initially struck gold pagodas to emulate the coinage used by Indian rulers. They came in various forms and metals. The most valuable were star pagodas.
rupee	Silver coin used throughout India and adopted by the East India Company.
ship's husband	A managing owner of a ship, usually owning a proportion of a ship but given managerial responsibility by other owners.

sicca rupee	Applied to rupees minted in the current year.
Westmerian	Native of Westmorland.
writer	East India Company appointees to the merchant and civil services.
writership	Junior position in the East India Company's merchant and civil services.

One

THE PROVINCIAL WORLD AND GLOBAL ENCOUNTERS

During the long eighteenth century thousands of men and women made their way from the British Isles to the East Indies. Most were appointees and licensees of the East India Company: factors, company and free merchants or military men and their wives and daughters. A few arrived in the East Indies through routes unregulated by the East India Company and established themselves as traders, shopkeepers, soldiers of fortune and providers of services from hairdressing to portraiture to the expatriate communities.[1] It was on the entrepreneurship, experiences and ambitions of these sojourners that British India was to be built. Without them, there would have been no India to substitute for the loss of the American colonies. There would have been no jewel in the British imperial crown.

The provincial origins, motivations and activities of these sojourners have been largely ignored in the history of the empire and emergence of the global world. Our understanding of the global world and imperial expansion has been principally framed by one of three concerns: the evolution and operations of the East India Company; the establishment and dynamics of British rule in India through the development of British official families; and cultural and political impacts of Anglo-Indian families, particularly nabobs. Those narratives situate eighteenth-century sojourners to the East Indies from the British Isles as either part of an emerging company state, servants pursing the interests and logics of a transnational company or part of a national imperial project in which Britain's empire-building was inextricably entwined with nation-building. Either way, the experiences, origins and motivations of eighteenth-century sojourners have been considered primarily within the interface between the global and the national.

[1] H. Furber, *Private Fortunes and Company Profits in the India Trade in the 18th Century* (Aldershot: Variorum, 1997), IV, pp. 255–284; S. Ghosh, *The Social Condition of the British Community in Bengal 1757–1800* (Leiden, E. J. Brill, 1970), pp. 9–32, 59.

Similarly, histories of regional and provincial change have given almost no attention to the East Indies. Yet the men and women who ventured to the East Indies came from somewhere, and that somewhere was, for many, the provincial world. Counties beyond London, provincial towns and rural villages made an enormous commitment of human, financial and social capital to ventures in the East Indies. For instance, the British Library India Office Family Search Index identifies close to a hundred men from Yorkshire over the long eighteenth century appointed or licensed by the East India Company. Similar numbers of entries are identified as originating from Devon and Lancashire. More than thirty men from Cornwall can be found among the Index's list of East India Company appointees and licensees with similar numbers of entries identified with Durham, Dorset, Warwickshire, Worcestershire, Norfolk and Shropshire respectively. The Index understates the East Indies connections in the provincial world. While it identifies only forty male appointees as originating in Cumberland, an enumeration of men compiled from piecing together multiple sources found in excess of two hundred. Similarly, an enumeration from multiple sources shows almost six times the number of Westmerians directly involved in the East Indies than those identified as having Westmorland origins.

The provincial and local dimensions of imperial and global encounters remain largely unexplored, even unrecognised. The potential articulations between the global world and domestic transformations such as the eighteenth-century renaissance of English provincial towns and the rise of middling folk remain largely neglected. Yet the provincial investment in East Indies sojourns raises a range of questions. Was it simply a provincial reflection of an East Indies encounter driven out of national preoccupations? Were these appointees simply members of the Anglo-Indian dynastic families, which some have described as British official families, for whom provincial attachments and identities were largely immaterial? Alternatively, were provincial sojourners thrust into the global arena by provincial aspirations, interests and conditions? To what extent did provincial attachments and networks provide the springboard for East Indies ventures? What was the impact of East Indies sojourns on the fabric of provincial life? This book applies a Cumbrian lens to the interface between the provincial and global worlds.

For more than a century, antiquarians and historians, amateur, academic and professional, have hinted at a Cumbrian encounter with the East Indies. Yet, unlike Cumbria's involvement in the slave-based Atlantic trade and ventures in the West Indies and North America, Cumbrian ventures in the East Indies have remained largely in the shadows. Neither the patterns nor protagonists have been traced. The imperatives that drove them, the sensibilities that shaped and were shaped by them, and the experience and impact of Cumbrians' East Indies ventures lie disregarded and unexplored.

If remarked on at all, the East Indies is typically an embedded note in the margins of Cumbrian regional and family histories. The significance of the death and burial in Cumbria of the Malayan Thomas Ellen, the Indian youth Richard Fletcher and the Indian woman Rosetta who died of smallpox in 1773[2] as sentinels of a broader Cumbrian interface with the East Indies in the global eighteenth century are barely noted. The threading of individuals with Cumbrian origins, attachments and interests in the historiographies of the East India Company, the commercial globalisation of shipping, banking and trade (including the opium trade) and the development of British imperial expansion, are rarely remarked on.

This book demonstrates that the social and economic life in the Cumbrian counties – Cumberland, Westmorland and Lancaster North of the Sands – was profoundly tied to the East Indies. It identifies over four hundred middling and gentry Cumbrian men and women who travelled to and sojourned in the East Indies during the long eighteenth century, as well as Cumbrians whose East Indies interests were operated from the British Isles. Piecing together that Cumbria–East Indies encounter generates a different rendition of Cumbria's social and economic development in the eighteenth century and subsequent trajectory than long-standing narratives focusing on stuttering, then extinguished, industrialisation. It exposes, too, the critical articulation between the provincial and the global.

Intersecting Narratives of Eighteenth-Century Worlds

Exploring the provincial–global articulation through Cumbria's encounter with the East Indies illuminates the intersection between fundamental social and economic shifts in the British Isles during the eighteenth century. As a consequence, this book is positioned at the intersection of four distinct historiographies: the particulars and re-visioning of Cumbria's regional history; the history of the East India Company, the East Indies and the creation of the second empire in the East; the rise of the middling ranks and transformation of the gentry and the dynamics of social position, expression and aspiration; and, finally, the emergence of the provincial town and its eighteenth-century renaissance. Those historiographies are not only constituted separately; they are mostly treated in isolation from each other. The following discussion traces out the key elements of each and highlights the potential for connections between them in the context of Cumbria's provincial encounter with the East Indies.

---

2   D. Rushworth, 'Tom Ellen: A Malayan in Cumberland and the Caribbean in the Later 18th Century', *Transactions CWAAS*, Third Series, VIII (2008), pp. 169–175.

Narratives of Cumbria's Economic and Social Change

In his classic work on North Country life, Hughes portrayed the East India Company as a haven for gentry Cumbrians hanging on to Jacobite allegiances in opposition to the Glorious Revolution and the Hanoverian succession.[3] Hughes's portrayal is consistent with a long-standing historiographical depiction of Cumbria as a region that failed to industrialise, retained feudal institutions, particularly customary tenure and rights, and showed limited agrarian improvement. It is a portrayal reflecting a regional historiography framed by questions around why proto-industrialisation was followed by de-industrialisation; and why Cumbria fell short of becoming a booming conglomeration of manufacturing like Manchester, Lancashire and the Midlands.[4] This book challenges such a picture.

The arguments in this book also fit with an emerging re-visioning of Cumbria's regional history. That re-visioning of Cumbria has involved placing activity at the centre rather than passivity and inactivity. It takes seriously that Cumbrian trade embraced the American colonies, the West Indies, Spain, the Baltic and Africa with products including rum, tobacco, fish, timber, textiles and slaves.[5] It recognises the dynamic potential associated with Beckett's demonstration of the interface between gentry ambitions and entrepreneurship.[6] The coastal ports, the coal trade and the tobacco trade were all important elements in, for instance, the Lowthers' search for regional

---

[3]   E. Hughes, *North Country Life in the Eighteenth Century Vol II Cumberland & Westmorland 1700–1830* (London, Oxford University Press, 1965), p. 105.

[4]   I. Whyte, '"Wild, Barren and Frightful" – Parliamentary Enclosure in an Upland County: Westmorland 1767–1890', *Rural History* 14, 1 (2003), pp. 21–38; J. Warren, 'Harriet Martineau and the Concept of Community: *Deerbrook* and Ambleside', *Journal of Victorian Culture*, 13, 2 (2008), pp. 223–246; C. E. Searle, 'Custom, Class Conflict and Agrarian Capitalism: the Cumbrian Customary Economy in the Eighteenth Century', *Past & Present*, 110, 1 (1986), pp. 106–133; C. E. Searle, 'Customary Tenants and the Enclosure of the Cumbrian Commons', *Northern History*, 29 (1993), pp. 126–153; J. D. Marshall, 'Stages of Industrialisation in Cumbria', in P. Hudson (ed.), *Regions and Industries: A Perspective on the Industrial Revolution in Britain* (Cambridge, Cambridge University Press, 1989), pp. 132–155; C. M. L. Bouch and G. P. Jones, *A Short Economic and Social History of the Lake Counties 1500–1830* (Manchester, Manchester University Press, 1961), Chapters IX and X; J. D. Marshall and J. K. Walton, *The Lake Counties from 1830 to the Mid-twentieth Century: A Study in Regional Change* (Manchester, Manchester University Press, 1981), pp. 1–54; J. D. Marshall, *Furness and the Industrial Revolution* (Beckermet, Barrow in Furness Library, 1958).

[5]   Hughes, *North Country Life Vol II*, pp. 28–57; Bouch and Jones, *The Lake Counties*, pp. 246–274.

[6]   J. V. Beckett, 'Regional Variation and the Agricultural Depression, 1730–1750', *Economic History Review*, New Series, 35, 1 (February 1982), pp. 35–51; J. V. Beckett, 'The Decline of the Small Landowner in Eighteenth- and Nineteenth-Century England: Some Regional Considerations', *The Agricultural History Review*, 30 (1982), pp. 97–111; J. V. Beckett, 'Absentee Land Ownership in the Later Seventeenth and Early Eighteenth Centuries: The Case of Cumbria', *Northern History*, 19 (1983), pp. 87–107; J. V. Beckett, 'The Eighteenth-Century Origins of the Factory System: A Case Study from the 1740s', *Business History*, 19, 1 (1977), pp. 55–67.

economic and political dominance.[7] The Senhouses too sought to sustain their economic position through trade, shipping and port developments.

The privileging of Cumbria's industrial development in its regional historiography has pushed to the margins Cumbria's middling and gentry mercantile activities, overseas trade and the development of service industries such as tourism. Re-visioning Cumbria's regional history has involved opening up the genesis of the tourism sector in the eighteenth century.[8] It means foregrounding trade networks inside and outside the British Isles including: the use of the Isle of Man as an entrepôt;[9] Kendal's Joseph Symson and his extensive network of national trade and his sometimes contentious aspirations for overseas expansion into the American colonies;[10] Isaac Fletcher's export of stockings to the American colonies;[11] Quaker networks that engaged middling and yeoman families, as well as wealthier merchants and their gentry associates in ventures in North America.[12]

Of course, these trade enterprises were inevitably precarious. Port expansion was limited by under-capitalisation and vulnerable to the rise of ports such as Bristol and Liverpool.[13] The decline of the slave trade was also relatively early in Cumbria although it lingered until abolition.[14] There were inevitably individual business failures, such as Peter How's financial collapse in the 1760s, which had repercussions for many others in Cumbria's small society.[15]

7 Beckett, *Coal and Tobacco*, pp. 102–155.
8 I. Thompson, *The English Lakes: A History* (London, Bloomsbury, 2010), pp. 19–43; Bouch and Jones, *The Lake Counties*, pp. 283–289; J. K. Walton and J. Wood (eds), *The Making of a Cultural Landscape: The English Lake District as Tourist Destination, 1750–2010* (Farnham, Ashgate, 2013); A. J. L. Winchester, 'The Landscape Encountered by the First Tourists', in Walton and Wood (eds), *The Making of a Cultural Landscape*, pp. 49–68.
9 M. Robinson, 'The Port of Carlisle: Trade and Shipping in Cumberland, 1675–1735', *Transactions CWAAS*, Third Series, VIII (2008), p. 153.
10 S. D. Smith (ed.), *'An Exact and Industrious Tradesman': The Letter Book of Joseph Symson of Kendal 1711–1720* (Oxford, Oxford University Press, 2002), pp. l–liii, lix, xcviii–ix, cvii–cvix, cxxix.
11 A. J. L. Winchester (ed.), *The Diary of Isaac Fletcher of Underwood, Cumberland 1756–1781* (Kendal, CWAAS Extra Series XXVII, 1994), pp. xxiv–xxvi.
12 A. J. L. Winchester, 'Ministers, Merchants and Migrants: Cumberland Friends and North America in the Eighteenth Century', *Quaker History*, 80, 2 (Fall 1991), pp. 85–99.
13 Bouch and Jones, *The Lake Counties*, p. 271; Marshall, *Furness*, pp. 85–88; Beckett, *Coal and Tobacco*, pp. 102–114; J. E. Williams, 'Whitehaven in the Eighteenth Century', *Economic History Review*, 8, 3 (1956), pp. 393–404; K. Morgan, *Slavery, Atlantic Trade and the British Economy, 1660–1800* (Cambridge, Cambridge University Press, 2000), pp. 85–86.
14 N. Tattersfield, *The Forgotten Trade: Comprising the Log of the Daniel and Henry of 1700 and Accounts of the Slave Trade From the Minor Ports of England 1698–1725* (Kindle edition, Pimlico, Random House, 1998), Chapter 20; D. Richardson, and M. M. Schofield, 'Whitehaven and the Eighteenth-century British Slave Trade', *Transactions CWAAS*, Second Series, XCII (1992), pp. 183–204; W. G. Wiseman, 'Caleb Rotheram, Ecroyde Claxton and their Involvement in the Movement for the Abolition of the Trans-Atlantic Slave Trade', *Transactions CWAAS*, Third Series, IX (2009), p. 154.
15 A. W. Routledge, *History & Guide Whitehaven* (Stroud, Tempus, 2002), p. 57; Beckett, *Coal and Tobacco*, p. 114.

But other enterprises emerged under the pressure of external shocks. The War of Independence, for instance, strained the Atlantic trade for a period but it drew capital back from the Americas and stimulated the Cumbrian ship-building industry.[16] In short, the ebb and flow in global interfaces should not be interpreted as a withdrawal of Cumbria from the global world.

That early industrial innovation in the Cumbrian counties was not transformed into mass industrialisation has distracted from the transformation of the Cumbrian counties over the long eighteenth century. Despite confiscations and reprisals after the 1705 and 1745 Jacobite rebellions, possibly because of them, Cumbria attracted new types of investment, technologies and economic enterprise. The first atmospheric pumps were introduced into Cumberland's coal pits in 1716.[17] The mid-eighteenth century saw a proliferation of mining, iron forges and smelting.[18] Whitehaven's turnpike trust was established in 1739 and from the 1750s followed by a rash of new road initiatives. In 1753, the London Lead Company invested in the extension of mines at Alston Moor.[19] Carriers were introduced in 1757 and the *Flying Machine* stagecoach service from Kendal to Carlisle started in 1763.[20] Kendal became a centre for theatre.[21] New roads, new industries, tourism, enclosure and pressures for agricultural improvements all encouraged extensive surveying and the development of more reliable maps in the 1770s.[22]

Those developments reflected and contributed to a considerable demographic expansion. Cumberland, Westmorland and Furness all grew between 1688 and 1801. Over that time, Cumberland's population almost

[16] Routledge, *History & Guide*, pp. 72–74; National Museums Liverpool, Maritime Archives & Library Information Sheet 18: Thomas & John Brocklebank, www.liverpoolmuseums.org.uk/maritime/archive/sheet/18.

[17] W. Rollinson, *A History of Cumberland and Westmorland* (Chichester, Phillimore Publishing Co., 1996), p. 77.

[18] A. Fell, *The Early Iron Industry of Furness and District* (London, Frank Cass & Co., 1968), pp. 207–222; Rollinson, *A History of Cumberland and Westmorland*, pp. 75–81; Bouch and Jones, *Lake Counties 1500–1830*, pp. 246–263.

[19] T. Sopwith, *An Account of the Mining Districts of Alston Moor, Weardale and Teesdale in Cumberland and Durham: Comprising Descriptive Sketches of the Scenery, Antiquities, Geology and Mining Operations in the Upper Dales of the Rivers Tyne, Wear and Tees* (Alnwick, W. Davison, 1833), p. 179; A. Raistrick, *Two Centuries of Industrial Welfare: London (Quaker) Lead Company, 1692–1905* (3rd revised edition, Littleborough, George Kelsall, 1988), p. 19.

[20] Rollinson, *A History of Cumberland and Westmorland*, pp. 96–107; A. White, *A History of Kendal* (Lancaster, Carnegie, 2013), pp. 126–148; J. K. Walton, 'Landscape and Society: The Industrial Revolution and Beyond', in Walton and Wood (eds), *The Making of a Cultural Landscape*, p. 74; P. Hindle, *Roads and Tracks of the Lake District* (Milnthorpe, Cicerone Press, 1998), pp. 149ff.

[21] M. Eddershaw, *Grand Fashionable Nights: Kendal Theatre 1575–1985* (Lancaster, Centre for North West Regional Studies, University of Lancaster, 1989).

[22] P. Hindle, 'The First Large Scale County Maps of Cumberland and Westmorland in the 1770s', *Transactions CWAAS*, Third Series, I (2001), pp. 139–141.

doubled to 117,230 by 1801. The Westmorland population increased from around 27,000 to almost 41,000. Furness saw similar rates of increase. Carlisle's population doubled between 1688 and 1801. From a little more than 10,000 people in 1801, it had climbed to 19,000 by 1831. Penrith's population, less than 1,400 in 1688, was 3,801 by 1801[23] and increased to 5,385 inhabitants by 1821.[24] Kendal's population was about 2,000 in the 1730s, 8,000 by the 1780s[25] and was claimed to be almost 12,000 by the 1820s.[26]

Ports along the western coast proliferated and even the smaller ports around Furness handled comparatively high tonnages of ships involved in coastal and foreign trade.[27] In 1756, Furness shipping handled 2,482 tons of trade and was reputedly the base for 150 vessels. Between 1766 and 1782, Piel and Ulverston dealt with no less than 1,100 tons of coastal trade annually.[28] Established as a customs port in 1685, Whitehaven developed a global presence. In 1712, 1.6 million pounds of tobacco were received there.[29] For much of the century, Whitehaven's trade, shipping and ship-building were comparable to Bristol and exceeded Liverpool.[30]

Shipping and trade supported flourishing coastal towns. The Workington population increased from less than 1,000 in 1688 to more than 6,000 by 1801.[31] In 1821 its population was almost 7,000 including the 500 sailors based at the port but away from home during the census. Despite competition from Liverpool, Whitehaven was still a major population centre in 1821. The resident population was well over 12,000 and there were about 8,000 sailors associated with the town but excluded from the town census. The Whitehaven population had increased almost ten-fold between 1693 and 1821. Including its sailors, Maryport's 1821 population exceeded 5,000.[32]

The diversification of the Cumbrian economy and the amenities of Cumbria's provincial towns supported opportunities in Cumbria but there were also opportunities elsewhere, in London, Europe, in the Atlantic trade,

---

23 Bouch and Jones, *The Lake Counties*, p. 217.
24 Pigot and Co., *National Commercial Directory for 1828–9: Cumberland Lancashire Westmorland* (Facsimile Edition, Norwich, Michael Winton, 1995), p. 25.
25 Including Kirkland; J. D. Marshall, *Kendal 1661–1801: The Growth of a Modern Town* (Kendal, Titus Wilson & Son, n.d.), p. 3.
26 Pigot and Co., *National Commercial Directory*, p. 315. See also White, *A History of Kendal*, pp. 172–175.
27 Bouch and Jones, *The Lake Counties*, p. 217.
28 Marshall, *Kendal 1661–1801*, pp. 86, 87.
29 Rollinson, *A History of Cumberland and Westmorland*, p. 108; Beckett, *Coal and Tobacco*, pp. 105–115.
30 R. C. Jarvis, 'Cumberland Shipping in the Eighteenth Century', *Transactions CWAAS*, New Series, LIV (1955), pp. 225–230; P. Skidmore, 'Vessels and Networks: Ship owning in North-West England's Coasting Trade in the Late Eighteenth and Early Nineteenth Centuries', *The Mariner's Mirror*, 99, 2 (2013), pp. 153–170.
31 Marshall, *Kendal 1661–1801*, p. 217.
32 Pigot and Co., *National Commercial Directory*, pp. 29, 30, 22.

in the American colonies, the West Indies and, gradually, the East Indies. The desire and capacity to take those opportunities were shaped by periodic shocks, including business failures such as those experienced by leading Whitehaven merchants Peter How in 1763 and Thomas Lutwidge before him.[33] Cumbria faced chronic problems of liquidity and other inertias. Until the development of a formal banking infrastructure in the 1800s, access to capital or even operating funds relied on the benefice and prudential assessments of individual lenders, including the domineering Lowthers.[34] Cumbria, despite the considerable expansion in infrastructure, remained often difficult to move around. It was a region that could be simultaneously isolating and crowded as it was increasingly exposed to the demands of tourists and the emerging tourism industry.

Far from a declining society resistant to change,[35] Cumbrians adapted to changing conditions. The re-visioning of Cumbria's regional history has shifted from portraying Cumbria as an inward-looking region isolated by a hostile topography and an economy inhibited by the vestiges of feudalism, to a region populated by people looking outwards, making connections and seeking success through generating and exploiting a diversity of opportunities. Cumbria's regional development, especially in its trade and manufacturing, suggests partnerships and business associations constituted across the social hierarchy: a dynamic amalgam of gentry, yeoman, trade and merchant families. Cumbrian gentry and middling ranks often invested together and took risks together. This is perhaps most obvious in shipping. There was a long-standing practice of ship ownership packaged into shares of one or more sixteenths.[36] It was a practice still evident in the 1800s. Take, for instance, the ownership of the Cumberland brig the *Amphion*, which included among its owners a number of gentlemen, mariners, a yeoman, a hairdresser and a gardener.[37]

Economic alliances between gentry and middling ranks were also evident elsewhere, including in the iron industry, manufacture and trade. Those

---

[33] Beckett, *Coal and Tobacco*, pp. 113–115.

[34] G. P. Jones, 'Some Sources of Loans and Credit in Cumbria before the Use of Banks', *Transactions CWAAS*, New Series, 75 (1975), pp. 275–292.

[35] J. Healey, 'Agrarian Social Structure in the Central Lake District, *c.* 1574–1830: The Fall of the "Mountain Republic"?', *Northern History*, 1, 2 (September 2007), pp. 73–75, 91; I. Whyte, 'Cumbrian Village Communities: Continuity and Change, c.1750–c.1850', in C. Dyer (ed.), *The Self-Contained Village? The Social History of Rural Communities 1250–1900* (Hatfield, University of Hertfordshire Press, 2007), pp. 96–113; Warren, 'Harriet Martineau and the Concept of Community', pp. 223–246; Bouch and Jones, *Lake Counties 1500–1830*, p. 218; M. A. Hill (ed.), *An Independent Woman's Lake District Writings: Harriet Martineau* (New York: Humanity Books, 2004), p. 11.

[36] Hughes, *North Country Life Vol II*, pp. 186–188; Jarvis, 'Cumberland Shipping in the Eighteenth Century', pp. 212–35.

[37] A. Forsyth, *Highway to the World: The People and Their Little Wooden Ships, Brigs, Brigantines, and Snows of Cumberland in the 18th and 19th Centuries* (Carlisle, Bookcase, 2011), p. 111.

enterprises were frequently innovative. From the mid-eighteenth century, Cumbrian ironmasters adopted business models still used today, including vertical integration and peripheralisation of production to economically marginal communities. The Cumbrian iron industry developed operations in Scotland to take advantage of secure fuel supplies and cheap labour.[38] There were technical innovations and diversification of both markets and products. Rather than aristocratic ventures, the iron industry was one 'capitalised by merchants and entrepreneurs'.[39]

The amalgam of gentry and middling ranks in trade, manufacturing and extractive industry has been ascribed to the sparsity of the Cumbrian aristocracy and the vulnerability of a gentry unable to improve its returns from land rents.[40] The constraints on land-based income, associated with persistent and often effective assertion of customary tenure,[41] contributed to a 'shelling out' of the gentry over the seventeenth and eighteenth centuries, although the rate of that decline is subject to some debate.[42] Some have interpreted these factors as creating conditions for inertia and stultification. Customary tenure and a region with a relatively small population and significant bio-physical limitations may similarly be seen as driving gentry and middling alliances into entrepreneurism and diversification.[43]

Middling Ranks and Gentry

The early melding of middling and gentry interests in Cumbria and in their East Indies encounters presents an opportunity to address broader questions around the aspirations, identity and positioning of gentry and middling ranks in the social hierarchy. There are already rich historiographical seams that cohere separately around middling ranks and gentry and their respective constitution, self-awareness and identity as a rank; the construction and nature of rank-based sensibilities; the trajectories and conditions of their rise or decline; and

---

[38] Fell, *The Early Iron Industry*, pp. 256–285.

[39] A. D. George, 'The Early Iron Industry in Furness – A Revolution in the 18th Century', *Cumbria Industrial History Occasional Papers*, 5 (2005), pp. 49–53; B. Tyson, 'Attempts to Smelt Metal with Coal Near Whitehaven Before 1700', *Cumbria Industrial History Occasional Papers*, 2 (1999), pp. 3–22; B. Tyson, 'Heavy Transport in Cumbria before 1800: Methods, Problems and Costs', *Cumbria Industrial History Occasional Papers*, 4 (2002), pp. 13–33.

[40] A. J. L. Winchester, 'Wordsworth's "Pure Commonwealth"? Yeoman Dynasties in the English Lake District', *Armitt Library Journal* (1998), pp. 91, 93, 97.

[41] Searle, 'Custom, Class Conflict', pp. 106–133; Searle, 'Customary Tenants', pp. 126–153; N. Gregson, 'Tawney Revisited: Custom and the Emergence of Capitalist Class Relations in North-East Cumbria, 1600–1830', *Economic History Review*, New Series, 42, 1 (February 1989), pp. 18–42.

[42] Whyte, 'Cumbrian Village Communities', pp. 96–113; A. J. L. Winchester, 'Personal Names and Local Identities in Early Modern Cumbria', *Transactions CWAAS*, Third Series, XI (2011), pp. 29–49.

[43] Winchester, '"Pure Commonwealth"', pp. 86–113.

the extent of mobility between ranks.[44] Cumbria's East Indies experience provides a setting to explore those dynamics, particularly one of the central historiographical themes of whether middling folk sought social advancement by adopting the styles and practices of those of higher social rank.

The debate around emulation has been multi-faceted analytically and empirically. However, at its heart is the pursuit of success and the way in which success was expressed. For many years, Veblen's concept of conspicuous consumption was a central, framing motif. Veblen argued that the consumption of certain goods was used to evidence wealth and 'conversely, the failure to consume in due quality and quantity … [was] a mark of inferiority and demerit'.[45] Proponents of emulation theory have suggested that the accelerating availability of consumer goods in the eighteenth century was both driven by the desire, and fuelled the ability, of middling folk to step outside the boundaries of sober protestant ethics of work, saving and investment. Consumer goods allowed middling people to pursue social status and mobility through the emulation of the gentry.[46]

The timing, regionality, shape and meaning of consumption have all been the subject of considerable debate.[47] A raft of empirical studies shows that the patterns of consumption and the array of goods found among gentry and middling folk overlapped, but they were by no means identical. Certain luxury goods appear to have attracted middling rather than gentry attention.[48] Moreover, while Veblen and his proponents defined consumption as

---

[44] There are extensive and cross-cutting historiographies around these themes including: P. Langford, *Polite and Commercial People: England 1727–1783* (Oxford, Oxford University Press, 1992); M. R. Hunt, *The Middling Sort: Commerce, Gender and the Family in England 1680–1780* (Berkeley, University of California Press, 1996); L. Davidoff and C. Hall, *Family Fortunes: Men and Women of the English Middle Class 1780–1850* (revised edition, Abingdon, Routledge, 2003); D. Wahrman, *Imagining the Middle Class: The Political Representation of Class in Britain, c.1780–1840* (Cambridge, Cambridge University Press, 1995); D. Wahrman, *The Making of the Modern Self: Identity and Culture in Eighteenth Century England* (New Haven, CT, Yale University Press, 2006); L. Stone and J. C. Fawtier-Stone, *An Open Elite? England, 1540–1880* (Oxford, Clarendon Press, 1984); H. R. French, *The Middle Sort of People in Provincial England, 1600–1750* (Oxford, Oxford University Press, 2007); K. Wrightson, *Earthly Necessities: Economic Lives in Early Modern Britain* (New Haven, CT, Yale University Press, 2000).

[45] T. Veblen, *The Theory of the Leisure Class* (reissued edition, Oxford, Oxford University Press, 2009), p. 53.

[46] P. Borsay, *The English Urban Renaissance: Culture and Society in the Provincial Town 1660–1770* (Oxford, Clarendon Press, 1991), pp. 316–317.

[47] C. Campbell, *The Romantic Ethic and the Spirit of Modern Consumerism* (Oxford, Blackwell, 1987), pp. 17–35; J. Brewer and R. Porter (eds), *Consumption and the World of Goods* (London, Routledge, 1994) provides a comprehensive review; M. Berg, 'Consumption in Eighteenth Century and Early Nineteenth Century Britain', in R. Floud and P. Johnson (eds), *The Cambridge Economic History of Modern Britain: Volume 1 Industrialisation, 1700–1860* (Cambridge, Cambridge University Press, 2004), pp. 257–387. See the extended discussions of regionality and consumption in H. Berry and J. Gregory (eds), *Creating and Consuming Culture in North-East England, 1660–1830* (Aldershot, Ashgate Publishing Limited, 2004).

[48] L. Weatherill, *Consumer Behaviour & Material Culture in Britain 1660–1760* (2nd edition,

a competitive activity explicitly directed to securing upward social mobility, there are other interpretations of middling and, indeed, gentry consumption. Bourdieu, for instance, argued consumption was a transactional activity shaped by tastes bounded by rank, a process of distinction rather than a process dedicated to climbing out of one's social rank.[49] Moreover, it has rightly been noted that while consumption in one rank may appear similar to that in another, those similarities are not necessarily emulation nor even imitation.[50] Weatherill and Vickery caution against abstractions. Both highlight the complex alignments between consumption and social position as well as the close interactions and sociability between people of middling rank and minor gentry. Under those conditions, they argue that consumption patterns need to be examined empirically within their specific context and referenced to explicit evidence of motivation and meaning.[51]

Although the emulation debate has been primarily associated with the historiography of consumption, it surfaces too in the historiography around production, innovation and industrialisation. The decline of Britain's industrial dominance has been tied to cultural explanations suggesting that the entrepreneurial and innovative spirit of early industrialists was replaced by a desire to emulate the norms and values of the gentry, including a preoccupation with land ownership.[52]

Cultural explanations of industrial decline and the notion of elite positions residing primarily in land have been vociferously criticised by Rubenstein. He questions the evidential basis for such claims. Rubenstein also argues that even in the most expansive industrial period, the British economy was and continued to be primarily one of an economy of commerce, finance and the service sector.[53] In short, Rubenstein argues the debate itself was misdirected and irrelevant.

Rubenstein's critique simultaneously opens up a new direction for exploring Cumbria's economic development while missing the heart of the issue. Usefully,

London, Routledge, 1996), pp. 166–189.

[49] P. Bourdieu, *Distinction: A Social Critique of the Judgement of Taste* (London, Routledge Kegan Paul, 1994), pp. 34–55.

[50] C. Campbell, 'Understanding Traditional and Modern Patterns of Consumption in Eighteenth Century England: a Character-Action Approach', in Brewer and Porter (eds), *Consumption and the World of Goods*, p. 41.

[51] L. Weatherill, 'The Meaning of Consumer Behaviour in Late Seventeenth and Early Eighteenth Century England' and A. Vickery, 'Women and the World of Goods: A Lancashire Consumer and Her Possessions 1751–1781', both in Brewer and Porter (eds), *Consumption and the World of Goods*, pp. 207–208, 210, 275–278; see also French, *The Middle Sort of People*, p. 121.

[52] M. Wiener, *English Culture and the Decline of the Industrial Spirit 1870–1980* (2nd edition, Cambridge, Cambridge University Press, 2004), pp. 1–10, 127–154; Stone and Fawtier-Stone, *An Open Elite?*, p. 283.

[53] W. D. Rubenstein, *Capitalism, Culture and Decline in Britain 1750–1990* (London, Routledge, 1994), pp. 24, 140–162.

for those concerned with the Cumbrian counties, he raises the possibility that the limited industrialisation of Cumbria represented not so much a failure of industrial spirit, but a choice by gentry and middling families to focus on alternative and well-established economic sectors. This aligns with a broader re-visioning of Cumbria as a diversified regional economy. But the argument around industrialisation also creates a distraction. The real issue is not about the relative importance of the industrial and financial sectors respectively. It is a debate around success and the pathways to influence. It is about whether business success, in and of itself, conferred dominant elite membership, or whether the income and wealth generated by business had to be invested in cultural capital: acquiring the right styles, learning certain behaviours, purchasing certain consumption goods, building domestic 'palaces', taking up the arts and taking on the mantle of authority. Crucially, it is about whether that cultural capital required the acquisition of land and landed estates. It is here that the historiography of the middling ranks and gentry meets with the historiography of provincial life and the development of urban provincial elites.

Provincial Life

Borsay, Sweet and French argue that the provincial urban renaissance that characterised the eighteenth century saw an assertion of middling ranks and the economic sectors of trade, professional services and manufacturing.[54] Their work contrasts with a succession of historians who portrayed provincial life as shaped by national imperatives and the desire to 'assimilate metropolitan cultures and values'. For the latter, provincial life was a pale imitation of London.[55] It is an argument difficult to sustain. It is countered by a raft of research showing agricultural productivity increased, provincial towns expanded, provincial medical and health services became increasingly professionalised,[56] leisure, consumption and cultural opportunities proliferated in the provinces, the provinces saw a spree of building and renovating, and a combination of improved transport and romanticism stimulated the emergence of new provincial economic sectors such as commercial tourism.

---

[54] Borsay, *The English Urban Renaissance*, pp. 225–256; R. Sweet, *The English Town, 1680–1840: Government, Society and Culture* (London, Routledge, 2014), pp. 178–191, 194–197; French, *The Middle Sort of People*, pp. 201–261.

[55] R. Porter, 'Science, Provincial Culture and Public Opinion in Enlightenment England', in P. Borsay, (ed.), *The Eighteenth Century Town, 1688–1820* (London, Longman, 1990), p. 251.

[56] A. Withey, '"Persons That Live Remote from London": Apothecaries and the Medical Marketplace in Seventeenth-and Eighteenth-Century Wales', *Bulletin of the History of Medicine*, 85, 2 (Summer 2011), pp. 222–247; A. Tomkins, 'Who Were His Peers? The Social and Professional Milieu of the Provincial Surgeon-Apothecary in the Late-Eighteenth Century', *Journal of Social History*, 44, 3 (Spring 2011), pp. 915–935; Langford, *A Polite and Commercial People*, p. 137.

Far from being simply fashion-followers emulating London, some provincial towns became fashion-leaders and fashionable centres.[57]

Moreover, Borsay and Sweet have demonstrated that provincial life was marked by a strong tendency to celebrate local identity and an emerging desire among provincial urban elites to represent provincial towns as progressive and modern. The legitimacy of local civic powers and privileges and the authority of local elites, both of gentry and of the middling sort, were promoted by reference to the history of provincial places. Local elites presented provincial towns as different from London but not at the periphery. They sought recognition of provincial towns as the bedrock of the British Isles, its innovation and, even, its global reach.[58] They were often resistant to the centralising control of London and parliamentary politics. For instance, gentry and middling folk in the North West were known for their sympathy with American colonial anxieties around taxation, representation and the desire to control their own civic affairs.[59]

The assertion of the middling sort in provincial life was, in part, a reflection of the expansion of their economic power and expanding populations. The middling population outside of London more than doubled over the eighteenth century. The provincial urban renaissance was accompanied by middling ranks increasing their influence through their participation in local governance and a network of clubs, societies and local charitable activities. Those changes set the scene for re-alignments and tensions between national and provincial politics and imperatives. Provincial politics, with its tussles among gentry and urban elites for local influence and position, also shaped the culture and practice of parliamentary politics.[60]

There are even instances of issues, trivial in national terms but driven out of provincial contests of status and influence, preoccupying and distracting key actors at Westminster. For example, in the build up to the Tea Act, legislation that was to contribute to the outbreak of the American War of Independence, Lord North was caught up in a very Cumbrian falling out between James Lowther and John Robinson, Lowther's own Member of Parliament for Westmorland. The dispute itself was over a piece of local patronage. Its resolution required the intervention of the Prime Minister, Lord North. The dispute prompted Robinson to give up the Westmorland seat and take Harwich on the Treasury interest.

---

[57] Marshall, *Kendal*; Borsay, *The English Urban Renaissance*, pp. 28–29.
[58] Sweet, *The English Town*, pp. 186–187, 260–266.
[59] A. Murdoch, *British History 1660–1832: National Identity and Local Culture* (Basingstoke, Macmillan Press, 1998), p. 114; K. Wilson, *The Sense of the People: Politics, Culture and Imperialism in England, 1715–1785* (Cambridge, Cambridge University Press, 1998), pp. 200–201, 237–284.
[60] Wilson, *The Sense of the People*, p. 437.

Ten years later, Lord North was again embroiled in this local dispute when Lowther threatened to join the opposition because the Earl of Abergavenny, John Robinson's grandson, would take precedence over himself.[61] These dynamics are consistent with, although of a different nature to, Wilson's exploration of the alignment and interface between metropolitan and provincial politics in the crucible from which eighteenth-century imperialism emerged. Wilson demonstrates how local dynamics shaped local opinion around certain imperial issues and those opinions, in turn, had an impact on government and the framing of government policy including imperial policy.[62]

The East Indies and British Imperialism

The different historiographies reviewed thus far have in common shifts involving re-positioning of people, sectors and regions previously treated as peripheral. A similar shift is evident in East Indies historiography. For many years it was dominated by a focus on the parliamentary politics of empire and geopolitics, the administrative, commercial and political operations of the East India Company, and the impacts of Company and colonial rule. All of those tended to reduce the encounter between the British Isles and the East Indies to the imposition of a metropolitan, effectively a London, agenda on the periphery.

That London, de facto, was treated as the metropole is hardly surprising. There is no doubt about its intense mix of social, economic and political dynamism in the eighteenth century.[63] London saw the struggles between Parliament and the East India Company for control of interests in India. London was the setting for a parade of scandals, rifts, impeachments and litigation through the 1770s involving some of the most prominent East India Company servants. London's broadsheet writers and artists, the public, literate and otherwise, and theatre-goers had an inexhaustible appetite for India, its plunder and the comedy afforded by the new caste of nabobs.[64] The East India Company fuelled the perception of its London-centeredness by building the new East India House to tower over London's commercial centre.[65] Moreover, London's economy was firmly enmeshed with the East India Company's operations.

---

[61] A. Connell, 'Appleby in Westminster: John Robinson, MP (1727–1802)', *Transactions CWAAS*, Third Series, X (2010), pp. 221–223; J. Cannon, *Aristocratic Century: The Peerage of Eighteenth-Century England* (Cambridge, Cambridge University Press, 1987), p. 176.

[62] Wilson, *The Sense of the People*, pp. 137–205.

[63] See J. White, *London in the Eighteenth Century: A Great and Monstrous Thing* (London, Bodley Head, 2012) for a recent portrayal.

[64] T. Nechtman, *Nabobs: Empire and Identity in Eighteenth-Century Britain* (Cambridge: Cambridge University Press, 2010); C. Smylitopoulos, 'Rewritten and Reused: Imaging the Nabob through "Upstart Iconography"', *Eighteenth-Century Life*, 32, 2 (Spring 2008), pp. 39–59.

[65] H. V. Bowen, J. McAleer and R. J. Blyth, *Monsoon Traders: The Maritime World of the East India*

Two-fifths of East India Company stock accounts were located in London or the Home Counties in 1756. The proportion rose to well over half of all stock by 1830.[66] In excess of 1,700 people worked in the Company's London warehouses, wharves and offices in 1785. Most of the Company's establishment of clerks in the British Isles were located in London. Straddling the worlds of finance, trade, administration and law, they commanded high salaries. Experienced clerks in East India House received on average an annual income of about £200 in the 1780s. By the 1820s an experienced East India clerk could expect an annual salary of £600. Their average real incomes increased 125 per cent between 1780 and 1815.[67]

The conflation between London and the East India Company has been so powerful that Mentz, in his history of English merchants in Madras, stated unequivocally that 'English society in Madras was thus entangled in a web of personal relationships which all began and ended in London'.[68] Mentz's view is only one, relatively recent exposition, of a long historiographic tradition of what Crosbie describes as metropolitan-focused imperial history drawing 'almost exclusively from the perspective of England or, more specifically, from London'.[69] Notwithstanding, unevenly and sporadically, historians have begun to capture the diversity of the engagement between the British Isles and the East Indies. That engagement is being increasingly explored within broader perspectives focusing on national and subaltern imperatives, as well as framed by concerns around globalisation and the emergence of modernity.[70]

Attempts to integrate debates around the metropolitan and the periphery, imperial power and the experiences of colonising and being colonised have shifted the gaze on to how empire, the global world and being a colonial power, impacted on the cultural, material, social, domestic and economic lives of those who were 'at home' in the British Isles.[71] Recent histories have

Company (London, Scala, 2011), p. 97.

66 H. V. Bowen, *The Business of Empire: The East India Company and Imperial Britain, 1756–1833* (Cambridge, Cambridge University Press, 2008), pp. 111–113.

67 H. Boot, 'Real Incomes of the British Middle Class, 1760–1850: The Experience of the Clerks at the East India Company', *Economic History Review*, LII, 4 (1999), pp. 639–640.

68 S. Mentz, 2005, *The English Gentleman Merchant at Work: Madras and the City of London 1660–1740* (Copenhagen, Museum Tusculanum Press, University of Copenhagen, 2005), p. 232.

69 B. Crosbie, 'Ireland, Colonial Science, and the Geographical Construction of British Rule in India, c. 1820–1870', *The Historical Journal* 52, 4 (2009), pp. 963–964.

70 P. J. Stern, 'History and Historiography of the English East India Company: Past, Present, and Future!', *History Compass*, 7, 4 (2009), pp. 1146–1180; K. Wilson, 'Introduction: Histories, Empires, Modernities', in K. Wilson (ed.), *A New Imperial History: Culture, Identity, Modernity, 1660–1840* (Cambridge, Cambridge University Press, 2004), pp. 5–13.

71 C. Hall and S. Rose (eds), *At Home with Empire: Metropolitan Culture and the Imperial World* (Cambridge, Cambridge University Press, 2009), pp. 22–30; see also *The East India Company at Home*, http://blogs.ucl.ac.uk/eicah/home/.

focused on Scottish and Irish mercantile networks in the seventeenth and eighteenth centuries, as well as the politics of the Union and empire.[72] Those provide a more nuanced analysis than Colley's influential argument that global threats drove Union and the imperial project served to forge the British Isles into Great Britain.[73]

The enmeshing of provincial societies, the East India Company and encounters with the East Indies has begun to attract attention. Thomas, for instance, has shown how the East India Company had a long history of contracting agents in provincial ports. The first agency was established as early as 1640.[74] Hampshire attracted two such agencies. These provincial Company agents were typically prominent men of the middling classes, often merchants working either on their own account or within a consortium. Successful commercially, many held provincial civic responsibilities. They integrated the East India Company into the fabric of provincial life. [75] The East Indies also established its infrastructure in the provincial world, including Haileybury College in Hertfordshire. It was provincial production that met the East India Company demand for European goods in its East Indies settlements.

According to Bowen, the Company expenditure on contracted commodities exported to the East Indies reached almost £28 million in the three and a half decades between 1756 and 1800.[76] Cloths, metals, particularly copper and lead, and a miscellany of goods referred to as general merchandise were almost entirely manufactured or produced in provincial centres throughout the British Isles. Lightweight worsted textiles, stuffs, were supplied by manufacturers mainly in Norwich. Broadcloth was supplied primarily out of Gloucestershire and long ells, a variety of serge, was supplied from Cornwall, Devon and Somerset. Iron was, for much of the eighteenth century, supplied by Sweden for export to the East Indies, but English

---

[72] D. Dickson, J. Parmentier and J. Ohlmeyer (eds), *Irish and Scottish Mercantile Networks in Europe and Overseas in the Seventeenth and Eighteenth Centuries* (Gent, Academia Press, 2007); B. Crosbie, *Irish Imperial Networks: Migration, Social Communication and Exchange in Nineteenth-Century India* (Cambridge, Cambridge University Press, 2012); G. McGilvray, *East India Patronage and the British State: The Scottish Elite and Politics in the Eighteenth Century* (London, Tauris Academic Studies, 2008).

[73] L. Colley, *Britons: Forging the Nation 1707–1837* (3rd revised edition, New Haven, CT, Yale University Press, 2009), pp. 79, 127–130.

[74] J. H. Thomas, 'East India Agency Company Work in the British Isles, 1700–1800', in H. V. Bowen, M. Lincoln and N. Rigby (eds), *The Worlds of the East India Company* (Woodbridge, Boydell Press, 2004), p. 35.

[75] Thomas, 'East India Company Agency', pp. 33, 42; J. H. Thomas, 'County, Commerce and Contacts: Hampshire and the East India Company in the Eighteenth Century', *Hampshire Studies*, 68 (2013), pp. 169–177.

[76] H. V. Bowen, 'Sinews of Trade and Empire: The Supply of Commodity Exports to the East India Company during the Late Eighteenth Century', *Economic History Review*, New Series, 55, 3 (2002), p. 484.

and, later, Scottish, mines supplied lead. By the 1790s, the lead supply was administered out of Newcastle upon Tyne[77] by way of the Quaker-affiliated London Lead Company with its mines in Wales and at Alston Moor in Cumberland.

Moreover, despite claims that the East India Company was primarily a London company, those at the core of the Company's governance, its directors, its chairmen and the politicians progressively asserting control over the Company in the late eighteenth century, had attachments and interests well beyond London. Stockholders might have been primarily London-based,[78] but they had limited sustained impact on the operations of the Company.[79] The policies, practices and culture of the Company were shaped at home by a directorship made up of a small group of individuals, their circle of business and familial networks. They had patronage to dispense and the extent of that patronage increased over the eighteenth century as vacancies for civil and military appointments increased.[80] If those dispensers of patronage originated in, were focused on, and attached primarily to, London, this would present a significant barrier to provincial participation in the Company and the East Indies. But this was not the case.

There were chairmen with Scottish and Irish connections: Laurence Sullivan was born in County Cork while Robert Gregory went to India from Galway and bought a significant estate in Galway on his return. Charles Grant, Hugh Inglis, John Michie and David Scott were all Scotsmen. Bowen notes three chairmen with active provincial attachments: George Wombwell, who used his India earnings to restore his family estate in Yorkshire; Francis Baring from Devon; and Henry Fletcher of Clea Hall, Cumberland[81] who, retiring from the Company's maritime service, served as an East India Company director virtually uninterrupted for thirteen years prior to taking the chairmanship.[82]

Although establishing the origins of chairmen and directors is by no means a trivial task, especially prior to 1758, between 1700 and 1829 over half of the chairmen came from outside London and the Home Counties. About a quarter were drawn from Scotland, Ireland and Wales. A significant minority

77 Bowen, 'Sinews of Trade and Empire', pp. 472–473, 478–482.
78 Bowen, *The Business of Empire*, pp. 109–116.
79 Bowen, *The Business of Empire*, p. 111; C. N. Parkinson, *Trade in the Eastern Seas 1793–1813* (Cambridge, Cambridge University Press, 2010), pp. 1–28; H. Furber, *John Company at Work: A Study of European Expansion in India in the Late Eighteenth Century* (New York, Octagon Books, 1970), pp. 268ff; H.V. Bowen, 'The "Little Parliament": The General Court of the East India Company, 1750–1784', *The Historical Journal* 34, 4 (1991), p. 859.
80 Ghosh, *The Social Condition of the British Community in Bengal*, pp. 17–20.
81 Bowen, *The Business of Empire*, p. 127.
82 J. Brooke, 'FLETCHER, Henry (c.1727–1807), of Clea Hall, Cumb.', in L. Namier (ed.), *The History of Parliament: The House of Commons 1754–1790* (1964), www.historyofparliamentonline.org/volume/1754-1790/member/fletcher-henry-1727-1807.

were from provincial counties (Figure 1.1). A similar pattern was evident among the directors (Figure 1.2).[83]

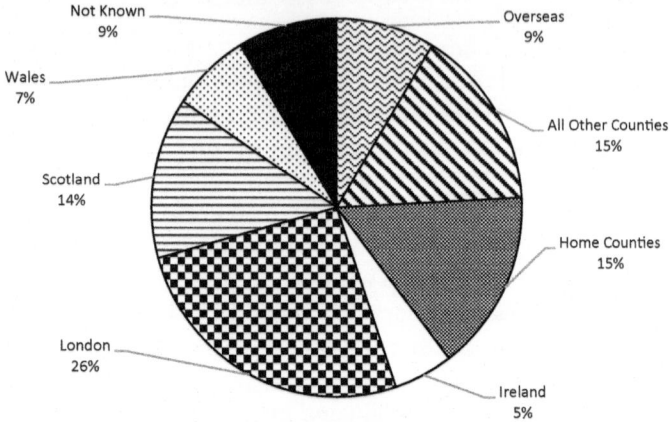

Figure 1.1 Origins of East India Company Chairmen, c. 1700–1829

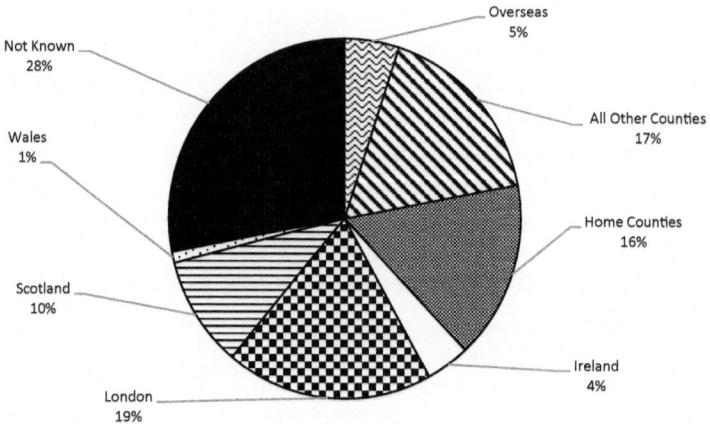

Figure 1.2 Origins of East India Company Directors, c. 1700–1829

In short, at the intersection between the historiography of the East Indies and the historiography of provincial eighteenth-century England there arises

[83] This analysis used biographical material from: C. G. Prinsep (ed.), *Record of Services of the Honourable East India Company's Civil Servants in the Madras Presidency, from 1741 to 1858...: Including Chronological Lists of Governors, Commanders-in-Chief, Chief Justices and Judges, of the Madras Presidency, Between 1652 and 1858 As well as Lists of the Directors of the East India Company; Chairmen and Deputy Chairmen of the Direction; and Presidents of the Board of Control* (Reprint, BiblioLife, n.d.); J. G. Parker, 'The Directors of the East India Company 1754–1790' (PhD thesis, University of Edinburgh, 1977); and C. H. Philips, *The East India Company 1784–1834* (2nd edition, London, Hesperides Press, 2006).

the possibility of a new viewpoint: one that treats neither provincial life and culture, politics and governance, nor economic development, nor the encounter with the East Indies as driven primarily out of national imperatives centred on London. It opens up the possibility that for the British Isles the global encounter was propelled and shaped by provincial preoccupations; that London functioned primarily as a way station in that encounter; and that national imperatives associated with global, colonial and imperial expansion were mediated and shaped by provincial dynamics.

'Piecing Together' a Picture of the Past

Taking a provincial lens to what is usually treated as a national encounter means taking attention away from high politics and London and turning to the local. That shift presents distinct challenges. Provincial connections with the East Indies must be excavated from, and linked across, a plethora of archives, records and material. This requires what Anderson refers to as a process of 'piecing together' 'archival traces' large and often disparate sets of data.[84] In that regard it differs from micro-history's intensive focus on a single event, individual, family or localised social system.[85] The Cumbrians involved in the East Indies have been identified through accessing a multiplicity of informational sites embracing formal archives, private collections and family histories, contemporary printed material, to non-traditional material such as portraits. The following discussion provides a brief description of those sources and the enumeration 'rules' that structured the enumeration of Cumbrian involved in the East Indies.

Reading across Archives and Materials

'Piecing together' 'archival traces' inherently means 'reading across' and referencing a substantial number and variety of primary records, manuscripts and contemporary print materials. Cumbrians eligible for enumeration may be found by the merest aside in a letter or report and each must be 'followed'. Inevitably there is a trawling through archival material, and in some cases close reading and transcription, before setting aside some material as not directly relevant or peripheral. The primary materials used and referenced are various but at their core are three types: letters (sometimes associated

---

[84] C. Anderson, *Subaltern Lives: Biographies of Colonialism in the Indian Ocean World, 1790–1920* (Cambridge, Cambridge University Press, 2012), pp. 4, 14–15, 41, 44–46, 122, 159.

[85] Two examples of micro-history involving encounters with the East Indies are found in the histories of the Midlands Shaw couple and the Scottish Johnstones respectively, in A. Popp, *Entrepreneurial Families: Business, Marriage and Life in the Early Nineteenth Century* (London, Pickering & Chatto, 2012) and E. Rothschild, *The Inner Life of Empires: An Eighteenth-Century History* (Princeton, NJ, Princeton University Press, 2012).

with accounts and journals), wills and inventories, and East India Company personal records including pension fund, licence, bond and service records.

Following individual Cumbrians and the way their kin, friendship and business connections prompted and shaped their East Indies encounters goes beyond a prosopographical approach, that is, compiling the social and economic characteristics of individuals who constitute a set milieu or set of historical actors.[86] The Cumbrian encounter with the East Indies explored in this book has been revealed by an approach more akin to anthropology where an 'ego's' or a subject's relationships are used to reveal kin, economic, community and social relations and structures. The latter approach allows the patterns and networks that structured the provincial encounter with the East Indies to be integrated with individual experience and biographical trajectories that illuminate the imperatives, logics and sensibilities associated with the encounter of Cumbria's middling folk and gentry with the East Indies.

The process of tracking down archival traces is by no means straight-forward. It requires dealing with the formal records which have, as Steedman notes, been consciously chosen to preserve records of the past for adminis-trative or other purposes, and material which are 'mad fragmentations that no one intended to preserve and just ended up there'.[87] There is no compelling logic for material related to the encounter of Cumbrians with the East Indies to be preserved, archived or catalogued. There was no administrative branch of the East India Company dedicated to Cumbria. Cumbrians are scattered across the Company's records, their Cumbrian connections sometimes evident, sometimes not. Individuals such as John Robinson, Henry Fletcher, Henry Fawcett and Richard Atkinson, repeatedly referred to in the histori-ographies of the East India Company and British India, are rarely associated with Cumbria. Even when those associations are acknowledged, their depth and influence are left unexplored and their significance unrecognised.

Similarly, the records of Cumbrians 'at home' found in the Cumbrian, Lancashire or national archives are not conveniently arranged or catalogued to distinguish sojourners to the East Indies from others. Even so, the remnants of that East Indies encounter are not as obscured in the provincial space as one might assume from the little attention given to it. It is, for instance, not infrequently etched in stone. Cumbrian churches whisper of Cumbrian ventures in the East Indies in the memorials by which families commemorate their dead, assert their connections and promote their virtues.

Excavating and piecing together the trajectories of Cumbrians involved in the East Indies, their lives, their social milieu and their networks has been

---

86 L. Stone, 'Prosopography', *Daedalus*, 100 (1971), pp. 46–79.
87 C. Steedman, *Dust: The Archive and Cultural History* (New Brunswick, NJ, Rutgers University, 2002), p. 68.

enabled by accelerating advances in digitisation and powerful search engines. The new digital world gives historians an extended reach, allows archives to be penetrated in new ways and facilitates access to remnants of the past residing outside formal archives and retained, preserved and protected by private individuals and families, as well as often unpaid local historians who have ferreted out material previously only rarely embraced by academic historians. The digital world has made accessible the catalogues and backlists of businesses dealing with the artefacts of the past: fine art, manuscripts, letters and personal ephemera. Formerly, serendipity brought these to the attention of historians. These artefacts and their statements of provenance are increasingly preserved and susceptible to systematic interrogation.[88]

Digitisation and flexible search modes provide an ability to track individuals and interrogate across the walls between archives and the rigidities within archives created through their systems of categorisation. Today's new technology-based capabilities open up new opportunities, just as historians have found technologies have in the past. The historiography of the 1970s, for instance, would have looked very different without computerisation. Computerisation enabled the extensive use of quantified data and the aggregated analysis of patterns and underpinned a burst of migration studies, household constitution studies and much economic history. In the future it is likely that the development of geospatial information systems will stimulate historical geography and the use of visualisation techniques to analyse historical dynamics through a spatial lens.[89]

This book is part of a burgeoning body of research taking advantage of the compression of time and distance enabled by digitisation and online access to primary sources. The enhanced ability to track individuals and their networks allows biographical narratives to be integrated with the analysis of aggregate patterns, profiles and characteristics and the thematic analysis of sensibilities. Researchers are increasingly following the way in which individuals threaded themselves through different global spaces as globalised systems were established and operated. That emerging approach is evident in the historiography of slaving,[90] Anderson's work on subaltern people and the

---

[88] Anderson, *Subaltern Lives*, pp. 187–188; M. King, 'Working With/In the Archives', in S. Gunn and L. Faire (eds), *Research Methods for History* (Edinburgh, Edinburgh University, 2011), pp. 13–29.

[89] See Gunn and Faire (eds), *Research Methods for History* and A. von Lünen and C. Travers (eds), *History and GIS: Epistemologies, Considerations and Reflections* (New York, Springer, 2013) for recent reflections on changing tools and the impacts on the practice of history.

[90] For example: C. Hall, N. Draper, K. McClelland, C. Donington and R. Lamb, *Legacies of British Slave-Ownership: Colonial Slavery and the Formation of Victorian Britain* (Cambridge, Cambridge University Press, 2014); L. A. Lindsay and J. Wood Sweet (eds), *Biography and the Black Atlantic* (Kindle Edition, Philadelphia, University of Pennsylvania Press, 2014); M. Dresser and A. Hann (eds), *Slavery and the British Country House* (Swindon, English Heritage, 2013).

development and operation of archipelagos of penal colonies[91] and *The East India Company at Home*.[92]

The new permeability of archival boundaries generated by the digital world provides new analytic possibilities. However, the researchers who have followed that path have also highlighted the fundamental limitations of 'the record'. 'Archival traces', and the narratives built on them, are still shaped by choices of the past. Past individuals and institutions have determined what is to be recorded and what is to be preserved. Irrespective of the power of the digital world, the digital world cannot re-create what was not created or retained. The digital world may extend the reach of the historian but it does not dismantle the fundamental and polarised character of the record. The traces of the past are either those consciously retained because they legitimate or facilitate prevailing ruling relations, or they are simply inexplicably surviving detritus of past lives and events.[93]

Enumerating Cumbrians

While the digital world provides a platform for piecing together the lives and encounters of Cumbrians involved in East Indies ventures, several questions need to be addressed if that encounter is to be systematically revealed. What are the boundaries of Cumbria? Who should be counted as a Cumbrian? How can a 'Cumbrian' be identified and distinguished? Was someone born out of Cumbria but to parents or grandparents born in Cumbria, 'in' or 'out' as a Cumbrian? Conversely, what of the child born in Cumbria but whose familial and kin connections lay outside the Cumbrian counties? What is defined as involvement in, venture to, and encounter with the East Indies? Decisions around those questions are contestable, but the task of framing an enumeration is inescapable.

The enumeration of 421 Cumbrian men found in Appendix A and twenty-three Cumbrian women found in Appendix B are framed both by temporal and place dimensions. The temporal boundary is the long eighteenth century. To be enumerated, individuals must have been involved as adults with the East Indies between 1680 and 1829, although that involvement may stretch before and beyond those boundaries. Individuals born in the long eighteenth century but not in the Company or the East Indies prior to 1830 have been excluded from the enumeration, although they may be referred to in the narrative.

The place-related boundary is more complex and more challenging to apply. Enumerated individuals were either born in the Cumbrian counties – Cumberland, Westmorland and Lancashire North of the Sands – or with

---

91 Anderson, *Subaltern Lives*.
92 *The East India Company at Home*, http://blogs.ucl.ac.uk/eicah/home/.
93 King, 'Working With/In the Archives', pp. 23f.

Cumbrian parents with an ongoing association with Cumbria; and individuals who lived or worked in Cumbria over a long period. The enumeration also includes a small set of individuals who integrated themselves into Cumbrian provincial life after sojourns in the East Indies, such as Alexander Nowell of Kirkby Lonsdale and John Charles Bristow who died at Eusmere.

The other dimension of the place-related boundary relates to the East Indies. Cumbrians also had to be directly involved in the East Indies. In this context, the East Indies takes an early meaning, that is, of India, South East Asia and the southern coast of China. Cumbrian men must have been: appointees to the East India Company in the British Isles or in the East Indies; or a Company director, agent, ship's husband, contracted supplier; or in a position of political power over the Company. Cumbrians with commercial ventures in the East Indies or licences to travel as free merchants are included. Excluded are those Cumbrian women and men who held East India Company stock but had no other direct or formal involvement in the East Indies or in the Company.[94] The enumerated Cumbrian women are those who lived in the East Indies for some period in their adult life and were either born in Cumbria, born elsewhere with a Cumbrian parent, or married men involved in the East Indies. Non-Cumbrian spouses, whether husband or wife, involved in the East Indies are excluded from the enumeration of Cumbrians although their children may be included if they meet the other criteria.

Mixed-race children, where they have been identified, are included in the enumeration if they meet the enumeration criteria but many do not. They are, nevertheless, often at the heart of some of the tensions that infused the Cumbria encounters with the East Indies. Thirty-eight mixed-race children have been identified including children by women whose backgrounds are opaque (Appendix C). For instance, one of the latter was referred to as Mary Smith. Three children born in India between 1806 and 1810 to Mary Smith and John Charles Bristow were baptised at St Marylebone on 25 July 1811.[95] Rather than the father's name being followed by the given name of the mother designated as 'wife', there is no such designation on these children's baptismal records. That, and Bristow's own background (he had at least three older half-siblings through his father's relationship with Mahondy Khanum of Patna), are hints that his own children may have been mixed race. The mother's name, consisting of two ubiquitous names 'Mary' and 'Smith', suggests that the baptismal records of these Bristow children may be an example of what Ghosh has revealed were widespread practices in which

---

[94] This is consistent with Philips, *The East India Company 1784–1834*, p. 340.

[95] *Church of England Parish Registers, 1538–1812*: London – Saint Marylebone, Day book of baptisms, Feb. 1811–Mar. 1812. Ancestry.com. *London, England, Baptisms, Marriages and Burials, 1538–1812* [online database]. Provo, UT, USA: Ancestry.com Operations, Inc., 2010, accessed http://home.ancestry.co.uk.

native women become erased from the sexual and family life of British men and, often, the lives of their own children.[96]

Making Sense

Steedman implies that the fragments of the past are so limited that the task of the historian is 'to conjure a social system from a nutmeg grater'. [97] Digitisation, search engines and connectivity combine to generate, however, an abundance of fragmentary, albeit uneven, material. If the process of enumerating the Cumbrians who fall within these time and place boundaries presents a challenge, so too does piecing together and interpreting the fragmentary material associated with each of the enumerated individuals. Inevitably their lives, trajectories, affiliations and associates are incompletely and unevenly rendered in the record. It is perhaps easiest to see their collective 'archival traces' as constituting a prism that allows the Cumbrian encounter with the East Indies to be refracted. Quantitative analysis gives attention to the aggregate patterns of the encounter across time, the implication of place attachments in those East Indies ventures, the social profile of Cumbrian East Indies sojourners, and the structure of connections between Cumbrians involved in the East Indies. Thematic, qualitative analysis, particularly of the remnants of personal correspondence but also of contemporary printed materials and administrative records including wills and inventories, provides an insight into the sensibilities of Cumbrians as well as economic, social and material drivers, expressions and outcomes of East Indies ventures.

Even within a single archive associated with a single organisation or institution or archives focused on a particular set of events or families, the problem of 'what is missing' is ever present. It is a problem multiplied when dealing with populations as aggregates of defined individuals. No doubt it has contributed to what Miller criticises as the tendency towards abstraction evident in social history and the 'cultural turn'.[98] Among the Cumbrians at the centre of this book, the density of material ranges from a simple, single reference connecting a Cumbrian to the East Indies but otherwise unconnected to any other individuals, to genealogies, to extensive collections of letters, wills and other records, as well as references in secondary sources. Some voices inevitably remain muted. Other voices are lost entirely. Their lives are reflected only in the official, public and private commentary

---

[96] D. Ghosh, *Sex and the Family in Colonial India: The Making of Empire* (Cambridge, Cambridge University Press, 2006), pp. 15–23, 76, 139, 144; D. Ghosh, 'National Narratives and the Politics of Miscegenation: Britain and India', in A. Burton (ed.), *Archive Stories: Facts, Fictions, and the Writing of History* (Durham, NC, Duke University Press, 2006), pp. 27–44.

[97] Steedman, *Dust*, p. 18.

[98] J. Miller, 'A Historical Appreciation of the Biographical Turn', in Lindsay and Wood Sweet (eds), *Biography and the Black Atlantic*, pp. 21, 23, 28–32, 41.

constructed by others. At least, however, their existence, and, for some, aspects of their lives, can be retrieved.

The material that has been generated by this process of accumulating 'archival traces' presents two interpretative tasks. The first is the task of taking into account the particular mode and rules by which material or the record was produced. Applications for appointment to the East India Company, to personal letters, to contemporary print material, to wills and inventories, to material sources such as portraits, houses and church memorials, are stylised in form and their meaning cannot always be interpreted directly. For instance, an East India Company applicant may state that his nomination was not secured by financial payment but the sale of nominations by Company directors was widespread.[99]

Such a declaration says little about the virtues, or even the compliance, of an applicant, his family or his friends. However, it says a great deal about the importance for the East India Company of personal relations, reputations and reciprocal obligations in regulating the behaviour of Company servants. Equally, declarations and the development of standardised applications, albeit unevenly used, reflect the Company's evolving bureaucratisation and its trans-formation from merchant company to territorial power, and, eventually, to administrative state across the eighteenth century.

Contemporary printed material, too, provides what might be termed 'information' but simultaneously articulates societal values, aspirations and ambition. Cumbrian house and estate advertisements, for instance, demon-strate the way in which estates that would be small and relatively insignificant in the southern counties were in Cumbria developed to support and reflect local social elites, including garden villas on the hinterlands of provincial towns. Similarly, guidebooks, whether of the Lake District, India, aristo-cratic estates or provincial towns, provide description but also sketch out the changing terrains of sensibility, taste and social position. So, too, do the many histories of provincial towns produced during the eighteenth century.[100]

Even in personal records the individual voice was not always prominent. Diaries were often little more than jottings of time, place, appointments, weather and, occasionally, expenditure. Wills, contracts and property settle-ments all had ritualised forms. So too did letters. On the other hand, it should not be assumed ritualised form embodies 'real' function or meaning, or prevents the expression of the individual voice. Of legal documents, wills and, where they are available, inventories, provide rich insights despite elements of linguistic ritual, for they express multiple dimensions of social, economic

---

99 Ghosh, *The Social Condition of the British Community*, pp. 21–23; Parkinson, *Trade in the Eastern Seas*, pp. 15–16.

100 R. Sweet, 'The Production of Urban Histories in Eighteenth-century England', *Urban History*, 23, 2 (1996), pp. 171–188; R. Sweet, *The Writing of Urban Histories in Eighteenth-Century England* (Oxford, Clarendon Press, 1997).

and cultural life: the values, mores and norms of property, expectations of and responsibilities to family and kin, bonds of friendship and consumption. Similarly, the historiography of eighteenth-century letter-writing shows the complex and multi-layered meanings embodied in letters.

Earlier analysis of eighteenth-century letter-writing conflated personal letters and letters for publication. They also treated letter-writing as primarily a vehicle arising from, and directed to reinforcing, the emergence of the culture of politeness and sociability. Brant, however, demonstrates a diversity of personal letter-writing genres in the eighteenth century and challenges the notion that letter-writing was designed merely to promote this new social paradigm of polite sociability. Despite ideals of politeness, the personal letter was still a vehicle for conveying frank demands, criticism, disdain and even abuse. The conventions of letter-writing were shaped by performance and the persona taken on by the correspondent and the circumstances of the correspondence.[101] The language of politeness, humility and, on occasions, servility took account of social hierarchy, but the same language could also be a gloss for impertinence, resistance or claims of disputed entitlement. Certainly, in the Cumbrian context, all those parts and passions are evident. The letter-rich records of the middling Cumbrian Cust family are especially resonant. In short, letters were shaped by prevailing conventions, but style and convention did not necessarily mute the writer's voice. In the world of global sojourns, letters conveyed that voice to maintain intimacy over considerable distance and long periods. As Popp points out, 'correspondence was… the child of absence'.[102]

Letters raise issues of interpretation, particularly where there is an abundance of correspondence. The Custs, the Senhouses and the Hudlestons are associated with bodies of correspondence that extended over time and were characterised by a multiplicity of correspondents ranging across family, friends, distant kin, colleagues, acquaintances and even strangers. The letters within those different bodies of correspondence embraced intimate correspondence to correspondence directed to matters of business. Some subjects or themes threaded their way through long sequences of letters. Other subjects, incidents or events were the focus of only brief attention. How are these to be analysed and interpreted? Does each letter, or each letter within a subset of letters, constitute the unit of analysis? Or is the unit of analysis the contours of one or more bodies of correspondence as a whole or an extended strand within it? If the latter, does this draw us back from a nuanced interpretation of sense within prevailing social, institutional and cultural contexts bound by time and place or demand quantification of phrases, references and words found in content analysis or analysis of the structure of the text?

---

[101] C. Brant, *Eighteenth-Century Letters and British Culture* (Basingstoke, Palgrave Macmillan, 2010), pp. 15, 23, 24–27.

[102] Popp, *Entrepreneurial Families*, p. 11.

In this book, these bodies of correspondence have been treated as 'places' in which themes central to Cumbria's East Indies encounter may be expressed. Those expressions are analysed across the multiplicity of sources. In addition, rather than formal textual analysis or transforming subjective expression into quantitative data and analysing it statistically, the analysis of these letters has involved a structured interrogation with interpretative judgements generated by qualitative thematic reading. That thematic reading has been structured by three considerations.

The first consideration was around establishing the range of experience, attitudes, expectations, perceptions and sensibilities expressed across the entire body of source material. The second consideration was to explore the extent to which letters across a multiplicity of correspondents show divergence or convergence in experiences, attitudes, expectations, perceptions and sensibilities. The third consideration was to understand those experiences, attitudes, expectations, perceptions and sensibilities by reference to the structural positions, interests and relational contexts of the correspondents themselves. The content of a letter is not, then, detached from the immediate circumstances of the correspondent, their relation with the recipient, or the explicit and sometimes less transparent function of a letter or a set of letters.

The application of those three considerations is iterative rather than sequential. Such a process of analysis and interpretation recognises that correspondence is not a simple, unproblematic body of material, even when elements of content appear to be records of events, activities, or 'facts'.[103] What, then, is expressed in the text are interpretative judgements generated out of that process rather than a description of its mechanics. I tend to provide contextual signals around the text of letters that are quoted because, while those quotes are designed to illustrate convergences (or divergences) with other correspondence, it needs to be remembered that specific letters were also embedded in the trajectories of people's lives.

That brings us to the second major interpretative task when piecing together these 'archival traces'. That is, the task of integrating and analysing the disparate and uneven material attached to individuals and their milieu into threads that contribute to a broader narrative that goes beyond the individuals themselves. This raises issues around the nature of the 'biographical turn', especially the distinction between biographical-based analysis and narratives as ways of exploring the 'particular' and the practice of traditional biography.[104]

---

[103] Popp, *Entrepreneurial Families*, pp. 19f.

[104] Anderson, *Subaltern Lives*, pp. 4–22, 187–189; Miller, 'A Historical Appreciation', pp. 28–32; C. Ginzburg, *Threads and Traces: True False Fictive* (Berkeley, University of California Press, 2012), p. 203.

In this book, biographical narratives are scattered throughout, although presented most formally in the final substantive section of Chapter 2. These narratives are not designed to simply 'humanise' history, although as Ogborn and others point out, this is an important antidote to reductionism and reification.[105] The approach used here reflects a view that history is constituted through, and, therefore, illuminated by, the choices and actions of individuals within the context of their immediate relations and structured positions. Unlike traditional biography, biographical fragments are not used here to constitute the individual and her or his life as reflecting a process of self-actualisation. Bourdieu refers to the latter as a biographical illusion.[106] Rather, each individual life is regarded as constituted through a series of trajectories.

While experienced personally, those trajectories are wrought by events, structures and processes beyond the control of an individual and, despite their efforts, of families and friends. At the same moment, lives, and the multiple trajectories that make up those lives, are shaped by purposeful decisions and conscious sensibilities. Each of those trajectories are only partially rendered in 'archival traces' and some trajectories within a single life are absent from the record altogether.[107] Nevertheless, the enriched empirical environment enabled by the digital world allows us to integrate biography into the analysis of structures, networks, practices and sensibilities.[108] Multiple biographical narratives provide a basis for reflecting on the transferability, representativeness or idiosyncrasy of the 'case' while capturing the nuances of individual experience and agency within the prevailing social, economic and political structures, networks and sensibilities.

Chapter Structure

This book is not about the life of Cumbrian provincials in India, but how the East Indies sojourn was tied to, and expressed, ambitions for life and position in Cumbria. It recognises and unwraps Cumbria's implication in the establishment and operation of East India settlements, the East India Company and the parliamentary response to commercial and military expansion in India throughout the long eighteenth century. It suggests that Cumbrian gentry and middling encounters with the East Indies lie on the connective

---

[105] M. Ogborn, *Global Lives: Britain and the World 1550–1800* (Cambridge, Cambridge University Press, 2008), pp. 9–14; Miller, 'A Historical Appreciation', pp. 46–47.

[106] P. Bourdieu, *The Logic of Practice* (Cambridge, Polity Press, 1990), p. 55.

[107] Anderson, *Subaltern Lives*, pp. 15, 16, 18.

[108] See the diverse biographies presented in N. Chaudhuri, S. J. Katz and M. E. Perry (eds), *Contesting Archives: Finding Women in the Sources* (Urbana, University of Illinois Press, 2010) for the application of biography as a means to illuminate women's experiences in a variety of socio-historical contexts.

edges between historiographies embracing English provincial life, the East India Company, British India and new imperialism, issues of continuity and change in the structure, practices and sensibilities of class, family and kinship, and social and economic development in Cumbria.

Under those circumstances, Cumbria provides a window on the interface between provincial life and the East Indies through the period over which 'British India' developed. It allows us to ask whether the East Indies encounter beyond London was an integral part of the social and economic life of the provinces. Was it anything more than a disparate set of individuals with provincial origins who happened to develop, adopt and operate primarily through Anglo-Indian identities and networks? Was the provincial encounter simply an experience of national imperialism felt at a local level and provincials' involvement in the East Indies driven, as some might suggest, by imperatives around union and British identity? Were the imperatives for Cumbrian middling and gentry families about sustaining, retaining, and sometimes, restoring their social and economic position within their provincial milieu?

This book presents an opportunity to test the common view that the eighteenth-century encounter between the British Isles and the East was primarily a combination of imperial ambition and the construction of a British identity in the context of a new United Kingdom. Equally, the lens of a provincial encounter with the East Indies provides a new way of looking at Cumbria, not as a 'failed' industrial economy but as a region in which opportunities 'abroad', whether in the British Isles or overseas, were taken by an amalgam of gentry and middling rank families.

The sequence of chapters reflects the particular combination of quantitative and structural analysis, biographical narrative and thematic analysis which has been enabled by the digital world. The pattern of the Cumbrian encounter set out in Chapter 2 has a three-pronged focus. The social characteristics, place origins and networks of Cumbrian men and their kin involved in the East Indies are presented. Those patterns are set within their chronological context and explored further through six short biographical narratives. Chapters 3, 4 and 5 turn to a broader canvas and follow the cycle of Cumbrians' anticipation of, passage to and return from the East Indies.

Chapter 3 explores how gentry and middling Cumbrian families saw the East Indies, its potential as a pathway to success and how they managed their ambivalences about the East Indies to establish for themselves an acceptable balance between risk-taking and reward-seeking. Because the new opportunities presented by the East Indies could not be realised by desire alone, Chapter 4 shows how the passage to the East Indies depended on a complex interaction between cultural, economic and social capital. Chapter 5 traces the pattern of success and disappointment for Cumbrian East Indies sojourners and their families and the way sojourners sustained, established or promoted their own position or the standing of their families within Cumbrian provincial society.

The final chapter comments on the materiality of the Cumbrian encounter with the East Indies. It comments too on how the lens of the Cumbrian encounter with the East Indies brings new insights into prevailing narratives of imperialism, the global world and nationhood as well Cumbrian regional social and economic development. In doing so, it underscores the importance of the regional or provincial case and how a provincial lens can illuminate aspects of national and global experience.

Two

CUMBRIAN CONTEXTS, PATTERNS AND LIVES

1885 – C. W. Bardsley:

> [S]he was married to Christopher Wilson, who had but recently purchased Bardsea Hall... Christopher was a sea captain in the Hon. East India Company's service, and like many another adventurer of that time, left it with his fortune made. He was a cadet... of a good Westmorland family... He wooed and won.[1]

1965 – E. Hughes:

> Ever since the days of Governor Pitt and 'Galloper' Curwen, Cumbrian youths of families with Jacobite or Non-Juror sympathies had entered the service of the East India Company.[2]

1981 – J. V. Beckett:

> By the late 1730s, with only Lowther and Edward Stephenson – a former East India Company nabob who had bought himself an estate near Keswick – lending money...[3]

The East Indies became enmeshed in Cumbrian life in the eighteenth century with well over 400 Cumbrian men and women identified as directly involved in East Indies trade, the East India Company or East Indies sojourns. They

---

[1] C. W. Bardsley, *Chronicles of the Town and Church of Ulverston* (Ulverston, James Atkinson, 1885), p. 91.

[2] E. Hughes, *North Country Life in the Eighteenth Century Vol II Cumberland & Westmorland 1700–1830* (London, Oxford University Press, 1965), p. 105.

[3] J. V. Beckett, *Coal and Tobacco: The Lowthers and the Economic Development of West Cumberland 1660–1760* (Cambridge, Cambridge University Press, 1981), p. 207.

were connected to, and supported by, many more Cumbrians. This chapter analyses the characteristics of the Cumbrians involved in the East Indies encounter, the structure of their relationships, and heralds the continuities as well as the heterogeneity of their East Indies encounters. It starts with a chronological overview of the context in which Cumbrians were operating, focusing on the alignment between the numbers of Cumbrian men appointed and licensed by the East India Company, the changing operations of the East India Company, and events shaping the British Isles in the global world.

The second section focuses on the patterns of encounter, compares rates of Cumbrian involvement in the East Indies with other counties, and explores the social characteristics and place origins of enumerated Cumbrian men. The social structure of Cumbria's encounter with the East Indies is uncovered by a systematic mapping of the networks between East Indies-involved families. The final section presents six chronologically arranged biographical narratives that highlight the way in which the pursuit of success in the East Indies comprised profound and persistent continuities, despite the social heterogeneity of Cumbrian sojourners, the diversity of their trajectories and outcomes for their families, and the chronological stretch of the long eighteenth century.

Company Contexts

Over the long eighteenth century, the numbers of Cumbrian men going to the East Indies accelerated. Four Cumbrian men were appointed or licensed by the East India Company in the twenty years prior to 1700. In the following two decades, a further eight Cumbrian men took up appointments or licences and entry. Levels remained similar for the next thirty years. The 1750s saw a jump in Cumbrian appointments and licences. Thereafter there was a broadly upward trend (Figure 2.1).

Those Cumbrians were in the midst of extraordinary change and were exposed to a succession of decisive events. Cumbrian families such as the Braddylls, Winders and Stephensons saw the East India Company struggle through the Glorious Revolution and expand under Union and the Hanoverian succession. William of Orange's accession and debates around royal assent to trade monopolies were associated with attacks on the Company's monopoly and 'interloper' trade in the East Indies outside of the Company's control flourished.[4] In 1698, two companies, the old East India Company and a new company, were each given royal assent to trade in the East Indies, although the new company was short-lived and a merger quickly occurred. One of the

---

[4]   J. Bohun, 'Protecting Prerogative: William III and the East India Trade Debate, 1689–1698', *Past Imperfect*, 2 (1993), pp. 63–86.

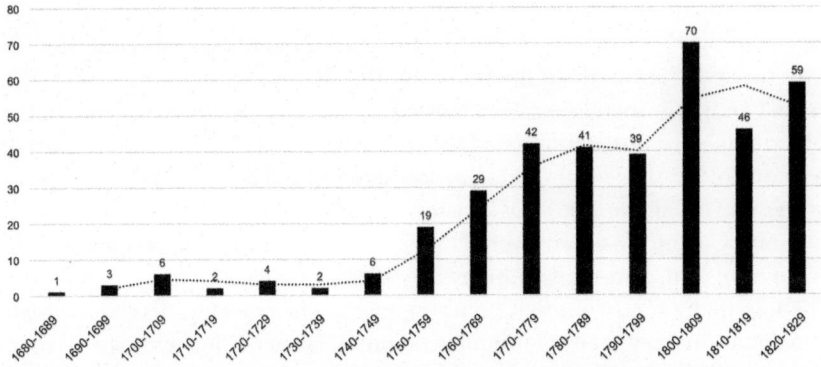

Figure 2.1 Number and Moving Average of Appointments/Licences of Cumbrian Men by Year of Initial Appointment or License to the East Indies, 1680–1829

key players negotiating that merger and re-stabilising a Company monopoly in the East Indies was the Cumbrian merchant Jonathan Winder.

From 1715 the Company was actively pursuing commercial advantages from the Mughal emperor. In 1717, a two-year, three-man Company delegation to Delhi was granted an imperial firman, waiving customs duties on the Company trade in Bengal. The Cumbrian Edward Stephenson, who is the subject of a biographical narrative later in this chapter, was part of that delegation. The extension of Mughal recognition provided the Company with more security in India. It also, importantly, amplified the Company's influence at home. In 1721 and 1723, parliament reinforced the Company monopoly. In 1726, the East India Company gained a new charter giving it authority over all British subjects operating within the East Indies. The key settlements Madras, Calcutta and Bombay were progressively endowed with the paraphernalia of local rule evident in English towns: corporations: mayors, recorders and aldermen.[5] In 1730, parliament again renewed the Company's monopoly in exchange for a Company payment of £200,000.[6] It followed by lending the British government a million pounds and effectively financed Britain's involvement in the Austrian War of Succession. The close relations between Company and Crown saw France returning Madras to the Company after a three-year occupation by the French under the Treaty of Aix-le-Chapelle.[7]

5   T. A. Mansfield, 'Calcutta, from Fort to City: A Study of a Colonial Settlement, 1690–1750' (PhD thesis, University of Leicester, 2012), pp. 107–111; Riddick, *The History of British India: A Chronology*, p. 6.
6   L. Sutherland, *The East India Company in 18th Century Politics* (Oxford, Clarendon Press, 1952), p. 30.
7   Sutherland, *The East India Company in 18th Century Politics*, pp. 30, 46.

A combination of European geopolitics, the fragmenting Mughal empire, the Company's close relationship with the British government, and its own anxieties around competition in the Indian market, saw the East India Company increasingly embroiled in military conflicts on the Indian sub-continent. Those culminated in 1756 with the loss of Calcutta and Fort William to the nawab of Bengal, Siraj-ud-daula, followed by Clive's defeat of the nawab at the Battle of Plassey in 1757. The conquest was a pivotal moment. Calcutta was retrieved, French influence on the India sub-continent was diminished, and the Company was given territorial powers over Bengal. The Company was, from that point on, moving from a commercial company to a fiscal-military state combining commercial activities with increasingly intense military, judicial and civil administrative operations.[8]

The considerable increase in the number of Cumbrian men appointed or licensed to the East Indies from the 1750s was aligned to a broader expansion of Company settlements in the post-Plassey era. The personnel collecting revenues in Madras numbered 175 Europeans in 1787, almost as many as the entire civilian European population, male and female, of Madras in 1740.[9] By 1787, the Madras Army had some 850 European officers. A third of the 6,000 rank and file were Europeans and there were around fifty military surgeons.[10] The pattern was similar in Calcutta. Prior to 1750 around fifty Company civilian men from the British Isles were at Calcutta at any one time.[11] After Plassey, the civil establishment reached seventy-six.[12] European merchants outside the Company, as well as European men captaining country trade ships and the populations of resident European women also increased.[13]

The British government became deeply implicated in, and benefitted from, the success of the East India Company. Co-dependency generated the complex articulation between the British government's and the Company's interests in the American colonies which climaxed in the American War of Independence. The taxation crisis with the American colonies had its roots in the government's attempt to simultaneously maintain its own tax revenues, relieve the East India Company of tax liabilities on imported and re-exported

---

[8] T. Roy, 'Rethinking the Origins of British India: State Formation and Military-Fiscal Undertakings in an Eighteenth Century World Region', *London School of Economics Working Papers*, No. 142/10 (2010), pp. 3, 8–11.

[9] H. Furber, *Private Fortunes and Company Profits in the India Trade in the 18th Century* (Aldershot: Variorum, 1997), IV, p. 284; S. Mentz, *The English Gentleman Merchant at Work: Madras and the City of London 1660–1740* (Copenhagen, Museum Tusculanum Press, University of Copenhagen, 2005), p. 244.

[10] Furber, *Private Fortunes*, IV, p. 287.

[11] P. J. Marshall, *East Indian Fortunes: British in Bengal in the Eighteenth Century* (Oxford, Oxford University Press, 1976), pp. 14–15.

[12] S. Ghosh, *The Social Condition of the British Community in Bengal 1757–1800* (Leiden, E. J. Brill, 1970), p. 1.

[13] Furber, *Private Fortunes*, VIII, p. 3.

tea, resolve the Company's over-supply of tea, and deal with the financial pressures on the Company associated with the Bengal famine.[14] The eventual loss of the American colonies prompted a new focus on the East Indies as an imperial domain.

The gaze shifted from proprietorial Atlantic colonialism to commercial and imperial rule in the East.[15] All those factors contributed to refocusing the Company from merchant operations supported by maritime and military services to something very different. By 1813, trading opportunities were pursued by free, rather than Company, merchants. The Company had been largely transformed into a professional administration of civil service, judiciary and military. By the early nineteenth century, the Company's transformation diversified career opportunities in the East Indies, but it also constrained private trade and the personal acquisition of plundered wealth.

Patterns of an Encounter

Within the broad sweep of change, Cumbria's involvement in the East Indies manifested three critical patterns. The first was the over-representation of Cumbrians in the East Indies compared to other English counties. The second was the dispersed pattern of Cumbrian origins found among Cumbrians appointed to or licensed by the East India Company. The third pattern was related to the social profile of Cumbrian appointees and licensees to India.

In the 1960s an analysis of the place-origins of officers in the Bengal military found that, while 6 per cent of the British population had London origins, London origins were found among almost twice that proportion of officers in the Bengal army.[16] Razzell's research reinforced a prevailing view that London was at the centre of the East India Company and, consequently, it was the interests of London merchants that drew the British Isles and the East Indies into a nexus of trade, colonialism and imperialism.

The methodological limitations of Razzell's analysis should have signalled caution. The dataset was limited to officers in the Bengal military. It excluded military appointments to the Madras and Bombay presidencies, appointments of people born in India, and civil appointments and licences to free merchants in Bengal as well as Madras and Bombay. Razzell's categorisation of origins also problematically used broad regional conglomerations,

14 B. W. Labaree, *Catalyst for Revolution: The Boston Tea Party* (Boston, MA, Massachusetts Bicentennial Commission Publication, 1973), pp. 5, 9, 11, 17-21.

15 A. Murdoch, *British History 1660–1832: National Identity and Local Culture* (Basingstoke, Macmillan Press, 1998), pp. 68–70; P. J. Marshall, *The Making and Unmaking of Empires: Britain, India and America, c.1750–1783* (Oxford, Oxford University Press, 2005), pp. 4–12, 373–379.

16 P. Razzell, 'The Social Origins of the Indian and British Home Army: 1758–1962', *The British Journal of Sociology*, 14, 3 (1963), pp. 248–260.

conflating counties with very different characteristics. The industrial conurba-
tions of Lancashire and Cheshire, for instance, were amalgamated with the
counties of Westmorland and Cumberland.

The British Library India Office Family Search Index provides a more
robust basis for analysing county origins and presents a somewhat different
picture (Figure 2.2). The county origins of around 1,600 men appointed or
licensed prior to 1804 can be found there. The rate of East India Company
appointment and licensing across all the counties was around 0.88 men per
10,000 of the 1801 population, but county rates varied considerably. The
London-proximate counties of Berkshire, Surrey, Essex, Hertfordshire and
Kent all had higher rates than the total counties population rate. However,
other London-proximate counties such as Middlesex, Buckinghamshire and
Sussex apparently had very low rates, although arguably Middlesex residents
may have been styled as Londoners in the records.

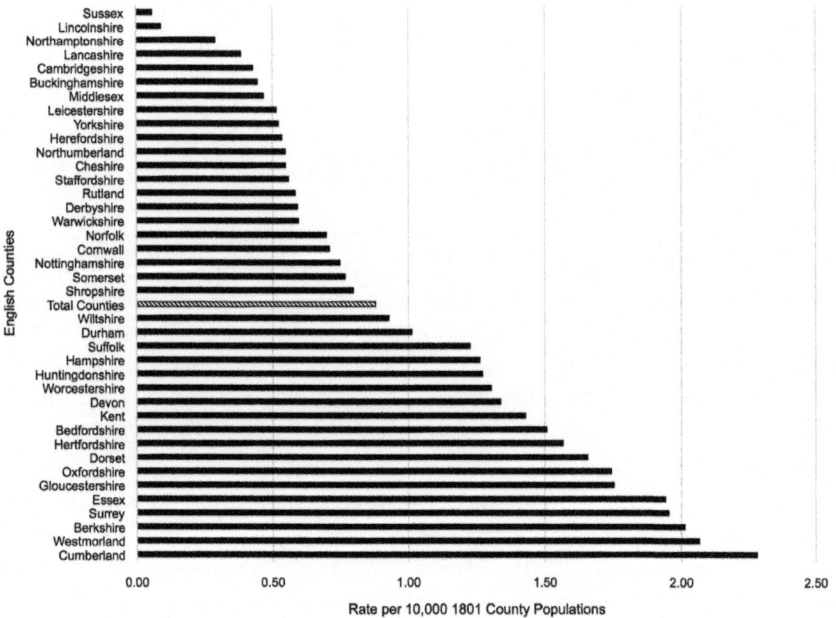

Figure 2.2 Rate of Male Appointment and Licences to the East Indies Prior to 1804

Westmorland and Cumberland had high rates compared to other English
counties with 2.07 and 2.28 men per 10,000 of their 1801 populations respectively. The sheer size of the London-proximate county populations compared
to the smaller populations of Cumberland and Westmorland meant that men
from London-proximate counties made up larger proportions of the English
men appointed and licensed to the East Indies. Nevertheless, Cumbrians

were over-represented. While Westmorland and Cumberland constituted less than 2 per cent of the English population in 1801, men from those counties made up 4 per cent of all the East India Company's English appointees and sojourners over the long eighteenth century.[17]

The over-representation of Cumbrian and their high rates of Company appointments and licences have two important implications. First, they suggest that the Cumbrian encounter with the East Indies was not simply a local expression of national imperatives. If it was so, the proportion of Company appointments and licences by county would be similar to the proportion of each county's demographic contribution to the national population. Second, it implies that many Cumbrians were exposed to people involved in the East Indies. That conclusion is also suggested by the spatial pattern of the births and baptisms of Cumbrian men appointed or licensed by the East India Company.

The vast majority of the enumerated Cumbrian men involved in the East Indies were born in Cumbria. They had their origins across almost a hundred Cumbrian towns and villages (Map 2.1). In some localities, East Indies involvement was dominated by a small set of resident families. For instance, the thirteen men involved in the East Indies and born or baptised in Crosby Ravensworth represented only four family names: Addison, Dent, Wilkinson and Rigg. The three men from Allonby were all Huddarts. Dalton-in-Furness was represented in the East Indies only by the Ashburners and James Romney. Gilcrux was similarly represented only by the Hall family and Maulds Meaburn by the Dent family. All but one of the men involved in the East Indies from Temple Sowerby were named Atkinson. Newby Bridge's encounter with the East Indies was dominated by the Taylors.

In most places, however, the patterns were much less concentrated and involvement in the East Indies was spread across a number of different families. For instance, in Bassenthwaite, Cartmel, Hawkshead, Bardsea, Barton, Brigham and Kirkby Thore, each of the enumerated men had different family names. Penrith was similar. In Whitehaven, only a quarter of the men involved in the East Indies shared a family name. There were twenty-five different family names among the thirty-nine enumerated men from Carlisle and its surrounds. Seven different family names were found among the men from Kendal and its surrounds. Two Stanleys were among the Workington men involved in the East Indies but the remainder were from different families. Overall, more than half of the Cumbrian settlements with East Indies connections contributed only a single man to the East Indies. Around a third of the enumerated Cumbrian men had no

17 The baseline 1801 population is taken from B. Mitchell, *British Historical Statistics* (Cambridge, Cambridge University Press, 2011), pp. 30–31; Razzell, 'The Social Origins of the Indian and British Home Army', p. 250.

Number of baptisms/births of enumerated Cumbrian men

·	·	·	•	•	•	●	●	●	●	●	●
1	2	3	4	5	7	8	9	10	13	15	22	39

Map 2.1 Cumbrian Natal Locations of Enumerated Men Involved in the East Indies

kinship or familial relationships with other Cumbrian men with East Indies interests. Those spatial patterns of birth and baptismal places indicate that provincial, rather than dynastic, dynamics drove the Cumbrian encounter with the East Indies.

British India and East India Company historiography has long portrayed British India as shaped by the succession of fathers and sons over many generations, marriages forged *in* India, and the creation of an Anglo-Indian identity among British official families.[18] A dynastic tendency was certainly evident in a few Cumbrian families, including the Ashburners, Pattensons of Melmerby Hall, the Bellasis family and Taylors of Newby Bridge. However, it should not be overstated. If the Cumbrian experience of the East Indies was principally driven by dynastic Anglo-Indian families, the births and baptisms of these men could be expected to concentrate around a few locations. Clearly, this was not the case. Indeed, far from a pronounced dynastic tendency, the fathers of around 80 per cent of the enumerated Cumbrian men were not themselves involved in the East Indies or the East India Company. The spatial dispersion of Cumbrians' East Indies involvement was matched by social dispersion. It has long been argued that East India Company appointees and licensees had primarily mercantile origins.

According to Ghosh, 86 per cent of writers and cadets appointed to the Company's Bengal Presidency in 1768, 1780 and 1800 respectively were from merchant, trader or professional families.[19] That profile was somewhat different from that of the Cumbrian men associated with the East Indies. By comparison, only 73 per cent of Cumbrian appointments and men licensed to the East Indies prior to 1830 can be categorised as from merchant, trader or professional families. Around 10 per cent of Cumbrian appointees and licensees were from artisan, craftsman and minor farming families compared to Ghosh's 3 per cent of appointees to Bengal. Men from gentry and landowning families accounted for 18 per cent of the Cumbrian appointees compared to 11 per cent of appointees to the Bengal army (Figure 2.3).

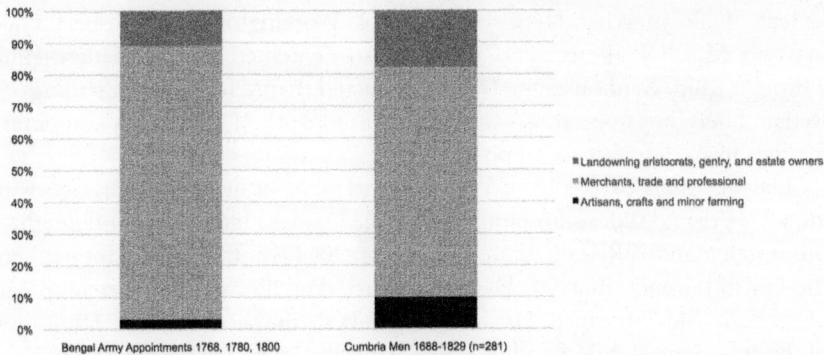

Figure 2.3 Comparative Social Composition of British-born Bengal Army Officers and Cumbrian East India Appointees and Licensees

---

18 Ghosh, *The Social Condition of the British Community in Bengal*, pp. 33–56; Mentz, *The English Gentleman Merchant at Work*, pp. 42–46, 215–259; J. G. Parker, 'The Directors of the East India Company 1754–1790' (PhD thesis, University of Edinburgh, 1977), pp. 354f; Marshall, *East Indian Fortunes*, pp. 11–12.

19 Ghosh, *The Social Condition of the British Community*, p. 31.

Those comparisons should be treated with caution. The database of enumerated Cumbrian men presented in this monograph stretches over the long eighteenth century. Ghosh's data were drawn from three periodic snapshots and his treatment of 'upper' class and 'middle' class categories is unclear. Nevertheless, it appears Cumbrians involved in the East Indies were more likely to be of higher or of lower rank. Certainly, the Lysons' 1816 list of gentlemen's seats in Cumberland show gentry families had strong East Indies associations (Table 2.1).[20] All but six of the Lysons' gentlemen had some kin-based involvement in the East Indies in the eighteenth century. Over a quarter of the residents of these 'gentlemen's seats' had at least one close relation (father, son, brother, grandfather, first cousin or uncle) who had served in the East India Company or lived in the East Indies. Four residents on the Lysons' list had lived in the East Indies.

Like the spatial dispersion of origins among the Cumbrian men involved in the East Indies, the heterogeneity of social rank among Cumbrians in the East Indies suggests that the East Indies penetrated deep into Cumbrian life. Moreover, Cumbria's early fusion between land, commerce, trade and manufacture was evident in many of the Cumbrian families involved in the East Indies. On the Lysons' list, for instance, the gentry Lawson family was connected to other gentry families such as the Curwens, Hudlestons and Musgraves. But they also became connected to the solidly merchant and middling Adderton and Addison families, and, eventually, to the prominent Whitehaven merchant family, the Gales. The Gales' trading operations embraced North America, London and St Petersburg from their base in Whitehaven. The Gales infiltrated gentry families in addition to the Lawsons. Isabella Gale married Henry Curwen of Workington Hall. Robert Gale married Mary Senhouse and in doing so cemented ties to Nether Hall. Through Mary Senhouse, the Gales connected themselves to the Flemings of Rydal. There are numerous examples of a network of marriages conjoining families from different social positions.

The Flemings of Rydal in Westmorland were drawn into marriage with an, albeit rising, statesman family when Sir Daniel Fleming's granddaughter Susannah married Rydal's estate steward Michael Knott in 1738. Her nephew, the fourth baronet, married Diana Howard, daughter of the fourteenth earl of Suffolk and Berkshire. Her niece Elizabeth married Andrew Hudleston of Hutton John, while another niece, Dorothy, married George Stanley of Ponsonby Hall. Susannah made a less socially exalted alliance, but then her early years had been precarious. Nonetheless, in marrying Michael Knott, the builder of Rydal Mount and steward to the Fleming estates, Susannah

---

[20] D. Lyson and S. Lyson, *Magna Britannia; being a Concise Topographical Account of the Several Counties of Great Britain – Volume the Fourth: Cumberland* (London, T. Cadell and W. Davies, 1816), pp. XCVIII–C.

Table 2.1 Lysons' Cumberland Gentlemen and Baronets Seats 1816 and the East Indies

Seats	Lysons' Owners or Occupiers	East Indies Connection
Armathwaite Castle	Robert Sanderson Milbourn, Esq.	Not known
Brayton	Wilfred Lawson, Esq.	Distant kin
Carleton-hall	Rt Hon. Thomas Wallace.	Kin
Calder Abbey	Miss Senhouse.	Kin
Corby-Castle	Henry Howard, Esq.	Not known
Dalemain	Edward Hasell, Esq.	Kin
Dovenby-hall	Joseph Dykes Ballantine Dykes, Esq.	Kin
Dalehead	Thomas Stanger Leathes, Esq.	Not known
Ewanrigg	John Christian, Esq.	Kin
Hayton-Castle	Mrs Joliffe (Rev. Isaac Robinson.)	Uncle and kin HEIC
Holmrook	Major Skeffington Lutwidge.	HEIC
Hutton-hall	Occupied by J.O. Yates, Esq.	HEIC
Hutton John	Andrew Hudleston, Esq.	Son in HEIC
Irton-hall	Edmund Lamplugh Irton, Esq.	Brother in HEIC
Isel	Property of Wilfred Lawson, Esq.	Distant kin
Justice-town	Thomas Irwin, Esq.	Son in HEIC
Kirkoswald	Timothy S. Fetherstonhaugh	Brother, India House, HEIC
Linethwaite	Thomas Hartley, Esq.	Not known
Melmerby	Rev. Thomas Pattenson.	Brothers in HEIC
Mirehouse	John Spedding, Esq.	Brother in HEIC
Moor-park	Joseph Liddell, Esq.	Great Nephew HEIC
Nether-hall	Humphrey Senhouse, Esq.	Kin
Newbiggin-hall	Rev. S. Bateman.	Kin
Ponsonby-hall	Edward Stanley, Esq.	Kin
Rickerby	James Graham, Esq.	HEIC

Seats	Lysons' Owners or Occupiers	East Indies Connection
Salkeld-Lodge	Lt Col. Samuel Lacy.	Not known
Staffold	Richard Lowthian Ross, Esq.	Not known
Skirwith Abbey	John Orfeur Yates, Esq.	HEIC
Tallantire-hall	William Browne, Esq.	Uncle in HEIC
Walton-hall	William Ponsonby Johnson, Esq.	Father in HEIC
Warwick-hall	Robert Warwick, Esq.	Son in HEIC
Woodside	Executors of late John Losh, Esq.	Grandson in HEIC
Workington-hall	John Christian Curwen, Esq.	Uncle and kin HEIC

Fleming made an alliance with a family, which Armitt describes as 'the cheerful (and unusual) spectacle of a rural family who rose by steady steps to wealth'.[21]

Armitt tellingly notes that the Knott's 'advance to riches and gentility was not by husbandry alone, but by trade, by office or by commerce'.[22] Michael Knott was, at the time of his marriage, already acquiring land beyond the tenements inherited from his father. He was dabbling in charcoal as well as timber. By 1746, Michael Knott was investing in the charcoal and iron industries. He actively supported his children's marital alliances with families in the developing iron industry in Furness. Knott kin were already involved in the East Indies. Michael's son George returned from the East Indies after Michael Knott had composed his will in 1772. Their close kinsman John Knott died in Calcutta.

In essence, Cumbria's East Indies ventures were built on an existing, structured network between middling and gentry families. The structure of that network can be exposed by examining the connections between kin-nodes which share a mutual relative in the East Indies (Figure 2.4). Kin-nodes are groups of kin sharing the same surname. While there were some enumerated Cumbrian men who shared no related East Indies sojourners with other families or kin, there were eighty-seven interconnected kin-nodes among the 421 enumerated Cumbrian men. Some kin-nodes were connected to only one other kin-node but some were connected to a multiplicity of other kin. The number of shared relations is signified by the size of the symbol associated with each kin name. The Gale and Benn families, with the largest symbols

---

[21] M. L. Armitt, *Rydal* (Kendal, Titus Wilson & Son, 1916), p. 341.
[22] Armitt, *Rydal*, p. 341.

in Figure 2.4, respectively shared East Indies-involved male relations with eighteen other extended families. The Hudlestons shared East Indies-involved men with seventeen other extended families, including those in Appendix D. Conversely, families like the Dockers were only connected to a small number of other kin-nodes by way of mutual relatives involved in the East Indies.

Kin-nodes were clustered within the network of families with shared relatives in the East Indies. Clusters are made up of kin-nodes with a higher probability of being connected to each other than the probability of being connected to other kin-nodes within the network as a whole.[23] Clusters are signalled by kin-nodes sharing a symbol. There were thirteen significant clusters among kin-nodes within a network of families involved in the East Indies. Close examination indicates that endogamous practices were prevalent among Cumbrians. That is, families of a particular rank tended to be connected to families of a similar rank.

For most gentry families, the probability was that they shared a kinsman in the East Indies with one or more other gentry families. The cluster of Yates, Hasell, Salmond, Pattenson and Aglionby showed endogamous practices among Cumbria's minor gentry families. Similarly, there were middling family clusters. The most obvious of those was a robust cluster involving the middling Stephenson, Winder, Ritson, Farish, Farrer, Pennington of

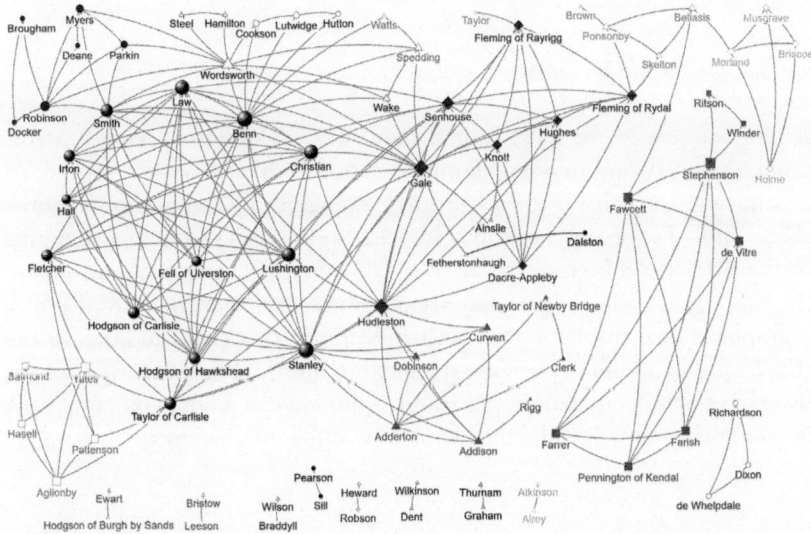

Figure 2.4 Kin-nodes and Connections through Cumbrian Men Involved in the East Indies, 1688–1829

23 The clusters are generated by the Girvan-Newman algorithm using NodalEXL. See A. Lancichinetti, and S. Fortunato, 'Community Detection Algorithms: A Comparative Analysis', *Physical Review E*, 80, 1 (2009), p. 056117–1.

Kendal and Fawcett families. That cluster was attached to the network as a whole by way of the socially and economically fragile Bellasis family. The tendency for rank endogamy combined with the linkages between ranks is consistent with a substantial body of research showing that English society was marked by both constrained movement between ranks in the eighteenth century and some social mobility. The latter drew gentry and middling ranks together.[24]

Notably the clusters within this Cumbrian network shows a pronounced predilection towards 'bridging'. That is, forming ties between kin-nodes of differing social positions or ranks. That bridging existed before, drove East Indies ventures and was particularly evident in the two largest clusters. One of those large clusters – denoted by the diamonds – shows that the gentry Hudlestons were conjoined to the gentry Senhouses and the prominent gentry Flemings of Rydal, Westmorland. But within the midst of that cluster lay the solidly merchant Gales and the middling Knotts. The other large cluster – denoted by the ovals – shows that the gentry Stanley family was closely connected to the gentry Fletchers, Irtons and Christians as well as a set of more socially ambiguous families including the Benns, with their connections to the prominent Whitehaven merchant and tobacco importer Timothy Nicolson[25] and the Law family. Within that cluster were also some solidly middling families based in Carlisle and Furness such as the Hodgsons, Taylors and Fells.

Lives and the Pursuit of Success

Pursuing success in the East Indies, then, was a shared experience across Cumbria's gentry and middling families, both merchant and professional. At the same time, the long eighteenth century saw significant changes in Cumbria, the East India Company the British Isles and its position within an expanding global world. Six biographical narratives illuminate how temporal conditions, place and social origins played out. These short narratives represent a 'biographical turn' insofar as they place individual experiences and trajectories at the centre of inquiry. They are designed to illustrate the way experiences, networks, attachment, identity, place and aspiration can mesh in different ways generating sometimes similar and sometimes different outcomes.

---

[24] G. E. Mingay, *English Landed Society in the Eighteenth Century* (London, Routledge, 2007), pp. 80–85; F. M. L. Thompson, *Gentrification and the Enterprise Culture: Britain 1780–1980* (Oxford, Oxford University Press, 2001), pp. 52–53; H. R. French, *The Middle Sort of People in Provincial England, 1600–1750* (Oxford, Oxford University Press, 2007), pp. 148–152; J. Black, *Eighteenth-Century Britain, 1688–1783* (2nd edition, London, Palgrave Macmillan, 2008), pp. 94f.

[25] J. V. Beckett, *Coal and Tobacco: The Lowthers and the Economic Development of West Cumberland 1660–1760* (Cambridge, Cambridge University Press, 1981), p. 112.

Presented chronologically these biographical fragments stretch across the long eighteenth century starting with the middling Edward Stephenson, whose career began as the East India Company was re-consolidating a single monopoly. His biography is followed by that of Catherine Holme, who, as daughter and wife, encountered the East Indies in the period immediately after Plassey. Thomas Cust, a fortune-seeker from a middling family, like Catherine Holme, pursued success in the post-Plassey India. Richard Ecroyd, as a posthumous, probably mixed-race, son of a Cumbrian ship's surgeon, shows both the attenuation and the persistence of Cumbrian identity in the East Indies late in the eighteenth century. Two men, the middling Montagu Ainslie and gentry Andrew Hudleston, started their Company careers early in the nineteenth century when the Company turned from trade to taxation and rule.

Edward Stephenson (1691–1768)

Edward Stephenson lies as if an aristocrat before the altar of Crosthwaite Church at Keswick. His merchant brother and his nephew are memorialised nearby (Plate 2.1). Both he and his brother had long Company careers in India. They were part of a network of Cumbrian families involved in global trade in the early part of the eighteenth century. Stephenson was possibly descended from a Whitehaven family involved in sea trade and the rope industry. His father was almost certainly providing wood and wine to the churchwardens at Keswick in the early 1700s. He married into another Cumbrian merchant family, the Winders of Lorton (Appendix E).

Edward was seventeen years old when he was sent to India, sponsored by his brother-in-law Jonathan Winder, then a London merchant and active in merging the two East India Company monopolies.[26] Winder himself had been a merchant to Calcutta, but unlike his nephew Edward, was a very experienced merchant at the time of his Company appointment. The Winders were trading in Barcelona as well as the West Indies and North Africa from the late seventeenth century.[27]

By 1714 Edward was appointed to the three-man Company delegation to Delhi in search of commercial privileges, which resulted in the firman of 1717.[28] For his success in Delhi, Edward was awarded £800 and promoted

---

[26] J. J. Fisher Crosthwaite, 'Some of the Old Families in the Parish of Crosthwaite', *Transactions Cumberland and Westmorland Association Advancement of Literature and Science*, 10 (1884–85), pp. 19–22; C. R. Wilson, *The Early Annals of the English in Bengal. Being the Bengal Public Consultations for the First Half of the Eighteenth Century. Vol. II, Part II: The Surman Embassy* (Calcutta, The Bengal Secretariat Book Deposit, 1911), pp. xi–xv; J. W. Kaye, 'Governor's House Keswick', *Transactions CWAAS*, New Series, LXVI (1966), p. 339.

[27] F. A. Winder, 'The Winders of Lorton', *Transactions CWAAS*, Old Series XII (1893), pp. 439–457; F. A. Winder, 'Further Notes on the Winders of Lorton', *Transactions CWAAS*, Old Series XV (1898), pp. 229–238.

[28] Wilson, *The Early Annals of the English in Bengal*, pp. xii–xiii.

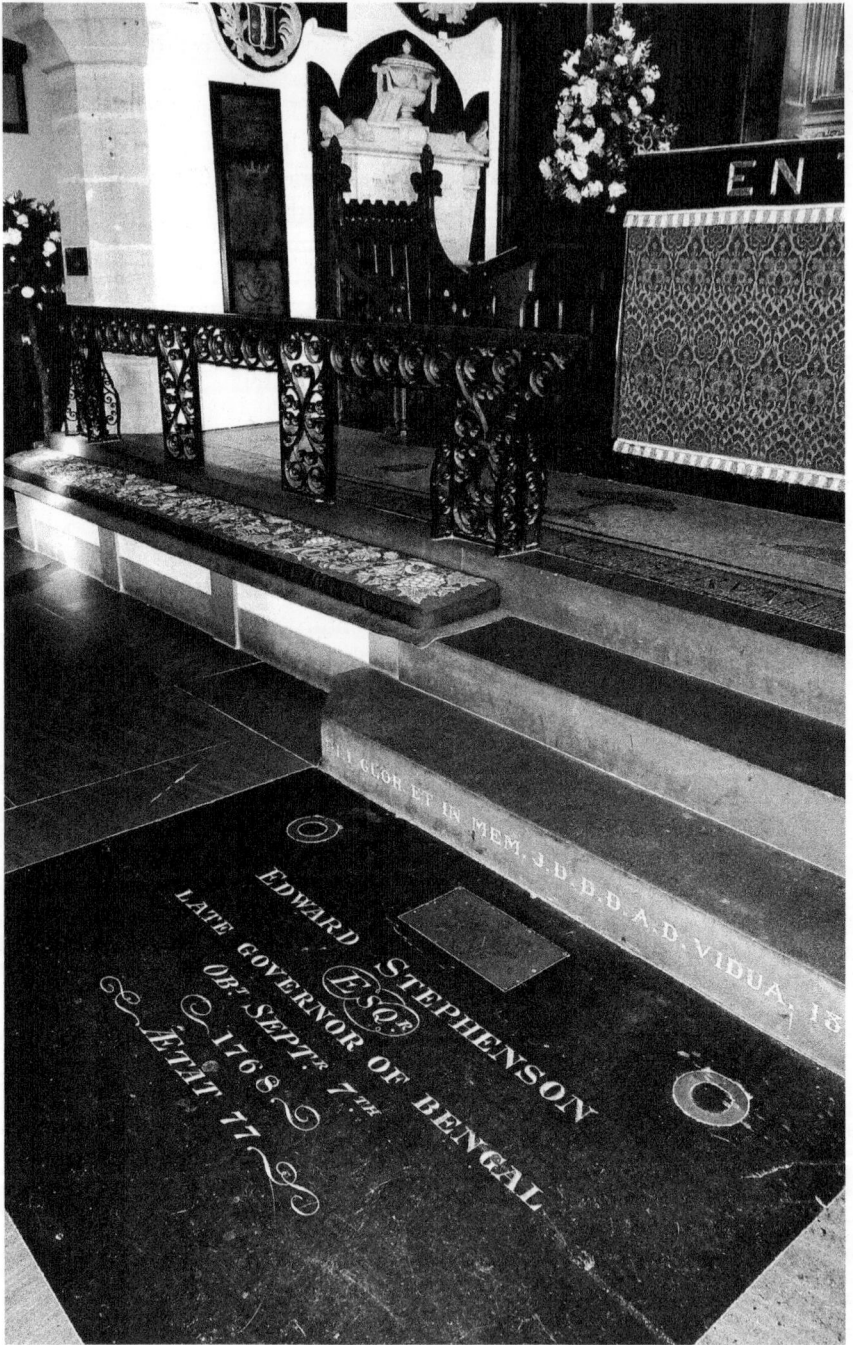

Plate 2.1 Memorial stone of Edward Stephenson before the altar of Crosthwaite
Parish Church, Keswick. Photo by the author

to a succession of factories. Appointed to the Bengal Council in 1720, he was second in Council by 1728. The death of Henry Frankland, the Bengal governor, saw Stephenson's appointment as governor. His governorship lasted less than two days. Unknown in Calcutta, the Company's Court of Directors had replaced Frankland with John Deane who arrived in Calcutta within two days of Stephenson's succession. Stephenson returned to his previous position. He resigned and returned to England the following year.[29]

Like most East India Company servants, Stephenson was involved in private trade while in India. It was built on a wider familial trading network. His Winder cousins were actively trading to and from Calcutta. In 1720 Samuel Winder sought to export to the East Indies three table clocks, a box of glasses and mathematical instruments valued at sixty pounds, as a 'a separate venture'.[30] The Winders maintained a trading presence in Barcelona.[31] Diverse and extensive trading ventures were typical of Cumbrian merchants involved in the East Indies at the time. In addition to the Stephensons and the Winders, there were too the Braddylls based near Ulverston. Long represented in the East India Company's operations and governance (Appendix F), in 1709 Roger Braddyll of Conishead could ship to the Cumbrian Gulston Addison in Madras twelve chests of wine, twenty-four gallons of Florentine oil, twelve dozen gallons of olives, sixteen dozen gallons of elder vinegar, six hams, six kegs of sturgeon and two barrels of herring.[32]

Stephenson's trading ventures made him a wealthy man. He acquired houses in London and Essex. He built in Keswick and acquired Holme Cultram, Scaleby Castle, Stonegarethside Hall[33] and the Royal Oak Hotel.[34] He was reputed to have purchased in Cumbria and elsewhere in the British Isles land 'sufficient to yield him an annual income of £1,245' by 1750.[35] Edward had enough economic power to worry the Lowthers and was a provider of credit to merchants and gentry in Cumbria at a time when there were few other substantial lenders.[36]

---

[29] Kaye, 'Governor's House Keswick', pp. 341–342.

[30] IOR/E/1/12 ff. 52-52v [20 Jan. 1721] – Letter 33 Samuel Winder to the Court requesting permission to ship out table clocks, glasses and mathematical instruments as part of his private allowance.

[31] Winder, 'Further Notes', pp. 229–238.

[32] IOR E 1/11 ff. 423–424 [9 December 1709] – Letter 240 Roger Braddyll to Thomas Woolley requesting permission to send several chests of wine to Governor Gulston Addison at Madras.

[33] Kaye, 'Governor's House Keswick', p. 344.

[34] Fisher Crosthwaite, 'Some of the Old Families in the Parish of Crosthwaite', p. 21.

[35] J. V. Beckett, 'English Landownership in the Later Seventeenth and Eighteenth Centuries: The Debate and the Problems', *Economic History Review*, New Series, 30, 4 (November, 1977), p. 571.

[36] Beckett, *Coal and Tobacco*, pp. 207–208.

Stephenson epitomised the aspirations of fortune-seekers in the East Indies. He, and indeed, his brother and Winder cousin all survived India, returned to the British Isles and lived long lives. Edward Stephenson died without children and his wealth passed first to his brother, John, and then to Rowland Stephenson of Scaleby Castle, one of the promoters of the Keswick regattas in the latter part of the eighteenth century.[37] He not only retained interests in Cumbria, but his East Indian fortune fuelled the economic, social and political influence of a network of Cumbrian middling families, including the prominent India merchant and shipping magnates the Fawcetts, well into the nineteenth century.

Edward Stephenson was of middling origin. He died a nabob. He acquired land in Cumbria and he built himself a large house in Keswick. His achievement was signalled by its styling as the 'Governor's House'. Some suggest that the fields outside Keswick known as the Howrahs referred to Stephenson's residence in Bengal.[38] The regalia of his success included the use of esquire and the prominent use of arms on his monumental slab. His burial in Keswick signalled simultaneously his deep attachment to Cumbria and the Indian pathway to his wealth and influence. There was no attempt here to acquire the persona of long-standing Cumbrian gentry. His success was referenced directly to trade and commercial ventures.

Catherine Holme (Mrs William Brightwell Sumner) (1736–1771)

Edward Stephenson was a nabob before the term became almost universally pejorative. When Catherine Holme returned from India, the nabob was increasingly the subject of envy, anxiety and ridicule. Nabobinas, the wives and daughters of nabobs, were perhaps doubly stigmatised, living as they did on the margins of a very male world and making fortunes through their connections to already suspect men.[39] Her memorial at East Clandon was perhaps, then, a testimonial designed to redress a prevailing public discourse:

> Those exemplary virtues which as a daughter, wife, parent and friend distin-guished and endeared her living are worthy of remembrance and imitation.[40]

Catherine Holme travelled at least twice to India. First as an unmarried daughter in the company of her widowed father and brother, and second, returning to India after a brief retreat in the British Isles. Her father, John Holme of The Hill, Dalston was a Carlisle attorney but also a minor gentry

---

[37] A. Hankinson, *The Regatta Men* (Milnthorpe, Cicerone Press, 1988).

[38] Kaye, 'Governor's House Keswick', p. 345.

[39] T. W. Nechtman, 'Nabobinas: Luxury, Gender, and the Sexual Politics of British Imperialism in India in the Late Eighteenth Century', Journal of Women's History, 18, 4 (Winter 2006), pp. 8–30.

[40] Church of St Thomas of Canterbury, Monumental Inscriptions, www.eastclandon.org.uk/PDF-Files/Monumental%20inscriptions_EC%20website.pdf.

landowner. His first sojourn in the East Indies had allowed him to return to Cumbria and marry the well-connected Catharine Brisco of Crofton Hill (Appendix G). They had two children, Catherine and John, who was educated with John Smith of Carlisle in 'Writing, Arithmetick and Merchant Accompts' and appointed as a Company writer around 1760.[41]

In 1764, John Holme returned to Calcutta with his children and became Notary Public and later Registrar of the Mayor's Court in Calcutta. Catherine was already married and a mother. She had also sojourned in the East Indies before. Her first child to William Brightwell Sumner was born in Calcutta in 1758.[42] Two children followed before the Sumners returned to England around 1762. Her children were painted in England by Zoffany around 1764, probably as Catherine left for Calcutta.

Clive encouraged William Sumner back to Calcutta, promising him eventual appointment as his successor there. But William and Catherine travelled apart. It was Clive who accompanied Catherine on the voyage and a tedious, ill-humoured journey it was. Clive complained of Catherine:

> To give you a Specimen of this Lady's Natural Abilities, she gave us to understand that she understood Music and could play upon the Harpsichord & to convince Us of this she has been playing two hum drum Tunes for four Hours every day since she has been on Board (Sunday excepted) without the least Variation or Improvement.[43]

Catherine gave birth to a short-lived son on arrival in Calcutta.[44] Her husband's career did not prosper, although his coffers did. He fell out with Clive who, suddenly anxious of his reputation in London, sought to distance himself from the purchasing and price-setting cartel, the Society of Trade, designed and managed by Sumner. Having encouraged him back to Calcutta and appointed him second in Council, Clive then persuaded Sumner to resign.[45]

The Society of Trade generated Sumner around £23,000 in two years.[46] Overall, Henry Verelst, a governor of Bengal, suggested Sumner accumulated £90,000 in India.[47] With it, Catherine Sumner was transformed from the provincial daughter of an ambitious father straddling the middling ranks and the minor gentry into a nabobina.[48] Like all nabobs, her husband

[41] IOR J/1/3 f.216 and J/1/4 f.44.
[42] IOR N/1/2 f.27
[43] G. Forrest, *Life of Lord Clive* (London, Gassell and Company, 1918), p. 248.
[44] IOR N/1/2 ff. 61–62.
[45] Marshall, *East Indian Fortunes*, p. 169.
[46] Marshall, *East Indian Fortunes*, pp. 131–133.
[47] Marshall, *East Indian Fortunes*, pp. 131–133, 237.
[48] Nechtman, 'Nabobinas', pp. 8–30; T. W. Nechtman, 'A Jewel in the Crown? Indian Wealth in Domestic Britain in the Late Eighteenth Century', *Eighteenth-Century Studies*, 41, 1 (2007), pp. 71–86.

successfully conformed to the eighteenth-century cultural aspiration of wealth but strained the boundaries of socially legitimate, and at times legal, means to achieve it. When the Sumners returned to England they acquired Hatchlands, Surrey. It was an ostentatious signal of success. Proximate to London, its interiors were designed by Robert Adam,[49] and it had the aura of its previous owner, that exemplar of British heroism, Edward Boscawen.[50] Catherine died the following year.

Superficially, Catherine's trajectory appears entirely different to that of Edward Stephenson's. There were, however, dimensions that bound them together. Both demonstrated to ambitious Cumbrians at home that the East Indies could be a pathway to success. The size of Catherine and William's fortune was probably widely known in Cumbria: Henry Verelst's secretary was the Cumbrian John Knott. Knott's cousin and future brother-in-law was George Knott, a lieutenant in the Bengal army. Also in the Bengal army were Catherine's cousins Horton and William, the Westmerians Thomas Pearson and John Stables, and William Gawith. In the civilian establishment, there were from Kendal Francis Drinkel and Richard Ecroyd. There were also John Johnson of Whitehaven and Ewan Law, the son of the Bishop of Carlisle and Mary Christian of Unerigg Hall.[51] The Cumbrian East Indiaman officers Henry Fletcher and John Orfeur Yates were part of the Calcutta circuit at the time.

Clive's letters mean that Catherine is destined to be characterised as pretentious, vulgar and 'troublesome'.[52] Yet she followed the marital patterns and practices of her family of forming marital connections with families of wealth, status or influence. Her mother's family, the Briscos or Briscoes, were long-standing gentry and assiduously contracted marriages with both gentry and merchant families.[53] Catherine Holme's maternal grandmother was a Musgrave, an aunt married Sir Christopher Musgrave of Edenhall[54] and another married into the Hiltons or Hyltons.[55] Through a tangle of marriages, they were also connected to the Morlands of Capplethwaite Hall.[56]

[49] E. Harris, *The Country Houses of Robert Adam: From the Archives of Country Life* (London, Aurum Press, 2007), pp. 24–27.

[50] 'G. H Sumner', *Gentleman's Magazine*, vol. 10 (1838), pp. 326–327.

[51] R. G. Thorne, 'LAW, Ewan (1747–1829), of Lower Brook Street, Mdx. and Horsted Place, Little Horsted, Suss.', in R. G. Thorne (ed.), *The History of Parliament: The House of Commons 1790–1820* (1986), www.historyofparliamentonline.org/volume/1790-1820/member/law-ewan-1747-1829.

[52] Forrest, *Life of Lord Clive*, p. 253.

[53] C. R. Hudleston and R. Boumphrey, *Cumberland Families and Heraldry: With a Supplement to an Armorial for Westmorland and Lonsdale* (Kendal, CWAAS, 1978), pp. 37f.

[54] Hudleston and Boumphrey, *Cumberland Families and Heraldry*, pp. 237f.

[55] Hudleston and Boumphrey, *Cumberland Families and Heraldry*, pp. 159f.

[56] R. S. Boumphrey, C. R. Hudleston and J. Hughes, *An Armorial for Westmorland and Lonsdale* (Kendal, Lake District Museum Trust and CWAAS, 1975), pp. 209f.

Like the Stephenson network of kin, all those families were involved in global trade. The Musgraves were early supporters of the new, second East India Company.[57] The Morlands were involved in the sugar trade with Barbados and became part of the Kendal elite.[58] The Briscos also had West Indies interests and received £10,600 compensation after the abolition of slavery.[59] The network of Musgrave, Morland, Holme and Brisco kin bridged Cumbria and the East Indies for much of the long eighteenth century.

In the context of her family's marital strategies and material ambitions, Catherine was almost certainly a success. William Brightwell Sumner may have failed in his quest to succeed Clive in Bengal, but great wealth was a great healer. When Sumner died in Bath in 1796, he was described as a 'gentleman of great respectability' who provided 'distinguished service' on the Council of the Bengal Presidency.[60] Whiffs of corruption and plunder had dissipated. If she had lived, Catherine would have shared in that distinction. Unlike Edward Stephenson, however, East Indies wealth drew Catherine Holme away from Cumbria. She had inherited her father's Cumbrian estate, but it was allowed to fall into disrepair and was eventually sold to another East Indies sojourner who had returned to Cumbria.

Thomas Cust (1752–1795)

If Catherine Holme realised the wealth generating opportunities presented by the East Indies, Thomas Cust did precisely the opposite. If Edward Stephenson provided an exemplar of aspirations fulfilled, Thomas demonstrated that the encounter with the East Indies could be marked by death and disrepute.[61]

Thomas Cust was appointed as a military cadet to the Bengal Presidency around 1768. He rapidly acquired a commission owing, according to his mother, to their good friends, probably Catherine Holme's brother or father.[62] But Thomas's career thereafter was slow. He was still a captain in the Bengal Native Infantry at his death in 1795.[63] He died at Barrackpore

57 E. Cruickshanks and R. Harrison, 'MUSGRAVE, Sir Christopher, 4th Bt. (c.1631–1704), of Edenhall, Cumberland', in D. Hayton, E. Cruickshanks and S. Handley (eds), *History of Parliament* (1802), www.historyofparliamentonline.org/volume/1690-1715/member/musgrave-sir-christopher-1688-1736.

58 S. Smith, 'The Provenance of Joseph Symson's Letter Book (1711–20)', *Transactions CWAAS*, Third Series, III (2003), pp. 157–168.

59 *Legacy of British Slave Ownership Database*, www.ucl.ac.uk/lbs/person/view/25598.

60 'Oxford, June 25', *Oxford Journal*, 4 June 1796.

61 Letter from Charlotte Crackenthorpe, Newbiggin Hall, to Richard Cust London, 3 May 1796, CAS DCART/C11/44iR.

62 A draught in favour of a Mr Holme for just over £173 had been given to Thomas when he left for India. Letter Elizabeth Cust to her son Thomas Cust, India, 1772, CAS DCART C11/42iR.

63 V. Hodson, *List of the Officers of the Bengal Army 1758–1834 Vol. 1* (Reprint, Eastbourne, A Naval and Military Press, 1927), p. 486.

after returning from extended sick leave at the Cape of Good Hope. His estate was complex. It took many years to establish that he had little capital after his extensive debts were paid. Thomas illegally left entailed property to illegitimate children, seeding an extended battle between his brother and his children's trustees, as well as resentments that lasted well into the 1870s.[64] There were liabilities to four native women and eight surviving mixed-race children. Thomas's brother Richard and his mother took care of a succession of Thomas's children. By 1794, Susan, Richard, Charles and possibly William were resident in England. The remaining children Charlotte, Elizabeth, Jane and Thomas were despatched to England a year after their father's death in 1797 (Appendix H).[65]

Thomas borrowed from whomever he could convince to lend to him, including the mothers of his children,[66] his younger brother, friends, fellow Cumbrians, colleagues and strangers. Peremptory letters to his mother demanded she honour various bills including £140 in 1775,[67] £80 in June 1776 and £80 the following month.[68] Strained financially, in April 1776 Elizabeth Cust refused a bill of £140 and another in September of £23.[69] A bill of £80 remained unpaid in November 1776.[70] Claims on his mother stopped after she refused a bill of Lady Hay of Pitfour's son in 1777, but Thomas continued to borrow. His Crackenthorpe relatives were repaid £200 in 1795.[71] A substantial twelve-month loan contracted in 1787 from James Graham of Rickerby, Carlisle,[72] was eventually repaid from his estate in 1804.[73]

Cutting the costs of the children's education was a preoccupation of Thomas's agents both before and after his death. The Mounseys demanded

---

64 IOR L/AG/34/29/9 f. 62; IOR L/AG/34/27/19 f.57; Letter Robert Mounsey to Richard Cust, 10 August 1796, CAS DCART C11/51xxiiiR.

65 Letter John Palling, Calcutta, to Richard Cust, Parliament street, London, 8 January 1797, CAS DCART C11/55fR.

66 Inventory of Thomas Cust's account with John Palling, Calcutta audited accounts 1800, CAS DCART C11/61/19b.

67 Letter Thomas Cust, Calcutta, to his mother Elizabeth Cust, Carlisle, 15 June 1775, CAS DCART/11/42ii.

68 Letter Thomas Cust, Calcutta, to his mother Elizabeth Cust, Carlisle, 9 July 1776, CAS DCART/11/42viii V.

69 Letter Elizabeth Cust, Carlisle, to John Watson, 1 September 1776, CAS DCART/11/42ix R.

70 Letter Kenneth MacKenzie, London, to Elizabeth Cust, 19 November 1776, CAS DCART /11/42xiR.

71 Letter Robert Mounsey, Carlisle, to Richard Cust, Parliament St, London, 12 August 1795, CAS DCART C11/51viiR.

72 Thomas Cust to James Graham, bond, Calcutta, 30 June 1787, DCART C11/54cm.

73 A lengthy correspondence between Richard Cust, Robert Mounsey in Carlisle, James Graham at Barrock Lodge and others over the period 1803–1804 is in CAS DCART C11/54ceR, C11/54ceV, C11/54/chR, C11/54chV, C11/54clR, C11/54ck, C11/54ciV, C11/54cnR.

that Richard remove the boys from Dr Burney's school in London and send them north for an education not exceeding £25 annually each for their entire 'Board, Cloathes and Learning'.[74] Thomas also sucked cash out of his Cumbrian estates. His agent wrote to one of his tenants that Thomas had no intention to 'interfere in the management of [the] Estate, but [required] his moiety of the rents and Profits from time to time becoming due'.[75] When Thomas unilaterally decided to sell the Woodside estate in Westmorland, his brother was forced to purchase it at auction at a price thought to be inflated.[76] It was rumoured that Thomas would break the Great Smeaton entail so the property could be sold.[77] In 1794, Mounsey recommended that the Rockliff Tithes be sold to pay off a £750 mortgage.[78]

Thomas's very conspicuous consumption explains his need for cash. Thomas's inventory included numerous neck cloths, shirts, breeches of all sorts, ten pairs of silk stockings, eight dressing gowns, a variety of military and civilian coats, household goods and furniture, glassware, silver domestic ware, silver and gold uniform accoutrements, and a variety of gold pieces including watches, seals, buckles and buttons. He had books, sporting equipment, musical instruments, carpets, liquor, pistols, a three-foot telescope, an opera glass, portable writing table, candlesticks and goats. Most extravagantly, in addition to his horse and palanquin, he owned an eight-oared budgerow, 'built of the best materials... [with] two bedrooms one 12 feet by 10 feet the other 8 by 6'.[79] Perhaps that display of wealth encouraged a number of dubious suitors to pursue his daughter Susan when she returned to Calcutta:

> One being a Gambler, who I judge had an Eye to Property, supposing it 10 Times more than ever I fear can be realized, the other a young Man of too high Rank in Society to have, as by his Conduct he evinced, any other design than that against her Honor.[80]

---

74 Letters G and R Mounsey, Carlisle, to Richard Cust, Parliament street, London, 21 July 1794 and 26 July 1794, CAS DCART C11/51iiR and CAS DCART C11/51iiiR, Robert Mounsey, Carlisle, to Richard Cust Parliament street, London, 13 March 1795, CAS DCART C11/51vR; Letter Robert Mounsey, Carlisle, to Richard Cust, Parliament street, London, 25 July 1795, CAS DCART C11/51viR.

75 Letter G and R Mounsey, Carlisle, to Thomas Cust, Great Smeaton, 29 March 1791, CAS DCART C11/55aR.

76 Purchase and contract by Edward Graves agent for Richard Cust, 12 March 1793, CAS DCART C11/57eR.

77 Letter Robert Ellis, Bolton, to Richard Cust, Parliament street, London, 2 May 1793, CAS DCART C11/54aR.

78 Letter Robert Mounsey, Carlisle, to Richard Cust, Parliament street, London, 12 August 1795, CAS DCART C11/51viiR.

79 IOR L/AG/34/27/18 f70.

80 Letter John Palling, Calcutta, to Richard Cust, Parliament street, London, 30 August 1798, CAS DCART C11/60/17R.

There was no fortune. John Palling, Thomas's agent in Calcutta, reported to the Mounseys and Richard Cust that there was probably no more than £800 to remit to England.[81] The Mounseys tried to persuade Richard that entailed property should be given to Thomas's illegitimate nieces and nephews.[82] He refused. In response they threatened to go to Chancery unless Richard took on the trust, which he reluctantly did.[83]

Elizabeth Cust's investment in her son's East Indies career never saw the return for which she hoped. Ultimately it was the younger son, apprenticed to the stationer's trade in London, not the son in the East Indies, who provided for Elizabeth Cust's old age. Thomas never returned to Cumbria although he despatched his mixed-race children there. His younger brother Richard did return to Carlisle. He styled himself 'esquire'.[84] The value of Richard's spinster daughter's estate in 1870 at more than £25,000 was a measure of his success.[85] The deaths and distress of his children were a measure of Thomas's failure. Susan and Charlotte died of consumption, Susan at sea returning from India and Charlotte in Carlisle. Elizabeth and Jane were apprenticed as milliners in Newcastle and married tradesmen.[86]

Richard purchased army commissions for the surviving boys. The eldest boy Richard was surprisingly successful in the 1820s and 1830s, a period in which it was increasingly difficult for mixed-race children.[87] He was described as of 'amiable disposition, mildness of manners and sincerity' when he died young.[88] His younger half-brother Charles, borrowed extensively and

---

[81] Letter John Palling, Calcutta, to Richard Cust, Parliament street, London, 30 August 1798, CAS DCART C11/60/17R.

[82] Letter Robert Ellis to Mr Frankland, 17 April 1797, CAS DCART C11/45xxxviiiR.

[83] Letter Robert Mounsey, Carlisle, to Richard Cust, Parliament street, London, 10 August 1796, CAS DCART C11/51xxiiiR; Letter Robert Ellis, Bolton, to Richard Cust, Parliament street, London, 10 October 1796, DCART C11/47ixR. Letter Robert Mounsey Carlisle, to Richard Cust, Parliament street, London, 6 August 1797, CAS DCART C11/51xxxR; Letter Richard Cust to Robert Mounsey, 31 October 1797, CAS DCART C11/45xxviiR; Letter Robert Mounsey Carlisle, to Richard Cust, Parliament street, London, 4 November 1797, CAS DCART C11/51xxxiiiR; Letter Robert Ellis to Robert Mounsey, 20 November 1797, CAS DCART C11/45xxviiiR; Letter Robert Mounsey, Carlisle, to Robert Ellis, Bolton, 10 December 1797, CAS DCART C11/45xxxiR; Draft letter Richard Cust to Robert Mounsey, 16 December 1797, CAS DCART C11/45xxxivR; Letter Robert Mounsey to Richard Cust, 17 April 1798, CAS DCART C11/49x; Letter Robert Mounsey to Richard Cust, Parliament street, 13 July 1798, CAS DCART C11/51xIR.

[84] *U.K. and U.S. Directories, 1680–1830.*

[85] PPR, *National Probate Calendar*, 1870.

[86] Statutory declaration R. H. Clutterbuck, 8 February 1879 and associated papers CAS DCART C11/32/64.

[87] C. Hawes, *Poor Relations: The Making of a Eurasian Community in British India 1773–1833* (Richmond, Curzon Press, 1996), pp. 62f.

[88] S. Hibbert, J. Palmer, W. Whatton and J. Greswell, *History of the Foundations in Manchester of Christ's College, Chetham's Hospital, and the Free Grammar School*, vol. 2 (London, William Pickering, 1834), p. 251.

eventually disappeared.[89] Thomas, the youngest boy, married, lost his wife and child, sold his army commission, re-joined as a private and was subsequently dismissed as 'unfit'.[90] He was imprisoned for three months at York and sentenced to death for cattle stealing.[91] The sentence was commuted. In August 1827, he arrived in Sydney, deported for stealing from a counting house.[92] Success, then, was not the only story associated with the Cumbrian East Indies encounter.

The East Indies presented risks and ambivalences, not least of which were mixed-race children. The latter were by no means rejected by Thomas's mother or brother. Richard provided for his mixed-race nieces and nephews, albeit reluctantly and often clumsily. Their presence had significant and ongoing repercussions for him which were emotional as well as material. Richard felt his brother's agents manipulated the children and was incensed when accused of profligately sending his servant with the children as they travelled to the Mounseys in Carlisle. He replied to those accusations angrily:

> As [my servant] had been a short time used to the children and seemed fond of them, I therefore thought her the properest person to attend them, your authority therefore I did not think necessary to obtain, and consequently did not pay you the compliment to consult you upon the Business, well judging that 4 young Children such as they are could not travel 300 miles unattended by any person. Common Humanity one should think would teach us this, but you it appears, think otherwise...[93]

He was almost certainly irritated when Charlotte Crackenthorpe congratulated him on sending Susan to her father in Calcutta:

> I think you be very happy that you had sent out Susan [to India]... poor thing she will have a melancholy arrival but by your account she is much properer for the East than England. I mean her Ideas.[94]

---

89 Undated note CAS DCART C11/32/78; Letter Richard Cust, Malta, to his uncle Richard Cust, 6 January 1802, DCART C11/54bqR and V.

90 Undated note CAS DCART C11/32/81.

91 *England and Wales, Criminal Registers, 1791–1892* [online database]. Provo, UT, USA: Ancestry. com Operations Inc, 2009. Original data: Home Office: Criminal Registers, Middlesex and Home Office: Criminal Registers, England and Wales; Records created or inherited by the Home Office, Ministry of Home Security, and related bodies, Series HO 26 and HO 27; The National Archives of the UK (TNA), Kew, Surrey, England., HO 27(28) p. 327; HO 27(30) p. 239; HO 27(34) p. 361.

92 *New South Wales Convicts Indents 1788–1842*, State Archives New South Wales Series: NRS 12188 Item: [4/4012] Microfiche: 665, online database.

93 Draft letter Richard Cust to Robert Mounsey, 16 December 1797, CAS DCART C11/45xxxivR.

94 Letter from Charlotte Crackenthorpe, Newbiggin Hall, to Richard Cust London, 3 May 1796, CAS DCART /C11/44iR

Richard was sensitive to implied criticism of the children's race and refused a request by relatives to change the children's surnames.[95] But he, especially after his eldest nephew's death, became resentfully distanced from the children and they, equally resentful and distressed, distanced from him. Their deaths, the shadows of disrepute, social decline and marginalisation presented a stark contrast to Richard's successful pursuit of Cumbrian respectability and gentility.

Richard Ecroyd (1766–1797)

A year after Thomas Cust's death, the Calcutta-born Richard Ecroyd was attempting to close the gulf between his life in India and his Cumbrian relatives. He wrote from Moorshedabad[96] to an aunt that he was searching for a Cumbrian wife:

> I should look out for a little Quaker wife – nor should I study her Wealth or Beauty; but her Goodness of Heart and Discretion… my sole Idea or prospect which I form to myself of future happiness is to close my life (after a total separation thus long) in the Centre of my Father's family.[97]

Whether this reflected material opportunism or psychological yearning cannot be established. But Richard had made contact with his father's family only after a failed attempt in 1791 to get Warren Hastings to find him 'some fixed Employ in which I may earn my Bread, either in Bengal or Europe'.[98]

Richard is an elusive figure. He was unnamed, sometimes unacknowledged, in family pedigrees.[99] Traces of his life are found in his father's will and, primarily, Richard's six letters to his widowed aunt Deborah Ecroyd. He was born posthumously in 1766 to Maria Seniour and named after his father. His parents were unmarried.[100] He was his father's second child. The surgeon Richard Ecroyd senior already had a child by a native woman, Manoo.[101]

Richard Ecroyd senior was the son of a Lancashire apothecary whose elder brother was a Kendal apothecary and surgeon. Richard senior's sister-in-law was the daughter of Dr Rotheram, a member of Kendal's middling, urban

---

95   Letter Richard Cust, 23 April 1799, CAS DCART C11/52gV.

96   Now Murshidabad.

97   Letter Richard Ecroyd junior, Moorshedebad, to his aunt Deborah Ecroyd, Kendal, 18 June 1796, CAS WDFA 2/1/37.

98   BL Add MS 29172 f. 362 – Letter Richard Ecroyd junior to Warren Hastings, 1791.

99   Ecroyd genealogical notes and correspondence, CAS WDFA 2/4/46.

100 Letter Richard Ecroyd junior, Calcutta, to Deborah Ecroyd (née Davies), Atherstone, Warwickshire, 20 March 1793, CAS WDFA 2/1/37.

101 Will of Richard Ecroyd, National Archives, *PCC* PROB 11 Piece 921.

and non-conformist elite. Richard senior's niece married the Kendal surgeon and apothecary, John Claxton. Their children were involved in the slave trade and contributed to its abolition.[102] Notably the East Indiaman *Royal George*, to which Richard senior was appointed as an East Indiaman surgeon, continued on to a slaving voyage after Ecroyd had disembarked in Calcutta.[103]

From about 1764, Richard senior was living in Calcutta. He died there in August 1765.[104] He left 400 rupees to the mother of the pregnant Maria. One thousand rupees was set aside for Maria if she should prove not to be pregnant. £1,000 was set aside for his expected child. Richard Barwell, known for his sexual relations with multiple women and one of the wealthiest nabobs in Calcutta, was appointed the child's guardian.[105] Richard junior was not, then, left unsupported although he claimed that he thought himself 'the only solitary one of the Name' until 'joyful tidings of' his aunt in Cumbria.[106]

Richard's version of his detachment from Cumbria seems disingenuous. It appears that neither Richard junior nor his relatives were keen to contact each other, although Richard senior's will indicates that they must have at least known of each other. In Cumbria there may have been discomfort about his illegitimacy and, possibly, his race. Richard claims his mother to be French, descended, he writes grandly, from the Comte de Flandres.[107] But there is no other mention of French kin. His mother and grandmother may have been of French-Indian descent. Richard repeatedly commented he was required to make provision for them in India. By his own account, Richard junior did not pursue contact with his Cumbrian relatives while being educated in England. Richard was in London under the care of Richard Barwell's brother until 1784. After nine years in England, he returned to Calcutta.[108] It was almost a decade later that an apparently chance meeting in Bengal with a Cumbrian, probably the mercenary Joseph Harvey Bellasis, allowed Richard junior to eventually contact his Ecroyd relatives.

In his correspondence, Richard junior assiduously promoted himself as a desirable family member: a man of education and respectability, a gentleman embedded in Europe but with standing in India. He referred to his residence as 'my seat at Culpee…'. He represented himself as a moral man caring for

102 W. G. Wiseman, 'Caleb Rotheram, Ecroyde Claxton and their Involvement in the Movement for the Abolition of the Trans-Atlantic Slave Trade', *Transactions CWAAS*, Series Three, IX (2009), pp. 153–160.

103 *Royal George* Journal, 11 Oct. 1764–1 Jul. 1767, IOR L/MAR/B/17H.

104 IOR N/1/2, p. 116.

105 Will of Richard Ecroyd, National Archives, *PCC*, PROB 11 Piece 921.

106 Letter Richard Ecroyd, Calcutta to Deborah Ecroyd, Atherstone, Warwickshire, 20 March 1793, CAS WDFA 2/1/37.

107 Letter Richard Ecroyd, Calcutta to Deborah Ecroyd, Atherstone, Warwickshire, 20 March 1793, CAS WDFA 2/1/37.

108 Letter Richard Ecroyd, Calcutta to Deborah Ecroyd, Atherstone, Warwickshire, 20 March 1793, CAS WDFA 2/1/37.

his mother, working hard despite economic adversity, committed to a simple life, and desirous of maintaining his virtuous life into the future. He would be satisfied:

> if by honest Means I can provide the Necessaries of Life for my family & self & have a Mite to contribute towards the Relief of the Distressed it's my utmost Ambition… And while with these I continue to keep my Place in the first & most respectable Society…[109]

Richard was persistently anxious to demonstrate that he could provide well for a Quaker wife. In February 1795, he described Bengal as 'very dull, very little or no trade going on' but he was, nevertheless, able to leave his mother with an annuity of more than £300 a year.[110] His inability to raise ready money for travel to England that year was balanced by the information that he had invested in an 'indigo Manufactory'.[111] Any aspiration to return to the British Isles ended when Richard died in May 1797. His estate was valued at 460 Sicca Rupees, around £57.[112]

Richard exemplified the simultaneous stretching and retention of connections between Cumbria and the East Indies. His trajectory showed, too, that while the East Indies was a pathway to success for Cumbrians, Cumbria offered a pathway for Richard Ecroyd to climb out of the liminal space created by his illegitimacy, posthumous birth, and, possibly, mixed-race. His desire to search out opportunities in Cumbria and a Cumbrian wife contrast with Montagu Ainslie's apparent desire to stay in India.

Montagu Ainslie (1792–1884)

Montagu was born into the confluence of a burgeoning Cumbrian middling professional class, Kendal's non-conformist elite, powerful local families in the Lowthers and the old gentry Flemings, local industrial enterprise, and connections to the East Indies. Like Thomas Cust and Richard Ecroyd, Montagu's origins were in the rising but socially ambiguous occupations of surgeons, apothecaries and physicians.[113] Both his grandfather and father

---

[109] Letter Richard Ecroyd, Calcutta to Deborah Ecroyd, Atherstone, Warwickshire, 20 March 1793, CAS WDFA 2/1/37.

[110] Letter Richard Ecroyd, Calcutta to Deborah Ecroyd, Kendal, n.d., CAS WDFA 2/1/37.

[111] Letter Richard Ecroyd, Calcutta to Deborah Ecroyd, Kendal, May 1795, CAS WDFA 2/1/37.

[112] Inventory of Richard Ecroyd, L/AG/34/27/21.

[113] A. Tomkins, 'Who Were His Peers? The Social and Professional Milieu of the Provincial Surgeon-Apothecary in the Late-Eighteenth Century', *Journal of Social History*, 44, 3 (Spring 2011), pp. 915–935; A. Withey, '"Persons That Live Remote from London": Apothecaries and the Medical Marketplace in Seventeenth-and Eighteenth-Century Wales', *Bulletin of the History of Medicine*, 85, 2 (Summer 2011), pp. 222–247; P. J. Corfield, *Power and the Professions in Britain 1700–1850* (London, Routledge, 2000), pp. 1–13.

were physicians. His father married Agnes Ford, a wealthy ironmaster's daughter. His aunt married the East Indies sojourner George Knott and the family had an ownership share in Cumbria's most dominant, and long-lived, iron company (Figure 2.5). Montagu's father formed at Cambridge a lasting friendship with William Lowther, the successor in 1802 to 'Wicked Jimmy', the Earl of Lonsdale. It was undoubtedly through Lonsdale that he was appointed to the East India Company. At Haileybury, Montagu won the Hindustani prize before leaving for Bengal where he was appointed to a variety of quasi-judicial positions.

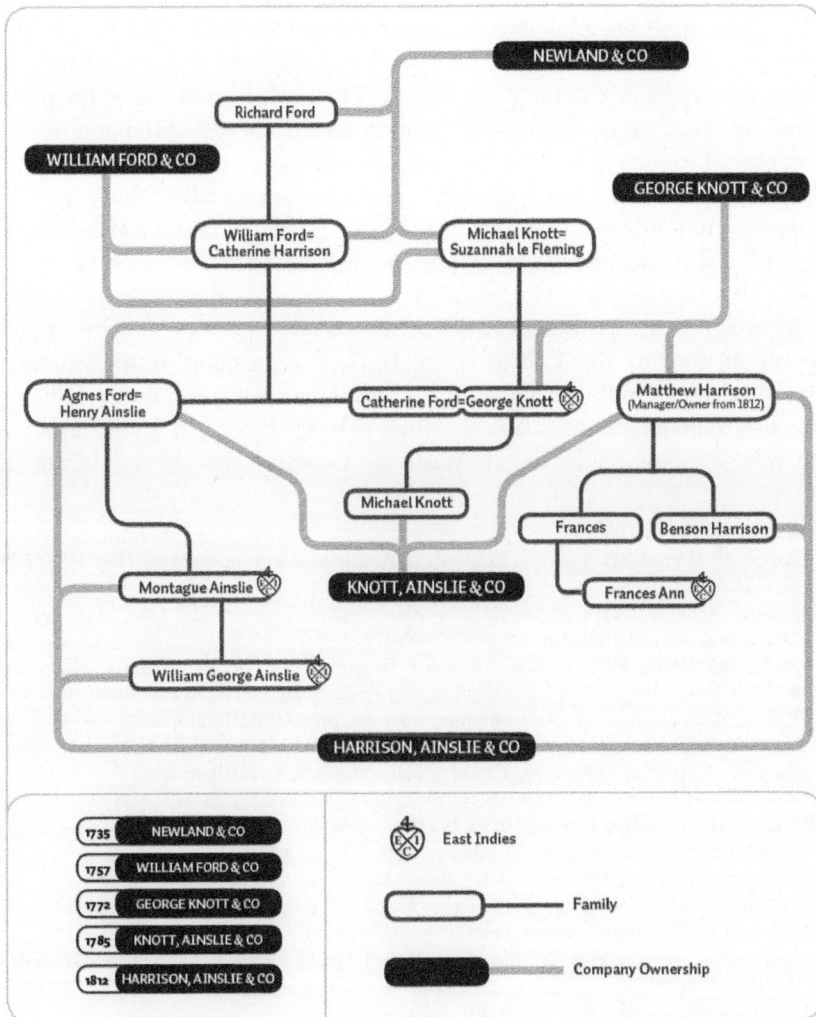

Figure 2.5 Ainslie Kin, the East Indies and the Cumbrian Iron Industry

Montagu married in India in 1818 and had six children with his wife who died from cholera, along with their youngest daughter, in 1833.[114] His surviving children were relocated to England and he remarried in 1834 before returning to Cumbria. Having sold his house at Humeerpore for 35,000 rupees,[115] but indebted to his father's estate, on return to Cumbria Montagu established himself at Ford Lodge, Grizedale which had descended to him through his mother. He then invested heavily in Cumbrian property. He purchased the Eagles Head at Satterthwaite in 1838. He had an ownership interest in the Ship Inn at Barrow. Among his landholdings were cottages around Satterthwaite and the 700-acre Hill Top Farm. By 1873, his landholdings in Lancashire were almost 2,600 acres.[116]

In association with his partners in Harrison, Ainslie & Co., he invested in shipping, including the schooner *Mary Kelly* in 1841.[117] In 1856 he took about a quarter share in the sloop *Melfort*.[118] In 1845, he was one of the provisional directors of the Furness & Windermere Railway.[119] Montagu was an agricultural improver, installing extensive drainage in the Grizedale state.[120] He promoted breed improvement by presenting various silver challenge cups and prizes to the North Lonsdale Agricultural Society[121] and the Windermere Agricultural Association.[122] He established a 1,200-acre plantation of trees[123] and built a new house at Grizedale.[124]

Montagu was appointed a justice of the peace, magistrate and, eventually, deputy lieutenant for Lancaster in 1852,[125] a position from which he promoted local militia such as the High Furness Mountaineer Rifles.[126] His son William George Ainslie, after a brief career in India, took on the management of Harrison Ainslie & Co. and was the establishment

[114] IOR N/1/10 f.533.17.

[115] East India Company Permission to Montagu Ainslie to sell his house, Jan.–Nov. 1834, IOR F/4/1524-60227.

[116] *England, Return of Owners of Land, 1873* [online database]. Provo, UT, USA: Ancestry.com Operations, Inc., 2010, Lancaster and Cumberland.

[117] A. Ainslie, 'Ainslie: History of the Ainslies of Dolphinston, Jedburgh, Grizedale, Hall Garth & Their Descendants' (Unpublished, Bradford Peverell, Dorset, A. Ainslie, 2008), p. 7.

[118] P. Sandbach, Harrison Ainslie's Shipping Interests, http://lindal-in-furness.co.uk/History/harrisonainslie.htm; A. Crocker and P. Sandbach, 'A Harrison Ainslie Gunpowder Stock Book of 1871-1876', *Transactions CWAAS*, Third Series, XX (2010), p. 26.

[119] 'Furness and Windermere Railway', *Westmorland Gazette*, 17 May 1845.

[120] J. Richardson, *Furness, Past and Present: Its Histories and Antiquities, vol. 1* (Barrow-in-Furness, J. Richardson London, Simpkin, Marshall, and Co., 1880), p. 109.

[121] 'North Lonsdale Agricultural Society', *Kendal Mercury*, 26 October 1844.

[122] 'North Lonsdale Agricultural Society', *Kendal Mercury*, 21 May 1859; 'Windermere Agricultural Exhibition', *Westmorland Gazette*, 20 September 1856.

[123] Richardson, *Furness, Past and Present*, p. 110; T. W. Thompson, *Wordsworth's Hawkshead* (London, Oxford University Press, 1970), pp. 27, 164.

[124] Ainslie, *Ainslie: History*, Part IVa, p. 11.

[125] *The London Gazette*, www.thegazette.co.uk/Edinburgh/issue/6208/page/744/data.pdf.

[126] 'High Furness Mountaineer Rifles', *Kendal Mercury*, 28 January 1860.

chairman of the North Lonsdale Iron and Steel Company, and represented North Lonsdale in parliament. Montagu's long life at Grizedale makes his return from India appear inevitable, part of an ordered cycle of seeking success through an East Indies sojourn and returning as a successful man. But Montagu's return was by no means certain. His father wrote to Lord Lonsdale that:

> The Agents of my son in India have stopped payments, & I know of no property he has which was not in their hands. I fear the loss of one half of his entire gains will prevent his return as he intended in Dec[r] 1834 & that I have very little chance of seeing him again.[127]

Montagu's substantial house at Humeerpore and his previous marriage in India left one of his siblings also unconvinced that he would return:

> I remember his saying long since, that if it was not for coming home to see <u>him</u> [Dr Henry Ainslie, his father] he should prefer staying where he was; though now he has lost his wife, he may now think differently, and should he remain in India, I should expect to hear of another Wife.[128]

Like Thomas Cust, Montagu sent his children back to England, dividing their care between his brother, sister and sister-in-law. Like Thomas Cust, this did not necessarily signal a return to Cumbria. It was a typical, although not universal, practice for children of sojourners to be sent to the British Isles. Montagu's remarriage in Simla just over a year after his first wife's death raised new questions among his siblings about his readiness to return:

> Now do you think he will entirely give up his situation in India? Will it not be kept open for his return there, should he find it expedient to, on account of an increase of his family: Now, it appears, he certainly intends to come home but are you sure that circumstances will not alter <u>cases</u>.[129]

Speculation about Montagu's intentions illustrated a deep ambivalence among Cumbrians 'at home' about Cumbria's East Indies sojourners. Material interests were involved. Montagu was in debt to his father's estate to the extent of £1,000. Just as Richard Cust found the expenses associated with the care of sojourners' children could be a strain so too did Montagu's brother.

---

[127] Letter Henry Ainslie to Lord Lonsdale, 9 October 1833 cited in Ainslie, 'Ainslie: History', Part IVa, p. 5.

[128] Letter Agnes Mansel, Barmouth to Gilbert Ainslie, 3 January 1835, cited in Ainslie, 'Ainslie: History', Part IVa, p. 6.

[129] Letter Agnes Mansel to Gilbert Ainslie, 26 January 1835, cited in Ainslie, 'Ainslie: History', Part IVa, p. 7.

Gilbert Ainslie, based at Cambridge and caring for his brother's two sons, complained that his house was 'scarcely fit for my own family. Else his two little boys are dear little fellows. They are now at School again.'[130] School may have provided some respite in Gilbert Ainslie's household, but it did not relieve the financial pressure. A little later, Gilbert noted with relief:

> I this morning received your letter dated 4th inst. Enclosing a bill for £157.5.5 on my brother's Account, which I have taken without delay to my Bankers. It has come opportunely as I have a school Bill to pay for his boys and I have had so much to pay lately my own finances are rather low...[131]

The entwining of fears about Montagu's ability and desire to re-attach himself to Cumbrian life, anxieties about the liabilities associated with caring for his orphaned children, and a sense that Montagu was refusing to realise the benefits associated with his East India career were all captured in his brother's exasperated note to their sister:

> You are right about Montagu – instead of coming home on his pension of £1,000 a year he is on furlough of £500 a year. This will enable him to return [to India] if he pleases – a plan to which I shall strongly object.[132]

The requirements of his family that he should come to and stay in Cumbria prevailed. He brought his valuable pension home just as his contemporary, but gentry, fellow Cumbrian Andrew Fleming Hudleston did a few years later.

Andrew Fleming Hudleston (1795–1861)

Montagu Ainslie and Andrew Hudleston were the same generation. Both returned to Cumbria after extended careers in India. Both were in the civil service and trained in the Company's new civil service college at Haileybury. They also had a common relative in George Knott.

The Hudlestons were particularly well connected. But the family struggled financially. Andrew's father was sent to London to practise law. Returning to Hutton John late in life, Andrew senior married Elizabeth Fleming, daughter of the third baronet of Rydal. Connections to the East Indies were dense (Figure 2.4 and Appendix D). Links with the Lowthers, Flemings and John Hudleston, the East India Company director, ensured Andrew Fleming Hudleston's Company appointment. East Indies money from Susannah

---

[130] Letter Gilbert Aislie to unstated, February 1835, cited in Ainslie, 'Ainslie: History', Part IVa, p. 7.

[131] Letter Gilbert Ainslie to Roper, 6 February 1835, cited in Ainslie, 'Ainslie: History', Part IVa, p. 5.

[132] Letter Gilbert Aislie to unstated, February 1835, cited in Ainslie, 'Ainslie: History', Part IVa, p. 7.

Knott, the daughter of John Knott, supplemented by his aunt Isabella Hudleston, ensured Andrew could afford to travel to India.[133]

In a career marked by prudence and order, in 1817 Andrew was appointed assistant collector of sea customs at Canara and Malabar.[134] Hudleston revelled in the diversity of the people and the climate.[135] He wrote enthusiastically, for instance, of a Jewish wedding at Cochin.[136] He delighted in the countryside. He visited and appreciated Jain and Hindu temples and pagodas.[137] After an interregnum as assistant to the Secretary of the Revenue and Judicial Department in Madras, he was allowed to return to Canara. In 1831 he was appointed principal collector and magistrate at Malabar and a year later was the third judge of the Provincial Court, Western Division.[138] His income was around £2,000–£2,500 annually and he was eligible for a pension of £600. He was determined, despite expressions of homesickness, to stay and maximise his earnings and his pension.[139]

Unlike his Hudleston cousins, who were born and raised outside of Cumbria and were busily establishing themselves among the dynastic, official families of British India, Andrew was explicit in his ambitions to provide his parents and, ultimately himself, with the means to maintain and live comfortably at Hutton John. He was careful with his expenditure. For many years he shared quarters to reduce costs.[140] Except for a very early request to his parents for additional funds when he first arrived in India, he did not seek funds from home. He used credit but stayed free of long-term debt. He had a detailed knowledge of his accounts and the workings of his household.[141] In 1821 and 1833, prompted by his father's, then his mother's, ill-health, Andrew took leave in England and had the means to do so.

---

[133] Letter Elizabeth Hudleston to her son Andrew Fleming Hudleston, 19 November 1829, DHUD 5/9/1; Letter Andrew Fleming Hudleston, to his mother, Hutton John, 19 September 1814, CAS DHUD 13/2/7R; Letter Andrew Fleming Hudleston, Cecil Street, Strand, to his aunt, Isabella Hudleston, Whitehaven, 28 February 1814, CAS DHUD 14/3R.

[134] Letter Andrew Fleming Hudleston, Madras, to his aunt, Isabella Hudleston, Whitehaven, 10 August 1816, CAS DHUD 14/10V.

[135] Letter Andrew Fleming Hudleston, Calicut, to his mother, Hutton John, 17 December 1817, CAS DHUD 13/6/5R and DHUD 13/6/5V.

[136] Letter Andrew Fleming Hudleston, Calicut, to his mother, Hutton John, 23–25 May 1819, CAS DHUD 13/6/11.

[137] Letter Andrew Fleming Hudleston, Madras, to his parents, Hutton John, 2 February–10 March 1815, CAS DHUD 13/3/1pp3.

[138] Letter to Andrew Fleming Hudleston, 15 March 1831, CAS DHUD 12/37/4; Letter Andrew Fleming Hudleston, Calicut, to his mother, Hutton John, 9 February 1831, CAS DHUD 13/3/12aR.

[139] Letter Andrew Fleming Hudleston to his mother, 24 October 1829, CAS DHUD 14/8.

[140] Letter Andrew Fleming Hudleston, Madras, to his parents, Hutton John, 2 February to 10 March, 1815, CAS DHUD 13/3/1/pp8.

[141] Letters from P. Calayanasoodarum to Andrew Fleming Hudleston, 1826–1830, CAS DHUD 12/19/1aR to DHUD 12/19/1xV.

While in India, Andrew Hudleston took an active interest in Cumbria and Cumbrians. He rejoiced in the receipt of Cumbrian newspapers.[142] He welcomed Cumbrian compatriots to India, although his mother warned him to be careful of the Cumbrian Mr Church who, sponsored by the Missionary Society, was a Methodist.[143] His letters pronounced on Cumbrian everyday life from marital alliances, how to manage Susannah Knott's predisposition to drink, and the importance of his parents acquiring a 'chay' or chaise. He was kept informed of the comings and goings at Hutton John and Whitehaven as well as the gentry and their estates – Ponsonby, Dalemain, Acorn Bank, Rydal, and, of course, the Lowthers. He commented on Cumbrian politics. A supporter of the Norfolk rather than the Lowther interest, he commented favourably on the Brougham candidature, although Brougham was described by his aunt Isabella in Whitehaven as a dangerous radical.[144]

He corresponded with the Knotts and the aristocratic Lady Diana le Fleming.[145] Lady Diana made Andrew a substantial bequest in her will.[146] He advised the reclusive Lady Anne Frederica le Fleming to reconsider her plan to evict the Wordsworths from Rydal Mount.[147] He helped her to lay the foundation stone for the new chapel at Rydal,[148] and she implicated him in the development even when he was living on the Malabar coast. In describing progress on Rydal chapel, she acknowledged his role in it by writing 'I ought to say our Chapel as we were both present at laying the foundation stone, and to your kind exertions much of its first progress was owing.'[149] She left him the entire Rydal estate at her death.[150]

While in India, Andrew Hudleston's correspondence was full of domestic matters at Hutton John. He commented and advised on estate planting at Hutton John and his father's estate improvements. He and his parents exchanged gardening notes. On return from India, Andrew continued estate

[142] Letter Andrew Fleming Hudleston, Madras, to his mother, Hutton John, 28 April 1816, CAS DHUD 13/3/5V.

[143] Letter Elizabeth Hudleston, Hutton John, to her son Andrew Fleming Hudleston, Madras, 2 October 1816, CAS DHUD 13/5/8R. See Church's obituary in the *Missionary Register*, May (1824), pp. 201–207.

[144] Letter Isabella Hudleston, Whitehaven, to her nephew, Andrew Fleming Hudleston, Coimbatore, 13 October 1819, CAS DHUD 11/2/7V.

[145] See A. Galbraith, *The Fleming Family of Rydal Hall* (London, Shoes With Rockets, 2006) for a useful description of the descent of the Rydal Estate, pp. 50–65.

[146] Annotated Will of Lady Diana le Fleming, 1816, CAS DHUD 5/12/5.

[147] Letter Andrew Fleming Hudleston to his mother, 28 June 1827, CAS DHUD 15/4.

[148] 'Westmorland News – Rydal Chapel', *Westmorland Gazette*, 5 July 1823.

[149] Letter Lady Anne Fredica Fleming to Andrew Fleming Hudleston, 12 December 1825, CAS DHUD 15/11/11.

[150] Letters Archdeacon William Jackson to Andrew Fleming Hudleston, 1861 regarding Ann Frederica le Fleming's legacy, CAS DHUD 15/26; 'Rydal', *Cumberland Pacquet, and Ware's Whitehaven Advertiser*, 30 April 1861.

improvement and supported various agricultural, educational and literary societies. In 1838 he joined the committee for establishing the Penrith and Carlisle Railway.[151] By 1846, Andrew was nominated among the sheriffs for Cumberland,[152] and in 1852, deputy lieutenant for Cumberland.[153]

His life in India and Cumbria had a certain symmetry. He was a keen attendee of balls and parties in Madras and Cumbria. He constructed a style in which India clearly stayed with him, not as an Anglo-Indian identity but, rather, as a Cumbrian gentleman returned from India. An obituary commented on his many eccentricities and his admired sociability:

> In private life he was hospitable, affable, lively of conversation, and full of anecdote. No man could tell a story with more grace or humour... Mr Hudleston will be a missed man, and much regretted in his own neighbourhood.[154]

The obituary went on to note that his property, including the Rydal estate, was bequeathed to a distant relative in the East Indies. One of Westmorland's most renowned estates, Rydal, as well as Cumberland's ancient Hutton John were thus embedded in the East Indies.

Conclusion

The county rates of East India Company appointment and licensing, the spatial pattern of enumerated men's origins, the social profile of enumerated men, and the Cumbrian network of connections between Cumbrian kin with mutual relatives in the East Indies, all reflect decisions made by families and individuals across four or five generations. The biographical fragments show that success was a persistent motif in the anticipatory logic that drove decisions to sojourn in the East Indies. But was this an unalloyed pursuit of nabobish wealth? Were East Indies encounters simply a fearful gamble or was there a more nuanced balancing of optimism and risk-taking? How, in the midst of a public discourse in which India and premature death appeared to be inextricably entwined, did Cumbrian middling and gentry families rationalise and seek to mitigate the risks of pursuing success in the East Indies?

---

[151] 'Cumberland and Westmorland Agricultural Society', *Carlisle Patriot*, 27 August 1853; 'Consecration of the New Christ Church at Penrith', *Carlisle Journal*, 1 November 1850; 'Christmas at Penrith &c,', *Westmorland Gazette*, 4 January 1851; 'Working Men's Reading Room, Penrith', *Carlisle Journal*, 19 October 1855; 'Queen Elizabeth's Grammar School', *Cumberland and Westmorland Advertiser, and Penrith Literary Chronicle*, 16 March 1858.

[152] 'High Sheriffs', *Lancaster Gazette*, 21 November 1846.

[153] 'The London Gazette, September 24', *Morning Chronicle*, 25 September 1852.

[154] 'Death of Mr Huddleston [*sic*] of Hutton John', *Kendal Mercury*, 7 September 1861; 'Death of Mr Hudleston of Hutton John', *Carlisle Journal*, 6 September 1861.

Three

WHY GO TO THE EAST INDIES?

In 1783, Edmund Burke thundered:

> In India, all the vices operate by which sudden fortune is acquired... Arrived in
> England, the destroyers of the nobility and gentry of a whole kingdom will find
> the best company in this nation... Here the manufacturer and the husbandman
> will bless the... hand that in India has torn the cloth from the loom, or wrested
> the scanty portion of rice and salt from the peasants of Bengal, or wrung from
> him the very opium... They marry into your families; they enter into your
> estates by loans; they raise their value by demand; they cherish and protect your
> relations which lie heavy in your patronage.[1]

It was a speech that brought together themes developed over three decades
of pejorative discourse about the East Indies and those who ventured there
from the British Isles. The men and women who went to the East Indies and
returned were portrayed as venal, uncouth nabobs and nabobinas. They
were depicted as disconnected from the moral restraints of polite society and
corrupted culturally with wealth unnaturally acquired. They were the stuff
of satire in pamphlet, picture and play. At best they were ridiculous in their
pretentions. At worst, they were disruptors of the rightful order, displacers of
the landed gentry and debasers of the middling ranks.[2]

No doubt the vociferousness of that public discourse persuaded some that
a career in the East Indies was to be avoided. But that same discourse also
conveyed and reinforced another motif which served to encourage rather than

---

[1] E. Burke, *Mr. Burke's speech, on the 1st December 1783, upon the question for the Speaker's leaving the chair, in order for the House to resolve itself into a committee on Mr. Fox's East India Bill* (London, J. Dodsley, 1784), pp. 32–33.

[2] T. W. Nechtman, 'Nabobinas: Luxury, Gender, and the Sexual Politics of British Imperialism in India in the Late Eighteenth Century', Journal of Women's History, 18, 4 (Winter 2006), pp. 8–30; P. Lawson and J. Phillips, '"Our Execrable Banditti": Perceptions of Nabobs in Mid-Eighteenth Century Britain', *Albion: A Quarterly Journal Concerned with British Studies*, 16, 3 (Autumn 1984), pp. 225–241; T. W. Nechtman, *Nabobs: Empire and Identity in Eighteenth-Century Britain* (Cambridge, Cambridge University Press, 2010), pp. 143–147; M. Edwardes, *The Nabobs at Home* (London, Constable, 1993), pp. 42–43.

dissuade; that of the East Indies as a place of abundant opportunities for the acquisition of wealth. Certainly, there appears to have been no appreciable difference in the propensity of Cumbrians to seek success in the East Indies. Prior to Burke's speech in 1783, around 129 Cumbrian men are known to have been appointed or licensed to the East Indies. At least a further 241 Cumbrian were appointed or licensed from 1783 to 1829. Nevertheless, the deep ambivalence evident in the British Isles about East Indies ventures cannot be ignored. It shaped the Cumbrian encounter with the East Indies. The way in which Cumbrians expressed and managed the ambivalences around the East Indies encounter demonstrates the nuanced and contingent nature of success.

Through Cumbrian letters, the first of which was written in 1695, this chapter explores how gentry and middling Cumbrian families saw the promise of the East Indies, what they hoped for and what they feared. It is concerned with the aspirations that drove Cumbrian families to risk the death of their children and financial loss. It is about how, in the context of an often lurid discourse about both death and wealth in the East Indies, Cumbrian gentry and middling families managed to balance their optimism and fears, their reward-seeking and their risk-taking. Those themes were most evident in Cumbrians' letters at three critical moments. First, the leave-taking of sojourners tended to prompt reflections on the purpose, hopes and fears associated with the East Indies. The second moment at which reflection was prompted was when some sort of crisis had arisen. That crisis might be in the East Indies or in Cumbria. Death, illness, debt or hardship were triggers for reflection. Reflection was also prompted when sojourners were making decisions to come home.

Women were frequent correspondents in the letters that reflect on those issues. Only a small number of Cumbrian women may have travelled to the East Indies, but as mothers, aunts, wives and sisters they were intimately connected with East Indies ventures. They were part of a correspondence with Cumbrian sojourners and others, which was notable by the way in which the pursuit of success was not reduced to economic success. There is no doubt that the acquisition of wealth, or at least a comfortable income, was a core element to the East Indies encounter. But the correspondence also shows other imperatives, both individual and familial. Concerns with status and reputation, as well as emotional attachments and material outcomes all surface. Implicit, and sometimes explicit, in this correspondence is a mutual negotiation and attempts to align individual with familial interests, the emotional with the instrumental.

What is clear is that the reasons for Cumbrians going to the East Indies cannot be simply understood as unproblematic economic decisions. This resonates with Popp's findings in his history of familial entrepreneurship. The decision of the Midlands family company Shaw and Crane to extend operations into Calcutta in the 1830s was one driven by entrepreneurial imagination rather than certain economic returns. It was shaped, too, by familial relations, not simply economic imperatives.[3] Likewise, the letters of Cumbrians involved in the East Indies show that the East Indies encounter was an imaginative venture supported by complex rationalisations of, and strategies to manage, risk and reward. Those were driven out of the social and emotional lives of the correspondents as much as by any calculative, economic logic. The discussion around those dynamics are structured around four central themes: the temptations of wealth, issues of respectability, death and loss, and, finally, the reconciliation of risk and reward.

Temptations of Wealth

Wealth was a powerful magnet in the eighteenth century. Wealth brought (and bought) power and position. According to Marshall, few travelled to the East Indies in the eighteenth century without a financial incentive to do so.[4] Yet the financial incentives for Cumbrians were never conceived of as unproblematic. There were anxieties around whether the economic promise of the East Indies would be realised. There were anxieties around the impacts of the pursuit of wealth on other aspects of a family's position, as well as concerns around the potential for loss.

The tensions around risk and reward, the promise of success and the fear of failure were recorded very early in the Cumbrian encounter with the East Indies. This was no more apparent than in the exchange between George Fleming (1667–1747) and his father Sir Daniel Fleming (1633–1701) of Rydal. George Fleming (1667–1747), scion of one of the leading gentry families in Westmorland, wrote to his father in 1695 expressing an intention to seek appointment as chaplain to a fleet of East Indiamen then readying for departure.[5] His father firmly refused permission.

George Fleming was at St Edmund Hall, Oxford at the time. He and three of his ten brothers followed their father to an Oxford education. Their father had entered Queen's College as a seventeen-year-old commoner in 1650. George, the fifth of Daniel's sons, was admitted to Oxford in 1688, completed a bachelor of arts in 1692, and was awarded a master's degree in March 1695.[6]

3   A. Popp, *Entrepreneurial Families: Business, Marriage and Life in the Early Nineteenth Century* (London, Pickering & Chatto, 2012), pp. 7, 60–68, 71–72.
4   P. J. Marshall, *East Indian Fortunes: British in Bengal in the Eighteenth Century* (Oxford, Oxford University Press, 1976), p. 214.
5   J. R. McGrath (ed.), *The Flemings in Oxford: Being Documents Selected from the Rydal Papers in Illustration of the Lives and Ways of Oxford Men* (Oxford, Oxford Historical Society, 1913), vol. 2, pp. 242–244.
6   *Oxford University Alumni, 1500–1886* [online database]. Accessed http://home.ancestry.co.uk/ Ancestry.com Operations Inc, 2007. Original data: Foster, Joseph. *Alumni Oxonienses:*

Perhaps because of his long and expensive education, George was at pains to assure his father of the benefits of an East Indies venture. So he noted that while the stipend of an East Indies chaplain was small, he had hope of acquiring wealth of a 'goodly sum': 'There are so many advantages, as have very well rewarded my predecessors' journeys [*sic*], particularly the last who brought £3000 home with him.'[7]

George's relatives were unconvinced of the benefits of modelling a career on an East Indies 'merchant parson'. Two days later, George's cousin Henry Brougham, also at Oxford, wrote to his kinsman and godfather, Daniel Fleming, in a panic:

> Yesterday, and not before, I was informed of my Cous George's intention to go to the East-Indies … I look upon it to be one of the most unaccountable projects that was ever Set a foot … 'Tis great odds but he looses his life in the voyage … [but] there is neither interest, improvement or reputation to be got by it.[8]

As the twelfth child of a long established but minor gentry family whose mother was the daughter of a Carlisle merchant, Brougham was well aware of the nuances and enmeshed nature of money, status and prospects. He once commented of his own situation as a commoner at Queen's College, that he had to live like a gentleman to ensure he could attract credit.[9]

Daniel Fleming's view of his son's East Indies aspirations was as disapproving as Brougham's. He wrote to George refusing his consent, in part, because of 'fearing that I shall then never see you more'. But just as importantly, Sir Daniel reminds his son that 'it is not for you to turn Trader, that was never raised in it'. Finally, Daniel Fleming points out to George that there was no need to go to India because 'you are not (God be praysed) in a Desperate condition'.[10]

For Daniel Fleming, the strands of life important to him, his love for his sons, his demand for obedience, his pride as one of Westmorland's ancient gentry families and his attachment to the north, combined with a calculation of the probabilities of a positive economic return.[11] Daniel Fleming

The Members of the University of Oxford, 1715–1886 and *Alumni Oxonienses: The Members of the University of Oxford, 1500–1714* (Oxford, Parker and Co., 1888–1892).

7   McGrath, *Flemings of Oxford*, vol. 2., p. 243.

8   McGrath, *Flemings of Oxford*, vol. 2, p. 245.

9   Cited in S. Wright, 'Brougham, Henry (*bap.* 1665, *d.* 1696)', *Oxford Dictionary of National Biography* (Oxford University Press, 2004); online edn, Jan. 2008: www.oxforddnb.com/view/article/3580.

10   McGrath, *Flemings of Oxford*, vol. 2, p. 247.

11   M. L. Armitt, *Rydal* (Kendal, Titus Wilson & Son, 1916), pp. 561–674; A. Galbraith, *The Fleming Family of Rydal* (London, Shoes With Rockets, 2006), pp. 30–39; B. Tyson (ed.), *The Estate and Household Accounts of Sir Daniel Fleming of Rydal Hall, Westmorland from 1688–1701* (Kendal, CWAAS Record Series Volume XIII, 2001), pp. xvii–xxvi.

reckoned the odds of his son surviving a venture in the East Indies was a hundred to one and the probability of making a fortune a thousand to one.[12] Twisted together, Daniel Fleming's negative assessment of the benefits and risks of an East Indies venture strangled George's East Indies ambitions.

Other Cumbrians made complex calculations around East Indies ventures, but they came to very different conclusions. Families already involved in the world of trade around the turn of the eighteenth century, the already mentioned Braddylls, Winders and Stephensons, saw the East Indies as a way of extending their existing business reach.

By the end of the 1760s success in the East Indies was represented by an accumulation of other examples. Christopher Wilson returned in 1726 from the East Indies with wealth enough to purchase property at Bardsea and marry the granddaughter of Miles Dodding of Conishead.[13] John Taylor, who had left Kendal for the East Indies in 1734 burdened by an indebted father, returned two decades later with a fortune and married the sister of the governor of Madras.[14] In 1768, one of Henry Fletcher's protégés, John Orfeur Yates commenced building a sizable house on his newly acquired estate, reputedly funded by an East Indian fortune accumulated in Bombay in less than eight years.[15]

Edward Stephenson was not the only Cumbrian who held high office in India. Thomas Braddyll was also the governor of Bengal, Gulston Addison was the president of Madras, William (Bombay) Ashburner from Dalton-in-Furness was warehouse keeper and a member of the Committee of Accounts in Bombay, George Tullie was the registrar of the Mayor's Court at Calcutta, Philip Tullie sat on the council of the Madras presidency. The Holmes had established themselves in Calcutta and Catherine Holme had married an East Indies nabob. Henry Fletcher, the seventh son of John Fletcher of Clea Hall, had retired from his East Indiaman command, made a lucrative marriage and been elected as a director of the East India Company. Other Cumbrians were common in the Company's court of directors. In this earlier period, they included Dodding Braddyll, Timothy Tullie and John Stephenson, kinsman of Edward Stephenson.[16]

For middling Cumbrians, then, accumulating a fortune in the East Indies was an ambitious aspiration, but not a fantastical one. For someone like the

---

[12] McGrath, *Flemings of Oxford*, vol. 2, p. 247.

[13] C. W. Bardsley, *Chronicles of the Town and Church of Ulverston* (Ulverston, James Atkinson, 1885), p. 91; N. Penney (ed.), *The Household Account Book of Sarah Fell of Swarthmoor Hall* (Cambridge, Cambridge University Press, 2014), pp. x, xv, 131, 375, 525, 555, 564.

[14] S. D. Smith, (ed.), *'An Exact and Industrious Tradesman': The Letter Book of Joseph Symson of Kendal 1711–1720* (Oxford, Oxford University Press, 2002), pp. cxviii.

[15] H. Summerson, *'An Ancient Squires Family' The History of the Aglionbys c. 1130–2002* (Carlisle, Bookcase, 2007), p. 124.

[16] See Appendix A for selected references.

young Thomas Cust, appointed, against his mother's wishes, to the Company's military service as a cadet, the East Indies was associated with fortune and freedom from the responsibilities of an eldest son to a mother widowed young. Although the salaries associated with military service were relatively modest, compared to the wealth someone like Thomas was likely to accumulate in Cumbria at the time, even the salary of an ensign was significant. The losses of his father and the debts of his mother meant his prospects of a significant income from already encumbered land and property were limited.[17] Elizabeth Cust's hopes for great wealth were limited, but she was clear as to her expectations of Thomas and her investment in his East Indies venture. He was to be self-sufficient in India:

> Your pay is more than sufficient for your maintenance, but if it were much less than it really is you must fall upon such a method of economy as to make it answer.[18]

Thomas was to support his family at home. After all, his mother writes, one old man in Penrith has already been returned £50 by his son who has been in a similar situation to Thomas in India for two years. Finally, Thomas was to revitalise the fortunes of his family and to provide for himself on his return home.[19]

The East Indies pull associated with prospects of wealth was a powerful one. Through the 1750s to the end of the 1770s, over thirty Cumbrian men like Thomas Cust and John Yates from middling and gentry families started their careers in the East Indies. In some cases, the East Indies presented a means by which long-standing financial difficulties within the family could be remedied or at least ameliorated. John Orfeur Yates was very aware of the familial expectations resting on him when he first travelled to India in 1762. He revelled in the role of his mother and sister's financial saviour. At his father's death he wrote to his sister promising to defend his family from his father's weakness of character and unworldliness, from a predatory world of lawyers and litigation, and to augment his sister's:

> slender prospects… on my own part I've reason, from my present situation, to hope it will soon be in my power to render you some service… I was often apprehensive my hon[d] Fathers open and generous Temper, unsuspecting of Deceit himself; would at some time lead him into difficulties in his office, which

---

[17] Letter Elizabeth Cust, Carlisle, to Thomas Cust, Barrackpore, 1772, CAS DCART C11/42iV.

[18] Letter Elizabeth Cust, Carlisle, to Thomas Cust, Barrackpore, 1772, CAS DCART C11/42iR

[19] Letter Elizabeth Cust, Carlisle, to Thomas Cust, Barrackpore, 1772, CAS DCART C11/42iR.

those vile retainers of the Law, void of conscience or equity themselves, are always ready to turn to their own purposes of advantage or Envy.[20]

Personal advantage and familial benefits went hand in hand. The Westmerian Reverend George Bellasis wrote to his brother John of Long Marton, Westmorland, who was about to leave for India as a military cadet in 1763 advising him to gain 'Honour, Friends and Preferment'. The acquisition of these was not seen as an end in itself. Rather, their achievement was desirable because they would enable John Bellasis 'to be useful to the Publick and your Relations'.[21] Twenty-five years later, John Bellasis, like John Yates, writes from Bombay in the role of financial saviour to his brother Hugh who was struggling on a Westmorland farm:

> I will help you out! I cannot positively say when but be assured the time is not long to come... [because] of late Years been very successful and flatter myself by the Year 90 I shall have it in my power to return to Europe with a very handsome Fortune and be assured (my dear Hugh) that the greatest Happiness I have in view, is the glorious idea I have of the good offices I shall be able to afford you all.[22]

John Wordsworth, the poet's brother, showed a similar desire. He saw the East Indies as both a pathway to personal wealth and as a platform for supporting his extended family.

In 1800, John Wordsworth wrote to Mary Hutchinson that he had been told he would be rich within ten years,[23] but he also wrote to his brother William of the way in which he intended to invest that wealth. 'I will work for you... Could I but see you with a green field of your own and a Cow and two or three other little comforts I should be happy.'[24] He was disappointed and in the frustration of disappointment of his financially disastrous first voyage as commander, John Wordsworth not only recognised the implications for his family and its circle of the losses, he sought to implicate them in his actions. He wrote, 'Oh! I have thought of you and nothing but you; if ever of myself and my bad success it was only on your account.'[25]

The interlocking concerns of individual and family were continuing motifs throughout the period. In 1810, Mrs Pattinson of Kirklinton wrote to her son

---

[20] Letter John Yates, Calcutta, to Jane Yates, Cumberland, 1 February 1763, CAS DAY/6/4/3/aR.

[21] Cited M. Bellasis, *Honourable Company* (London: Hollis & Carter, 1952), p. 47.

[22] Letter John Bellasis, Bombay, to Hugh Bellasis, Long Marton, 6 January 1785, CAS WDX 1641/1/1/p28b.

[23] C. Ketcham (ed.), *The Letters of John Wordsworth* (Ithaca, NY, Cornell University Press, 1969), p. 77.

[24] Ketcham, *The Letters of John Wordsworth*, p. 57.

[25] P. J. Kitson, 'The Wordsworths, Opium, and China', *Wordsworth Circle*, 43, 1 (2012), p. 3.

in Bombay saying she had heard news that he would soon be promoted and reinforced the importance of success for the sake of his 'worthy father' and sisters:

> The happiness of so many depends on you – It is now five years since you arrived in India I hope and expect that in five more we shall have the comfort the unspeakable happiness of seeing you at Kirklinton.[26]

But by the time Mrs Pattinson was reminding her son of his obligations, what constituted financial success and the financial incentives associated with the East Indies had changed. By the late 1780s, the ambition for the acquisition of vast wealth through entrepreneurial and military adventure was less conspicuous. Particularly in the East India Company's civil and military appointments, the windfall fortune was being gradually replaced with the more modest, but compared to home, substantial incomes attached to what was emerging as a 'professional' career course.[27]

Those developments were evident to Cumbrians at the time. In 1788, John Bellasis noted to his brother in Westmorland that opportunities in the army were limited, particularly for men unable to get an appointment as an officer. It was better for such a young man to attach himself to a free merchant if he was to acquire an 'independency'.[28] Even so, for women marriage to a senior member of the East India Company offered security. As Andrew Hudleston advised in 1813:

> Tell Miss Fleming India is a very fine place for getting married & she cannot do better than to come out…[29]

Four years later, however, Andrew suggested that a young man in India had very diminished prospects compared to the two generations before him. He wrote from Madras to his parents at Hutton John, Cumberland:

> Fortunes are not now so rapidly made in India as formerly; many of the great situations having been cut down, & those which fluctuated reduced to fixed Salaries. Still however a person with prudence & economy may look forward to the time when he may return to his Native Country, not with a large fortune, but with a comfortable Independence. This is as far as regards the Civil Service; but the prospects of the Military are bad in the extreme.[30]

---

26 Letter Mary Pattinson, Kirklinton, to Thomas Pattinson, 31 August 1810, CAS DX 249/14iR.

27 P. Spear, *The Nabobs: A Study of the Social Life of the English in Eighteenth Century India* (London, Curzon Press, 1980), pp. 39–41.

28 Letter John Bellasis, Bombay, to Hugh Bellasis, Long Marton, 21 December 1788, CAS WDX 1641/1/1/29a and WDX 1641/1/1/29b.

29 Letter Andrew Fleming Hudleston, Madras, to Isabella Hudleston, Whitehaven, 8 October 1813, CAS DHUD 11/8R.

30 Letter Andrew Hudleston, Madras, to his mother, 19 March 1817, CAS DHUD 13/4/2V.

Whatever the fluctuations in the financial opportunities presented by the East Indies across the eighteenth century, hopes of great wealth and the memories of Cumbrian nabobs who made their fortunes persisted for decades. An instance lies in the landlady of the Royal Oak in Keswick sending one of her sons, John Janson, to the East Indies as a military cadet in 1807,[31] reputedly in the hope he would return with a fortune similar to that of the Cumbrian nabob, Edward Stephenson.[32] There is some evidence that Mrs Janson's judgement was idiosyncratic and unreliable. In 1810 Southey writes that Keswick has only two items of news. One was the Keswick Regatta was to be hosted by William White (1753–1811), another Cumbrian nabob. The other was Mrs Janson:

> She, poor deluded woman, a few days since turned away a Noble Lord from her own door before she had glanced her eye at the Coronet upon his Carriage which she did not discover until he was on the wing, but her despair was witnessed by some of her servants who relate the story with no small glee.[33]

But even if Mrs Janson was, as Southey delights in portraying her, a mix of commercial opportunism, social pretension and inept discernment, she was by no means the only Cumbrian who believed that India provided prospects of worthwhile careers. Gentry such as Humphrey Senhouse (c.1731–1814) and his wife Kitty supported both their orphaned great nephews Humphrey Senhouse Gale and William Gale into careers in the East Indies. William was bonded as a free mariner in 1817 and Humphrey Senhouse Gale entered as a military cadet. Descended from the prominent Whitehaven merchant family and related to the Flemings of Rydal as well as the Senhouses of Netherhall, William and Humphrey were orphans. When appointed to the East Indies they were not being deserted by their kin, as these were appointments designed to secure their futures.

Issues of Respectability

The pursuit of financial success was accompanied by fears of loss and failure. The ramifications went beyond material losses. The articulation of pursuing financial success, the acquisition of wealth and the risks of financial failure were all suffused by a motif of respectability. Material acquisition was not

---

31   IOR L/MIL/9/117 f.221.

32   J. Fisher Crosthwaite, 'Some of the Old Families in the Parish of Crosthwaite', *Transactions Cumberland and Westmorland Association Advancement of Literature and Science*, 10 (1884–85), p. 22.

33   Letter 1805. Robert Southey and Edith Southey to Elizabeth Browne, 12 September 1810, *The Collected Letters of Robert Southey*, L. Pratt, T. Fulford and I. Packer (eds), www.rc.umd.edu/editions/southey_letters/ Part_Four/HTML/letterEEd.26.1805.html#.

the only preoccupation of gentry and middling families involved in the East Indies; anxieties around respectability thread their way through the letters of Cumbrian families and their circles. It is evident, for instance, when Mary Pattinson, wife of the Reverend Thomas Pattinson of Kirklinton, wrote to her son Thomas in Bombay in 1813:

> You must always remember, you are our <u>only Son</u>, & you know your Father's family as well as mine (tho' not rich) are very respectable, & that you should be a credit to both.[34]

Here success was less about riches, and more about approval within one's social milieu. Mary Pattinson was so pleased to have received favourable comments by the middling but influential and wealthy Fawcetts on her son's progress in Bombay, that she 'stay'd late, and came home quite happy' from her visit to Scaleby Castle.[35] A similar theme of not compromising respectability by an unfettered pursuit of wealth was expressed by Isabella Hudleston to her nephew Andrew Fleming Hudleston. He received his aunt's letter while he prepared to leave for India for the first time. For this gentry family, despite having battled declining material circumstances for some generations, the pursuit of wealth was to be balanced with the maintenance of honourable conduct. Isabella Hudleston wrote:

> Your Ancestors my Dear, were never famed for possessing great riches, but they possessed what was much better, an Honest, Honorable, & upright Conduct, without which Riches are of little avail.[36]

Part of that conduct involved publicly and privately acknowledging the support of and duty to family. The opportunity for success in the East Indies depended on the sacrifices and 'kindnesses' of others who, in turn, deserved a reciprocal commitment. So, Isabella Hudleston reminds her nephew Andrew that:

> kindness has placed you in a situation to make a fortune, & from your present good intentions & conduct & your own good sense, I trust please God will inable you to be a good Man, remember the first step towards it, is Duty towards your Parents.[37]

---

[34] Letter Mary Pattinson, Carlisle, to Thomas Pattinson, Bombay, 21 August 1813, CAS DX 249/14/gR.

[35] Letter Mary Pattinson, Kirklinton, to Thomas Pattinson, Bombay, 31 August 1810, CAS DX 249/14iR.

[36] Letter Isabella Hudleston, Whitehaven, to Andrew Hudleston, Bath, 7 March 1814, CAS DHUD 14/2/iR.

[37] Letter Isabella Hudleston, Whitehaven, to Andrew Hudleston, Bath, 7 March 1814, CAS DHUD 14/2/iR.

Respect for parents, kin and their social position was expressed, in somewhat different circumstances, by Joseph Huddart when he exhorted Kitty Senhouse not to be too indulgent when dealing with the entreaties of her great nephew Humphrey Gale. Humphrey had requested additional financial assistance to pay off his debts in India. Huddart advised Kitty Senhouse that:

> He has no right to expect [more] after what you have done for him, he ought to look at those Cadets who have landed with a little money and a little credit, instead of those gentlemen who have money and credit at will.[38]

Here Huddart was not merely being curmudgeonly, but reinforcing the notion that respectability involved living within one's means. Consistent with Bourdieu's view that taste and consumption are about distinction not mere emulation,[39] Huddart was expressing the view that the practices of one's own social milieu should be maintained. He raised the spectre of debt as not merely carrying with it the risk of financial failure, but as compromising the Senhouse's social standing and constituting a threat to respectability.

Uncontrolled indebtedness was one of the great fears of families sending their children to the East Indies. There was a continuing theme that easy money would 'seduce' sojourners into activities that would bring disrepute. There were both economic and social dimensions to that anxiety. Respectability was the platform on which credit was built and credit, in turn, was absolutely critical to the business of personal life as well as to trade and manufacturing in Cumbria, as it was in many provincial towns throughout the eighteenth century.[40] Provincial businesses and households frequently operated on credit and spent considerable time managing both their own indebtedness and those to whom they had provided credit.[41] Borrowing and lending were critical to the pursuit of business as well as day-to-day living in the East Indies. But uncontrolled debt in the East Indies could easily rebound on families at home, as Thomas Cust's biographical narrative in Chapter 2 indicates.

Interest rates were higher in the East Indies than at home and writers and junior military appointments could easily accumulate debts beyond the ability to repay. In 1811, for instance, the Madras rate of interest was around

---

[38] Letter Joseph Huddart, Greenwich, to Kitty Senhouse, Edinburgh, c. March 1811, CAS DSEN 5/5/1/9/57cV.

[39] P. Bourdieu, *Distinction: A Social Critique of the Judgement of Taste* (London, Routledge & Kegan Paul, 1994), pp. 34–55.

[40] M. Finn, *The Character of Credit: Personal Debt in English Culture, 1740–1914* (Cambridge, Cambridge University Press, 2007), pp. 76–80; J. D. Marshall, 'Agrarian Wealth and Social Structure in Pre-Industrial Cumbria', *Economic History Review*, New Series, 33, 4 (1980), pp. 514–515.

[41] Finn, *The Character of Credit*, pp. 76–80.

6 per cent.[42] Rates of 12 per cent were not unknown, as Richard Ecroyd reported to his Cumbrian aunt in the 1790s and as Thomas Cust's 1787 debt to James Graham of Rickerby testifies.[43] In Britain the bank rate or minimum lending rate was 5 per cent in 1797 and the rate for consols in 1811 was 4.7 per cent.[44] More importantly, credit in the British Isles largely rested on, and was regulated by, a network of long-standing reciprocities, friendship, business and familial connections.[45] By contrast, credit in the East Indies created dependencies on strangers, both native and European. Strangers were unconstrained by any broader commitments, obligations or connections to the interests of a debtor's family and kin.

Even where there were local connections between creditor and borrower, the outcome could be unpalatable to the borrower's family. For instance, while difficult to disentangle, it is clear that Thomas Cust was more and more in the power of the Mounseys, his Cumbrian agents, who themselves had a family member in India. Thomas Cust was attempting to sell land in Cumberland to pay for debts he contracted in India. Some of those debts in India were with George Stephenson Mounsey, a fellow officer in Bengal. At his death, Cust's debt to Mounsey in India was about £500.[46]

Some of the impacts of Thomas's debt have been noted in the previous biographical narrative, but the profound threat to reputation generated by debt and the deep distress debt caused was illustrated by the reaction of his mother and her friends to Thomas's bills. There was considerable moral pressure put on debtors' families. Elizabeth Cust, for instance, found it hard to resist a bill drawn on her by her son Thomas when it was eventually presented in London with the following correspondence penned by the creditor's father:

> I intended returning [the Bill] to my Son, protested, but recollecting that the Drawer is an Officer, that he has received the money from the paymaster General of his Brigade, on the Assurance that his Bill would be honoured in England... I am convinced it will do him great Disservice, in regard to his future Credit... To convince you of my readiness to do everything in my Power to prevent such Consequences I therefore wish to know whether Mistress Cust will pay any part, or the whole at a longer date to prevent the Disgrace that must attend her Son if the Bill is sent back.[47]

[42] Letter Joseph Huddart, Greenwich, to Kitty Senhouse, Edinburgh, c. March 1811, CAS DSEN 5/5/1/9/57cR.

[43] Letter Richard Ecroyd, Calcutta to Deborah Ecroyd, Kendal, May 1795, CAS WDFA 2/1/37; Thomas Cust to James Graham, bond, Calcutta, 30 June 1787, DCART C11/54cm.

[44] B. Mitchell, *British Historical Statistics* (Cambridge, Cambridge University Press, 2011), pp. 678–679.

[45] M. R. Hunt, *The Middling Sort: Commerce, Gender and the Family in England 1680–1780* (Berkeley, University of California Press, 1996), pp. 22–34.

[46] Inventory of Thomas Cust's account with John Palling, audited accounts 1800, CAS DCART C11/61/19b.

[47] Letter William Brooke, St Albans, to Charles Nevinson, London, 20 June 1776, CAS

In 1776, the Cumbrian Charles Nevinson, then operating an apothecary business from Duke Street, Westminster, wrote to Elizabeth Cust notifying her that a Major Brooke had arrived from India with a duplicate of a bill of credit against her made out by her son Thomas. His advice was not to pay:

> I took the Liberty of opening the Letter for which I ought to beg your pardon, but expected it might contain some Explanation of the matter and for what purpose the money was taken up and might therefore serve as some Rule how to proceed, but finding in it nothing satisfactory in that way, neither Explanation or Apology. It confirmed, I confess my former opinion that you ought not to distress yourself by answering it... No one Reason being assigned makes one rather suspect the debt had been incurr'd in some extravagant way... I think you ought not to pay it.[48]

Refusing to pay bills of credit presented a profound risk that went beyond the individual who contracted the debt. Andrew Hudleston was undoubtedly aware of these sensitivities when applying to his parents for financial assistance on arrival in India in 1814:

> I may require in addition to my pay for the first few months of my setting up for myself. Indeed it gives me the greatest concern to be under the necessity of writing to my Parents for the Sum of a hundred pounds, after their having been so kind & liberal to me, even though attended with inconvenience to themselves; However I think it more agreeable to myself, & I am sure it will be more pleasing & satisfactory to you, & my Father; that I have made my application to you; than if I had contracted debts or borrowed money of my own accord.[49]

Elizabeth Cust's exchange with Lady Hay of Pitfour illustrates the depth and emotional, material and reputational complexity of refusing a bill.

In 1777, Elizabeth Hay of Pitfour appealed to Elizabeth Cust to honour Thomas's debts to her son Charles. Before approaching Elizabeth Cust, she sought advice from Captain Thomas Conway recently returned from India. Conway's advice was clear. Charles's mother had a moral duty to pursue the matter, not for the creditor but for the debtor. He wrote that it would be:

> cruel that he [Thomas] should be disappointed in the Bill – when an Officer's Character is hurt the world will know the consequences it may be the young mans last Drafts and for a trifle his Mother if capable should endeavour beyond a Doubt to discharge it, if not you must return one with the Protest to Charles the Lieut's credit will be ever ruined inevitably... [Payment would] be the

DCART C11/42viR.

[48] Letter Charles Nevinson, London, to Elizabeth Cust, 15 July 1776, CAS DCART C11/42xiiR.

[49] Letter Andrew Hudleston, Madras, to Elizabeth Hudleston, Hutton John, 19 September 1814, CAS DHUD 13/2/7V.

making of him and he may shortly in Return remit ten times the sum to his Parents...[50]

When Lady Hay forwarded Conway's advice to Elizabeth Cust, she received an emotional but uncompromising response, which called on their shared positions as mothers:[51]

> I could not Comply to my sons demand... oh Madam – what shall I say – we and our situation in life are unknown to you. I have two sons he in India is the Elder I have already Raised too large a share of My little fortune for my Eldest son Had I properly considered Myself or my other son. He in India has had many cautions not to draw Bills on me as I could not Raise them ... tis surprising that mine should be so distressd... he has had a lieutenancy above these three years past and friends also who would be very attentive to his welfare if he has prudence... [I hope] Madam never experience[s] the distress of mind wch I do My happiness was centrd in my children...[52]

Elizabeth Cust knew that dishonouring her son's bills called into question her commitment as a mother and her position as a respectable person.

Nothing was more likely to raise protective hackles among Cumbrian men at home than when young Cumbrian men in India applied to their mothers or aunts to honour their bills. So when Humphrey Senhouse Gale sought his great aunt Kitty Senhouse's agreement to be drawn upon for debts in India in 1811, the Cumbrian Joseph Huddart, an East Indiaman commander, navigator, shipbuilder, entrepreneur and merchant who based himself in London, advised against complying with his request. Humphrey Gale had accumulated his debts as a young ensign in Madras. It was not an unusual story. His great aunt was an indulgent and loyal correspondent to Humphrey Gale and perhaps he was confident of her response. His request foundered in the face of Huddart's advice because of the long-term intimacy of Huddart's relations with the Gale and Senhouse families and Huddart's own India experience.

Huddart had risen from being the son of a farmer and shoemaker to an East Indiaman commander, a celebrated hydrographer, adviser to the building of the East India Dock and rope manufacturer. Kitty Senhouse was the sister-in-law of Sir Joseph Senhouse (1749–1829) with whom Huddart had attended school and maintained a lifelong friendship. Huddart's boatbuilding and early ventures into trade with North America had been undertaken out of Maryport, the Senhouse family's port development designed to rival

---

[50] Letter Thomas Conway to Lady Hay, Pitfour, 7 January 1777, CAS DCART /11/42xiv R and CAS DCART /11/42xiv V.

[51] Letter Elizabeth Cust to Lady Hay, Pitfour, CAS DCART /11/42xv.

[52] Letter Elizabeth Cust to Lady Hay, Pitfour, 15 March 1777, CAS DCART /11/42xvi R and DCART /11/42xvi V.

Lowther-controlled Whitehaven. Huddart had direct experience of conditions in Madras. He had a strong prudential sense and clear views around the 'proper' expectations and requirements of a young ensign. When he heard that Humphrey Senhouse Gale had sought relief from his creditors, Huddart was incensed. He wrote to Kitty Senhouse:

> sorry to hear... [he] has got involved in debt... he did say he had an ensign's pay about £200 per annum in a country that every article of provisions that the country supplies is cheaper than in England, and sufficient for the necessaries of life, and he certainly has it in his power to support himself directly on an ensigns pay... I am afraid if you advance this sum readily, you or his friends may be called upon again.[53]

Huddart advised that Humphrey Gale should immediately dispose of unnecessary accoutrements including his horses which, Huddart pointed out, would relieve Gale of the costs of grooms, grasscutters and a raft of other servants.

While for Cumbrians at home the East Indies were associated with a menace of debt and reputational degradation, paradoxically the East Indies also presented a solution to dealing with individuals bringing familial reputations at home into disrepute. The East Indies became a repository for disreputable family members and thus a way of shifting them out of local society. For instance, the gentry Hasells of Dalemain were relieved when John Hasell was driven to return to Bombay sometime in 1779. His elder brother Edward wrote that John:

> behaved very ill... He has made a great debt. My father and Messrs Musgrave will lose a great sum of money by him. His affairs have taken up much of my time in writing about them to London, Dalemain etc.[54]

The dissociation that followed was profound and inexorable. Even his death remained unknown to his family. A recent detailed history of the Hasells speculates that it may have been in 1782.[55] John Bellasis, from a distinctly middling family, however, notes in a letter to his brother at Long Marton, Westmorland, that John Hasell's death occurred soon after arrival back in Bombay around May 1781.[56]

A similar withering of familial connections is evident with two of Thomas Cust's children. The previous chapter notes that Thomas junior was

---

53 Letter Joseph Huddart, Greenwich, to Kitty Senhouse, Edinburgh, c. March 1811, CAS DSEN 5/5/1/9/57cR and DSEN 5/5/1/9/57cV.

54 F. Wilkins, *Hasells of Dalemain: A Cumberland Family: 1736–1794* (Kidderminster, Wyre Forest Press, 2003), p. 101.

55 Wilkins, *Hasells of Dalemain*, p. 101.

56 Letter John Bellasis, Bombay, to Hugh Bellasis, Long Marton, 16 May 1781, CAS WDX 1641/1/1/p. 27b.

eventually deported to Australia. His elder brother's trajectory was equally problematic. Charles was arrested in 1800 for debt and bailed by his uncle, Richard Cust. In 1802, having lost or sold his commission in the British army, he was reduced to working a transport ship, the *Carlisle Bridge*. His half-brother Richard, an ensign with the 33rd Regiment, was deeply shamed by meeting Charles in Malta and wrote to his uncle seeking financial assistance:

> Little can you conceive how it hurt me when he called to see me that Charles should be placed in a Situation worse than a Servant. Several of the Officers of our Reg.ᵗ that knew him when at Chatham and whilst with me at Canterbury now slyhts him and myself too. I have hardly the power of walking with him in his distress. He has not an atom to change himself or fit to appear in.[57]

Charles Cust was reported dead in 1813 but was subsequently reputed to be commanding a ship in the East Indies. In 1815 he was rumoured to be in London with a wife and two children in 'great distress' and in 1816 imprisoned. By 1820 he was believed to be in Calcutta.[58] The uncertainties around his life and death suggest no one sought to sustain the relationship, even among his mixed-race siblings. His father's relatives also saw the return to the East Indies as more appropriate for Thomas Cust's mixed-race children.[59]

Others, despite misbehaviour or failure at home, were desperate when in the East Indies to sustain or repair relations with family in Cumbria. For instance, the Gilpin involvement in the East Indies was prompted by debt.[60] John Losh was sent to Madras in 1824 after his academic career at Queen's College, Cambridge was curtailed less than two years after admission.[61] Jeremiah Adderton of Workington, related to the prominent gentry Curwen family, was probably always destined for India. Nevertheless, his appointment in 1778 was in the context of some scandal of his own making.[62] In an attempt to repair his relations with his family, he writes from Pondicherry to his uncle Henry Curwen and assures him:

---

[57] Letter Richard Cust (II), Malta, to his uncle Richard Cust, 6 June 1802, CAS DCART C11/54bqR.

[58] Anon. undated memorandum, CAS DCART C11/32/78.

[59] Letter from Charlotte Crackenthorpe, Newbiggin Hall, to Richard Cust London, 3 May 1796, CAS DCART/C11/44iR; Draft letter Richard Cust to Robert Mounsey, 16 December 1797, CAS DCART C11/45xxxivR.

[60] Letter John Addison junior to Francis E Barker regarding Richard Gilpin, 1814, CAS BDBROUGHTON/19/39/2.

[61] *Cambridge University Alumni, 1261–1900* [online database]. Provo, UT, USA: Ancestry.com Operations Inc, 1999. Original data: J. A. Venn (comp.), *Alumni Cantabrigienses* (London: Cambridge University Press, 1922–1954). Accessed http://home.ancestry.co.uk/; J. Uglow, *The Pinecone: The Story of Sarah Losh, Forgotten Romantic Heroine – Antiquarian, Architect and Visionary* (London, Faber and Faber, 2012), p. 166.

[62] Letter from Jeremiah Adderton, Pondicherry, to Henry Curwen, Workington, Hall, 4 September 1778, CAS DC/3/7.

That heedlessness of which led me into innumerable troubles at home, I have long felt myself totally divested of, and trust my conduct in this country has been such, as if known, would more than atone for the follies that have preceded… I again take the liberty to request you will indulge me with a letter.[63]

Loss and Death

Pursuing an East Indian fortune was not so much a gamble but an adventure: an activity known to be risky. Investments could be lost, wealth squandered and earning potential left unfulfilled. Shipwrecks, bankruptcies, dismissal (although many of the merchants dismissed by the East India Company returned with substantial fortunes),[64] indebtedness, the inability to transfer their fortunes from the East Indies to the British Isles, disputes over the Company's terms of payment, and even draining litigation on return to the British Isles, were all features of the East Indies encounter.[65] The following discussion highlights the uncertainties and disappointments associated with East Indies ventures before turning to what has become accepted as one of the greatest fears for those going to the East Indies: death.

Perhaps Cumbrian correspondents avoided commenting on loss and disappointment in their letters. As Popp points out, letters were semi-communal and not all private troubles, sometimes self-inflicted and sometimes inflicted by others, would have been paraded in letters likely to be circulated to many.[66] The disappointments of Thomas Cust's brother and mother have already been noted. There is a voluminous correspondence involving Thomas's brother Richard, Thomas's India agent John Palling, and his disapproving cousin, the elderly lawyer Robert Ellis.[67] But little new is added by rehearsing those further in detail. The tone in those letters was similar to the tone evident in Edward Hasell's previously cited exasperated letter regarding the activities of his brother John Hasell.

The losses and disappointments associated with the trajectories of those men were, in part, at least in the public arena. But this was not always the case. Failures in East Indies ventures were not always apparent. Such was the case of John Orfeur Yates, who married into the minor gentry Aglionby and less minor Musgrave families. Having entered the Company's service initially as one of Henry Fletcher's recruits on his East Indiaman, Yates remained in Calcutta for a handful of years. He had returned to Cumberland in

63 Letter Jeremiah Adderton, Pondicherry, to Henry Curwen, Workington, Hall, 4 September 1778, CAS DC/3/7.

64 Marshall, *East Indian Fortunes*, pp. 230, 230n, 237.

65 Marshall, *East Indian Fortunes*, pp. 214–256 and see examples in H. Furber, *Bombay Presidency in the Mid-Eighteenth Century* (London, Asia Publishing House, 1965), pp. 3–4, 15–17.

66 Popp, *Entrepreneurial Families*, pp. 12–13.

67 Wilkins, *Hasells of Dalemain*, p. 101.

1768 and proceeded to build Skirwith Abbey reputedly with his East Indies fortune. It was not until years later that his wife, children and friends found that their nabob's expenditure might have been conspicuous in its lavishness but it depended on unsecured credit and inaccessible assets he claimed were in India. His annual income in 1800 was a mere £464 annually and he was living on a series of loans provided by his brother.[68]

Yates attributed his financial difficulties to the insolvency of others. It seems more likely that insolvencies among agents in India precipitated the disclosure of, rather than caused, the parlous state of his finances. Nevertheless, it was true that complications in remitting funds and losses due to the failure of agents in India were persistent problems for sojourners, both while in India and after they returned home. In 1821, the very successful East Indies merchant who operated particularly in Java, Cumbrian Robert Addison, told a select committee that remittances from trade in the East Indies remained difficult.[69] There were, too, periodic banking crises. Yates died too early to have been affected by the collapse of Palmer & Co., when it went bankrupt in 1820, but many others were caught up in it.[70] It is quite possible that Montagu Ainslie's losses and fragile financial position was attributable, in part at least, to the collapse of Palmer & Co.[71]

Losses associated with business risks were not, however, the only source of disappointment for Cumbrian sojourners. For some, the East India Company itself was seen as the perpetrator of misfortune. For instance, John Addison of Whitehaven wrote repeatedly to the East India Company directors in 1720 requesting payment of a gratuity of one hundred pounds he claimed was in lieu of commission agreed by Council in Surat. He cites ill-treatment by a commander of an East Indiaman, the continuing liability for the interest he now has to pay on borrowing to meet the expenses of his voyage, recurrent illness in India, and the loss of social and economic opportunities at home:

> I am obliged to humbly further acquaint you that through several dangerous and frequent sicknesses in India with other impediments to that most expensive voyage on board *Godolphin*, it has cost me (without extravagance) not less than the sum of five hundred pounds sterling from my going from London in your service till my return... the great part of which I am now to pay... and besides all these hardships have spent above eleven years of my precious youthful days

---

[68] Summerson, 'An Ancient Squires Family', pp. 124–125.

[69] Parliamentary Papers, *House of Commons and Command*, Volume 6 HM Stationery 1821, House of Commons, p. 228.

[70] A. Webster, *The Richest East India Merchant: The Life and Business of John Palmer of Calcutta, 1767–1836* (Woodbridge, Boydell Press, 2007), pp. 110–112, 122–131.

[71] Letter Henry Ainslie to Lord Lonsdale, 9 October 1833, cited in A. Ainslie, 'Ainslie: History of the Ainslies of Dolphinston, Jedburgh, Grizedale, Hall Garth & Their Descendants' (unpublished, Bradford Peverell, Dorset, A. Ainslie, 2008), p. 5.

in your services which by sad experience I am conscious that I could have spent with God's blessing in Great Britain among my relations and known friends to good advantage.[72]

John Addison's sense of injury arises not simply from his losses or foregone income, but from the sense of betrayal by the Company of a mutual compact to share the risks and rewards of the East Indies venture. A similarly anxious, if less combative tone, is to be found forty years later in George Knott's plea to Clive's private secretary that his status and re-appointment as an officer to the Bengal army be resolved:

> I cannot avoid begging the favour of you to lay before his lordship and the general distress I have for some time suffered [despite] the solicitations that have been made... by H Verelst and myself in relation to my being readmitted to the service... I have [been in] Monghier since the 20th June and as you know how disagreeable such a situation must be I beg you would take the first opportunity to inform me of my fate...[73]

There are no surviving records as to why George Knott (1743–1784), son of the Rydal Fleming's steward and kinsman Michael Knott (1696–1772), found himself constrained to seek readmission. He had been appointed as Company cadet in 1762 and made relatively rapid advancement. In August 1763 he was appointed ensign and then, a little over six months later, lieutenant. His fragile circumstances in June 1766 almost certainly arose from the double batta mutiny among European officers the month before, another example where the Company's employees felt their compact with the Company had been abused.[74]

George Knott's role in the mutiny is unknown. What is known is that the resolution came swiftly. Six days after his letter, George Knott was not only readmitted but appointed to a captaincy.[75] No doubt his readmission and promotion was eased by John Knott (d. 1779), George's cousin and brother-in-law, who was secretary to a senior member of the Bengal Council and eventual successor to Clive, Henry Verelst. When George Knott returned to England sometime between 1768 and 1772, he almost undoubtedly had already remitted or brought back with him a substantial amount of capital.

72 IOR E/1/12 138-139v [1 March 1720] – Letter 78 John Addison at Whitehaven to William Dawsonne and the Committee of Correspondence concerning a £100 gratuity for his work in the Company's service at India and St Helena.

73 IOR Mss Eur G37/41/1 f.3 [2 July 1766] – Letter Henry Strachey and George Knott 2 July 1766.

74 L. S. S. O'Malley, *Bihar and Orissa District Gazetteers: Monghyr* (New Delhi, Concept Publishing, 2007), p. 48; R. Holmes, *Sahib: The British Soldier in India 1750–1914* (London, Harper Perennial, 2005), pp. 53f, 272f.

75 V. Hodson, *List of the Officers of the Bengal Army 1758–1834 Volumes 1–4* (Reprint, Eastbourne, A Naval and Military Press, 1927), vol. 2, p. 605.

He died within a decade, quickly followed by his wife. His early death in Cumbria was a proof that excess mortality was by no means restricted to the East Indies.

Nevertheless, there was a persistent motif of impending death associated with India. Indeed, the East Indies featured in one of the earliest obituaries in English print; an account of an East India Company captain who was killed during a skirmish at sea with the Portuguese in 1621.[76] Thereafter, expatriate deaths in the East Indies and the deaths at home of those with East Indian connections were regularly featured in print. From about 1780, English language newspapers and journals in the East Indies also printed birth, marriage and death notices. Deaths in particular provided a substantial amount of easy copy. They contributed to a perception of the East Indies as a place in which survival was constantly in the balance. Stories of individuals transformed within a day from robust health to a moribund state with no hope of recovery were widely circulated, including by Andrew Hudleston writing from Calicut to his aunt at Whitehaven in 1819:

> Many people apparently in good health, while walking along the road, have been seized with a giddiness in the head, fallen down, vomited & died in the short space of half an hour, but in general the disease does not prove fatal in under 5 or 8 hours.[77]

For Europeans the rapidity of death in the East Indies contrasted starkly with what had become one of the most common causes of adult death in the British Isles by the latter part of the eighteenth century, the slowly progressing tuberculosis. By then it had become, unlike cholera, a thoroughly romantic disease linked to poetic sensibility.[78]

It has been estimated that over half the 645 covenanted Company servants appointed to the Bengal presidency between 1707 and 1775 never returned to the British Isles and died in India. The proportion of non-covenanted residents who never returned to the British Isles was higher again.[79] The net mortality above that which would have occurred if these individuals had stayed in the British Isles would have been less dramatic than these estimates suggest. Nevertheless, it is clear that many families held reasonable fears that they would never see their East Indies-bound kin again.

---

[76] E. Barry, 'From Epitaph to Obituary: Death and Celebrity in Eighteenth-Century British Culture', *International Journal of Cultural Studies*, 11 (2008), p. 259; N. Starck, *Life after Death: The Art of Obituary* (Melbourne, Melbourne University Press, 2006), p. 5.

[77] Letter Andrew Hudleston, Calicut, to Isabella Hudleston, Whitehaven, 15 March 1819, CAS DHUD 14/16V.

[78] P. Bourdelais, *Epidemics Laid Low: A History of What Happened in Rich Countries* (Baltimore, MD, Johns Hopkins University Press, 2006), p. 115; C. Lawlor, *Consumption and Literature: The Making of the Romantic Disease* (Basingstoke, Palgrave, 2006), pp. 2, 51–55.

[79] Marshall, *East Indian Fortunes*, pp. 218–219.

The sense of the uncertainties of life for those leaving the British Isles for the East Indies was reinforced by early travelogues complaining of the unhealthy locations of principal settlements. In 1727, the Scotsman Alexander Hamilton claimed a third of Calcutta's European population had been buried in a period of less than six months.[80] Although European mortality rates in the East Indies declined over the next century, the probability of death remained substantially higher than in the British Isles. In the 1830s, the annual death rate among soldiers stationed in Britain was a little over fifteen deaths per thousand, compared to forty-eight deaths per thousand for British soldiers on 'peacetime' service in India.[81]

Death, then, was the preoccupying fear of Cumbrian families sending their children to the East Indies, but the chances of returning home increased over the long eighteenth century. The 175 Cumbrian men appointed or licensed to the East Indies between 1800 and 1829 entered the East Indies at a time when significant falls in mortality were being achieved. The probability of death from disease, despite Andrew Hudleston's description of rapid death, was declining rapidly even among those most vulnerable to death, soldiers. Military peacetime deaths fell from seventy per thousand of population per year in the period 1806–1809, to forty-eight deaths per thousand of population per year in the period 1827–1838.[82] Even so, death rates were twice as high as those in the British Isles. That was reflected in the death or burial places of Cumbrian men appointed to the East Indies during the long eighteenth century. Many did not return. Fifty-one per cent of the men for whom deaths or burials can be established, died outside the British Isles.

It was in the context of the threat of death that, notwithstanding the multiple exemplars of successful Cumbrian careers in the East Indies, Thomas Cust's mother conjured a vision of the East Indies. For Elizabeth Cust, India was loaded with ambivalences. Hopes of gain were mixed with fears. She feared that her younger son's future, and her own, would be compromised by her elder son's recklessness far away from the moderating influences of family. She feared he would predecease her. That anxiety was not simply around the grief of losing a son. Elizabeth Cust was apprehensive about how her old age would be supported if her eldest son did not return. For her, Thomas's death would have undermined any possibility of a financial return on her considerable investment in Thomas's Company bonds, his fitting out and travel.[83]

Anxiety was an inherent part of the encounter with the East Indies. For Cumbrians, loss and disappointment were part of their correspondence

80 R. Travers, 'Death and the Nabob: Imperialism and Commemoration in Eighteenth Century India', *Past and Present*, 196 (August 2007), p. 87.

81 P. Curtin, *Death by Migration: Europe's Encounter with the Tropical World in the Nineteenth Century* (Cambridge, Cambridge University Press, 1989), pp. 7, 23.

82 Curtin, *Death by Migration*, p. 23.

83 Letter Elizabeth Cust to Thomas Cust, India, 1772, CAS DCART C11/42iR.

throughout the long eighteenth century and evident in letters with business associates, family and friends. There were persistent references to illness, to the loss of ships and narrow escapes from death. The tone of those references ranged from a sort of 'matter of fact' asides to expressions of sorrow and grief. Perhaps as a forerunner of the Victorian fascination and celebration of death and its intersect with an increasingly militaristic pursuit of imperial dominance in the nineteenth century, there were instances where death was connected to a compensatory heroic legacy. That compensatory heroism was obvious in the public memorial in the *Bombay Courier* to Thomas Pattinson, killed at Corry Gaum in 1818, and private condolences to his parents from the East Indies merchant and owner of Scaleby Castle, Henry Fawcett:

> Lieutenant Pattinson was early in the action, shot through the body, and put in a place of safety, where his heroic spirit would not allow him to remain. When he conceived the overwhelming numbers of the enemy must overpower us, he appeared again noble exerting the noble strength left him, and encouraging the men, until another wound in the breast totally disabled him, and finally caused the death of as gallant officer who ever lived.[84]
>
> Oh I wish to say be <u>comforted</u>! "Casting all your <u>care</u> upon him who careth for you." "<u>Thy will be done</u>" but it is hard <u>practically</u> to learn that lesson, <u>so often repeated</u> with our lips. M^r F continues better, w^h I know will give you some comfort – he sends you a letter, received yesterday Even^g from James Graham – making such kind & affectionate mention of your dear Son & also of his Gallant & noble conduct, in the trying hour & manifesting the <u>love</u> of his bro^r Officers so as must be gratifying and consoling to his <u>dear parents.</u>[85]

Reconciling Risk and Reward

Fears that those bound for the East Indies would never return were firmly based in material experience. So too were fears of loss and failure, rather than success and wealth. At the same time, the individual and familial opportunities presented by the East Indies were by no means illusionary. Cumbrians were neither unaware of the risks nor the rewards of the East India encounter. Nor were these Cumbrian families driven by instrumental considerations unalloyed by affection. Indeed, adventurous youths were frequently more enthusiastic about the East Indies than their families. Thomas Pattinson's parents, for instance, were willing to forego the considerable investment that must have been made into his fitting out and travel. Even at the point of departure to India in 1805, Thomas's parents were providing him with opportunities to change his mind. His father writing on one side of a sheet of paper was followed by Thomas's mother writing on the other side of the page:

---

[84] Enclosed in CAS DX 249/16a.
[85] Letter Mr Fawcett to Mary Pattinson, no date, CAS DX 249/14wV and DX 249/14wR.

My dear Boy, My Mother receiv'd your letter last night, which gave us all very real pleasure to hear you were well, and that your inclination is still to go to India...

We are happy to find you are well & that you write in good spirits. I longed to know what your sentiments now are in regard to going abroad, for if you had in the least disliked it you should not have gone. No! Not for all the <u>Indies</u> but as you write me that you still prefer it I will endeavour to rest satisfied...[86]

Gentry and middling Cumbrian families contextualised the risks of an East Indies encounter with alternative activities in global trade as well as conditions at home. They rationalised risk at a multitude of levels and had accepted a view that the East Indies were not only survivable but liveable. Some families, it appears, adopted a pattern of sending younger rather than elder sons to the East Indies. It is difficult to establish precisely how common this was. However, among the gentry families prominent in Cumbrian affairs, such as the Senhouses, the Fletchers, the Christians, the Stanleys, and the Flemings, the East Indies venture was very much the domain of younger sons. There were exceptions. Notably, Andrew Hudleston of Hutton John sent not only his eldest son but his only child to India.[87] His second cousin, John Hudleston (1749–1837), descended from a younger line of the Hutton John family, was experienced in India and as a director and influential member of the India faction of the Company found positions for a multitude of his own sons, as well as the sons of a wide circle of kin and friends.

It is possible, but unlikely, that choices about which children went to India were constituted around prudential concerns and designed to manage East Indian risk. It is more likely that the East Indies presented for the Cumbrian gentry another solution to the problem of supporting younger sons.[88] Certainly, a prudential approach is not obvious among those Cumbrians involved in the East Indies trade. Very early in the eighteenth century, John Braddyll, eventually of Conishead Priory, was active in the East Indies. Of John Braddyll and Sarah Dodding's five surviving sons, four were in the East Indies prior to 1750. Similarly, Edward Stephenson of Keswick, as well as his only brother, were in India around the same time, along with multiple Winders and Addisons. John Taylor, who returned to Cumbria after service

---

86 Letter Thomas and Mary Pattinson, Kirklinton, to their son Thomas Pattinson, 16 February 1805, CAS DX 249/14vR.
87 IOR J/1/27 f.97.
88 In Cumbria this is noted by Hughes, *North Country Life Vol II*, p. 89 and explored by D. R. Hainsworth, 'The Lowther Younger Sons: A 17th-Century Case Study', *Transactions CWAAS*, New Series, 88 (1988), pp. 149–160. The difficulties for middling and gentry families of supporting younger sons and business is an ongoing motif in R. Grassby, *Kinship and Capitalism: Marriage, Family, and Business in the English-Speaking World, 1580–1740* (Cambridge, Cambridge University Press, 2006), pp. 78, 190, 198, 208–210.

as a surgeon with the East India Company, subsequently committed his three sons to the East Indies in 1770, 1778 and the 1790s respectively.

Similar to Quaker families operating in the North American colonies, many Cumbrians in the East Indies relied on familial networks to operate their ventures.[89] This was certainly evident in the connected Dent and Wilkinson as well as the Fawcett families who situated sons across both the Indian sub-continent and China to maintain their extensive trading, shipping and agency businesses, including opium. James Graham, the Carlisle banker, repeatedly spent time in India with his children. The Bellasis, Huddart and Wordsworth families, ambitious middling families all, sent multiple offspring to the East Indies. This pattern was part of a broader tendency among merchant and trading families to place close kin in overseas posts. The management of Cumbrian business interests in this way was evident in the West Indies, Africa, the Baltic and Europe as well as the East Indies.[90] By the nineteenth century, the East India Company had become part of the accepted career options for gentry and middling ranks. Gentry and middling families in Cumbria were, as Andrew Hudleston's mother notes in 1821, despairing when depressed trade meant that even the influence of Lord Lonsdale could not deliver East India Company appointments.[91]

Perhaps, too, people simply accepted that life was short, whether in the East Indies or at home. The observations of deaths in Carlisle from 1779 to 1787 reported by the Carlisle physician John Heysham, suggest that average life expectancy was a little under thirty-nine years.[92] Under those circumstances, perceptions of the risk of death in the East Indies were perhaps mitigated by views about the uncertainties of life at home and the other places to which Cumbrians were connected globally. Certainly, India was not seen as presenting the same risks as some other parts of the world. In 1806, Ann Pattinson, when writing to her brother Thomas in Bombay, noted:

> David Story is ordered to the West Indies. He is just going to sail for Barbados. They are all very anxious about him here. It is so unhealthy a climate.[93]

---

[89] A. J. L. Winchester, 'Ministers, Merchants and Migrants: Cumberland Friends and North America in the Eighteenth Century', *Quaker History*, 80, 2 (Fall 1991), pp. 85–99.

[90] See for example, E. Hughes, *North Country Life in the Eighteenth Century Vol. 11 Cumberland & Westmorland 1700–1830* (London, Oxford University Press, 1965), pp. 335–354; F. A. Winder, 'The Winders of Lorton', *Transactions CWAAS*, Old Series XII (1893), pp. 439–457; F. A. Winder, 'Further Notes on the Winders of Lorton', *Transactions CWAAS*, Old Series XV (1898), pp. 229–238; Wilkins, *Hasells of Dalemain*, pp. 22–25, 28–29, 55–58.

[91] Letter Elizabeth Hudleston to Andrew Hudleston, 1821, CAS DHUD 13/11/1.

[92] W. A. Armstrong, 'The Trend of Mortality in Carlisle between the 1780s and the 1840s: A Demographic Contribution to the Standard of Living Debate', *Economic History Review*, New Series, 34, 1 (February 1981), p. 99.

[93] Letter Ann Pattinson, Penrith, to Thomas Pattinson, Bombay, 14 January 1806, CAS DX 249/14sR.

The issue of climate should not be neglected. It has become axiomatic that the Indian climate was one of the determinants of the British imperial model in India. In particular, official interest in developing India as a settlement colony waned as acclimatisation was increasingly seen as degrading to the British constitution and likely to engender effeminacy.[94] That developing view among government and Company officials did not necessarily align with the views expressed by Cumbrians. In their correspondence, Cumbrians expressed a broader 'everyday' or 'common sense' discourse around the interaction between health and weather. Certainly, views around the deleterious effects of the climate were by no means restricted to the Indian climate.

Cumbrians 'at home' and Cumbrian sojourners in the East Indies similarly expressed anxieties about the climates of both parts of the world. Neither the climate in the British Isles nor the climate in the East Indies were portrayed in universalistic terms. The effects on health of Cumbrian cold and wet were repeatedly referenced, as were a parade of family, friends and neighbours moving around the British Isles to find weather that would restore health. Similarly, some areas of, and seasons in, India were described as climatically trying, uncomfortable and unhealthy, while other places, seasons or times of day were described as pleasant. There was undoubtedly a sense of an 'English constitution' but the impacts of climate were also frequently personalised. Andrew Hudleston, for instance, wrote that Madras was unsuited to his constitution, but he found that the Malabar Coast and Mysore were much more amenable.[95]

The risks of ill-health and death from the Indian climate were, then, treated by Cumbrians as variegated rather than uniform, and contingent rather than inevitable. Indeed, there was a continual theme in Cumbrian correspondence that presented parts of India as relatively healthy. As Thomas Pattinson prepares to leave for India in 1805, he received from his mother both blessing and reassurance when she stated 'I will trust in the Almighty for your preservation and humbly hope, yes ardently, long for your safe return. Bombay is said to be a healthy climate...'[96] A decade later, Isabella Hudleston writing from Whitehaven to Andrew Fleming in Madras commented:

[94] M. Harrison, *Climates and Constitutions: Health, Race, Environment and British Imperialism in India, 1600–1850* (New York, Oxford University Press, 2000), p. 19; J. Beattie, 'Health Panics, Migration and Ecological Exchange in the Aftermath of the 1857 Uprising: India, New Zealand and Australia', in R. Peckham (ed.), *Empires of Panic: Epidemics and Colonial Anxieties* (Hong Kong, Hong Kong University, 2015), pp. 87–110.

[95] Letter Andrew Hudleston, Calicut, to his aunt Fleming, 29 December 1817, CAS DHUD 14/12R and DHUD 14/19V.

[96] Letter Thomas and Mary Pattinson, Kirklinton, to Thomas Pattinson, 16 February 1805, CAS DX 249/14vR.

> I think if the object you went to India can be acompleashed at Calicut I wou'd not wish you to make a change as all I know that have been in Calicut says it is the most Healthy place for the English Constitution.[97]

Half a century before, Elizabeth Cust, while disputing her son's notion that India was ruining his constitution, stressed 'Gentlemen that have returned from India are the healthyest men that I am acquainted with in the Little Circle of my acquaintance.'[98]

This is not to suggest that Cumbrians ignored the exposure of their kin to new diseases and a very different climate. They accepted that diseases largely unknown in England, as well as the heat, presented challenges to the Cumbrian constitution. At the same time, it was also believed that the challenges of climate and disease could be managed in much the same way as illness was managed at home. That is, through physic, travel to healthy climes and spas, and prudence.

Even the most feared of epidemic diseases, cholera, was susceptible to physic and the expansion of medical expertise.[99] In 1818, Andrew Hudleston writes to his aunt Isabella of the efficacy of treatment during a cholera outbreak:

> At present nine cases have occurred in Calicut but from being taken in time only two of them were fatal. The dose which is usually given, (& which is taken within an hour from the time the patient is first attacked rarely fails to effect his cure) consists of 18 grams of Calomel taken in powder, to be washed down by 15 drops of essence of peppermint & 80 or 100 drops of Laudanum in a wine glass of water.[100]

Elizabeth Cust was also confident in medical intervention. Almost undoubtedly influenced by the popularisation of the inoculation for smallpox which had been practised in Carlisle since the mid-1750s,[101] she cautioned Thomas against exaggerating the dangers of India:

> Every Body says you have kept your Health vastly well, the violent fever you had at your first arrival was what you were to Expect and is undoubtedly of service to you and to every Body at their first arrivals.[102]

---

[97] Letter Isabella Hudleston, Whitehaven, to Andrew Hudleston, Madras, 20 January 1821, CAS DHUD 14/2/13R.

[98] Letter Elizabeth Cust to Thomas Cust, 1772, CAS DCART C11/42iR.

[99] P. Chakrabarti, '"Neither of meate nor drinke, but what the Doctor alloweth": Medicine amidst War and Commerce in Eighteenth-Century Madras', *Bulletin of the History of Medicine*, 80 (2006), pp. 1–38.

[100] Letter Andrew Hudleston, Calicut, to Isabella Hudleston, Whitehaven, 30 September 1818, CAS DHUD 14/15.

[101] Armstrong, 'The Trend of Mortality in Carlisle', p. 105.

[102] Letter from Elizabeth Cust, Carlisle, to Thomas Cust, Barrackpore, 1772. CAS DCART

In both Cumbria and the East Indies the unwell travelled to find cures in healing climes and natural treatments. In the British Isles, Cumbrians travelled to Harrogate, Bath, Brighton and Cheltenham. Isabella Hudleston wrote to her nephew Andrew in Calicut, 'Your friend Henry Lowther has lost His beloved Wife, has been in a very bad state of Health, ordered to Bath & from there to Brighton.'[103] Notably Andrew Hudleston, who returned to Cumbria in the 1830s after a long career in India, travelled from Cumberland to Brighton thirty years later in an effort to improve his declining health. It was unsuccessful. He died there and his body had to be transported back to Cumbria for burial at Greystoke.[104]

In search of health, Cumbrians sojourning in the East Indies similarly travelled to the Cape of Good Hope, mountain towns in India, the Malabar Coast or simply took a local sea voyage. Andrew Hudleston's cousin William frequently had recourse to sea voyages and the Cape.[105] Thomas Cust spent considerable time at the Cape in the year before his death in 1795.[106] Three years later, his daughter Susan, who had undoubtedly contracted consumption in England before returning to Calcutta, was pronounced to be in need of a sea voyage:

> It is with much concern that I inform you that for some months past, Miss Cust's state of Health has been so bad, that an immediate Voyage to Sea has been in the Opinion of the medical Gent who attends her, Dr Hare, became absolutely necessary and the only prospect there is of saving her life.[107]

Others, such as John Bellasis, appeared to remain in rude health. While advising his brother Hugh to add their lately departed brother's name to the family tombstone, John Bellasis, already close to forty years in India, added:

> One Day or another, my name may be added to the List – at present I have very good Health. I have scarcely had one Days Illness since I left England and have almost forgot the taste of Physic.[108]

C11/42iV.

103 Letter Isabella Hudleston, Whitehaven, to Andrew Hudleston, Calicut, 21 February 1819, CAS DHUD 14/2/6V.

104 'Death of Mr Hudleston of Hutton John', *Carlisle Journal*, 6 September 1861.

105 Letter Andrew Hudleston, Madras, to Andrew and Elizabeth Hudleston, Hutton John, 9 June 1815, CAS DHUD 13/3/3V.

106 G. Theall, *Records of the Cape Colony 1793–1831 Copied for the Cape Government, from the Manuscript Documents in the Public Record Office* (London, Cape Colony Government, 1897), pp. 115, 123.

107 Letter John Palling, Calcutta, to Richard Cust, 6 April 1798, CAS DCART C11/61/11R.

108 Letter John Bellasis, Bombay, to Hugh Bellasis, Long Marton, 1 July 1802, CAS WDX 1641/1/1/37c.

Retaining one's health was seen by Cumbrian families as necessary if sojourners were to successfully realise the opportunities presented to them by the East Indies. Health was not taken for granted. But premature death and debility were also seen as preventable. Of particular importance to the retention of health was avoiding excess. In 1814, Isabella Hudleston expressed the contingent nature of health in the East Indies when she reported to her nephew Andrew, then in Madras, that she:

> met the other day a Mr Hall Brother to the late Vicar of Ponsonby who had been 27 years in Madras. He gave me a most pleasing account of the Place, & said it was he believed the Healthiest Situation in the World, if it was not counteracted by intemperance; Keep this in remembrance, I am sure he has, for a Healthier looking Gentleman I don't know.[109]

Moderation and health were imbued with moral dimensions. Health was associated with wealth. Ill-health was connected to excess, debt and disgrace. Debt and disgrace were, indeed, the manifestations of over-indulgence, extravagance and a lack of moderation. Nowhere is that connection more evident than in the Ulverston physician John Fell's description of Christopher Wilson to the eminent physician William Cullen from whom he was seeking advice regarding Wilson's gout and heart problems in 1773. In his eighty-fourth year at the time of Fell's enquiry, Wilson had married Margaret Braddyll and acquired Bardsea as well as the Braddyll's Conishead Priory, having returned in 1726 in his late thirties after a career in the East India Company army:

> Mr Wilson is descended from healthy Parents, who never had the Gout. He has enjoyed a very strong & vigorous Constitution and took great Care of it, being remarkably temperate, both in Respect to Eating and Drinking. He mostly drank Water and seldom took more than two or three Glasses of Wine a Day. He has spent a good Deal of his Life in the service of the East-India-Company, in which he was a Captain for many Years, and acquired a plentiful Fortune with an excellent character. When he quitted this service, he bought a large Estate, & amused himself with Hunting...[110]

The sentiments expressed in the letters of Cumbrians in the long eighteenth century persisted well into the late nineteenth century. Hull's vade mecum for Europeans bound for India published in 1878 warned that the 'problem' with India was not so much its climate but that 'every facility is afforded the

---

[109] Letter Isabella Hudleston, Whitehaven, to Andrew Hudleston, Bath, 7 March 1814, CAS DHUD 14/2/1V.

[110] Letter from John Fell, Ulverston, to Dr William Cullen, Edinburgh, 1 November 1773, ID 857, *The Cullen Project: The Consultation Letters of Dr William Cullen (1710–1790) at the Royal College of Physicians of Edinburgh*: http://cullenproject.ac.uk/.

thoughtless and self-indulgent for getting into debt in India... and no habit is more apt to grow, than one of gratifying every wish as it occurs...'.[111] Avoiding excess and maintaining health in the East Indies consequently provided not only a rich vein of subject matter in private correspondence but in print throughout the long eighteenth century and thereafter. Thomas Williamson in his 1813 advisory publication *The European in India* stated unequivocally that:

> A young person of good health, disposed to moderation in general, and avoiding the sun during the great heats, may expect to live as long in Calcutta as in any part of the world... many have not been blessed with strong constitutions; but they have, by prudence and forbearance, obviated the greatest dangers...[112]

Conclusion

Ambivalence was at the heart of Cumbrians' encounters with the East Indies. Fears of social marginalisation were accompanied by even more pressing anxieties that an East Indies venture would culminate not in vast wealth, but in loss, disaster and death. The tension between risk and reward was a persistent feature of the Cumbrian encounter with the East Indies. Wealth, respectability and success were the entwined hopes of Cumbrian families as they dispatched their children to the East Indies. Loss, debt, disgrace and death were their greatest fears.

Cumbrians were by no means ignorant of the risks of an East Indies sojourn. But the East Indies offered a promise of wealth beyond that which could be achieved in Cumbria or elsewhere in the British Isles. For Sir Daniel Fleming there were opportunities to place a son with East Indies ambitions advantageously at home. He was influential enough for George to be installed as a canon at Carlisle Cathedral. George's career culminated in appointment as Bishop of Carlisle.[113] For others, both gentry and middling class, the balance between risk and reward meant that the East Indies were not so obviously unacceptable. Middling Cumbrians, often in consort with gentry kin, were already operating within an extensive network of global trade in which the risks of loss, debt and death were familiar. Opportunities for younger sons in particular were limited. For both families and individuals

111 E. Hull, *The European in India, or, an Anglo-Indian's Vade-Mecum* (New Delhi, Asian Educational Services, 2004), p. 70.

112 T. Williamson, *The East India Vade Mecum or the Complete Guide to Gentlemen Intended for the Civil, Military or Naval Service of the Hon. East India Company, vol. 1* (London, Black, Parry and Kingsbury, 1810), p. 2.

113 W. Gibson, 'Fleming, Sir George, Second Baronet (1667–1747)', *Oxford Dictionary of National Biography* (Oxford, Oxford University Press, 2004); online edn, Oct. 2007: www.oxforddnb.com.ezproxy.lancs.ac.uk/ view/article/9698.

with access to the resources necessary to the pursuit of opportunities in the East Indies, there was the promise of success. Individuals were not thrust out to the East Indies without consideration of the nature of success or the risks associated with East Indies ventures.

Nor was being 'put out' to India simply a means by which the obligations associated with kinship could be avoided and young men and women sent off to 'go it alone'. Within the exception of Bombay, which was considered particularly inhospitable to young men without connections, there was considerable emphasis placed on providing hospitality in the East Indies.[114] An East Indies sojourn was a strategy to deliver mutual benefits to the sojourner and his family. Certainly, it was one riven with anxieties, hopes and ambivalence about whether the venture would deliver a worthwhile return of its costs.

The outcome of an East Indies venture was not treated fatalistically. The perceived risks associated with the East Indies were conceived of as manageable: risks mitigated through prudence and healthy living and rewards grasped through ambition and hard work. Many Cumbrians believed that the balance between risk and reward could be struck, that the rewards were worthwhile, and that there would be benefits stretching beyond individual sojourners to their families at home and their position within provincial society. Those beliefs are apparent in the way in which these provincial families mobilised a raft of resources to take family members to the East Indies.

[114] Spear, *The Nabobs*, pp. 73f.

Four

'PASSAGE TO INDIA'

> Unworthy, brutish Captain Carter and an officer of his has been pleased to beat me abt purely to let me know their powers – John Addison, Whitehaven, 1720.[1]

John Addison was one of many passengers on their voyage to or from the East Indies who protested treatment by the captains and officers of East Indiamen. Indeed, travellers' anxieties about possible abuse was a theme that persisted across the long eighteenth century. Almost a century later Cruikshank caricatured the voyage (Plate 4.1) and Williamson's *East India Vade Mecum* provided extensive instructions about how to select a ship, a captain, fellow travellers and a cabin to avoid the journey to India becoming a nightmare of filth and mistreatment.[2]

But the passage to India was not simply a matter of preparing for, or surviving, what could be a tedious, sometimes frightening and often uncomfortable trip. Travel to the East Indies was merely one, relatively brief, phase in a much more extended process. The high rate of Cumbrian engagement with the East Indies had its genesis in the comparatively high levels of educational achievement among young Cumbrians. They had to meet, too, the burden of the financial demands associated with preparation, fit-out, travel and the provision of venture capital for private trade. The passage to India was determined by the extent to which Cumbrian gentry and middling families could mobilise a network of friends to: gain patronage appointments into East India Company; financially support them in their East Indies venture; and provide care and support to preparations for an orderly and successful departure for and arrival in the East Indies. In short, the passage to India was paved by a complex interaction between what Bourdieu would describe as cultural, economic and social capital.

---

[1] IOR/E/1/11 ff. 184–185v [3 May 1720] – Letter 113 John Addison in London to Thomas Woolley.

[2] T. Williamson, *The East India Vade Mecum or the Complete Guide to Gentlemen Intended for the Civil, Military or Naval Service of the Hon. East India Company* (London, Black, Parry and Kingsbury, 1810), vol. 1, pp. 31–60.

An Interesting scene, on board an East-Indiaman, showing the Effects of a heavy Lurch, after dinner.

Plate 4.1 An Interesting scene on board an East-Indiaman, showing the Effects of a heavy Lurch, after dinner, circa 1818. Reproduced by permission of the National Maritime Museum, Greenwich

For Bourdieu, cultural capital is produced out of the intersection between family and the institutional structures of education. Cultural capital are assets in the form of competencies, qualifications and skills which allow (or deny) individuals opportunities to connect to the processes of economic capital accumulation. Cultural capital also provides the foundations of taste which, in turn, both constructs and maintains social distinctions. According to Bourdieu, social distinction feeds the processes of identity and identification that underpin institutionalised 'relationships of mutual acquaintance and recognition'.[3] It is those which bind class, kin and place networks together and generate social capital. That is, the material and symbolic resources and benefits that amass because individuals and groups share social spaces recognisable in common interests, tastes and mores.[4]

This chapter explores the splicing and re-splicing of these forms of capital and how they shaped the passage to India of Cumbrian sojourners. It starts with the way in which Cumbria's educational opportunities provided Cumbrians

---

[3] P. Bourdieu, 'The Forms of Capital', in J. Richardson (ed.), *Handbook of Theory and Research for the Sociology of Education* (New York, Greenwood, 1986), p. 88.

[4] Bourdieu, 'The Forms of Capital', pp. 81–95; P. Bourdieu, *Distinction: A Social Critique of the Judgement of Taste* (London, Routledge & Kegan Paul, 1994), pp. 112–125.

with particular advantages in the pursuit of Company and other appointments. The chapter then turns to the financial challenges of seeking success in the East Indies and the way in which comparatively under-resourced gentry and middling Cumbrians dealt with the burden of costs. Finally, the discussion then focusses on how the social capital embedded in Cumbrian networks, and the eighteenth-century concept of friends, combined to lever patronage, influence and resources to drive forward the pursuit of success in the East Indies.

Cumbria's Educational Landscape and Cultural Capital

In November 1783, East India Company director Francis Baring wrote that the Company's Cumbrian chairman and Member of Parliament for Cumberland Henry Fletcher was 'neither capable of forming accounts himself nor of digesting those which are formed by others'.[5] It was a pronouncement written in the heat of Fox's East India Bill designed to establish parliamentary control over the East India Company and constrain its patronage. Baring and Fletcher were on opposing sides. The two embodied persistent tensions between the Company's city faction, London-based merchant directors like Baring, and the India faction made up of directors who had themselves sojourned and operated in the East Indies. Under those circumstances, what is interesting is not so much that Baring chose to make a pejorative comment about Henry Fletcher, but that comment has served as the summary motif of Henry Fletcher's career in *The History of Parliament*.

It is an assessment at odds with a man who sustained his parliamentary position in opposition to the Lowther interest, a man who was an influential director of the East India Company after a successful career as an East Indiaman, and a man who both made and married a fortune. It is, however, an assessment consistent with a common portrayal of the provincial North as less literate than the South[6] and Cumbria as an isolated backwater with Cumbrians stultified and resistant to innovation.[7] Yet propositions of widespread illiteracy, limited intellectual opportunities and innovation sit, for Cumbria's middling and gentry classes at least, uneasily with the evidence.

5   Cited in J. Brooke, 'FLETCHER, Henry (c.1727–1807), of Clea Hall, Cumb.', in L. Namier (ed.), *The History of Parliament: The House of Commons 1754–1790* (1964): www.historyofparliamentonline.org/volume/1754-1790/member/fletcher-henry-1727-1807.

6   R. Houston, 'The Development of Literacy: Northern England, 1640–1750', *Economic History Review*, 35, 2 (May 1982), pp. 199–216.

7   C. L. M. Bouch and G. Jones, *A Short Economic and Social History of the Lake Counties 1500–1830* (Manchester: Manchester University Press, 1961), p. 218, present examples of this view expressed in 1790. A similar view is expressed by Martineau in the 1840s: see M. A. Hill (ed.), *An Independent Woman's Lake District Writings: Harriet Martineau* (New York: Humanity Books, 2004), p. 11.

In 1820 Henry Brougham declared Westmorland to be a beacon in the gloom of English educational performance. He asserted that one in seven of Westmorland's children accessed elementary education compared to a national average of one in sixteen children. Westmorland, he claimed, was superior to the rest of England in its rate of educational provision. He went on to claim Westmorland's ratios of child education were in excess of Holland, Scotland and Switzerland where there was one educated child to every eight to eleven children in the population.[8] Subsequently, historians have shown that while the precision of Brougham's estimates might be debated, his claim that the Cumbrian population was literate has some substance.

Analysis of northern circuit assizes, which included Cumberland and Westmorland, found that literacy rates in the northern English counties increased among male deponents and was over two-thirds by the 1730s. All the gentry and professional male deponents between the 1720s and 1740s were literate. Among the middling classes involved in crafts and trades or yeoman, around three-quarters of male deponents were literate. The proportions of women who were literate were smaller, but were nevertheless substantial. Over 80 per cent of women deponents from gentry families between 1640 and 1750 were literate.[9] Literacy unquestionably underpinned middling Cumbrian women's involvement in business.[10] The extent and depth of literacy undoubtedly varied. A flavour of the educational limitations for Cumbrian gentry women in the mid-eighteenth century can be found in the letters of Andrew Fleming Hudleston's faithful correspondent, his unmarried aunt Isabella.

Born in 1741, and resident in Whitehaven for much of her adult life until her death in 1823, Isabella Hudleston's education was patchy at best. Avidly interested in political affairs and news, public and private, Isabella plaintively comments in replying to one of her nephew's letters from India:

> Your Letters are all most charming do pray continue to favor me with them you have quite the power of letter writing tis quite uphill with me having never been properly taught how to spell I am quite ashamed to write & send a Letter but to you I do it because I love you & you will excuse… tis true I might turn to the Dictionary but my eyes fail me & I find that I have wrote all this Letter without spectacles I cou'd not see to read that small print without them & that takes up much time & makes writing very troublesome if it was not for the above I

8   H. Brougham, 'Education of the Poor', *House of Commons Debate 28 June 1820, vol 2., Hansard*, cc. 49–91; M. G. Jones, *The Charity School Movement: A Study of Eighteenth Century Puritanism in Action* (Cambridge, Cambridge University Press, 2013), pp. 321–322.

9   Houston, 'The Development of Literacy', pp. 206–213.

10 C. Churches, 'Putting Women in Their Place: Female Litigants at Whitehaven, 1660–1760', in N. E. Wright, M. W. Ferguson and A. R. Buck (eds.), *Women, Property and the Letters of the Law in Early Modern England* (Toronto, University of Toronto Press, 2004).

shou'd have great pleasure in sending letters to you but it was not the Fashion in my Day to teach Ladies the Grammar.[11]

By contrast, gentry and middling Cumbrian men had a myriad of opportunities for both elementary and vocational education. Indeed, such was the proclivity to schooling, the Cumbrian Thomas Rumney of Melfell wrote that the northern counties became: 'quite a manufactory for Bankers' and Merchants' clerks' for London in the eighteenth century.[12] Indeed, Cumbria was exporting schoolmasters to other counties. 'Expatriate' Cumbrian schoolmasters teaching at private schools and successfully preparing pupils for Cambridge and Oxford included Adam Barnes at Higham, Suffolk, William Bordley from Hawkshead who ran a school at Lancaster, and the Westmerians Robert Shaw and Robert Dent who headed schools at Burnley and Ottrington respectively in the early half of the eighteenth century. Later there was John Kendall of Whitehaven who had a school in Warwickshire and Thomas Lancaster of Barton who established schools in Fulham and Wimbledon. The most prominent was William Gilpin appointed as headmaster of Cheam in 1757 and succeeded by his son twenty years later.[13]

Cumbria was simply awash with schools. Sixty-two of the eighty-one grammar schools in England's northern counties operating during the eighteenth century were situated in Cumberland and Westmorland.[14] Opportunities for vocational training were rich. There were formal apprenticeships and vocational placements. Young Cumbrian men were situated in counting houses, the offices of merchants and tradesmen, articled to attorneys or taken on as midshipmen and mates on coastal or international shipping. Oxford and Cambridge, the vocational training grounds for young men destined for the church, had long-standing connections into Cumbria. Queen's College, Oxford was particularly prominent in the education and the provision of livings to middling and gentry Cumbrians.[15]

This plethora of academies, private schools and grammar schools had a reputation for providing a quality, affordable education for gentry and middling class sons.[16] It was a reputation that went beyond the Cumbrian counties. William Senhouse wrote from Barbados in 1787 that his

---

11 Letter Isabella Hudleston, Whitehaven, to Andrew Hudleston, Coimbatore, 13 October 1819, CAS DHUD 14/2/7R.

12 Cited in Bouch and Jones, *Lake Counties*, p. 201.

13 N. Hans, *New Trends in Education in the Eighteenth Century* (London, Routledge & Kegan Paul Limited, 1951), pp. 121–127 and Appendix 1.

14 F. Robinson, 'Trends in Education in Northern England during the Eighteenth Century: A Biographical Study' (PhD thesis, University of Newcastle, 1972), vol. 3. Frontispiece.

15 For example, Benjamin Hill and his kinsman George Bellasis, Ewan Law and the Flemings of Rydal.

16 E. Hughes, *North Country Life in the Eighteenth Century Vol 11 Cumberland & Westmorland 1700–1830* (London, Oxford University Press, 1965), pp. 293f.

acquaintances there 'whose connexions are principally with the Southern parts of England are surprised at the very moderate expense of [educating their] boys'.[17] In Cumbria itself middling and gentry families showed an almost feverish desire to provide their boys with an education that would deliver successful careers. Towards the end of the century, some gentry families sent their sons to public schools such as Eton, Harrow or Winchester or private schools such as Cheam. For instance, George Stanley's mother, Mildred the daughter of Sir George Fleming, Bishop of Carlisle, moved her son from the Carlisle Grammar School with only nominal fees in 1757 to the care of William Gilpin at Cheam. Gilpin himself had been educated at Carlisle Grammar School.

At Cheam, Gilpin was charging £25 per annum for basic tuition and about the same amount again for board and additional subjects. By 1760, George had been shifted to Eton at about a cost of £100 annually to his mother.[18] But the costs were high and the advantages questionable. Typically, Cumbrian gentry and middling families sent their boys to local grammar schools for elementary education. Some families admitted their sons to a succession of schools or supplemented school with private tuition.[19] Most importantly, Cumbrian middling and gentry families commonly 'finished' their sons with vocational training.

Navigation and other applied sciences related to seafaring were taught throughout Cumbria. Rebanks was teaching navigation in 1728 at Kendal and in 1760 Rowland Wetherald was teaching navigation at Great Salkeld, near Penrith. In Whitehaven John Scott was teaching navigation and mathematics as early as 1753. He tutored William Senhouse prior to his admittance to the navy. In the 1770s, navigation and ancillary subjects were offered in Whitehaven by Ward's Academy, William Chambers who published a textbook on navigation in 1774, John Drape and Joseph Wood. Joseph Fullerton, who started a school in Whitehaven in 1800, included navigation in its curriculum. Joseph Gilbanks taught navigation for two decades at Cockermouth from 1775. Navigation was being taught at Underbarrow and at Brampton. Navigation was accompanied by an array of applied sciences central to success in the emerging world of global enterprise. John Dalton was teaching mechanical and civil engineering in Kendal in 1787. Green-Row Academy offered navigation, astronomy, geography and drawing.[20] Many schools and academies combined classics and modern languages with

17 Cited in Hughes, *North Country Life Vol II*, p. 293.
18 F. Robinson, 'The Education of an Eighteenth Century Gentleman: George Edward Stanley of Dalegarth and Ponsonby', *Transactions CWAAS*, New Series, 70 (1970), pp. 181–191.
19 Robinson, 'The Education of an Eighteenth Century Gentleman', pp. 183–185.
20 Robinson, 'Trends in Education in Northern England', vol. 2, Appendix 1; F. Robinson and P. Wallis, 'Early Mathematical Schools in Whitehaven', *Transactions CWAAS*, New Series, 75 (1975), pp. 262–274.

disciplines fundamental to commerce and trade. Robert Hood, for instance, established a school in Brampton advertised in 1777 as specifically directed to preparing boys for a 'mercantile' life. Ten years later Septimus Hodgson of Whitehaven advertised a curriculum of English, writing and spelling, branches of mathematics and arithmetic, as well as surveying, measurement and 'the use of globes'.[21]

Evidence around school attendance among Cumbrians appointed to the East India Company is fragmentary but even those taking up seafaring careers were commonly educated at local grammar schools. For instance, Joseph Huddart, who joined the service in 1771 after many years seafaring, had been educated at the local clergyman's school at Allonby. Carlisle Grammar School delivered a number of its pupils into the maritime service of the East India Company including Patricius Curwen, who joined the Company in 1702, and a number of the Tullies who attended in the subsequent decade or so. Other pupils of Carlisle Grammar school among the East Indies mariners were William Boak, appointed to the Company in 1758, John Aglionby appointed in 1763, Thomas Dobinson, Henry Adderton who entered service in 1772, and Robert Robson appointed in 1796.[22]

Joshua Langhorne, appointed in the 1780s, attended Bampton School. Peter Crosthwaite attended Crosthwaite Grammar School and entered the Company service in 1758. Of a similar age, although very different social standing, Joseph Senhouse was educated at Cockermouth Grammar School. John Hasell, also appointed in the 1750s, attended Appleby Grammar School, along with his contemporary Richard Pearson. The latter's son also attended Appleby Grammar School before entering the Company's service in the 1780s. Charles Cust, the son of Thomas Cust and Noor Begum Bibby, was sent to St Bees for his education at the insistence of his father's agents, the Mounsey brothers of Carlisle.[23] The ill-fated John Wordsworth attended, like his brother, Hawkshead Grammar School, before his appointment to an East Indiaman in the 1780s.[24]

After completing a grammar school education, Cumbrian families then invested in 'finishing' their young men. There was a raft of tutors employed in 'finishing' young men specifically for the East Indies. The result was that, unlike some applicants to the Company,[25] many Cumbrians came with extensive certification of their educational history and skills. In 1759, John Holme was certificated by John Smith, as having successfully completed a

---

[21] Robinson, 'Trends in Education in Northern England', vol. 2, Appendix 1.

[22] Robinson, 'Trends in Education in Northern England', vol. 2, Appendix 1.

[23] Letter George and Robert Mounsey, Carlisle, to Richard Cust, London, 26 July 1794, CAS DCART C11/51iiiR.

[24] T. Thompson, *Wordsworth's Hawkshead* (London, Oxford University Press, 1970), p. 32.

[25] S. Ghosh, *The Social Condition of the British Community in Bengal 1757–1800* (Leiden, E. J. Brill, 1970), p. 29.

study in 'Writing, Arithmetick and Merchants Accompts'.[26] In 1770, William Douglas referred to expertise developed through Mr Smith's courses in 'Book Keeping and Merchants Accounts'.[27] Abraham Brown cited tuition prior to his appointment as a writer in 1754 in bookkeeping with a Daniel Blaney and in Kendal with Gilbert Crackenthorp and Thomas Rebanks.[28] Thomas Edmunds, after private schooling in Ambleside, took a course of mathematics and classics at Green Row Academy, Cumberland to ready him for a cadetship.[29] Reverend William Addison and his wife Isabella Curwen were less interested in a classical education. They sent their son to Thomas Abraham of Workington for instruction in arithmetic, book keeping 'in the Italian manner' and 'merchants accounts by double entry' in the 1770s.[30] A little earlier, Edward Ritson, a younger cousin of Edward Stephenson and Jonathan Winder, attended George Mackreth at Lamplugh, Cumberland to undertake a:

> regular course of mathematical learning in the following branches Viz Arithmetic Vulgar & Decimal, Mensuration, trigonometry, navigation and Merchants Accompts after the Italian method of Double entry.[31]

The education of Cumbrians appointed by the East India Company raises questions around the balance between patronage and education typically promoted in the historiography of the East India Company. Suresh Ghosh states that the inability of candidates to provide certificates of educational attainment were set aside where the familial interests of Company directors were concerned.[32] There is an implication in Ghosh and others that patronage and the vested interests of certain families were the primary factors shaping access to Company appointments.[33] There is, however, a considerable difference between being prepared to forego certification of educational attainment compared to being willing to appoint irrespective of educational attainment. Patronage, as the later discussion will show, was critically important, but it appears that it was not sufficient in itself. That a vocational education was crucial to a career in the East Indies is highlighted by John Bellasis. In 1794, John Bellasis, by then commander in chief of the Bombay Presidency's army, suggested his nephew:

---

26 IOR J/1/3 f.215.
27 IOR J/1/8 f.214.
28 IOR J/1/2 f.231f.
29 IOR L/MIL/9-166 ff.471.
30 IOR J/1/8 f.410.
31 IOR J/1/6 f.222.
32 Ghosh, *The Social Condition of the British Community*, pp. 28–30.
33 S. Mentz, *The English Gentleman Merchant at Work: Madras and the City of London 1660–1740* (Copenhagen, Museum Tusculanum Press, University of Copenhagen, 2005), pp. 229–232; Ghosh, *The Social Condition of the British Community*, pp. 33–56.

go on with writing and Accounts to the last moment and if you have an opportunity for him to learn navigation do not neglect it, also Geometry and Trigonometry, it will be of very great consequence to Him, if it can be accomplished. One day or other, please God, you may both live to see him return with independence.[34]

The superior educational opportunities of middling and gentry Cumbrians positioned them in relation to the Company's Indian appointments. It also positioned them well in London. London was, for some, an intermediary step to the East Indies. James Denis Hodgson, for instance, the son of a Carlisle grocer was apprenticed to John Chapman, oilman and salter of Broken Wharf, Upper Thames Street, prior to being appointed as a writer to the East India Company.[35] Shared education and the cultural capital associated with it underpinned a raft of Cumbrian connected businesses in London in banking, legal practice, insurance and ship brokerage. The Dents, Borradailes, Atkinsons, Winders, Fawcetts, Sowerbys and Stephensons, all used London as a way-station to success in India. Those families operated across a triangle connecting Cumbria, London and the East Indies.

Cumbrians' accumulation of the cultural capital necessary to secure appointments to the East Indies was undeniably facilitated by the relatively low cost of Cumbrian education. Attendance at Cumbrian grammar schools incurred relatively minimal costs, even when boys were boarding. In the 1750s, Joseph Ritson was charging a guinea a year for teaching at the grammar school in Cockermouth. St Bees was charging a little more than £7 annually for teaching in the 1770s with a weekly fee for board of five shillings.[36] In the 1780s, John Wordsworth, along with his brothers, was boarding in Hawkshead and attending the grammar school there. Grammar school subjects were free, although fees were charged for additional tuition in 'specialist' subjects. Fees varied but appear to have been around a little over a pound a year for writing tuition in the mid-1780s. Board was in the region of six shillings weekly.[37] In 1797, the grammar school at Blencowe was charging a little over £21 for board over the school year with tuition fees per subject set at £1.10s.[38]

Vocational subjects of interest to the East India Company and apprenticeships attracted more substantial fees. Even so, the base tuition fee at Green Row Academy at Abbey-Holme was only 25 guineas annually as late as 1817. By way of contrast, Elizabeth Cust estimated that educating Thomas, most

[34] CAS WDX 1641/1/1/34b Letter General John Bellasis, Bombay, to Hugh Bellasis, Long Marton, Westmorland, 16 March 1794.
[35] IOR J/1/11 f.191.
[36] Hughes, *North Country Life Vol II*, pp. 293–296.
[37] Thompson, *Wordsworth's Hawkshead*, pp. 89 and 89n.
[38] Robinson, 'The Education of an Eighteenth Century Gentleman', p. 129.

likely at the Kensington Academy, in the 1760s cost her £120. This was more than her annual income.[39] There is a certain irony that two decades later, Thomas was himself complaining from Calcutta of the costs associated with educating his sons sent from India to reside with their uncle in London. Mounsey, Thomas's agents in Carlisle, advised the children's uncle that the boys should be removed from Dr Burney's and sent to St Bees grammar school to reduce the financial burden on their father.[40]

Financing Success

The considerable price variation between education in Cumbria and education elsewhere, combined with Cumbria's reputation for superior educational opportunities, meant that Cumbria's gentry and middling families had some discretion around educational costs. There were, however, other costs associated with an East Indies career over which they had less choice. In the case of appointments to East Indiamen, commands were openly purchased until 1796 and quite probably more discreetly thereafter.[41]

The cost of a command varied in the latter quarter of the eighteenth century but was claimed to be as high as £9,000[42] although more typically in the region of £3,000.[43] Ship-owners or shareholders who could provide a discount on the price of a command or could gift a command found that they could simultaneously promote the interests of family and friendship while securing the loyalty of the commanders they had appointed.[44] Kin and place attachments between Cumbrian commanders, officers and ship-owners were important. The younger John Wordsworth's captaincy of the *Earl of Abergavenny* was virtually certain because of the ship's Cumbrian connections. Two of Wordsworth's cousins, John Wordsworth and Hugh Parkin, each had a sixteenth share in the ship and William Dent was the managing owner.[45]

---

[39] Letter Elizabeth Cust, Carlisle, to Thomas Cust, Barrackpore, 1772, CAS DCART C11/42iR.

[40] Letter George and Robert Mounsey, Carlisle, to Richard Cust, London, 26 July 1794, CAS DCART C11/51iiiR.

[41] C. H. Philips, *The East India Company 1784–1834* (2nd edition, London, Hesperides Press, 2006), p. 86.

[42] W. Medland and C. Weobly, *A Collection of Remarkable and Interesting Criminal Trials, Actions at Law, &c: To which is Prefixed, an Essay on Reprieve and Pardon, and Biographical Sketches of John Lord Eldon, and Mr. Mingay, vol. 2* (London, J. D. Dewick, 1804), pp. 184–185.

[43] E. Keble Chatterton, *A World for the Taking: The Ships of the Honourable East India Company* (Tucson, Fireship Press, 2008), pp. 84–85.

[44] Medland and Weobly, *A Collection of Remarkable and Interesting Criminal Trials*, pp. 184–185.

[45] C. N. Parkinson, *Trade in the Eastern Seas 1793–1813* (Cambridge, Cambridge University Press, 2010), pp. 186–187.

There was no equivalent legitimate pathway into the Company's merchant or military services. Indeed, applicants, nominating directors and those recommending an applicant, were all required to swear that they had neither given nor received payment to promote a nomination for a cadetship or writership. Notwithstanding, such payments did occur. A number of Bengal appointments involved inducements to directors of between £2,000 and £5,000 in the 1770s. Between 1800 and 1808 these shady payments varied from £150 to £3,500.[46] There is no direct evidence of such payments among the Cumbrian men appointed to the East Indies. Nevertheless, it is reasonable to assume that they were not unknown.

Whether inducements were being paid or not by Cumbrian families, there is no doubt that some families went to considerable expense to present their candidates well to Company directors. The cost of travel to, and accommodation in, London could be significant, especially when individuals destined for the East Indies found themselves cooling their heels in the South for considerable periods. Many families relied on the hospitality of Cumbrian relatives, friends and acquaintances to reduce the burden of those costs. But expense was unavoidable.

The costs of fitting out and travel to the East Indies could be substantial. For instance, the embittered John Addison suggested that his voyage on the *Godolphin* and operating in the East Indies on behalf of the Company for eleven years between about 1709 and 1720 had cost him 'not less than the sum of five hundred pounds sterling'.[47] Fifty years later, Elizabeth Cust estimated her expenditure on her son Thomas's travel to India was in excess of £550. In addition to £123 which appears to have been the expenses associated with travel to and residence in London while awaiting departure, there was £65.15.0 for passage. Fitting out was at a cost of £142.8.0. Thomas also borrowed against her £17 lent by his brother in London, £33 at the Cape of Good Hope and £173.5.0 in India on arrival.[48] The latter had been provided by a Mr Holmes, probably the father of Catherine Holme from Carlisle and registrar of the Mayor's Court in Calcutta. Notably the needs of Thomas's daughter, Susan, were calculated to be significantly less by her father's agents when she was returning from England to Calcutta thirty years later. As Robert Mounsey wrote to Susan's uncle, Richard Cust:

[46] Ghosh, *The Social Condition of the British Community*, pp. 20–27.

[47] IOR E/1/12 138-139v [1 March 1720] – Letter 78 John Addison at Whitehaven to William Dawsonne and the Committee of Correspondence concerning a £100 gratuity for his work in the Company's service at India and St Helena.

[48] Letter from Elizabeth Cust, Carlisle, to Thomas Cust, Barrackpore, 1772, CAS DCART C11/42iR.

I rec^d yours by last Post and agreeable to your request inclose you £85 viz. a Bank Bill value £55 and a draft value £30 which will discharge the two Bills drawn on you by Captain Cust and leave £40 towards fitting out his Daughter.[49]

In 1794, General John Bellasis estimated that an expenditure of £150 would be required to fit out his nephew, William, in a fashion that would allow him to 'appear in a proper manner' in India. His letter implies that passage and ancillary expenses would be no more than an additional £50.[50] A year later, John Wordsworth required eight guineas for a new uniform when promoted to fourth mate on the *Osterley*. He had previously been given £30 for fitting out in 1789 and another £100 in 1791 to fit him out and as venture capital on a possible voyage to China.[51] In 1812, Susannah Knott appears to have gifted her cousin Elizabeth Hudleston about £500 to fund Andrew Fleming Hudleston's fit out and the expenses of taking up a writership in Madras. It appears that those costs were around £350, for Hudleston notes to his aunt that he arrived in Madras with £150 pounds.[52] He subsequently had to ask for another £100 from his parents to set himself, despite staying with his cousin William Hudleston in Madras.[53]

The financial burdens of an East Indies venture were not easily sustained. Access to ready money was persistently problematic in eighteenth-century Cumbria.[54] Both Cumbrian gentry and middling families could be stretched by the costs of a Company appointment. There were some, of course, in the most desperate of conditions. John Hasell has already been mentioned. There was Richard Gilpin whose family had suffered almost three generations of economic decline and debt. He sold the Eccleriggs estate to set up a career in India.[55] Nevertheless, the significant sums invested in East Indies ventures suggest that families supporting those ventures were not in deep distress or unable to access credit.

Some middling families used mortgages to fund their children's East Indies ventures. Thomas Cust's appointment as a cadet to Bengal appears to have contributed to his mother mortgaging properties in Penrith and Carlisle.

---

[49] Letter Robert Mounsey, Carlisle, to Richard Cust, London, 8 February 1796, CAS DCART C11/51xvii.

[50] Letter John Bellasis, Bombay, to Hugh Bellasis, Long Marton, 16 March 1794, CAS WDX 1641/1/1/34a.

[51] C. Ketcham (ed.), *The Letters of John Wordsworth* (Ithaca, NY, Cornell University Press, 1969), pp. 11, 13, 17.

[52] Letter Andrew Fleming Hudleston, Madras, to Isabella Hudleston, Whitehaven, 8 October 1813, CAS DHUD 14/8V.

[53] Letter Andrew Hudleston, Madras, to Elizabeth Hudleston, Hutton John, 19 December 1814, CAS DHUD 13/2/7V.

[54] J. V. Beckett, *Coal and Tobacco: The Lowthers and the Economic Development of West Cumberland 1660–1760* (Cambridge, Cambridge University Press, 1981), p. 207.

[55] Letter John Addison junior to Francis E Barker regarding Richard Gilpin, 1814, CAS BDBROUGHTON/19/39/2.

She complained to her son later that the interest on those mortgages at 4 per cent was 'lessening my little income thirty pounds a year [from £100 per annum]... I keep but one servant and very little company as you may suppose I can't afford to do otherwise'.[56] Local gentry families were applied to for funds as Anthony Sharpe's letter to Henry Curwen of Workington Hall illustrates:

> I have had some late difficulties in fitting out my Son who is going Officer in the Hector East India man to overcome with I have a present want of £30 I have applied to Mr Charles Udale to be relieved he says he does not lend money without your knowledge & consent, & and that he wd mention my request first time he saw you but as the matter requires dispatch I presume upon this freedom humbly desiring that you'll be graciously pleased to signifie your consent by a line and that your benevolent temper will excuse this liberty and attribute it to faithful motives.[57]

Financial facilities were also sought from Cumbrian merchants, bankers and East Indiamen owners operating in London and India. In 1806, Thomas Pattinson's family drew on the Routledges to ensure that Thomas had £20 for voyage expenses over and above his passage and another £40 for use on arrival in India. This was not enough to fit him out for his appointment as ensign in Bombay. Thomas Pattinson required a further £30, the provision of which was facilitated by Henry Fawcett's reputation and influence as a member of the Bombay Council, as a merchant and as an owner of a tranche of ships including the East Indiaman *Scaleby Castle*, the largest ship at Bombay.[58]

Perhaps the most challenging aspect of the East Indies was accumulating venture capital. For those with maritime careers, the rewards of command were substantial but remuneration was insufficient until the rank of second mate had been reached.[59] Even then the promise of wealth resided in mariners' private trade, as it did for writers and cadets for much of the eighteenth century. Army officers benefitted from access to batta. Batta was a range of compensatory payments and additional allowances and it was jealously guarded. Periodic attempts by the Company to withdraw batta sparked several mutinies among European officers. George Knott of Coniston was probably caught up in one such incident during the 1760s.[60] Army officers

56 Letter Elizabeth Cust to Thomas Cust, India, 1772, CAS DCART C11/42iR.
57 Letter Anthony Sharpe to Henry Curwen, Workington Hall, 30 March 1776, CAS DCU 3/7.
58 Letter from Bombay to Henry Fawcett, 25 August 1806, CAS DX 249/14nR; Parkinson, *Trade in the Eastern Seas*, p. 337; A. Bulley, *The Bombay Country Ships, 1790–1833* (Richmond, Curzon Press, 2000), pp. 189f.
59 Chatterton, *A World for the Taking*, p. 85.
60 IOR Mss Eur G37/41/1 f.3 [2 July 1766] – Letters Henry Strachey and George Knott, 2 July 1766.

and seamen could also look to shares of plunder captured in military engagements to compensate for long periods of low and often irregular payment.[61]

Although remuneration for writers and army officers gradually became more regulated towards the end of the eighteenth century, Company appointments were frequently associated with continued demands on families for financial support. That support included what was effectively venture capital to pursue private trade. Private trade could involve a range of activities: import and export on one's own account to the British Isles; taking advantage of the high rates of interest prevailing in the East by lending to fellow Europeans but also to locals in East Indies businesses and nawabs; trading in silver; developing coffee and indigo estates; opium distribution; ship-building and brokerage; and building business partnerships with the already thriving trading and manufacture of the East Indies. All these held the promise, not always realised, of wealth.

The goods transported to and from the East Indies by Cumbrians were diverse. In 1709, the Braddylls were requesting Company permission to take wine, olives, oil, vinegar, fish and cured meat to India for private trade.[62] It has already been noted that in 1720, Samuel Winder sought permission to carry a range of European domestic goods to India with him.[63] In 1768 John Hasell brought 1,800 pieces of East Indies cloth in handkerchiefs back from his voyage to the East Indies with the expectation of selling them into the West African market.[64] The goods he was attempting to collect off Brazil in 1770 for private trade are unclear. What is clear that as commander of the *Duke of Portland*, private rather than Company trade was Hasell's primary concern. He overstepped the line between that which was acceptable to the Company and that which was not. He was dismissed from the Company and only reinstated after intervention by the Musgraves.[65]

Twenty-five years later, John Wordsworth was dealing in Spanish dollars in China and bought cloth, fibre and china in Canton for trade in England. Similar goods probably made him a £400 profit in 1798. In 1802 he was attempting to sell woollen goods in Canton and brought tea, among other goods, back to England. In what was to be his final voyage, Wordsworth

61 See R. Holmes, *Sahib: The British Soldier in India 1750–1914* (London, Harper Perennial, 2005), pp. 272ff.

62 IOR E 1/11 ff. 423-424 [9 December 1709] – Letter 240 Roger Braddyll to Thomas Woolley requesting permission to send several chests of wine to Governor Gulston Addison at Madras.

63 IOR/E/1/12 ff. 52-52v [20 Jan. 1721] – Letter 33 Samuel Winder to the Court requesting permission to ship out table clocks, glasses and mathematical instruments as part of his private allowance.

64 F. Wilkins, *Hasells of Dalemain: A Cumberland Family: 1736–1794* (Kidderminster, Wyre Forest Press, 2003), p. 54.

65 Wilkins, *Hasells of Dalemain*, p. 58.

determined to privately trade in rice and illegal opium between India and China and to return with tea.[66]

The acquisition of venture capital was by no means easy. Capital was in short supply in Cumbria. There were some Cumbrians whose ventures in the East Indies drew on wealth previously generated by India. The Stephensons and Fawcetts, Dents, Wilkinsons, Riggs and Addisons undoubtedly leveraged their businesses in the late eighteenth century off extravagant fortunes acquired in India in the earlier part of the century. The Winders, Braddylls, Wilsons, Taylors and, of course, Edward Stephenson were all advantaged by their comparatively early operations in India. Henry Fletcher and the elder John Wordsworth were positioned to take advantage of the rapid expansion of global trade in the mid-eighteenth century.

For many, however, venture capital was a matter of stitching together small sums, often from immediate family. In 1695 when George Fleming of Rydal ill-advisedly sought his father's permission to go to the East Indies, he also desired that his father would assist:

> with a sum of monies to venture by ye way of trade (for yet I am allowed) & I hope you will not refuse to grant me, what my Vicarage will in 2 years, or $2^{1/2}$, repay. I desire you S^r to direct yours to the Blew-Bell in War. Lane Lond. the Fleet goes within a Month at the Longest.[67]

John Hasell turned to his relatives for venture capital. His alcoholism and inability to turn the considerable investments made by the Musgraves and Edward Hasell into his trading ventures into profit left him bereft. His brother Edward Hasell wrote to their sister Elizabeth in 1779 that John:

> I know not what he will do or if he goes to Bombay or not… He has acted very dishonestly… and went to Dalemain to get more money from my father but did not succeed. He does not owe me much. I shall not be at all surprised that he takes some desperate step, so you may be prepared for it.[68]

John Wordsworth also turned to his relatives for venture capital. His uncle Kit Crackanthorpe, his grandmother Cookson, the elder John Wordsworth by way of a bond in 1801, his uncle Richard, his sister Dorothy and brother William all contributed to successive voyages. He drew on credit provided by local and London tradesmen and attracted support from William Lowther. Despite some losses and indifferent profits in the past, his long connections

---

66 Ketcham (ed.), *The Letters of John Wordsworth*, p. 41; P. Kitson, 'The Wordsworths, Opium, and China', *Wordsworth Circle*, 43, 1 (2012), pp. 2–12.

67 J. R. McGrath (ed.), *The Flemings in Oxford: Being Documents Selected from the Rydal Papers in Illustration of the Lives and Ways of Oxford men* (Oxford, Oxford Historical Society, 1913), Letter DCXXXI, pp. 242–244.

68 Cited in Wilkins, *Hasells of Dalemain*, p. 101.

in Cumberland and the Company, combined with a widespread belief in the profitability of the East Indies trade, allowed Wordsworth to raise venture capital to the extent of £20,000.[69] It was lost when the *Earl of Abergavenny* was wrecked in 1805, still in British waters at the Portland Roads.

The Importance of Friends

Critical to managing the economic burdens of East Indies ventures, as well as taking advantage of the opportunities offered by the East Indies, were friends. Friends were Bourdieu's 'durable network of more or less institutionalised relationships' characterised by recognition and direct or indirect acquaintance that generated the resources that can be referred to as social capital.[70] It was through friends that formal patronage and informal influence were mobilised to access Company appointments and pursue success in the East Indies. Cumbrian friends in London were crucial to successfully managing the intricacies of departure and ensuring sojourners were given the best chance of a successful arrival. Cumbrian friends welcomed sojourners at ports across the East Indies from Java to China, Ceylon and the Indian sub-continent.

Socio-culturally, friends and friendship were broadly positioned in the eighteenth century. Friends could embrace kin and family members, but equally importantly the concept of friends embraced non-related individuals. As Tadmor shows, friends were those who were supporters. They were 'patrons, guardians, employers and other allies... well-wishers, companions, members of social circles and intimates'.[71] The essence of friendship and being a friend lay in its active quality and that lay in service. It was sustained sometimes by instrumental reciprocities and sometimes by affection. The eighteenth-century idea of friends and the practice of friendship could involve those in intimate, affectual relationships with an individual. Friends could equally comprise a diffuse set of people, many who had little contact with a particular individual who might benefit from the exercise of friendship, but a group whose loyalties and support were generated and accessed by way of common acquaintances.[72]

The exercise of patronage and influence within the Company on behalf of Cumbrian nominees was not simply mobilised by kinship, but framed by the language of friendship. So too were the acquisition of venture capital and necessary financial resources. The importance of friends is alluded to by John Bellasis in discussing the future of his nephew:

---

[69] Ketcham (ed.), *The Letters of John Wordsworth*, p. 41.
[70] Bourdieu, 'The Forms of Capital', p. 248.
[71] N. Tadmor, *Family and Friends in Eighteenth Century England: Household, Kinship and Patronage* (Cambridge, Cambridge University Press, 2001), p. 167.
[72] Tadmor, *Family and Friends in Eighteenth Century England*, pp. 179, 213–215.

I mentioned to you a Plan of William's being sent out to me [in Bombay] and wrote at the same time to Cap' Christie and some of my other Friends in London respecting his appointments, outfits &c – I also wrote to my Brother at Kendal to consult with you respecting it, and desired He would correspond with Cap' Christie for you on the Business.[73]

The desperate need for friends, the way in which it was spliced with kinship, its potential fragility, and its importance in establishing one's social position beyond intimate circles is expressed in a letter from Humphrey Senhouse Gale to his great aunt Kitty Senhouse not long after his arrival in India. Reflecting on his past requests for financial assistance, Gale writes:

My [great] Uncle I knew very well would never have indulged me so far... In all probability he would have withdrawn his protection from me and cast me off upon the World, and where to look for a friend afterwards it is hard to say.[74]

Patronage

Friendship forged the chains of patronage and influence which in turn produced appointments and facilitated success in the East Indies.[75] Those chains were not always easy to discern even at the time.[76] The links in a chain of patronage can be even more opaque in retrospect. Nevertheless, the importance of provincial attachments in the nominations of Cumbrians to Company appointments is clear.

The nominating directors for fewer than forty of the Company's over 400 Cumbrian appointments during the long eighteenth century have been identified. Among those, about a fifth of the enumerated Cumbrian cadets and writers were nominated by a set of Cumbrian directors: Henry Fletcher, John Bladen Taylor, John Hudleston and James Law Lushington. All those Cumbrian nominating directors had sojourned in the East Indies. Henry Fletcher was an East Indiaman commander. John Bladen Taylor was born in Calcutta and returned to Westmorland after an army career in Madras.[77] John Hudleston, connected to Hutton John, was sent to Madras in 1766 as a writer. The Company recognised his long service with a bonus of 10,000

---

73 Letter General John Bellasis, Bombay, to Hugh Bellasis, Long Marton, 16 March 1794, CAS WDX 1641/1/1/34a.

74 Letter Humphrey Senhouse Gale, Wallajaput, to Kitty Senhouse, Netherhall, 1 January 1812, CAS DSEN 5/5/1/9/57hR and CAS DSEN 5/5/1/9/57hV.

75 J. M. Bourne, 'The Civil and Military Patronage of The East India Company 1784–1858' (PhD thesis, University of Leicester, 1977), pp. 9–10, 62, 162–164, 188.

76 Ghosh, *The Social Condition of the British Community in Bengal*, pp. 14–29.

77 J. W. Anderson, 'TAYLOR, John Bladen (1764–1820)', in R. Thorne (ed.), *The History of Parliament: The House of Commons 1790–1820* (1986): www.historyofparliamentonline.org/volume/1790-1820/member/taylor-john-bladen-1764-1820.

star pagodas.[78] He was a director from 1803 to 1826. James Law Lushington, whose great grandparents brought together the Christians and the Senhouses, was appointed in 1796 to Madras. On his return he entered parliament to support the East Indies interest, then contested and won Carlisle against the Lonsdale interest in the 1827 by-election. He entered the Company's Court of Directors in the same year. A director until 1854, Lushington chaired the Company three times between 1838 and 1849.[79]

These and other Cumbrians were at the heart of the East India Company. Cumbrians maintained a presence in the Company's Court of Directors over much of the long eighteenth century. Dodding Braddyll was elected to the directorship in 1728, served as deputy chairman in 1744 and was chairman from 1745 until his death in 1748. John Stephenson was a director from 1765 to 1768.[80] Richard Atkinson was elected to the Court of Directors in 1783. John Stables followed a lucrative civil and military career in India before appointment as a director in 1774.[81] Robert Clerk, a director from 1812 until his death in 1815,[82] was brother-in-law to Dorothy Taylor the daughter of Cumbrian nabob and owner of Abbott Hall, John Taylor and his wife Dorothy Rumbold.

These directors undoubtedly enhanced not only the probabilities of Cumbrian appointments but also the advancement of Cumbrians. John Brownrigg Bellasis writes tellingly in 1825 of the importance of influence to mitigate the usual rigid adherence in the Company to promotion by way of seniority: 'Unless assisted at first as I was by my Uncles, promotion goes by seniority and is consequently slow...'[83] But non-Cumbrian directors could also promote Cumbrian interests. Friendship, business and political associations were all activated by Cumbrians to promote Cumbrian prospects with East India Company directors. Humphrey Senhouse Gale was, for instance, recommended by the Cumbrian Joseph Huddart to the non-Cumbrian director and East Indiaman ship's husband Joseph Cotton in 1808. Huddart and Cotton both shared the experience of East Indiaman command. They

[78] Petition John Hudleston and response East India Company directors, 1787–1788, IOR J/1/6, ff.7–13; J. W. Anderson and R. G. Thorne, 'HUDLESTON, John (1749–1835), of Bathwick, Som.', in R. Thorne (ed.), *The History of Parliament: The House of Commons 1790–1820* (1986): www.historyofparliamentonline.org/volume/1790-1820/member/hudleston-john-1749-1835.

[79] M. Escott, 'LUSHINGTON, James Law (1780–1859), of 14 Portman Square, Mdx.', in D. R. Fisher (ed.), *The History of Parliament: The House of Commons 1820–1832* (2009): www.historyofparliamentonline.org/volume/1820-1832/member/lushington-james-1780-1859.

[80] M. Drummond, 'STEPHENSON, John (?1709–94), of Brentford, Mdx.', in L. Namier and J. Brooke (eds), *The History of Parliament: The House of Commons 1754–1790* (1964): www.historyofparliamentonline.org/volume/1754-1790/member/stephenson-john-1709-94.

[81] J. G. Parker, 'The Directors of the East India Company 1754–1790' (PhD thesis, University of Edinburgh, 1977), pp. 263–264.

[82] Philips, *The East India Company 1784–1834*, p. 336.

[83] John Brownrigg Bellasis's letterbook and diary, 1825, IOR and Private Papers Mss Eur Photo Eur 035, p. 37.

also had a series of interlocking interests in the East India Dock Company and as Elder Brothers of Trinity House.[84] Cotton's son joined Joseph's innovative cordage manufacturing company in Limehouse and was admitted as a partner to Huddart & Co. in 1807.[85]

Similarly, George Canning's support of Patrick French was occasioned by a member of parliament who noted he was well acquainted with Patrick's Cumbrian family and their connections. The East India Company director George Millett declared that his nomination of the orphaned William Dent reflected his 'long friendship' with William's uncle.[86] Likewise, John Manship stated that James de Vitre's nomination in 1808 was because de Vitre's uncle was the Cumbrian Henry Fawcett of Scaleby. Manship declares Henry Fawcett to be 'my very old acquaintance and whom I also sent to Bombay'.[87] The non-Cumbrian director Abram Robarts states that his nomination of the younger John Sowerby was prompted by 'long acquaintance with and friendship for [the Cumbrian] John Sowerby Esq who is stated by the Petitioner to be his uncle'.[88]

More opaque and attenuated chains of influence can be gleaned although they are difficult to establish definitively. For instance, George Colebrooke nominated two Cumbrians in 1770. If Colebrooke had Cumbrian sympathies, they were probably bound up in his relations with Thomas Rumbold. Rumbold's East Indies career culminated in the governorship of Madras and was inextricably linked to Cumbria. He was reputed to have been propelled from boot boy at the London club Whites to the East Indies by the Westmerian bookmaker and usurer Robert Mackreth.[89] It was said that in 1752, an embarrassed debtor to Mackreth and Rumbold was able to commute the debt by facilitating Rumbold's cadetship.[90] In 1762, Rumbold's sister married the Westmerian and Company surgeon John Taylor.[91] Ten years later Rumbold himself married the daughter of Dr Edmund Law, the Bishop of Carlisle.

---

84 H. V. Bowen, 'Cotton, Joseph (1745–1825)', *Oxford Dictionary of National Biography* (Oxford, Oxford University Press, 2004); online edn, Jan. 2008: www.oxforddnb.com/view/article/6421; S. Fisher, 'Huddart, Joseph (1741–1816)', *Oxford Dictionary of National Biography* (Oxford, Oxford University Press, 2004); online edn, Jan. 2008: www.oxforddnb.com/view/article/14023.

85 A. C. Howe, 'Cotton, William (1786–1866)', *Oxford Dictionary of National Biography* (Oxford, Oxford University Press, 2004); online edn, Oct. 2006: www.oxforddnb.com/view/article/6432.

86 IOR J/1/28 f.249.

87 IOR J/1/23 f.78.

88 IOR L/MIL/9/120 f.28.

89 R. Thorne, 'Mackreth, Sir Robert (*bap.* 1727, *d.* 1819)', *Oxford Dictionary of National Biography* (Oxford, Oxford University Press, 2004); online edn, Jan. 2008: www.oxforddnb.com/view/article/17629.

90 T. H. Lewis (ed.), *The Lewin Letters: A Selection from the Correspondence & Diaries of an English Family 1756–1884*, vol. 1 (London, Archibald Constable & Co Ltd, 1909), p. 17.

91 IOR N/1/2/78.

In addition to promoting the interests of Cumbrians to George Colebrooke, the Rumbold connection may have contributed to James Law Lushington's East Indies career. Lushington was a nephew of Rumbold's wife, Joanna Law. Similarly, it is difficult not to conclude that John Bellasis's long and successful career was triggered by connections with Robert Mackreth and Rumbold. While preparing for a career, Bellasis had been sent from Cumbria to reside with his maternal uncle, the Cumbrian Ben Hill and vicar of Monk Sherborne in Hampshire.[92] The church at Monk Sherborne memorialises Robert Mackreth who acquired the surrounding estate of Ewhurst in 1761 and became a generous patron of the church's restoration.[93] In 1765, Bellasis was appointed as a Company cadet.[94]

There were also convoluted connections between non-Cumbrian directors and powerful Cumbrian interests. Lowther was probably implicated in a number of appointments. For instance, in 1759 John Stables was recommended to the East India Company by his kinsman John Robinson for appointment as a cadet.[95] Although the nominating director is unclear, it was probably pressed by James Lowther to whom Robinson was agent. Lowther had already supported Robinson's cousin Charles Deane into a position on the *Bombay Castle*, the same ship on which Clive travelled to India that year.[96] Lowther's interests here were part of a broader strategy around the control of provincial loyalties. Charles Deane was the son of Whitehaven's tide surveyor, a position very much influenced by Lowther interests.[97]

Half a century later, the Lowther connection was probably associated with the nominations of brothers William and Montagu Ainslie. Their father, Henry Ainslie, a physician and ironmaster, was kin to the Knotts and through them connected to the Flemings of Rydal as well as the Knotts' past involvement in India. Henry Ainslie sustained a long friendship with William Lowther, the successor to the Lowther estates. Lowther, in turn, was a parliamentary colleague of Robert Smith, Baron Carrington, who recommended the Ainslie boys of Kendal to his brother and Company director George Smith.[98]

That aristocratic and upper gentry support was believed to be critical to appointments of provincials to the supposedly London merchant driven East India Company is illustrated by Helena Adderton's (née Curwen) repeated applications to the Duke of Portland for assistance in securing East India

92 M. Bellasis, *Honourable Company* (London: Hollis & Carter, 1952), pp. 45–46.
93 W. Page (ed.), 'Parishes: Ewhurst', *A History of the County of Hampshire: Volume 4* (London, Victoria County History, 1911), pp. 247–249.
94 Bellasis, *Honourable Company*, p. 46.
95 See Plate 5.2 for Romney's portrait of John Stables.
96 A. Farrington, *A Biographical Index of East India Company Maritime Officers 1600–1834* (London, British Library, 1999), p. 209.
97 A. Connell, 'Appleby in Westminster: John Robinson, MP (1727–1802)', *Transactions CWAAS*, Third Series, X (2010), p. 221.
98 IOR J/1/22 f.176 and IOR J/1/21/part 2.

Company appointments for her sons.[99] Similarly, in 1785 Edward Wilson applied to Sir Michael le Fleming of Rydal, providing instructions as to where le Fleming's influence might be most effectively directed. Wilson wrote:

> Not meeting with the encouragement in the Country I was taught to expect I therefore have with the advice of a friend and consent of my parents returned to London and entered as a Volunteer in the Honble East India Company's service and being informed that I can with the least Recommendation from such a gentleman as your Honour soon meet with preferment... [I am] praying your Honour will condescend as far as to procure me a Recommendation to Lord McCartney... but provided your Honour should not have any particular acquaintance with him, the interest your Honour may have with George Johnston, I doubt not but a letter from him would soon procure me a situation in India.[100]

There were appeals made to some of the Company's most powerful characters, many of whom were themselves of provincial origins. For instance, in 1765 Clive was requested by his cousin that he consider the merits of Francis Drinkel when distributing his favours in Bengal. The appeal referred to Drinkel's connection with a friend, the banker Rowland Stephenson, a cousin of governor Edward Stephenson:

> Mr Stephenson being an old acquaintance of mine and a friend of ours in India Affairs I take the liberty of introducing his Brother Mr Francis Drinkel who is going out a Free Merchant to Bengal to your Lordships Notice and I hope he will deserve your favour in India...[101]

As secretary to the Treasury, the Westmerian John Robinson actively promoted relatives and Cumbrians to the East Indies. In addition to those noted previously, Hugh Parkin was appointed to an East Indiaman at Robinson's request in the 1770s,[102] John Benn (later Benn Walsh) was appointed as a writer in 1776 to Bengal[103] and Myles and James Lowther Cooper were appointed after Robinson bought their father's estate in 1784.[104]

99 Letter Helena Adderton, Carlisle to 3rd Duke of Portland; 9 December 1769, NUM Pw F 52; Letter Helena Adderton, Carlisle to 3rd Duke of Portland, 5 September 1770, NUM Pw F 53; Letter Helena Adderton, Carlisle to 3rd Duke of Portland, 24 September 1770, NUM Pw F 54; Letter Helena Adderton, Carlisle to 3rd Duke of Portland, 29 January 1772, NUM Pw F 55; Letter Helena Adderton, Carlisle to 3rd Duke of Portland, 22 July 1772, NUM Pw F 56.
100 Letter Edward Wilson to Sir Michael Fleming, 21 May 1785, CAS WDRY 3/3/8.
101 IOR Mss EUR G37/33/3 f.22, 25 March 1765, Letter George Clive, probably to Clive.
102 C. B. Norcliffe, *Some Account of the Family of Robinson of the White House, Appleby, Westmorland* (Westminster, Nichols & Son, 1874), p. 92.
103 IOR J/1/9 f.229; B. Murphy and R. G. Thorne, 'BENN WALSH, John (1759–1825), of Warfield Park, Berks.', in R. Thorne, *The History of Parliament: The House of Commons 1790–1820* (1986): www.historyofparliamentonline.org/volume/1790-1820/member/benn-walsh-john-1759-1825.
104 T. Cockerill, 'Myles Cooper, President of King's College, New York', *Transactions CWAAS*, New Series, LXIV (1964), p. 341.

There were other pathways to success in India. The Riggs, for instance, were sponsored by their kinsmen, the Addisons, into agency and trading around Java. They were enabled to become proprietors of the Jasinga plantation on Java.[105] The Dents and the Wilkinsons assiduously maintained control over their operations, including the sale and distribution of opium, in India and China through intermarriage in Cumbria and the subsequent appointment of kin to their East Indies business interests.[106] John Robinson of Kirkby Thore found a place in his Bombay business for Thomas Cooper of Long Marton.[107]

Of particular importance in the Cumbrian encounter with the East Indies were appointments to East Indiamen. Those appointments resided in the hands of managing owners as Company director George Colebrooke reminded the Duke of Portland when the latter sought to advance Jeremiah Adderton on behalf of the Curwens:

> My Lord, I rec'd your Grace's letter by Mr Adderton recommending him to be advanced from third mate… if, upon inquiry he found out a vacancy, and would inform me of it, I would do all that I could to secure him, which is to apply to the owners on his behalf, in Case I had any Connection with them which would intitle Me to apply to them. Perhaps your Grace imagines that an appointment of Captains or Mates to be a Directors. Appointment is in a husbands and we are obliged to solicit their favour in matters of Mates appointments like any other persons.[108]

Once appointed as a commander to an East Indiaman, a man was effectively transformed from being the recipient of patronage to being a dispenser of it. Take for instance, Henry Fletcher, seventh son of John Fletcher and Isabella Senhouse.

After experience of coastal and Atlantic shipping, Henry Fletcher entered the Company's maritime service as a fifth mate on the East Indiaman *Lynn* in 1745.[109] In 1758, possibly with the support of Christopher Musgrave, he was appointed captain to the East Indiaman *Stormont*. Immediately, he set about constituting its officers and crew. He sought assistance from his cousin Humphrey Senhouse and mentioned the possibility that one of Humphrey's

[105] D. M. Campbell, *Java: Past & Present A Description of the Most Beautiful Country in the World, its Ancient History, People, Antiquities and its Products*, vol. 1 (London, William Heinemann, 1915), p. 650.

[106] P. K. Law, 'Dent Family (*per. c.*1820–1927)', *Oxford Dictionary of National Biography* (Oxford, Oxford University Press, 2004); online edn, Jan. 2015: www.oxforddnb.com/view/article/53862.

[107] Letter John Bellasis, Bombay, to Hugh Bellasis, Long Marton, 21 December 1788, CAS WDX 1641/1/1/29a.

[108] Letter George Colebrooke, Company director to the 3rd Duke of Portland, 22 September 1770, NUM PwF 2991.

[109] IOR L/MAR/B f.627.

own sons might be recruited. Senhouse agreed and Fletcher also recruited his cousin John Orfeur Yates as purser.[110] Even when Henry's complement of seamen was almost complete, he still saw the recruitment of experienced seamen with local attachments he could trust as a means of promoting his own career. In December 1758, Henry wrote again to Senhouse at Netherhall:

> I beg you would not give yourself any further trouble about any seamen, as they are now pretty plenty here; But if you should meet with any good clever compleat seamen, that one would have some credit in promoting, I should be glad if you could recommend them...[111]

Other Cumbrian East Indiamen commanders showed a similar pattern. The elder John Wordsworth's commands of the East Indiaman *Earl of Sandwich* and the *Earl of Abergavenny* were through the influence of Charles Deane, a protégé and mutual kinsman, of a past secretary to the Treasury and Westmerian, John Robinson of Appleby.[112] It was a career supported by the Gales, the Whitehaven merchant family with significant shipping and trading interests in the Atlantic, London and Russia,[113] and the Cumbrian London-based East Indiaman owner William Dent.[114] In turn, John Wordsworth appointed his cousin John Wordsworth as a mate on voyages to Bombay and China.[115] After his retirement he supported the younger John Wordsworth's nomination as commander to the *Earl of Abergavenny*.[116] Joseph Wordsworth, another cousin, was subsequently appointed third mate on John Wordsworth's disastrous last voyage.[117] With the Cumbrian attached Dents, Borradailes,[118] Hotham, Haistwell, and, even earlier, the Braddylls, all owning ships involved

---

[110] Letter Henry Fletcher, London, to Humphrey Senhouse, Netherhall, 4 November 1758, CAS DSEN 5/5/1/4/12cR.

[111] Letter Henry Fletcher, London, to Humphrey Senhouse, Netherhall, 5 December 1758, CAS DSEN 5/5/1/4/12eR and CAS DSEN 5/5/1/4/12eV.

[112] H. C. Hardy, *A Register of Ships, Employed in the Service of the Honorable the United East India Company, from the Year 1760 to 1810: With an Appendix, Containing a Variety of Particulars, and Useful Information Interesting to Those Concerned with East India Commerce* (London, Black, Parry, and Kingsbury, 1811), pp. 55, 82, 156, 169, 183.

[113] Wordsworth's first wife Anne Gale was sister to John Gale merchant of Whitehaven, London and St Petersburg and Thomas Gale who, after considerable maritime experience, was approved for an East Indiaman appointment in 1774 and sailed as second mate on the East Indiaman *Osterley* (II) in 1777/8. See Farrington, *A Biographical Index of East India Company Maritime Officers 1600–1834*.

[114] Hardy, *A Register of Ships*, p. 137.

[115] J. H. Thomas, *The East India Company and the Provinces in the Eighteenth Century Volume II: Captains, Agents, and Servants: A Gallery of East India Company Portraits* (Lewiston, NY, Edwin Mellen Press, 2007), vol. 2, Chapter 2; Hardy, *A Register of Ships*, pp. 212.

[116] Ketcham (ed.), *The Letters of John Wordsworth*, pp. 28–29.

[117] Thomas, *The East India Company and the Provinces*, vol. 2, pp. 59, 96–98.

[118] A. Borradaile, *Sketch of the Borradailes of Cumberland* (London, MacClure and MacDonald, 1881).

in the East Indies, Cumbrians were particularly well endowed with opportunities to find their way to the East Indies.

London Friends

Nowhere was the mobilisation of friendship as explicit as over the period immediately prior to sojourners' departures for the East Indies. It was through friends that sojourners and their families sought a well-ordered leaving characterised by passage on a safe ship with a decent commander, well fitted out with the clothing, books and kit that would make the voyage bearable, equipped to avoid ill-health and able to deal with temptations of excess and profligacy. Friends, too, were instrumental in furnishing sojourners with letters of introduction which, on arrival, would ensure they were not only welcomed but could aspire to good prospects at their destination.

The importance of friends was highlighted when the circumstances surrounding the separation of sojourners from family in Cumbria were fraught. For them departure was, or at least felt to be, friendless. For these young men, communications with home were characterised by apologetic letters and a desire for reassurance that, irrespective of the circumstances, their friends and family would forgive and re-embrace them.[119] The desperation associated with being friendless was conveyed in Jeremiah Adderton's letter from an encampment in Pondicherry to his uncle Henry Curwen of Workington Hall:

> I did myself the pleasure of writing to you by the ships of last year... and have been not a little mortified at finding they have procured me no letter in return. You will naturally suppose, leaving me destitute of all feeling, that the manner of my leaving England three years ago was such as must have cost me many anxious moments, and that it must be proportionally pleasing for me to hear that I have in any degree regained the good opinion of my Friends, and that while they are disposed to inform me so I must conclude myself most fortunate.[120]

For the most part, however, in the weeks and sometimes months prior to departure, sojourners were surrounded by friends, related and non-related, determined to smooth the way. The Cumbrian community in London, in particular, was galvanised by the opportunity to act as way-station between Cumbria and the East Indies. London-based Cumbrians took letters, both optimistic and apologetic, from the hands of embarking cadets and writers and sent them to variously anxious, angry or optimistic parents in the North.

---

[119] Letter John Ritson, Chatham Barracks, to his sister Elizabeth Ritson, Carlisle, 16 June 1815, CAS DX38/38.

[120] Letter Jeremiah Adderton, Pondicherry, to Henry Curwen, Workington, Hall, 4 September 1778, CAS DC/3/7.

They made sure that young Cumbrians were fitted out, able to organise passage and accommodated over the long wait before weather and full cargos allowed East Indiamen to leave. These London-based Cumbrian friends guided candidates for writerships and cadetships around London to interviews with the Company directors, to the docks, and to meet their own and their charges' relatives also residing in London. They took their charges sightseeing, lent them money, introduced them to banks and agency houses, acted as guarantors and paid bonds to the Company. They corresponded with parents and relatives about the progress, virtues and futures of the young people left in their care.

Facilitating East Indies departures by London-based Cumbrian friends was a pattern that persisted across the long eighteenth century. The experience of the young Joseph Senhouse in 1758 was not dissimilar to the experience of his great nephew Humphrey Senhouse Gale in 1809 or Andrew Hudleston's experiences when he waited to board the *Bengal* as a writer in 1814. For Joseph Senhouse, waiting to board the *Stormont*, his cousin Fletcher's ship, the primary friend was Richard Machell, a London lead merchant living at Knightrider Street, Blackfriars. It was with Machell that Joseph resided for the three months prior to departure. If this was an imposition, it was one that Machell sought. It had been Richard Machell who, on hearing of Joseph's likely arrival in London, initiated a correspondence with Humphrey Senhouse:

> I understand one of your sons is to come up [to London]... I shall be very glad if you will let me have the pleasure of his Company... I this day [saw] Capt. Fletcher who told me you were desirous of master Senhouse should be with him, but he said he was not quite certain that they could make room for him in their house, if not he would be glad to have him with me.[121]

By offering to bring Joseph into his own household, Machell gave Senhouse the opportunity to save a guinea a week in accommodation costs. For Machell, the offer reinforced his ties with Cumbria. He used his acquaintance with Fletcher to recommend himself to the gentry Senhouses and ingratiated himself with that up and coming East Indiaman commander Henry Fletcher.

Machell was assiduous in his care. Joseph wrote to his father expressing how grateful he was for Machell's advice on fitting out costs.[122] Anxious to ensure that Joseph remained safe in London, although Joseph himself rather boasted of his own ability to find his way around, Machell accompanied

---

[121] Letter Richard Machell, London, to Humphrey Senhouse, Netherhall, 18 November 1758, CAS DSEN 5/5/1/4/12dR.

[122] Letter Joseph Senhouse, London, to Humphrey Senhouse, Netherhall, 1 March 1759, CAS DSEN 5/5/1/4/12mR.

Joseph to Blackwall to see the *Stormont*.[123] Joseph wrote home that Machell took him sightseeing: 'On Monday we had the curiosity to go and see the armoury and lyons [*sic*] at the Tower, Mr Machell was so obliging as to go with us.'[124] The experience and provision of friendship as these young men were being sent to the East Indies shows continuities over many years.

Fifty years later, Joseph's great nephew Humphrey Senhouse Gale was the object of similar care.[125] He was accommodated by the retired East Indiaman commander Joseph Huddart in Huddart's house in the prosperous, gated suburb of Highbury Terrace, Islington.[126] Close to the eve of his departure, Gale wrote to his great aunt Kitty Senhouse of Nether Hall:

> I take this opportunity of writing to you to inform you that Captain H[uddart] came along with me down to Gravesend and saw me safe on board my ship on Wednesday last.[127]

Andrew Hudleston's preparations were framed by the care of Cumbrian friends in London in much the same way as Humphrey Gale's a decade or so before and Joseph Senhouse's almost fifty years previously.

Andrew's preparations were undertaken under the supervision of his second cousin, retired Company servant and East India Company director John Hudleston. Andrew stayed with Hudleston at his home in Old Windsor until his last few weeks in London. At that point his mother came down from Hutton John with her cousin Susannah Knott and they took lodgings with Andrew at Cecil Street off the Strand.[128] Together John Hudleston and Susannah Knott, whose father had served in the East Indies, prepared Andrew for the voyage.[129] As Andrew wrote to his aunt, John Hudleston was 'very kind in assisting me in getting all things necessary for my outfit for India'.[130]

---

[123] Letter Joseph Senhouse, London, to Humphrey Senhouse, Netherhall, 23 January 1759, CAS DSEN 5/5/1/4/12jR.

[124] Letter Joseph Senhouse, London, to Humphrey Senhouse, Netherhall, 19 January 1759, CAS DSEN 5/5/1/4/12iR.

[125] Letter Humphrey Senhouse Gale, London, to Kitty Senhouse, Netherhall, 30 March 1809, CAS DSEN 5/5/1/9/65y.

[126] A. P. Baggs, D. K. Bolton and P. Croot, 'Islington: Growth: Highbury', in T. Baker and C. R. Elrington (eds), *A History of the County of Middlesex: Volume 8: Islington and Stoke Newington Parishes* (London, Victoria County History, 1985), pp. 37–41.

[127] Letter Humphrey Senhouse Gale, London, to Kitty Senhouse, Netherhall, 16 April 1809, CAS DSEN 5/5/1/9/65x.

[128] Letter Andrew Fleming Hudleston, Cecil Street, Strand, to Isabella Hudleston, Whitehaven, 28 February 1814, CAS DHUD 14/3V.

[129] Letter Andrew Fleming Hudleston, on board the East Indiaman *Asia* to Elizabeth Hudleston, Hutton John, 19 September 1814, CAS DHUD 13/2/7R; Letter Andrew Fleming Hudleston, Cecil Street, Strand, to Isabella Hudleston, Whitehaven, 28 February 1814, CAS DHUD 14/3R.

[130] Letter Andrew Fleming Hudleston, Cecil Street, Strand, to Isabella Hudleston, Whitehaven, 28 February 1814, CAS DHUD 14/3V.

The help of experienced friends was necessary. Their care was more effective than that of anxious parents. As Williamson complained in the *East India Vade Mecum* of 1810, there was a tendency for cadets and writers to be weighed down with paraphernalia by nervous families:

> I cannot deprecate more forcibly the practice of burthening young folks with a variety of useless apparel... The grand object should be to provide what may be efficient after arrival in India.[131]

Even so there was a lot to purchase before leaving. Apparently the necessities for men seeking their fortunes in the East Indies included, but was not limited to, no fewer than four dozen calico shirts, two pairs of thick pantaloons, two pairs of thin pantaloons along with four pairs of long cotton drawers, a dozen pairs of worsted half-stockings, three dozen cotton half-stockings, a dozen pairs of silk stockings, breeches, waistcoats, a greatcoat, two pairs of boots, one pair of heavy shoes, a pair of light shoes, coats and a quantity of blankets, sheets and a raft of other impedimenta.[132]

A complete review of the ships, captains and travellers before committing to a particular ship was also advised. In particular, foreign ships were to be avoided. Although Williamson admitted that there might be some exceptions, the foreign ship was, he wrote:

> rarely sea-worthy; they are badly equipped, and worse manned; their decks are low' their accommodations dark, dismal and offensive; their water execrable; their provision scarce and bad; their commanders ignorant, avaricious, mean, proud and deceitful![133]

Andrew Hudleston was protected from these horrors no doubt by his cousin's interventions. Andrew was secured a berth on the rather new *Bengal* under the command of Captain George Nicholls who had been a midshipman under Captain John Wordsworth.[134] He also had secured a place at the captain's table. With sixty live sheep on board, there was the prospect of numerous mutton dinners. Even so, despite the guidance of his director cousin, the sheep and the captain's connection with John Wordsworth, now a prominent investor in East Indiamen, Andrew still felt he was treated stingily.[135]

By contrast, John Bellasis remembered his first voyage to India under the supervision of fellow Cumbrian John Hasell with fondness and remained

---

131 Williamson, *The East India Vade Mecum*, p. 8.

132 Williamson, *The East India Vade Mecum*, pp. 8–15.

133 Williamson, *The East India Vade Mecum*, p. 24.

134 Farrington, *A Biographical Index of East India Company Maritime Officers 1600–1834*.

135 Letter Andrew Fleming Hudleston, St Helena, to Andrew Hudleston, Hutton John, 21 June 1814, CAS DHUD 13/2/2.

Hasell's friend until his death despite the inconveniences of doing so. In 1781, Bellasis wrote that Hasell's death was a:

> fortunate circumstance both to himself and Friends;... He was very different person to this, at the time I was a Voyager to India with Him, so that I could not help pittying Him, and inconsequence has a great deal of trouble with him.[136]

London-resident Cumbrians ensured that young provincial Cumbrians in transit to the East Indies fulfilled obligations to friends. There was a whirl of visiting prior to departing London for the East Indies. Some visiting involved paying respects to, and receiving largesse from, relatives. In 1757, Joseph Senhouse went with Aglionby and the other Cumbrian mates to toss pancakes with his cousin Captain Fletcher at Fletcher's lodgings.[137] He repeatedly met with his aunt Fleming,[138] and visited with Captain Fletcher's sisters.[139] Andrew Hudleston had a similar flurry of visits. This sociability in London prior to leaving for the East Indies was not simply about reinforcing kinship connections. Visits frequently involved socialising with Cumbrians, either themselves visiting from the Lake Counties, or resident in London. Joseph Senhouse, for instance, was taken by Mr Sharp, a Cumbrian friend of Machell's, to drink tea with a Mr Watson of Carlisle.[140]

Cumbrians in London did more than simply supply board, lodgings, entertainment and supervision. They also acted as moral guardians, intelligence gathers and assessors. Reports were sent from London to the Cumbrian counties on sojourners' characters, prospects and behaviours. Machell, for instance, informed the Senhouses at Netherhall that Joseph Senhouse was 'well and in great spirits... he is a charming young Gentleman... no doubt he will turn out greatly for your satisfaction...'[141] Thomas Pattinson was staying with the Routledges in Cheapside prior to leaving for India in 1805 when he received a letter from his mother writing from Kirklinton stating: 'Your friends in London M\u02b3 Routledge & M\u02b3 Latimer & Co say you conduct yourself with great propriety which believe me is a great comfort to us all.'[142] Some

---

[136] Letter John Bellasis, Bombay, to Hugh Bellasis, Long Marton, 16 May 1781, CAS WDX 1641/1/1 pp. 27b–27c.

[137] Letter Joseph Senhouse, London, to Humphrey Senhouse, Netherhall, 1 March 1759, CAS DSEN 5/5/1/4/12mR.

[138] Letter Joseph Senhouse, London, to Humphrey Senhouse, Netherhall, 19 January 1758 [1759], CAS DSEN 5/5/1/4/12h and CAS DSEN 5/5/1/4/12iR.

[139] Letter Joseph Senhouse, London, to Humphrey Senhouse, Netherhall, 4 April 1759, CAS DSEN 5/5/1/4/12oR.

[140] Letter Joseph Senhouse, London, to Humphrey Senhouse, Netherhall, 1 March 1759, CAS DSEN 5/5/1/4/12mR.

[141] Letter Richard Machell, London, to Humphrey Senhouse, Netherhall, 14 January 1759, CAS DSEN 5/5/1/4/12g.

[142] Letter Mrs Pattinson, Kirklinton, to Thomas Pattinson, London, 25 March 1805, CAS DX 249/14tR.

old India hands interceded on behalf of Cumbrian families by mobilising Cumbrians in India itself. For instance, when Humphrey Senhouse Gale got into debt not long after his arrival in India, Huddart promised Kitty Senhouse that he would request his Cumbrian friend, almost certainly Henry Hall:

> to advise Mr Gale to consider what you have done for him, and the little right he has to expect more at your hands... Mr Hall ought to advise him to adapt his expenses to his income...[143]

For Cumbrian expatriates in London, providing these supports and services was an opportunity to show off their success. Joseph Huddart was reinforcing the fact of his positive social trajectory from son of a shoemaker to a man of considerable influence when he reported to Kitty Senhouse that he had sent Humphrey Gale's new flute to India 'under the care of Mr Durham who I got appointed a cadet'.[144] The services provided by London-based Cumbrians reached to the core of reciprocity and identity. Being a Cumbrian in itself constituted friendship and generated social capital. Cumbrians in London, related or unrelated, even strangers, were implicated in the project of ensuring that sojourners got the best possible departure, voyage and chances in the East Indies.

The benevolence extended to Cumbrians departing to the East Indies was an extension of, and mirrored, the mutual assistance and sociability encouraged by both the Cumberland and the Westmorland societies established in London in 1734 and 1746 respectively.[145] Those societies were active throughout the long eighteenth century and beyond. Society events were about attachment and identity. Provincial patriotism was celebrated in song at well-attended annual dinners.[146] Both the Cumberland and the Westmorland societies established charitable operations in London. The societies were middling affairs, but the Lowthers and the Flemings were prominent in London's Cumbrian societies. So, too, were Cumbrians involved in the East Indies. Henry Fletcher, having only recently relinquished the chairmanship of the East India Company, took the chair of the annual Cumberland Society dinner in April 1785. More than 150 attended at the Globe Tavern in Fleet Street.[147] The sixty-seventh Cumberland Society dinner was held at

---

143 Letter Joseph Huddart, London, to Kitty Senhouse, Netherhall, undated, CAS DSEN 5/5/1/9/57cV.

144 Letter Joseph Huddart, London, to Kitty Senhouse, Netherhall, 20 June 1813, CAS DSEN 5/5/1/9/67nR.

145 J. D. Marshall, 'Cumberland and Westmorland Societies in London, 1734–1914', *Transactions CWAAS*, New Series, 84 (1984), p. 239.

146 'Poetry for the Lancaster Gazetteer: The Following Provincial Song', *Lancaster Gazette*, 20 March 1802; 'Westmorland Society, London', *Lancaster Gazette*, 20 March 1802.

147 'Untitled', *Newcastle Courant*, 23 April 1785.

the Crown and Anchor on the Strand in 1802.[148] The Duke of Norfolk, John Christian Curwen and Henry Fletcher led proceedings.[149]

The ties evident in the Cumberland and Westmorland societies were also evident in the generosity shown to Cumbrian families sending children to the East Indies. London-based Cumbrians were part of a chain of Cumbrians involved in the East Indies stretching from returned sojourners living in the Cumbrian counties, to East Indies involved Cumbrian ship-owners, insurers, contractors, politicians and bankers, to Cumbrians operating in Madras, Bombay, Calcutta, China and South-East Asia. They not only ensured that sojourners worked their way through the intricacies of fit out, voyage and credit, they also organised letters of introduction to Cumbrians in India.

East Indies Friends

Friends in India were important. Elizabeth Cust put down her son's early commission on arrival in Bengal to the influence of friends:

> You have been more lucky than most young men. You met with very good friends and a commission immediately on your arrival – many you know were not so fortunate.[150]

It was a diffuse network in which letters of introduction were as important as a letter of credit. Mrs Pattinson reminded her son Thomas to take the greatest care of the letters of introduction written by their Cumbrian friends in England to their friends' Cumbrians friends in India:

> M[r] Fawcett's Father [in-law, John Bellasis] is great in the Army there and M[r] Fawcett has wrote us that he will give you a letter of introduction to him, this is truly kind of M[r] Fawcett & we hope it will be a means of your getting better forward. The two letters we have already sent you will we hope also do you great service, so pray seal them all up together & take the greatest care of them & always deliver these letters yourself & if the person be not at home leave a Card with your Name upon it, & where you are to be found – be sure you do this for fear of a mistake.[151]

Forty years previously, George Knott's India career was reactivated by letters from his cousin to Henry Verelst, Clive's successor as governor. Andrew Hudleston had a raft of introductions as well as his cousin's hospitality when

[148] 'Cumberland Society', *Carlisle Journal*, 8 May 1802.
[149] 'Cumberland Society', *Carlisle Journal*, 22 May 1802.
[150] Letter Elizabeth Cust to Thomas Cust, India, 1772, CAS DCART C11/42iR.
[151] Letter Mrs Pattinson, Kirklinton, to Thomas Pattinson, Cheapside, 16 February 1805, CAS DX 249/14vR.

he arrived in Madras. Similarly, Joseph Docker's career in 1827 was no doubt assisted by the following letter to William Jardine at Canton which mention the writer's and recipient's mutual friendship with another Cumbrian sojourner in the East Indies, Robert Addison:

> My dear Willie, The bearer of this is Mr Docker, surgeon of the *Windsor*, a very Gentlemanlike young man. He is the nephew of my old cronie Rob Addison formerly *one of you*. I chin chin you to be kind to him.[152]

The importance of introductions and connection are illustrated by Humphrey Senhouse Gale's constant search for further letters of introduction. He wrote to his great aunt Kitty Senhouse:

> Could you possibly get me a Letter of Introduction to the Governor, Commander in Chief, Counsellors, or to any of the Men in power on the Madras Establishment... Interest is everything in Madras... more particularly in India two or three Letters to some of our Fashionable fair ones... would not altogether be superfluous, by the way Ladies have nearly as much say in Government as Gentlemen... I cannot too often repeat how very necessary they [letters] are to anyone who expects to rise in the World.[153]

This anxiety was persistent in Gale's surviving letters and at first glance lies oddly with his kin connections. On his maternal line he was the great-great-grandson of Sir George Fleming, the Bishop of Carlisle. His great-grandmother married Humphrey Senhouse. His paternal line was the prominent merchant Gale family.

Humphrey Gale, however, was the son of Gustavus Gale who was prohibited from his Senhouse grandmother's house due to his 'undutiful elopement' from university.[154] Having conceived two children out of wedlock, marrying a widow against his family's wishes and subsequently deserting her and his children, as well as failing as a private schoolmaster, Gustavus avoided his responsibilities altogether by dying young and estranged in York.[155] His wife and numerous children were thrust upon the charity of the Senhouses.

The Senhouses activated their network of friends to find places in the East Indies for two of Gustavus Gale's boys. But one of them, Humphrey Gale,

152 Letter J. Gledstanes, London, to William Jardine, London, 16 April 1827 cited in A. Le Pichon, *China Trade and Empire: Jardine, Matheson & Co. and the Origins of British Rule in Hong Kong, 1827–1843* (Reprint, Oxford, Oxford University Press, 2007), p. 64.

153 Letter Humphrey Senhouse Gale, Wallajaput, to Kitty Senhouse, I January 1812, CAS DSEN 5/5/1/9/57hV.

154 Hughes, *North Country Life Vol II*, p. 314.

155 Prerogative & Exchequer Courts of York, *Probate Index, 1688–1858*: http://search.findmypast.co.uk.

was clearly largely ignorant of his wider kin. After arriving in India he wrote to his great aunt:

> I wish you would inform me how my Father became connected or related to my Uncle Senhouse my ignorance of my own family is a great source of uneasiness to me.[156]

Without a clear sense of his position within his own kin network, Gale struggled to make the connections that he felt would be advantageous to him. He had to ask his great aunt if he was related to Wilson Bradyll because a Colonel Hare, who was about to be made a general, had an acquaintance with Braddyll and Humphrey was unsure of whether to approach him for support. Humphrey Gale also enquired whether he was related to a 'General Gale'.[157]

It was the anxiety around his familial status and his uncertainty about whether he could make claim to friends that makes Humphrey Gale stand out. Introductions, making connections, seeking the support of friends and finding and making connections with fellow Cumbrians were routine. Cumbrians in the East Indies provided credit to other Cumbrians, they found positions for newcomers, they gave advice and they used fellow Cumbrians as a convenient postal service whenever one of them returned home. Cumbrian sojourners avidly reported home on the doings, circumstances and fates of other Cumbrian sojourners. Sojourners' letters became a sort of Cumbrian 'who's who', partly as a way of retaining attachments at home and partly because that information acted as a list of contacts for those coming out to India. As John Bellasis in Bombay noted when referring to Humphrey Hall of Gilcrux among a long list of Cumbrians he was in contact with or knew about:

> He belongs to [the] Madras [army]… We have troops from every port of India, so that Country [Cumbrian] Men soon find each other out.[158]

Conclusion

Access to affordable schooling and vocational education gave middling and gentry Cumbrians a unique platform from which to launch their East Indies ventures. They also had friends. They used their shared identity as

---

[156] Letter Humphrey Senhouse Gale, Wallajaput, to Kitty Senhouse, Netherhall, 1 January 1812, CAS DSEN 5/5/1/9/57hR and CAS DSEN 5/5/1/9/57hV.

[157] Letter Humphrey Senhouse Gale, Wallajaput, to Kitty Senhouse, Netherhall, 1 January 1812, CAS DSEN 5/5/1/9/57gV.

[158] Letter John Bellasis, Bombay, to Hugh Bellasis, Long Marton, CAS WDX 1641/1/1 p. 27c.

families from Cumberland, Westmorland and Furness to secure the patronage necessary for appointments or licence to operate in the East Indies. Cumbrian sojourners were supported through a chain of business connections, social relations and familial relations that stretched from Cumbria through London, across the fleet of East Indiamen and into European settlements across the East Indies. Just as Cumbrians living in the Lake Counties retained active contacts with expatriates in London, so London Cumbrians served as a way-station for East Indies sojourners.

In London, Cumbrians destined for the East Indies were fed, watered and bundled up with letters, equipment and advice. When they reached the East Indies, they were embraced by the fellow Cumbrian men and women who had gone before them. Many of those who went to the East Indies shared mutual experiences in education. They often had intimate friends in common. Inevitably, they had a wide circle of shared acquaintances. It was the ability of gentry and middling Cumbrian families to bring together their cultural, economic and social capital that got them to the East Indies. The challenge thereafter was to bring home the wealth and prestige to which sojourners and their families aspired.

Five

RETURNING AND RETURNS

Near this place lye the remains of John Braddyll, Esq., descended from an ancient family long seated at Portfield and Conishead, in Lancashire, who from his youth traversed the oceans of Europe and the Indies as a merchant, and having made a handsome fortune, the due reward of honest industry, and learned therewith to be content, he retired to this village, and enjoyed the fruits of his labour with temperance and moderation. Born at Conishead, 1695. Died at Carshalton, 13 May, 1753, aged 58 – Memorial in Tower, All Saints Carshalton, Surrey.

The splendid Indian Pagoda, recently presented to the [Carlisle] Museum, with so much munificence, by Sir Simon Heward, was the theme of general admiration and wonder – *Carlisle Journal*, 1842.[1]

This chapter is about the legacy of East Indies sojourns. It traces the pattern of bodily return, or failure to return, among the Cumbrian women and men who went to the East Indies. It explores the financial and social outcomes for sojourners and their families after often years of physical separation and emotional and material investment in East Indies ventures. It is about how returning Cumbrians reinserted themselves and expressed their success in the Cumbrian world. It also considers how the East Indies infiltrated the fabric of provincial Cumbria in civil society, its politics and the day-to-day institutions of local authority.

At the heart of those processes was a dynamic interplay between place attachment, identity and expressions of success. As previous chapters have shown, going to the East Indies was fundamentally about returning and returns. Yet as sojourners prepared, and were prepared for the East Indies, not coming home was as probable as returning. Financial failure was a constant anxiety. Returning and returns, therefore, cannot be considered without giving attention to the issue of those who did not return to Cumbria. Consequently, the discussion starts with the pattern of bodily return to Cumbria. It notes that some returning sojourners resided outside of Cumbria when they returned to

---

[1] 'Horticultural Society Show', *Carlisle Journal*, 24 September 1842.

the British Isles. It notes, too, how the cycle of aspiration, passage and return was interrupted for many by death. It is in the context of death and the way in which Cumbrian sojourners were memorialised, that issues of Cumbrian attachment and detachment associated with the East Indies is initially explored.

Straddling the experience of both bodily return and non-return were the financial pay-offs associated with East Indies ventures. This is the focus of the second part of the discussion. Again, death becomes a pivot point for the analysis with the value of personal estates, bequests and the inventories of sojourners providing, albeit fragmented, insights into the patterns of wealth among East Indies sojourners, even where Cumbrian sojourners' returns were prevented by death. The analysis then turns to those sojourners who did return to Cumbria and the ways in which they expressed their success in the midst of Cumbrian provincial life. The focus is initially on the interlock between East Indies experience and positions of local authority followed by a consideration of how East Indies wealth was implicated in the politics around Cumbria's political representation. The discussion then enters the realm of consumption and social positioning. It gives particular attention to East Indies returners' commitment to housebuilding and their pursuit of recognition as gentlemen through the exercise of benevolence and sociability.

Bodily Return, Residence, Death and Attachment

Of the Cumbrian men and women who went to the East Indies, many did not return. About 30 per cent of enumerated men cannot currently be accounted for. Of the remaining 70 per cent, almost half died in the British Isles and of those over half died in Cumbria. Some, like Andrew Fleming Hudleston, died while temporarily away from Cumbria but were buried in Cumbria. Others were buried elsewhere. The largest proportion, albeit still a minority, were buried in the East Indies. Notably, enumerated Cumbrian women sojourners were less likely than enumerated men to die in Cumbria; nine are known to have died in India or at sea and eight of the other twelve known to have returned to the British Isles died outside of Cumbria.

A tranche of returners resided or had businesses in London including Jonathan Winder, Edward and John Stephenson, the Routledges, Dents, Fawcetts and Sowerbys. East Indies-involved Cumbrians with parliamentary interests maintained London addresses or properties in proximate counties, including Henry Fletcher, John Robinson and Alexander Nowell. The Braddylls bought lands at Woodford in Essex and both Thomas and his brother Dodding died and were buried there.[2] Huddart was for very many

---

[2]   D. Lysons, *The Environs of London: Volume 4, Counties of Herts, Essex and Kent* (London, T. Cadell and W. Davies, 1796), p. 278.

years established at Islington and then Greenwich. His ropery was built near the East India Company warehouses and docks on the Thames. John Hudleston lived mainly at Windsor.

Residence or businesses in London should not be interpreted as detachment or disconnection from Cumbria. Previous chapters have shown, along with Marshall's seminal analysis of county societies,[3] that this residential dispersion generated a network of Cumbrians with strong provincial attachments and identity. Most East Indies returners maintained property and business interests in the Cumbrian counties. Indeed, John Hudleston died in Whitehaven while on a business excursion from the south. As Beckett has pointed out, Cumbria's absentee landowners, including successive Lowthers, could be, and were at times, more innovative and effective managers of their businesses and property in Cumbria than full-time residents.[4]

In his history of the parish, identity and belonging, Snell argues that memorials and gravestones show that parish loyalties were particularly strong prior to the nineteenth century, with county loyalties increasing during the Victorian era. He attributes that tendency to a proliferation of multiple residences among a rising middle class and the impacts of global mobility.[5] If that is the case, Cumbrian East Indies returners in the eighteenth century were forerunners in an emerging trend. The Westmorland and Cumberland county societies were some of the earliest established in the British Isles. Cumbrian East Indies sojourners carved their connections to Cumbria in stone.

John Braddyll's handsome memorial, the inscription of which was quoted at the beginning of this chapter, was only one example. Catherine Holme's memorial at East Clandon notes her father's estate at Holme Hill, Cumberland. Even earlier, Jonathan Winder marked connections with Cumberland, the marital alliance between the middling Winders and the Cumberland gentry Williams, and the East Indies, with a wall monument resplendent with signs of status and accomplishment: an ionic column, arms, a crest and elaborate carving. Its inscription was prepared as a narrative of success and connection:

> Near this Place lieth interred the Body of John Winder of Grays Inn Esqr. Barrister at Law Eldest Son & Heir of John Winder, Gent. of Lorton in ye County of Cumberland where ye Family flourished, in a Lineal Succession, above 300 Years. He married Lettice, one of ye Coheirs of William Williams of Johnby Hall in ye same county Gent.by whom he had two Children, William and Mary, and died 27 Jul. 1699 Aged 41. And also the Body of Jonathan

3   J. D. Marshall, 'Cumberland and Westmorland Societies in London, 1734–1914', *Transactions CWAAS*, New Series, 84 (1984), pp. 239–254.

4   J. V. Beckett, 'Absentee Land Ownership in the Later Seventeenth and Early Eighteenth Centuries: The Case of Cumbria', *Northern History*, 19 (1983), pp. 93–106.

5   K. D. M. Snell, *Parish and Belonging: Community, Identity and Welfare in England and Wales, 1700–1950* (Cambridge, Cambridge University Press, 2006), pp. 21, 464.

Winder, Esqr. his 3d Brother, sometime Agent for ye Hon E. India Com' at Bengal who departed this Life, unmarried, 12 Jan 1717, in the *48th*. Year of his Age. Pursuant to whose Will and Desire, his Executors erected this Monument. And likewise the Body of Samuel Winder.[6]

There were, too, memorials in the Cumbrian counties designed to commemorate Cumbrian East Indies sojourners buried elsewhere. John Bellasis's career was recorded in the church at Long Marton, as well as on a grand affair in St Thomas' Cathedral, Bombay.[7] Interred at Mysore, Jonathan Moorhouse was memorialised at Clifton, Westmorland. Charles Denton was memorialised at Crosthwaite, Keswick. At Kendal, James Pennington's memorial commemorating his death in India was 'erected by his three surviving brothers as a tribute of their sincere affection'.

In the East Indies, there were memorials explicitly connecting individuals to Cumbria. James Fawcett was memorialised in the cathedral at Bombay with an inscription that tied Cumbria, London and Bombay.[8] Carlisle connections were evident, too, in the South Park burial ground in Calcutta where Catherine Holme's brother was memorialised:

> The Remains of JOHN HOLME, Esq. of the City of Carlisle, Cumberland, who died the 2 day of January 1779, are here deposited, Aged 49 years. This Monument was erected To perpetuate the Memory of A Sincere Friend and Honest Man by his surviving Friends as a Testimony of their regard for his virtues.[9]

Memorial and gravestone inscriptions were purposeful and meaningful. They could be costly. Even on the simplest of memorial stones, the inscription itself attracted a separate charge, costed by the letter.[10] As Buckham points out gravestones and memorials were 'social markers. They embodied the memory of the deceased as a member of a family unit which was in turn located in a wider social structure.'[11] Snell notes that place references on memorials and gravestones increased over the eighteenth century, but for much of the long eighteenth century, references were largely around the parish.[12] This was not the case with many memorials of Cumbrians who failed to return

---

6　G. H. Gater and W. H. Godfrey (eds), *Survey of London: Volume 15, All Hallows, Barking-By-The-Tower (Part II)* (London, London County Council, 1934), p. 88.

7　B. Groseclose, *British Sculpture and the Company Raj: Church Monuments and Public Statutory in Madras, Calcutta, and Bombay to 1858* (Newark, DE, University of Delaware Press, 1995), p. 63.

8　Groseclose, *British Sculpture and the Company Raj*, p. 43.

9　P. Bailey, *South Park Street Cemetery, Calcutta: MIs Up to 1851* (CALCUTTA, HOLMES & CO., 2009).

10　Snell, *Parish and Belonging*, p. 457.

11　S. Buckham, '"The men that worked for England they have their graves at home": Consumerist Issues within the Production and Purchases of Gravestones in Victorian York', in S. Tarlow and S. West (eds), *The Familiar Past: Archaeologies Britain, 1550–1950* (London, Routledge, 1999), p. 199.

12　Snell, *Parish and Belonging*, pp. 471–476.

from India. Those memorials positioned Cumbrian sojourners within a Cumbrian identity while simultaneously referencing their global ventures. Their elaborate memorials were a 'proof' of success and indicative that, for some at least, East Indies ventures paid off.

The Pay-offs

The financial 'pay-offs' associated with East Indies ventures are neither easily established nor interpreted. Evidence is fragmentary and disparate. An array of records associated with deceased estates – wills, probate values, inventories, probate accounts and death duties – all provide a window on to the wealth and material circumstances of Cumbrians with East Indies interests, but they bring with them a raft of difficulties.

The most commonly available documents are wills and probate values. Probate values are problematic insofar as they only value personal estates. There are issues of comparative reliability too because valuation audits could be variable. East Indies sojourners sometimes had estates in multiple jurisdictions, consequently, there may be uncertainty about whether a single probate value represents the whole of their personal estate.[13] Wills tended to be standardised in form but the value of bequests may or may not be made explicit and estate residuals could not, in any case, be quantified. Inventories can be powerful evidence, but for comparative purposes over a large dataset such as the enumerated Cumbrians they are less consistently available. Inventories were gradually removed from the formal process of issuing probate or administration, although they persisted in India. In addition, lack of standardisation in accounting practices can make them difficult to interpret.

There are also questions of attribution. What part of William Wilson's probated personal fortune at more than £200,000 can be credited to his East India sojourn compared to that inherited from his grandfather, father and elder brother, all of whom were involved in hosiery manufacture and banking interests in Cumbria?[14] Can wealth accumulated by the end of life

---

13   J. Cox and N. Cox, 'Probate 1500–1800: System in Transition', and N. Goose and N. Evans, 'Wills as a Historical Source', in T. Arkell, N. Evans and N. Goose (eds), *When Death Do Us Part: Understanding and Interpreting the Probate Records of Early Modern England* (Oxford, Leopard's Head Press, 2004); L. Weatherill, *Consumer Behaviour & Material Culture in Britain 1660–1760* (2nd edition, London, Routledge, 1996), pp. 2–6; W. D. Rubenstein, *Men of Property: The Very Wealthy in Britain Since the Industrial Revolution* (2nd edition, London, Social Affairs Unit, 2006), pp. 18–24; C. Hall, N. Draper, K. McClelland, C. Donington and R. Lamb, *Legacies of British Slave-Ownership: Colonial Slavery and the Formation of Victorian Britain* (Cambridge, Cambridge University Press, 2014), pp. 48f.

14   Christopher Wilson left his wife cash in excess of £300. J. Satchell and O. Wilson, *Christopher Wilson of Kendal: An Eighteenth Century Hosier and Banker* (Kendal, Kendal Civic Society & Frank Peters Publishing, 1988).

be attributed to the East Indies when a sojourner has spent a considerable time back in the British Isles? John Hudleston, for instance, left a personal estate of considerable value in 1823.[15] He entered the East India Company as a writer in the Madras Presidency in 1766 and returned to the British Isles in 1787. The Company's directors awarded him a bonus of 10,000 star pagodas in 1788.[16] He was briefly a member of parliament and twenty-three years a director of the East India Company. Between 1774 and 1776, he held one of the largest holdings of stock by director.[17] He had business interests in Cumbria and London. It is doubtful whether the fraction of personal wealth that can be attributed to the East Indies will ever be established for men who had career cycles such as Hudleston. What is certain is that John Hudleston believed that India made him and he sought to provide those opportunities to his sons, relatives and friends.

Despite the problems associated with the paraphernalia of wills and probate, their relative accessibility and coverage makes them too rich to ignore.[18] The value of estates associated with Cumbrians with East Indies connections are treated here as reflecting East Indies activities, if not entirely attributable to them. In doing so, it follows the approach used by Hall and her colleagues in analysis of slave-generated wealth and its lasting implications after the abolition of slavery.[19] Some sense of the wealth associated with East Indies sojourners can be grasped from the sworn estates of those dying after 1857. Of the fifty-five enumerated Cumbrian men identified as dying after 1857, all but nine had estate values listed in the National Probate Calendar. Those are set out in Table 5.1. The smallest estates were those noted as restricted to property situated in England, implying that those men had wealth falling into other jurisdictions. The average value across personal estate values was about £38,500. The median value was £11,000.[20]

Those values can be placed in a broader perspective. Green and Owens suggest that 89 per cent of London men's wills in 1830 were valued at £10,000 while 94 per cent of men's wills across England and Wales were valued at £10,000 in 1859.[21] By comparison, none of the three East Indies Cumbrian men dying in 1859 and probated only in England had a probate value less than £10,000. Indeed, over the period 1858 to 1890, only 47 per

---

[15] Valued at around £120,000.

[16] Around £4,000.

[17] H. Furber, *Private Fortunes and Company Profits in the India Trade in the 18th Century* (Aldershot, Variorum, 1997), III, p. 145.

[18] See Arkell et al., *When Death Do Us Part: Understanding and Interpreting the Probate Records of Early Modern England* and Appendix A of Hall et al., *Legacies of British Slave-Ownership* for extended discussions.

[19] Hall et al., *Legacies of British Slave-Ownership*, pp. 48f and Appendix 1.

[20] Table 5.1 and Figure 5.1 compiled from PPR, *National Probate Calendar*.

[21] D. Green and A. Owens, 'Gentlewomanly Capitalism? Spinsters, Widows and Wealth Holding in England and Wales, c. 1800–1860', *Economic History Review*, LVI, 3 (2003), p. 517.

Table 5.1 Probate Values East Indies Cumbrian Men Dying After 1857 in England and Wales

Enumerated Cumbrian Men	Death	Probate Value (£)
Francis Warwick[a]	1857	£300
Richard Benson	1858	£120,000
Michael Falcon	1858	£6,000
James Law Lushington	1859	£12,000
James Steel	1859	£25,000
William Wilkinson	1859	£14,000
Jonathan Fallowfield	1860	£7,000
Alfred Borradaile	1861	£1,000
Andrew Fleming Hudleston	1861	£12,000
Robert Addison	1862	£140,000
William Page Ashburner[a]	1862	£5,000
George Hutchins Bellasis	1862	£1,500
John Boustead	1862	£20,000
John Losh	1862	£9,000
James Masterson Pennington	1862	£6,000
Jonathan Rigg	1862	£2,000
William James Symons	1863	£3,000
Josiah Andrew Hudleston[a]	1865	£450
William Simonds	1865	£12,000
Henry Cookson Airey	1866	£6,000
Joseph Ashley Senhouse	1867	£3,000
Montagu Watts	1867	£20,000
Thomas Wilkinson	1867	£35,000
Charles Hamilton Wake	1871	£4,000
Thomas Dent	1872	£500,000
Frederick Clerk	1873	£18,000
Robert Clerk	1873	£1,500
James Farish	1873	£20,000
James Denis de Vitre	1875	£25,000
Edward Gordon Fawcett	1875	£10,000
William Dent	1877	£45,000
Robert Burland Hudleston	1877	£1,500
George Cumberland Hughes le Fleming	1877	£18,000

Enumerated Cumbrian Men	Death	Probate Value (£)
Robert Lowther	1879	£12,000
Robert Addison	1880	£2,000
James Bell	1880	£2,000
David Ewart	1880	£45,000
William Wilson	1880	£200,000
John James Watts	1883	£6,800
Montagu Ainslie	1884	£84,400
James Gandy Gaitskell	1885	£9,343
Wilkinson Dent	1886	£183,400
Joseph Carleton Salkeld	1886	£48,400
Robert Wilkinson	1887	£73,103
John Brownrigg Bellasis	1890	£2,122
Patrick Theodore French	1890	£2,038

[a] In England.

cent of the probated East Indies Cumbrian men returning to England had probate values of personal estates less than £10,000.

Some comparison can be made between the value of the personal estates of Cumbrian men who went to the East Indies and those who did not. All the estates of the 300 men from Westmorland or Cumberland, excluding the East Indies returners, who died in the month of April for each year from 1858 to 1867 were analysed. The average estate value of those men was £2,000 and ranged between £5 and £160,000. Among the East Indies associated Cumbrians dying over the period 1858–1867, probate values ranged from around £1,000 to £140,000. This tendency for estates of Cumbrian men associated with the East Indies to be higher than other Cumbrians is graphically demonstrated in Figure 5.1.

Enticing though it might be to attribute the higher probate values among East Indies returners to East Indies wealth, those values were almost certainly generated by an interplay between multiple factors. As previous chapters have shown, East Indies ventures relied on access to both social and financial capital. Under those conditions, a wealth differentiation could be expected between these men who became involved in East Indies ventures and those who did not. What Figure 5.1 suggests, then, is that East Indies ventures reinforced and augmented the pre-existing advantages of the Cumbrian men who went to the East Indies.

Comparisons need to be treated with caution, but caution should not allow the difference the East Indies made to people's material situation to be understated. A direct illustrative biographical comparison is helpful here. Take, for

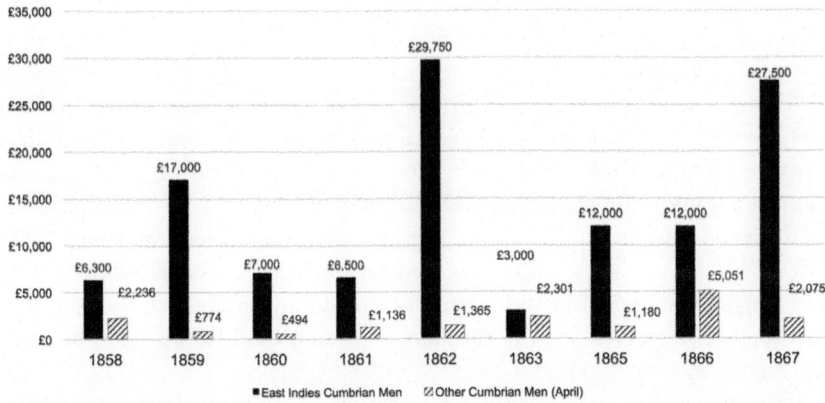

Figure 5.1 Average Probate Value (England and Wales) of East Indies Cumbrian Men and Westmorland and Cumbrian Men with Probate Dying April 1858–1867

instance, the considerable financial success of John Bellasis described later in this chapter, which was unequivocally attributable to his East Indies career. The financial outcomes of his career can be compared to his elder brother George Bellasis. George Bellasis was educated at Oxford. As a Doctor of Divinity he was appointed to a series of desirable livings. Nevertheless, his career ended in financial ruin. In 1772, George Bellasis was forced to leave the living of Yattenden and subsequently his other livings were sequestrated. The family became homeless. His wife returned to her parental home and George Bellasis was reduced to preaching engagements at Oxford and tutoring his own children.[22]

Although East Indies ventures tended to amplify wealth and income, deceased estates show the pay-offs for Cumbrians were variable. Take, for instance, Humphrey Senhouse Gale who was part of a wide middling and gentry network of kin.[23] His central desire was to rise to a position of independence and relieve his relatives of the burden of him.[24] He estimated it would take twelve years to return to Cumbria with a fortune.[25] He barely completed eight years in the East Indies, dying in 1819. Gale's will, made two years before his death, shows he was aware that his fortune had yet to be made. His specific bequests were small – 500 Spanish dollars and 500 pagodas bequeathed to his 'girl', Chindanah. The value of Gale's cash bequests was

---

22 M. Bellasis, *Honourable Company* (London, Hollis & Carter, 1952), pp. 53–56.
23 See Appendices C and D.
24 Letter Humphrey Senhouse Gale, Madras to Humphrey Senhouse, Netherhall, 30 July 1811, CAS DSEN 5/5/1/9 57eV; Letter Humphrey Senhouse Gale, Madras to Kitty Senhouse, Netherhall, 17 October 1811, CAS DSEN 5/5/1/9 57fR.
25 Letter Humphrey Senhouse Gale, Vellore to Kitty Senhouse, Netherhall, 31 March 1812, CAS DSEN 5/5/1/9 57iR.

a little over £210.[26] By comparison Eldred Addison who died in 1787 after a career as a writer in Calcutta specified cash bequests to family and friends in excess of £11,000.[27]

Multiple factors contributed to the gap between the two men. Addison was a favoured son of the respected clergyman and the grandson of Eldred Curwen of Sella Park. Gale was a 'poor orphan', the son of a disreputable man thrust upon the charity of his Senhouse relatives.[28] Gale was appointed to the army, Addison to the civil service. Addison's career was more than twice as long as Gale's. Gale was under-capitalised, or as Huddart saw it, extravagant, on arrival in India and became entangled in high-interest debt. It is unlikely that Gale ever accumulated enough funds to invest in lucrative private trade.

This pattern of contrasting fortunes was persistent among Cumbrian men dying in the East Indies. John Bellasis's estate was valued in excess of 160,000 rupees or in the region of £18,000 in 1808.[29] It can be compared to the estate of the thirty-year-old Westmerian Thomas Rumbold Taylor, an East Indiaman commander, who died in Madras in 1804. Taylor's inventory contained an impressive list of chattels and promissory notes, but there was an equally impressive list of liabilities. From a gross value of almost 12,500 pagodas, after the debts were paid, the estate proved to be worth less than 800 pagodas or around £290.[30]

Indeed, the estates of some Cumbrians did not meet their liabilities. William Varty of Hawkshead, a lieutenant for twelve years in India, died intestate in Madras. Varty's estate had net liabilities of more than 3,500 Madras rupees.[31] Captain Thomas Birkett of Moresby, Cumberland, similarly intestate at his death at Barrackpore in 1836, was found to have over 12,000 rupees in claims against his estate that had to 'remain unsatisfied' despite a career of twenty-eight years in the Bengal Army.[32]

Other deceased estates did allow for substantial remittances 'home'. George Hutchins Bellasis, based at Holly Hill, Windermere, received a substantial allowance from his father in Bombay of around £6,000 annually.[33] Even men with modest careers could direct substantial sums back to the British Isles and Cumbria. For example, Jonathan Moorhouse, who died in Madras in 1823 after twenty-four years in the army, had a respectable but

---

26   IOR L/AG/34/29-219 f.1.
27   National Archives, *PCC* PROB 11 Piece 1158.
28   E. Hughes, *North Country Life in the Eighteenth Century Vol II Cumberland & Westmorland 1700–1830* (London, Oxford University Press, 1965), pp. 314–315.
29   IOR L/AG/34/29/343 f.7.
30   IOR L/AG/34/29/205 f.41.
31   IOR L/AG/34/27/267 f.133.
32   IOR L/AG/34/27/116 f.82.
33   IOR L/AG/34/27/389 f.1.

not lofty career. His estate was valued at 313,024 rupees. Some monies stayed in India. There was a payment to a local woman, Fattemah, with whom Moorhouse was probably in a sexual, and possibly domestic, arrangement. She received eighty pagodas at five pagodas per month to cover the period between Moorhouse's death and probate. Fattemah received about 280 pagodas in compensation for her 'allowance ceasing'. There were payments to shopkeepers, servants and a substantial payment for probate fees and a memorial. Around 3,700 rupees remained in India in the form of a 4 per cent loan. Moorhouse's local executors received a little over 11,000 sicca rupees, about a £1,000, which they lodged with Binny & Co., for transfer to England. The vast majority of the remaining estate of around £26,000 was remitted to the care of Moorhouse's executors, William James and Thomas Law, both of Penrith, for distribution to his Westmerian cousins.[34] No doubt a small portion funded the memorial to Moorhouse and his parents found in St Cuthbert's at Clifton.[35]

Many Cumbrian East Indies returners brought with them little more than debts, as John Addison complained in the 1720s as he tried to wring compensation out of the East India Company.[36] More than a century later, in 1843, the Cumbrian East Indiaman commander Joseph Douglas was incarcerated at Fleet Street for debts arising from his actions in the first Opium War. In his case, compensation was sought not from the Company but from the 'nation'. Douglas claimed he lost £30,000 through arming and deploying his East Indiaman as a warship for the British government in the China Sea.[37] The nature of his losses, whether he had received government compensation or not, and the reasonableness of his expenditures were long contested by his creditors. What is clear, is that his previous, reputedly large, fortune was never recovered. In 1865 prior to his death, Douglas's debts were estimated at £194 secured against property to the value of £50.[38]

Addison and Douglas were not unique, but nor were they typical. Thomas Braddyll returned after thirty-one years in Bengal, quitting as its governor. Just prior to his death in 1747 he purchased the Woodford estate in Essex for £19,500; in his will he made cash bequests of almost £8,000 and his personal estate was reported as in excess of £70,000.[39] He died with in excess of

---

34 IOR L/AG/34/27/256 f.24 and IOR L/AG/34/29/222 f.55.

35 E. Bellasis (ed.), *Westmorland Church Notes: Being the Heraldry, Epitaphs and other Inscriptions in the Thirty-two Ancient Parish Churches and Churchyards of that County Volumes 1 and 2* (Kendal, Titus Wilson, 1889): Clifton.

36 IOR E/1/12 138-139v [1 March 1720] – Letter 78 John Addison at Whitehaven to William Dawsonne and the Committee of Correspondence concerning a £100 gratuity for his work in the Company's service at India and St Helena.

37 'National Ingratitude', *Worcester Journal*, 30 March 1843.

38 'Court of Bankruptcy', *Berkshire Chronicle*, 29 July 1865.

39 National Archives, *PCC* PROB 11 Piece 758.

£10,000 in Bank of England stock.[40] In addition to the estate John Braddyll left to his youngest son, Braddyll made a generous payment of £100 annually for the care of his oldest son. Along with annuities, he also set aside £15,000 for his daughter.[41] The value of Dodding Braddyll's estate is not known, but he had £3,333 in Bank of England stock in 1748.[42] Edward Stephenson was reputed to have returned from India with a considerable fortune in 1730. He was reputed to have £150,000 ready to spend on the acquisition of property in Cumbria in 1744.[43] Edward's younger brother John, a merchant in Calcutta, made bequests in his will to the value of £2,620 in addition to a commitment of £1,000 annually to be paid from his estate for the upkeep of his son who suffered from some sort of mental disorder.[44] Hugh Parkin, at his death in 1838, bequeathed an annual annuity of £1,400 to his wife living at Skirsgill.[45]

Among the Cumbrian men returning in the latter part of the long eighteenth century, at least seven died with personal wealth in excess of £100,000. They included the merchant and opium dealer brothers Thomas and Wilkinson Dent; Sir John Benn Walsh, also a dealer in opium and reputed recipient of £80,000 of 'gifts' as resident at Benares, a £10,000 dowry at his marriage to the niece of the nabob John Walsh, and eventually the latter's fortune through inheritance to his wife;[46] William Wilson, appointed as a writer to Madras in 1829; the Java coffee grower and merchant, Robert Addison; Richard Benson, a major-general in the Bengal Army and son of a Cockermouth attorney;[47] and John Hudleston from the gentry family of Hutton John which had struggled and feuded over declining financial fortunes over many generations.[48]

---

[40] *Bank of England Wills Extracts 1717–1845*, Film 65/2 N Reg. 54.

[41] National Archives, *PCC* PROB 11 Piece 801.

[42] *Bank of England Wills Extracts 1717–1845*, Film 65/2 N Reg. 208.

[43] J. V. Beckett, 'The Making of a Pocket Borough: Cockermouth 1722–1756', *Journal of British Studies*, 20, 1 (Autumn 1980), p. 147; J. W. Kaye, 'Governor's House, Keswick', *Transactions CWAAS*, Second Series, LXVI (1966), pp. 339–346.

[44] National Archives, *PCC* PROB 11 Piece 968.

[45] National Archives, *PCC* PROB 11 Piece 1897. The PPR, *National Probate Calendar* records Sarah Parkin's personal wealth as sworn about £2,000 in 1859 after an initial probate value of about £3,000 in 1858.

[46] P. J. Marshall, *East Indian Fortunes: British in Bengal in the Eighteenth Century* (Oxford, Oxford University Press, 1976), pp. 165, 206; H. Furber, *John Company at Work: A Study of European Expansion in India in the Late Eighteenth Century* (New York, Octagon Books, 1970), pp. 91, 121; K. Smith, 'Warfield Park, Berkshire Longing, Belonging and the Country House', *East India Company at Home* (August 2014), p. 11: http://blogs.ucl.ac.uk/eicah/files/2013/02/Warfield-Park-Final-PDF-19.08.14.pdf.

[47] See Table 5.1.

[48] W. D. Rubenstein, *Who Were the Rich? A Biographical Directory of British Wealth-holders Volume One 1809–1839* (London, Social Affairs Unit, 2009), p. 405.

Authority and the Politics of Parliamentary Representation

At the core of anxieties around East Indies wealth during the eighteenth century was a fear that this wealth would threaten existing national and local elites.[49] There can be little doubt that East Indies experience or connections were common among those in positions of local authority in the Cumbrian counties. East Indies returners were found among or connected to mayoralties and aldermen in both Westmorland and Cumberland.

In Appleby, Westmorland's county town, the East Indies sojourners in mayoral office included Robert Addison, and the opium dealers Wilkinson Dent and William Wilkinson. Families combining connections to the East Indies with representation within Appleby's town corporation were the Atkinsons, the Robinsons and the Parkins. Hugh Parkin's father James was mayor in 1748, again in 1756, twice in the 1770s, three times in the 1780s, in 1790 and died in office at the age of seventy-seven years in 1793. The tradition was maintained by Hugh's son who became mayor in 1860.

In Kendal, the connection with the East Indies started early. John Taylor, the East India Company surgeon who made a fortune enough to purchase Abbot Hall, was the grandson of Joseph Symson who was appointed mayor twice. Francis Drinkel, three times mayor of Kendal, sent his son to Calcutta in the 1760s. His daughter married into the long-standing East Indies and banking family, the Stephensons of Keswick. Kendal's mayor, William Berry, sent his son to Madras where he died. His mayoral successor three years later, Christopher Wilson, had a grandson return from a successful merchant career in the East Indies. Thomas Holme Maude, brother-in-law to the East Indies returner George Hutchins Bellasis of Holly Hill, was appointed mayor in 1799 and again in 1813.[50]

A similar pattern was evident in Carlisle. Lowther's supporters Henry Aglionby and Humphrey Senhouse both served as mayors. Both had sons who went to the East Indies with Henry Fletcher. Indeed, Humphrey's son Joseph also became a mayor of Carlisle. But the most pronounced intermeshing of Carlisle's city corporation and the East Indies was in the Hodgson family. Richard Hodgson, a mercer, was an alderman of Carlisle. He had at least thirteen children between 1744 and 1764. The eldest boy, William, appears to have entered the East India Company although records of his career are sparse. His second son, Richard, established a successful brewery and became the mayor of Carlisle. He was eventually knighted. The third son, George, was sent to Bengal where he died in 1780 as secretary to

---

49 T. W. Nechtman, 'A Jewel in the Crown? Indian Wealth in Domestic Britain in the Late Eighteenth Century', *Eighteenth-Century Studies*, 41, 1 (2007), p. 72.

50 C. Nicholson, *The Annals of Kendal: Being a Historical and Descriptive Account of Kendal and the Neighbourhood: with biographical sketches of many eminent personages connected with the town* (2nd edition, London, Whitaker & Co., 1861), pp. 286f.

the revenue department, leaving legacies to his mother, siblings and kin of about £6,000.[51] The youngest son was sent to Bengal as a cadet in 1782, returning sometime in the early 1800s and formally retiring from the East India Company in 1822. He was elected alderman of Carlisle in 1808.[52]

Many of those returning from East Indies sojourns met the property qualifications necessary to act as magistrates. East Indies sojourners were also prominent members of grand juries established for the assizes. For instance, in 1802, Joseph Senhouse, Hugh Parkin, James Graham of Barrock Lodge, John de Whelpdale and Charles Fetherstonhaugh were all East Indies returners on the grand jury for the Cumberland assizes. The grand jury for August 1818 consisted of the East Indies sojourners John Wordsworth and Thomas Salkeld as well as John de Whelpdale, and Charles Fetherstonhaugh.[53] Andrew Fleming Hudleston was on the grand jury along with the perennial Hugh Parkin and Charles Fetherstonhaugh in 1822.[54]

There was, too, a long-standing interlock between those appointed as sheriffs and those with East Indies connections. For instance, Westmorland's High Sheriff appointed in 1851, Edward Wilson, married the daughter of the governor of Bombay in 1843. His younger brother William was an East India Company writer. Five years later, William Wilkinson, one of the five sons of James Wilkinson of Flass who went to the East Indies and was part of the Dent trade, banking and opium network throughout India, China and Hong Kong, was appointed sheriff. He was followed, in 1858, by the Java merchant, Robert Addison of The Friary in Appleby. The East Indies-involved Tullies, Lutwidges and Hasells accounted for a succession of sheriffs in Cumberland. Edward Stephenson was a sheriff in 1757. John Brisco, John de Whelpdale, Thomas Salkeld, Fretchville Ballantine-Dykes and Andrew Hudleston were all East Indies returners subsequently appointed as sheriffs of Cumberland. Some sheriffs were the fathers of Company appointees and other sheriffs had parents who were East Indies returners. Charles Fetherstonhaugh has two sons appointed county sheriff. John Johnson's son William Ponsonby

51 F. Jollie (ed.), *A Political History of the City of Carlisle from the Year 1700 to the Present Time* (Carlisle, F. Jollie jun. and J. Jollie, 1820), pp. 10, 17; B. Bonsall, *Sir James Lowther and Cumberland and Westmorland Elections 1754–1775* (Manchester, Manchester University Press, 1960), p. 62; S. Jefferson, *History of Carlisle* (Carlisle, S. Jefferson, 1836), p. 448; R. S. Ferguson and W. Nanson (eds), *Some Municipal Records of the City of Carlisle : viz., the Elizabethan Constitutions, Orders, Provisions, Articles, and Rules from the Dormont Book, and the Rules and Orders of the Eight Trading Guilds, Prefaced by Chapters on the Corporation Charters and Guilds : Illustrated by Extracts from the Courtleet Rolls and From the Minutes of the Corporation and Guilds Extra Series (Cumberland and Westmorland Antiquarian and Archaeological Society)*, no. 4 (Carlisle, C. Thurnam & Sons, 1887), p. 116; *Monthly Magazine Or British Register*, vol. 22 (1806), p.190; IOR N/1/2 f.172 and IOR L/AG/34/29/4 f.9.
52 'Untitled', *Lancaster Gazette*, 3 December 1808.
53 'Cumberland Assizes', *Carlisle Patriot*, 15 August 1818.
54 'Grand Jury', *Westmorland Gazette*, 24 August 1822.

Johnson of Walton House was appointed as a county sheriff in 1815. In 1762, Thomas Braddyll, the son of Dodding Braddyll, was appointed as a sheriff of Lancashire.[55]

Those interlocks had their roots in Cumbria. The East Indies consolidated and amplified provincial influence. The social and economic influence that facilitated East Indies ventures also underpinned access to positions of local authority in Cumbria. In that sense, East Indies wealth acted to support existing institutions and indeed may have stabilised provincial elites. At the same time, however, East Indies wealth could be a disruptive and often unpredictable element on the politics of parliamentary representation. It is a thread that has been noted but not addressed in the various analyses of Cumbria's parliamentary politics and the complexities of the aristocratic manoeuvrings and interests of the Lowthers, Tuftons, Cavendish-Benticks and later the Howards.[56] The machinations of those aristocratic families are not detailed here, except to note that the resistance to the Lowther interest from the Dukes of Portland and Norfolk, and later Brougham, reflected not only their own ambitions but also a broader constituency. There was widespread concern among Cumbrian freeman, both gentry and urban, with Lowther dominance.[57] This discussion focuses on the enduring presence of an East Indies strand in struggles for control over Cumbrian parliamentary representation.

The first evidence of anxiety around the potential threat of East Indies wealth was Lowther's wariness of the nabob Edward Stephenson's interest in Cockermouth in 1744.[58] The Lowther interest was humiliated by resistance cohering around Henry Curwen and Henry Fletcher for the Cumberland election in 1768. Henry Fletcher of Clea Hall, a successful, retired East Indiaman commander who had promoted the East Indies careers of the Senhouse, Hasell and Aglionby boys, claimed a Cumberland seat and retained it for forty years. He was for much of that time an East India Company director. The Curwen–Fletcher alliance that mortified Lowther was sustained beyond the 1768 election. It was an alliance that manifested the complex reciprocities emerging from the interaction between the East Indies and parliamentary representation. Local alliances around parliamentary representation could shape East Indies careers. That dynamic was illustrated by Curwen's later careful entwining of the politics of parliamentary representation with appreciation of past East Indies patronage. In 1770, Curwen wrote to the Duke of Portland:

---

55 Compiled from *The London Gazette* online database.
56 Bonsall, *Sir James Lowther and Cumberland and Westmorland Elections 1754–1775*, pp. 62–73; J. R. McQuiston, 'The Lonsdale Connection and its Defender, William, Viscount Lowther 1818–1830', *Northern History*, 11, 1 (1979), pp. 143–163.
57 Bonsall, *Sir James Lowther and Cumberland and Westmorland Elections 1754–1775*, pp. 69–70.
58 Beckett, 'The Making of a Pocket Borough', pp. 146–147.

I should not have been so long in returning your Grace my best thanks for your great kindness to my Nephew Adderton which I beg leave now to do: but waited until I had returned Sir Joseph Pennington's visit at Muncaster. Sir Joseph publically declares this it is his fixed determination to give his interest against sir J L at any future selection and dropped some hints in private that it would be agreeable to him to be nominated a candidate at the next election for the county and said he did not suppose that Mr Fletcher could ever expect that honor again on the whole I am pritty confident he is aiming to get a nomination in his favour…[59]

A similar interweaving of parliamentary alliances with East Indies careers perhaps accounts for the stalling of Joseph Senhouse's East India career. Having been sponsored by Henry Fletcher into East Indiamen, Joseph returned to Cumberland in 1768. He and his father were previously on the warmest terms with Fletcher. Joseph's father had previously invested in East Indiamen in partnership with Fletcher. As a director of the East India Company, it seems likely that Fletcher supported Joseph's subsequent promotion to second mate on an East Indiaman. It is no coincidence then that Fletcher's candidature in opposition to Lowther in the 1768 elections and Lowther's reactive recruitment of Joseph's father as a candidate to oppose Fletcher jeopardised Joseph's career prospects. Joseph Senhouse was forced to look away from the East India Company to the West Indies.[60]

There were other instances of Lowther's political ambitions being thwarted by East Indies returners. For example, despite stacking the Carlisle city corporation, Lowther lost control of Carlisle, first to John Christian Curwen[61] and then to Rowland Stephenson in 1786. The latter was a banker cousin and eventual recipient of the fortune of the Bengal governor, Edward Stephenson of Keswick. Stephenson was succeeded by another opponent to the Lowther interest, Wilson Braddyll, whose fortune also descended from the East Indies. In 1812, the prominent Bombay ship-owner, merchant and banker, Henry Fawcett of Scaleby Castle, nephew of Rowland Stephenson, was elected to Carlisle, again in opposition to the Lowther interests. Fawcett's East Indies operations were presented as benefiting Carlisle trade.[62] Notably, for the

---

[59] Letter of Henry Curwen to the Duke of Portland, Workington, 7 October 1770, NUM PwF 3.236.

[60] Hughes, *North Country Life Vol II*, pp. 108–109, 109n; S. D. Smith, *Slavery, Family and Gentry Capitalism in the British Atlantic: The World of the Lascelles, 1648–1834* (Cambridge, Cambridge University Press, 2006), p. 113.

[61] Added Curwen, the maiden name of his mother, to his birth surname of Christian when he became to the Lord of the Manor of Workington, that of the Curwen family.

[62] J. W. Anderson and R. G. Thorne, 'FAWCETT, Henry (1762–1816), of Scaleby Castle, nr. Carlisle, Cumb.', in R. Thorne (ed.), *The History of Parliament: The House of Commons 1790–1820* (1986): www.historyofparliamentonline.org/volume/1790-1820/member/fawcett-henry-1762-1816; A. Drummond, 'STEPHENSON, Rowland (?1728–1807), of Scaleby Castle, nr. Carlisle, Cumb.', in L. Namier and J. Brooke (eds), *The History of*

Madras-born great-grandchild of John Christian and Bridget Senhouse, James Law Lushington, East Indies connections gave him no such benefit. He won the 1827 election for Carlisle narrowly against Lonsdale's candidate but was derided as an 'Indian juggler'.[63]

East Indies success and interests also allowed some to disentangle themselves from Lowther control. John Robinson's decision to take a treasury seat in the south, rather than stay under Lowther parliamentary patronage, was enabled by his importance to Lord North in managing the parliamentary relationship with the East India Company.[64] A very different, but equally telling, example was Alexander Nowell's snubbing of Lowther in the 1831 Westmorland election.

The son of a Lancashire attorney, Alexander Nowell made a fortune through indigo growing, manufacture and distribution.[65] In 1808, he purchased Underley at Kirkby Lonsdale. Nowell was looking to cement and build on his hitherto London-based and cordial relationship with Lowther. It was a step towards standing for parliament with Lowther patronage. He actively supported Lowther's interests in Carlisle, Lancashire and Westmorland for almost two decades. But his support was unrewarded. He was overlooked as a candidate for Lowther in the 1827 Carlisle by-election. He was ignored again by Lowther for nomination in a Westmorland seat in 1831. It was then that Nowell used his East Indies wealth to transform his disappointment and anger into a direct political challenge. Despite his previously conservative stance, Nowell acquired support as a candidate for reform and won the Westmorland seat on an independent ticket.[66]

Parliament: The House of Commons 1754–1790 (1964): www.historyofparliamentonline.org/volume/1754-1790/member/stephenson-rowland-1728-1807.

63 M. Escott, 'LUSHINGTON, James Law (1780–1859), of 14 Portman Square, Mdx.', in D. R. Fisher (ed.), *The History of Parliament: The House of Commons 1820–1832* (2009): www.historyofparliamentonline.org/volume/1820-1832/member/lushington-james-1780-1859.

64 A. Connell, 'Appleby in Westminster: John Robinson, MP (1727–1802)', *Transactions CWAAS*, Third Series, X (2010), pp. 217–236; A. Connell, 'John Robinson 1727–1802 – Clarification and Lines for Further Enquiry', *Transactions CWAAS*, Third Series, XI (2011), pp. 248–251.

65 V. Hodson, *List of the Officers of the Bengal Army 1758–1834* (Reprint, Eastbourne, A Naval and Military Press, 1927), vol. 3; A. Nowell, Copy of the petition of Alexander Nowell, esq. to the Honourable the Court of Directors of the East India Company, dated the 15th April 1811, with enclosures nos. 1. & 2., on the subject of advances by the Bengal Government to the indigo planters – together with copy of the reply of the Court of Directors to the said petition, dated the 14th June 1811, *Papers Relating to East India Affairs: Advances by the Bengal Government to Indigo Planters: Financial Letter from Bengal and One from the Court of Directors in Answer Thereto; Supplies Furnished from India to China; Merchandize and Bullion* (London, House of Commons, 10 July 1813), pp. 1–5.

66 McQuiston, 'The Lonsdale Connection and its Defender', pp. 169, 177; M. Escott, 'NOWELL, Alexander (1761–1842), of Underley Park, Kirkby Lonsdale, Westmld. and Wimpole Street, Mdx.', in D. R. Fisher (ed.), *The History of Parliament: The House of Commons 1820–1832* (2009): www.historyofparliament online.org/volume/1820-1832/member/nowell-alexander-1761-1842.

Social Place

Nowell's pursuit of a parliamentary seat and his feelings of humiliation at Lowther's failure to support his candidacy were more about his social aspirations than any political agenda. The following discussion explores two dimensions of East Indies returners' pursuit of social place in Cumbria's provincial world. The first is housebuilding and the associated expression of taste and the second is the way in which East Indies returners constructed their social position through benevolence and sociability.

The acquisition of country estates, 'country houses' and, towards the latter years of the long eighteenth century, 'houses in the country', and the meaning of those acquisitions, have been central motifs in both the emulation debate and the historiography concerning consumption and social hierarchy in the eighteenth century.[67] The acquisition of country estates has also been tied to global imperialism.[68] The acquisition of land by nabobs was a recurrent theme in popular and political discourse. Nabobs through their purchase of country estates were cited as agents of degeneration, undermining the moral framing of authority and potentially social and political authority as well.[69]

Acquiring, building and renovating houses in town and on country estates characterised the activities of men returning from the East Indies to Cumbria right across the long eighteenth century. In 1732, Christopher Wilson purchased Bardsea Hall, having returned from an army career in India in 1726. Edward Stephenson built the Governor's House in Keswick. In 1763, Dodding Braddyll's son Thomas made improvements to Conishead.[70] John Orfeur Yates commissioned John Addison to build an impressive but

---

[67] R. Wilson and A. Mackley, *Creating Paradise: The Building of the English Country House, 1660–1880* (London, Hambledon, 2000), pp. 11–46; C. Christie, *The British Country House in the Eighteenth Century* (Manchester, Manchester University Press, 2002), pp. 4–20; N. Zahedieh, 'An Open Elite? Colonial Commerce, the Country House and the Case of Sir Gilbert Heathcote and Normanton Hall', in M. Dresser and A. Hann (eds), *Slavery and the British Country House* (Swindon, English Heritage, 2013), pp. 69–77.

[68] S. Barczewski, *Country Houses and the British Empire, 1700–1930* (Manchester, Manchester University Press, 2014); Dresser and Hann (eds), *Slavery and the British Country House*; *The East India Company at Home*: http://blogs.ucl.ac.uk/eicah/home/.

[69] P. Spear, *The Nabobs: A Study of the Social Life of the English in Eighteenth Century India* (London, Curzon Press, 1980), pp. 32, 33, 37, 43; M. Edwardes, *The Nabobs at Home* (London, Constable, 1991), pp. 43–43; T. Nechtman, *Nabobs: Empire and Identity in the Eighteenth-Century Britain* (Cambridge, Cambridge University Press, 2010), pp. 165–170; J. Holzman, 'The Nabobs in England, a Study of the Returned Anglo-Indian, 1760–1785' (PhD dissertation, Columbia University, New York, 1926), pp. 70–87; P. Lawson and J. Phillips, '"Our Execrable Banditti": Perceptions of Nabobs in Mid-Eighteenth Century Britain', *Albion: A Quarterly Journal Concerned with British Studies*, 1, 16, 3 (Autumn 1984), pp. 225–241.

[70] S. E. Holmes, *The Paradise of Furness: The Story of Conishead Priory & Its People* (Sedbergh, Handstand Press, 2012), pp. 26–28.

uncomfortable house in 1767.[71] Thomas Pearson built a house in Burton in 1770 before he returned to and died at Calcutta.[72] Between 1789 and 1794, John Johnson, who left Whitehaven for Bengal in the 1750s, built the sumptuous Castlesteads near Carlisle.[73] John Sowerby, who established a successful career investing in East Indiamen,[74] purchased Dalston Hall for more than £15,000 in 1795. He sent his nephew as a cadet to Bengal in 1808.[75] The value of his entire estate was rumoured to be a million pounds.[76] Thomas Salkeld acquired Holme Hill and was probably responsible for its additions.[77] Andrew Hudleston undertook the first significant renovations at Hutton John for a century when he added a wing in 1830.[78]

The purchase, building and renovating of country houses and houses in the country was very much a Georgian affair, fuelled by increasing disposable incomes, land sales, resource exploitation, industrial activities and global trade.[79] Wilson and Mackley estimate that the investment in building or remodelling English country houses between 1770 and 1800 was about one and half times the fixed capital investment in the cotton industry.[80] For Cumbrians, estates and houses were important expressions of social and economic success and reflected the reconstitution of local elites. Take for instance the Scaleby estate and, in particular, Scaleby Castle.

The Scaleby estate was racked by uncertainty over the seventeenth century. In an effort to repair family fortunes ravaged by Catholic and royalist loyalties, the Musgraves sold the estate to the Gilpins. Richard Gilpin inherited it in 1724. Already heavily indebted, Richard made the situation worse by using Scaleby Castle as security for a variety of undisclosed loans. In doing so, he implicated many of Cumberland's most prominent merchants and gentry, including the Hudlestons of Hutton John. The largest debt was to the nabob Edward Stephenson, a mortgage of £7,000 contracted sometime around

---

71 H. Summerson, 'An Ancient Squires Family' The History of the Aglionbys c. 1130–2002 (Carlisle, Bookcase, 2007), p. 124.
72 'Some Account of Major Thomas Pearson', *The European Magazine and London Review*, 45, 180 (1804), p. 243.
73 M. Hyde and N. Pevsner, *Cumbria: Cumberland, Westmorland and Furness* (London, Yale University Press, 2010), p. 657.
74 C. R. Hudleston, and R. Boumphrey, *Cumberland Families and Heraldry: With a Supplement to an Armorial for Westmorland and Lonsdale* (Kendal, CWAAS, 1978).
75 Jefferson, *History of Carlisle*, p. 394; G. A. Cooke, *Topography of Great Britain Being an Accurate and Comprehensive Topographical and Statistical Description of all the Counties in England, Scotland and Wales, with the Adjacent Islands: Illustrated with Maps of the Counties, Which Form a Complete British Atlas*, vol. 22 (London, Sherwood, Neeley and Jones, 1820), p. 87.
76 'Untitled', *Sussex Advertiser*, 30 June 1823.
77 Hyde and Pevsner, *Cumbria*, p. 326.
78 Hyde and Pevsner, *Cumbria*, p. 418.
79 G. E. Mingay, *English Landed Society in the Eighteenth Century* (London, Routledge, 2007), p. 101f.
80 R. Wilson and A. Mackley, 'How Much Did the English Country House Cost to Build, 1660–1880?', *Economic History Review*, New Series, 52, 3 (1999), pp. 463–464.

1741.[81] In the midst of claim, counter-claim and threats of litigation, Scaleby Castle fell into disrepair. Stephenson eventually acquired it in the 1750s without encumbrance and Gilpin's trustees and other creditors were released from liabilities and reimbursed their lending.[82]

For the Stephensons and associated families, accumulating ancient estates like Scaleby and investing in their modernisation, often in Gothic style, was not uncommon. Rowland Stephenson made 'a complete reparation' of Scaleby Castle before 1794. It was modernised again in 1838 by Henry Fawcett. Nearby Scaleby Hall was built in 1834 by Henry Farrer, an East Indiaman commander who married Fawcett's first cousin, returned from Bombay and took the 1,500-acre estate.[83]

Another middling Cumbrian with East Indies connections, Hugh Parkin, similarly relieved the chaotic Whelpdale family of Skirsgill in the 1770s. Part of the Westmerian urban elite whose father was a mayor of Appleby, Parkin's Company career was sponsored by his cousins John Robinson and John Wordsworth.[84] In 1795 Parkin rebuilt Skirsgill[85] and the estate became very desirable:

> The Mansion House, is Stone Built, of Modern Structure, and in excellent Repair, and is well adapted for the residence of a Family of Distinction. The Ground Floor comprises a handsome Entrance Hall, Dining, Breakfast and Drawing Rooms, Library and Butler's Pantries, Kitchen and all convenient. Servants' Apartments. The First Floor, five excellent Bed Rooms, and Dressing Rooms and Water Closets etc; and the Upper Story Six airy and convenient bedrooms. The West wing of the Mansion contains an excellent Laundry and Wash House, Brew House, and spacious Servants' Apartments, detached from the rest of the Mansion. The Out-Houses are well arranged and at a convenient distance, and consist of excellent Stabling for Thirteen Horses, Three Loose Boxes and Coach House, Harness Rooms, Dog Kennels, Butching House, Barns, Byers and Other Farm Buildings.[86]

Parkin and Skirsgill were included in Neale and Moule's second series of *Views of the Seats of Noblemen and Gentlemen* published in 1826.[87] After Parkin's death, Skirsgill was purchased by Lancelot Dent, whose East Indies career centred on the opium trade. He too extended Skirsgill before commencing, with his brother, the building of Flass House at Maulds Meaburn in 1851.

---

81 J. F. Curwen, 'Scaleby Castle', *Transactions CWAAS*, New Series, XXVI (1926), pp. 404–405.
82 Correspondence and lawsuit papers: Edward Stephenson, 1747–1757, CAS DHUD 8/21.
83 Curwen, 'Scaleby Castle', p. 411.
84 'London, August 22', *Leeds Intelligencer*, 26 August 1793.
85 Hyde and Pevsner, *Cumbria*, p. 575.
86 'Mansion House and Valuable Estates in Cumberland Westmorland', *Carlisle Journal*, 9 October 1841.
87 J. P. Neale, *Views of the Seats of Noblemen and Gentlemen*, vol. 3 (Second Series, London, Sherwood, Gilbert and Piper, 1826), pp. 24, 12.

Flass was sumptuous in the extreme with an eleven-metre galleried hall, a saloon eighteen metres long, and a heady mix of gilt, iron and marble.[88]

The acquisition of estates was for some East Indies returners a reparation of the failures of previous generations. For John Yates, Skirwith Abbey was a symbol of resurrected fortunes and reassertion of position within Cumbria's gentry.[89] John Taylor, the Company surgeon and one of five children orphaned and dispossessed by a hard drinking, indebted father, retrieved his father's estate at Landing, Finsthwaite, which had been sold to pay substantial debts.[90] John Bellasis's search from Bombay for an estate in Westmorland was prompted in part by reputational anxieties associated with his mother's admission to the free hospital for the poor in Appleby. Vexed, Bellasis had written to his brother at Long Marton in 1781:

> I have thought of purchasing a small Estate, from 50 to 100 pounds a Year... The produce of it, I mean in the first place to make my Mother independent for life... I think it is a great shame for us all, that my Mother should remain at Appleby, indeed it is a shame that she ever went thither, situated as she is amongst her Sons & and Daughters. Her support could not have made much difference; I must confess I think the Earl of Thant's [*sic*] institution greatly abused... in all probability [she is] the means of keeping out some one or other... absolutely starving for want of common necessaries... I am persuaded it was her own choice, but she was certainly wrong, and it ought not to have been permitted, for no doubt the Neighbours cry out (privately) shame at it.[91]

For others, landed estates were undoubtedly an assertion of a new social position. James Graham returned to Cumbria from Bengal and improved two Cumbrian estates. His father was an ambitious Carlisle surgeon.[92] Graham went to the East Indies in 1780 and on return purchased the Barrock estate. He built a house in 1791 described as a 'pleasant, modern-built house... standing on the verge of a high bank, half surrounded by the river Peterill, and looking down a fertile vale inclosed with wooded eminences'.[93] After another period in India, where he operated as a moneylender to Thomas Cust among others, Graham returned to Carlisle. Instrumental in the establishment of the Carlisle New Bank, by 1810 Graham had let Barrock Lodge. Through his wife he acquired the Rickerby estates previously owned by William Richardson, another London-based Cumbrian with East Indies

---

88 Hyde and Pevsner, *Cumbria*, pp. 518, 574.

89 Letter John Yates, Calcutta, to his sister Jane Yates, 1 February 1763, CAS DAY/6/4/3/aR.

90 S. D. Smith (ed.), *'An Exact and Industrious Tradesman': The Letter Book of Joseph Symson of Kendal 1711–1720* (Oxford, Oxford University Press, 2002), pp. cxvii–cxviii.

91 Letter from John Bellasis, Bombay to his brother Hugh at Long Marton, 16 May 1781, CAS WDX 1641/1/1 pp. 27a–27b.

92 W. Hutchinson, *The History and Antiquities of the City of Carlisle: and its Vicinity* (Carlisle, F. Jollie, 1796), p. 96.

93 F. Jollie, *Jollie's Cumberland Guide & Directory* (Carlisle, F. Jollie & Sons, 1811), p. 81.

interests.[94] Graham was credited with turning it into an elegant, stately mansion and improving 'the appearance of the country, by adopting the best modes of modern agriculture'.[95]

About the same time, Alexander Nowell bought Underley and commissioned the Websters to build an extravagant mansion costing £30,000.[96] The average cost of a new house on a large estate in excess of 10,000 acres was around £22,000.[97] The Underley estate was less than 1,844 acres at its height.[98] A new house on such an estate could be expected to cost less than a sixth of that reputed to have been spent by Nowell.[99] Montagu Ainslie on his return from India built an enormous house consisting an uneasy mix of Gothic cottage, Lakeland traditional and Indian verandas.[100]

Townhouses also attracted East Indies investment. Nowell built a townhouse at Kirkby Lonsdale. It was modest compared to the building John Robinson undertook many years before in Appleby. The White House at Appleby dominated the town with three unusually tall storeys and elaborate windows.[101] Appleby also saw the renovation of The Friary by Robinson's distant relative Robert Addison, a free merchant with substantial interests in Java. In addition, Addison invested in a number of Cumbrian country estates including Littlebeck in Morland and Barwise Hall.[102] Kendal provided a town residence for John Taylor. It took twenty years for John Taylor to return with a fortune and strategic marriage to the sister of the nabob Thomas Rumbold (1736–1791). In addition to re-purchasing his father's lost estates, in 1772 he purchased Abbot Hall for £4,500.[103]

---

[94] J. Godwin, 'Rickerby: An Estate and its Owners – Part 1', *Transactions CWAAS*, New Series, 92 (1992), pp. 236–240.

[95] Anon., *A Picture of Carlisle and Directory: Containing an Historical and Topographical Account of that City, its Public Buildings and Institutions; also a View of the Progress of Commerce and Manufactures; Arts, Literature &c., With a short description of the most remarkable seats and curiosities in the adjoining parts of Cumberland* (Carlisle, A. Henderson, 1810), pp. 83–84.

[96] J. Battle (ed.), *Underley Hall Kirkby Lonsdale – Westmorland: A History of House and Occupants* (no publisher, 1969); Webster's drawings CAS WDX 1514. See also CAS WDPP 8/1; A. Taylor, *The Websters of Kendal: A North-Western Architectural Dynasty*, CWAAS Record Series 17 (edited Janet Martin, Kendal, CWAAS, 2004), p. 115.

[97] Wilson and Mackley, *Creating Paradise*, p. 294.

[98] 'Mr Alderman Thompson and the Executors of Alexander Nowell', *Kendal Mercury*, 12 August 1843.

[99] Wilson, and Mackley, *Creating Paradise*, p. 294.

[100] A. Ainslie, 'Ainslie: History of the Ainslies of Dolphinston, Jedburgh, Grizedale, Hall Garth & Their Descendants' (unpublished, Bradford Peverell, Dorset, A. Ainslie, 2008), Part IVa, p. 11.

[101] Hyde and Pevsner, *Cumbria*, p. 111.

[102] W. Whellan, *The History and Topography of the Counties of Cumberland and Westmorland, Comprising their Ancient and Modern History, A General View of their Physical Character, Trade, Commerce, Manufactures. Agricultural Condition, Statistics, Etc.* (Pontefract, W. Whellan and Co., 1850), pp. 721, 802.

[103] Smith, *'An Exact and Industrious Tradesman'*, pp. cxvii–cxviii.

The East Indiaman commander John Wordsworth (1754–1819), an older cousin of William and John Wordsworth, resided in a semi-detached, ornately carved sandstone Penrith townhouse built in 1791.[104] In Carlisle, Sir Simon Heward purchased 73 Castle Street to house himself and his two mixed-race daughters. Nearby on Abbey Street was a 'commodious' mansion suited to a 'family of distinction' owned by Thomas Salkeld.[105] Richard Hodgson, who left for Bengal destined for the army around 1782, had taken Moorhouse Hall on the outskirts of Carlisle by 1809.[106] Jonathan Fallowfield, the East India Company surgeon, also resided near Carlisle at Brisco Hill.

The acquisition of estates and the building of houses was not simply emulation of the styles of old gentry. Returners were avid participants in the picturesque, the Gothic and the growing preoccupation with the suburban villa. George Knott's East Indies service almost undoubtedly prompted the building of houses such as Thurstonville at Lowick Green and, indirectly, his son's much-admired villa at Water Head built on the Monk Coniston estate.[107] Ullswater was a particular magnet. John Bristow acquired Thomas Clarkson's house at Eusmere Hill.[108] Nearby James Salmond, descended from the Hasells of Dalemain and the Musgraves, built Waterfoot House in 1820 after twenty-three years in the Bengal army.[109] Jonathan Fallowfield was established at Watermillock by 1834.[110] General Benson returned from Bengal to Haseness at Buttermere.[111] The attorney John Edmunds, whose widow sent her third son Thomas to India as a cadet in 1827, established himself at The Gale, Ambleside.[112] William White, the Bombay attorney, settled himself and his mistress as a neighbour of Robert Southey at Keswick.[113]

---

[104] B. C. Lindley and J. A. Heyworth, *Penrith Through Time* (Stroud, Amberley Publishing, 2013).

[105] 'Elegant Mansion in Abbey Street, Carlisle, for Sale', *Carlisle Patriot*, 15 October 1825.

[106] Hodson, *List of the Officers of the Bengal Army 1758–1834*, vol. 2; 'Cumberland and Westmorland', *The Monthly Magazine: Or, British Register*, vol. 28 (1809), p. 536.

[107] A. Menuge, '"Inhabited by Strangers": Tourism and the Lake District Villa', in J. K. Walton and J. Wood (eds), *The Making of a Cultural Landscape: The English Lake District as Tourist Destination, 1750–2010* (Farnham, Ashgate, 2013), pp. 144–149.

[108] E. Baines, *A companion to the Lakes of Cumberland, Westmorland, and Lancashire: In a Descriptive Account of a Family Tour and Excursions on Horseback and on Foot: With a New, Copious, and Correct Itinerary* (London, Simpkins and Marshall, 1834), p. 201.

[109] J. Otley, *A Concise Description of the English Lakes and Adjacent Mountains: With General Directions to Tourists; Notices of the Botany, Minerology, and Geology of the Distinct; Observations on Meteorology; The Floating Island in Derwent Lake; And the Black-Lead Mine in Borrowdale* (5th edition, Keswick, J. Otley, 1835), pp. 8f.

[110] Baines, *A Companion to the Lakes of Cumberland, Westmorland, and Lancashire*, p. 343.

[111] Hodson, *List of the Officers of the Bengal Army 1758–1834*, vol. 1; Lorton & Derwent Fells Local History Society Archive Reference ldf/pr2/3 St. Bartholomew's Churchyard, Loweswater, Cumbria.

[112] IOR L/MIL/9/166 ff.468-72.

[113] Letter 2174. Robert Southey to Wade Browne, 5 November 1812, L. Pratt, T. Fulford and I. Packer (eds), *The Collected Letters of Robert Southey*: www.rc.umd.edu/editions/southey_letters/Part_Four/HTML/letterEEd.26.1805.html#.

These 'Lake Villas' attracted considerable investment. Holly Hill, overlooking Windermere near the expanding village of Bowness, was built by Cumbria's premier architectural and building company, the Websters of Kendal for George Hutchins Bellasis on his return from India. Holly Hill had six bedrooms, a dining and a drawing room, a breakfast room and study, two servants' rooms, a water closet, cellars, various pantries and closets, a scullery and kitchen, a veranda, and both front and backstairs. 'Holly Hill' was not a modest house, but nor was it a country house. It commanded 'beautiful views of Lake Windermere and its surrounding scenery. – The adjacent village of Bowness contains the Parish Church and two good inns. – Post, daily. – Market, twice a week. – Distance from Kendal, nine miles.'[114]

Holly Hill was, like other 'Lake Villas', organised around access to village and town amenities and had similarities with European 'Garden Houses' in India. Chattopadhyay notes that the 'Garden House' 'represented the whole landscape',[115] while according to Menuge the 'Lake Villa' in Cumbria was 'central to a novel kind of landscape'.[116] Both the 'Garden House' in India and the 'Lake Villa' in Cumbria provided for commercial and professional families. They combined private comfort with proclamations of financial success and superior taste. George Bellasis's Holly Hill in Bowness had its counterpart in his father John's Randall Lodge in Bombay on the promontory to Malabar Point (Plate 5.1).

The similarities in material character and amenities of 'Lake Villas' and 'Garden Houses' were striking. The 'Garden House' desirably had 'a well-planted garden... laid out as it would have been for a farm'.[117] The typical 'Lake Villa' had a kitchen garden, sometimes an orchard and:

> a cow-house with a loft above for hay storage, sometimes combined with the stable and coach house required by every rural gentleman's residence. Large villa estates might also include a gate lodge, summer house or ornamental building. Every lakeside villa had one or more boathouses.[118]

John Teasdale's inventory of goods associated with his 'Garden House' at Dinapore highlights the similarities. Apart from the grounds of his 'Garden House' providing for two elephants, Teasdale's inventory echoed the array of

---

[114] 'Delightful Residence Near the Lake, Windermere to be Sold by Private Treaty', *Lancaster Gazette*, 4 May 1822.

[115] S. Chattopadhyay, 'The Other Face of Primitive Accumulation: The Garden House in British Colonial Bengal', in P. Scriver and V. Prakash (eds), *Colonial Modernities: Building, Dwelling and Architecture in British India and Ceylon* (London, Routledge, 2007), p. 173.

[116] Menuge, '"Inhabited by Strangers": Tourism and the Lake District Villa', p. 144.

[117] Chattopadhyay, 'The Other Face of Primitive Accumulation: The Garden House in British Colonial Bengal', p. 174.

[118] Menuge, '"Inhabited by Strangers": Tourism and the Lake District Villa', pp. 143–144.

Plate 5.1 John Bellasis's Randall Lodge, Malabar Hill, Bombay. Reproduced by permission of the British Library

chattels that would be familiar with a town or small estate of any Cumbrian gentleman: a buggy horse, three horses, two bullocks, almost a hundred sheep, two terriers and three setters.[119]

Houses were part of a broader project of social positioning. They were not merely domestic environments, but a place in which refinement and superior aesthetic sensibility could be displayed. A fine balance was required here.[120] Nowell, for instance, was no better thought of because he stuffed Underley with paintings. His collection ranged across the Italian Renaissance through the French, Dutch and Flemish baroque to the prolific English painters of animals and romanticised country life, George Morland and George Stubbs. Works of Caravaggio, Tintoretto, van der Meer and Reubens were in his collection.[121] It was a collection indicative of his wealth, but also a desire to be seen as a man of taste and refinement rather than a rough indigo grower. Libraries and books were also goods which conveyed refinement.[122]

---

[119] IOR L/AG/34/27/19 f.115.

[120] The historiography of consumption has moved from simplistic views of conspicuous consumption and emulation being adopted by middling and lesser gentry to promote their social status and secure their position within local elites. Consumption was important to maintaining social position, but care was taken to ensure the line between success and excess was not crossed. See I. Tague, *Women of Quality: Accepting and Contesting Ideals of Femininity in England, 1690–1760* (Woodbridge, Boydell Press, 2002), pp. 133–161; L. Bailey, 'Consumption and Status: Shopping for Clothes in a Nineteenth-Century Bedfordshire Gentry Household Midland History Prize Essay 2010', *Midland History*, 36, 1 (2011), pp. 89–114; A. Vickery, 'Women and the World of Goods: A Lancashire Consumer and Her Possessions, 1751–1781', in J. Brewer and R. Porter (eds), *Consumption and the World of Goods* (London, Routledge, 1994); A. Vickery, *The Gentleman's Daughter: Women's Lives in Georgian England* (London, Yale University Press, 2003), pp. 164, 181–182.

[121] 'Sale of a Genuine Collection of Pictures', *Kendal Mercury*, 9 July 1842.

[122] See J. Seed, 'Commerce and the Liberal Arts', in J. Wolff and J. Seed (eds), *The Culture of Capital: Art, Power and the Nineteenth-Century Middle Class* (Manchester, Manchester University Press, 1988), pp. 45–65 for a discussion of the consumption of fine art and books in

John Bellasis commissioned and managed, largely from Bombay, the publication of his father-in-law's history of Dorset. John Knott compiled an extensive library in Calcutta including over 300 books embracing histories, including Engelbert Kaempfer's *History of Japan*, numerous travel books including Sir John Chardin's,[123] Arabic and Persian language instruction, grammar, classical and contemporary poetry, Christian and Islamic texts and 'lives', philosophy and books on sciences from astronomy to medicine to fossils.[124] Thomas Salkeld set up a library in his houses in Abbey Street, Carlisle.[125] After a decade in Bengal, Thomas Pearson returned to Westmorland in 1771 and built a 'spacious and ornamental' house in Burton incorporating an extensive library. When the library contents were sold in London seven years after Pearson's death, the sale took twenty-two days.[126]

East Indies returners were attracted to books, portraiture and patronage of the arts. The Westmerian Sir Thomas Bowser was painted in military dress uniform by Thomas Hickey, probably in Madras.[127] Christopher Wilson's grandson commissioned family portraits from Joshua Reynolds.[128] In addition to capturing the children of Catherine Holme, Zoffany painted the ill-fated John Hasell of Dalemain[129] and the Cumbrian banker and landowner James Graham.[130] Zoffany shows the latter sitting rotund with satisfaction. In the foreground a hookah, along with an accounts book, speak to the origins of Graham's wealth. In his hand is the banker's accoutrement, a bill or indenture, which connects Graham to the land in the background.

But it was George Romney, who, by virtue of his own roots in Dalton-in-Furness, brought Cumbria and the East Indies together in portraiture. Romney's work was redolent with Cumbria and the East Indies. Henry Verelst, Clive's successor, commissioned a full-length portrait of his new wife,[131]

---

provincial cities in the early to mid-nineteenth century. Both books and art were popular in the East Indies: see N. Eaton, 'Excess in the City? The Consumption of Imported Prints in Colonial Calcutta, c.1780–c.1795', *Journal of Material Culture*, 8, 1 (2003), pp. 45–74.

[123] John Chardin was the father-in-law of Sir Christopher Musgrave of Eden Hall.

[124] IOR L/AG/34/27/1 f.19.

[125] '"Elegant Mansion" in Abbey Street, Carlisle, for Sale', *Carlisle Patriot*, 15 October 1825.

[126] 'Some Account of Major Thomas Pearson', *The European Magazine and London Review*, 45, 180 (1804), p. 243; H. B. Wheatley, *Prices of Books: An Inquiry into the Changes in the Price of Books Which Have Occurred in England at Different Periods* (Cambridge, Cambridge University Press, 2015), p. 142.

[127] www.nicholasbagshawe.com/view-artwork.asp?id=186.

[128] Holmes, *The Paradise of Furness*, pp. 37–38.

[129] F. Wilkins, *Hasells of Dalemain: A Cumberland Family: 1736–1794* (Kidderminster, Wyre Forest Press, 2003), p. 51.

[130] See cover illustration, James Graham of Barrock Park and Rickerby 1786 by Johan Zoffany, Tullie House Museum and Art Gallery, Carlisle.

[131] Ann Wordsworth (1751–1835), the daughter of the Yorkshireman and East India Company director Josiah Wordsworth and distant kin of the Cumbrian Wordsworths. A. Kidson, *George Romney, 1734–1802* (Princeton, NJ, Princeton University Press, 2002), pp. 90–91.

probably on Thomas Pearson's advice. Pearson was Verelst's military secretary in Bengal. Verelst's private secretary was another Cumbrian, John Knott. Verelst had already been exposed to Romney's work. Rowland Stephenson, cousin of Governor Stephenson and brother-in-law of the Kendal-born Francis Drinkel who died in Calcutta, presented Verelst, in a rather extreme form of men's eighteenth-century gifting behaviour, with Romney's *Death of General Wolfe*. It was hung in the Council Chamber at Calcutta.[132]

Romney's East Indies connections were extensive. His brother James went to Bombay. A portrait of the Bishop of Carlisle was commissioned by the bishop's son-in-law, the nabob Sir Thomas Rumbold. Romney portrayed James Ainslie and his wife Margaret Farrer, the grandparents of Montagu Ainslie.[133] John Stables commissioned a portrait of himself and his wife and children, having spent the 1760s in India and returning to serve as Company director until his death in 1795. Portraits did more than show off financial success. They 're-presented' returners from the East Indies. A raft of family portraits presented these East Indies sojourners, not as corrupted nabobs, but as sober business men and respectable progenitors of delightful, innocent and beloved children (Plates 5.2 and 5.3).

Romney's portrayal of Thomas Pearson in *An officer conversing with a Brahmin* contradicts both the notion of Cumbria as a place of the wild and primitive and the popular discourse around nabobs. Exhibited in 1771, it, and the preparatory cartoons, contrasted with the public discourse portraying nabobs as extravagant, simultaneously abusive of and seduced by an exotic India.[134] Instead, Pearson is dressed modestly and engaged in intellectual discussion, albeit in a composition which seems to embed the superiority of Englishman over Indian. Rather than extravagant and venal, Pearson is presented as:

> a gentleman of an elegant and cultivated mind, who wisely and praise-worthily applied the riches which he had acquired in India, to the advancement of science and the improvement of taste.[135]

That pictorial message mirrored the view promoted by Cumbrian East Indies sojourners in their memorial inscriptions. That is, of men and women who strove for success but who were moderate in taste, polite, benevolent and sociable.

---

[132] M. Finn, 'Men's Things: Masculine Possession in the Consumer Revolution', *Social History*, 25, 2 (2000), pp. 133–155; Kidson, *George Romney, 1734–1802*, pp. 90–91; H. Ward and W. Roberts, *Romney: A Biographical and Critical Essay, with a Catalogue Raisonné of His Works*, vol. 1 (London, Thomas Agnew & Sons, 1904), p. 22.

[133] Ward and Roberts, *Romney: A Biographical and Critical Essay*, pp. 83–85.

[134] Kidson, *George Romney, 1734–1802*, p. 87.

[135] J. Romney, *Memoirs of the Life and Works of George Romney Including Various Letters and Testimonies to his genius &c., Also, Some Particulars of the Life of Peter Romney, his Brother, A Young Artist of Great Genius and Promising Talents but of Short Life* (London, Baldwin and Cradock, 1830), p. 69.

Plate 5.2 John Stables by George Romney. Reproduced by permission Hulton Archive, Getty Images

Plate 5.3 Mrs Stables and her daughters Harriet and Maria, engraved by J. R. Smith from painting by George Romney

Plate 5.4 Major Pierson and the Brahman. Reproduced by courtesy of the Yale
Center for British Art, Gift of Mr and Mrs J. Richardson Dilworth, Yale BA 1938,
transfer from the Yale University Art Gallery

Historians have given considerable attention to issues of taste and their expression in consumption over the long eighteenth century. There are still debates around concepts such as the consumer revolution, the extent to which consumption was driven by bodily desire enabled by rising standards of living, emulation or distinction. Notwithstanding those debates, three aspects of consumption are clear. First, while there were regional differences in the levels and goods consumed, there was burgeoning consumption both by individuals and by households, much of which drove and reflected the expansion of the eighteenth-century global world.[136] Cumbria was implicated in those dynamics as the discussion around houses and the expression of taste indicates. Second, consumption drove local and national economic expansion.[137] And finally, that consumption was caught up in broader expressions of values and social position. The latter does not imply emulation of 'higher' ranks, but rather that consumption was used to project core aspects of one's own rank.

A number of historians have demonstrated that middling families and lesser gentry families as elites in their provincial societies made careful decisions around appropriate levels of consumption and the range of goods that should be consumed. Consumption could be a pleasure but it was also a duty. Certainly, for Cumbrian East Indies sojourners, the consumption of houses and the way in which they were furnished was part of a broader strategy of social and economic leadership within their local communities. It involved an often tense integration of the elements central to being a 'gentleman' and to gentility: social distinction, benevolence and sociability.[138]

Alexander Nowell undoubtedly used Underley as an almost theatrical set to express a public persona. The public purpose of many of his activities was indicated by the publicity associated with them. The press noted at Christmas in 1831 Nowell's local largesse:

> From sixty to seventy poor families in Kirkby Lonsdale and the neighbourhood, have this Christmas been presented with beef in proportion to their families, and a peck of potatoes each by Mrs Nowell, of Underley. Mr Nowell's workmen have also been presented with a portion of beef and potatoes, and clothing. On Christmas day, from the same bountiful source, the inmates of the workforce... were entertained with a dinner of roast beef, and a pint of ale each. From forty to fifty children breakfasted on Christmas day in the school room at Keastwick,

---

136 I. McCabe, *A History of Global Consumption: 1500–1800* (Abingdon, Routledge, 2015), pp. 2–11, 187–220.

137 M. Berg, 'Consumption in Eighteenth-century and Early Nineteenth-century Britain', in R. Floud and P. Johnson (eds), *The Cambridge Economic History of Modern Britain Volume 1: Industrialisation, 1700–1860* (Cambridge, Cambridge University Press, 2004), pp. 357–387.

138 H. R. French, *The Middle Sort of People in Provincial England, 1600–1750* (Oxford, Oxford University Press, 2007), pp. 207f.; Vickery, *The Gentleman's Daughter*, pp. 192–222, 287f.

established by Mrs Nowell, and had some necessary article of clothing given
to them. Deeds like these speak for themselves, and require neither note nor
comment. [139]

The press also reported that local sportsmen were provided access to
Underley's grounds for coursing competitions and Nowell donated a Silver
Snuff Box as the winner's prize.[140] To celebrate Victoria's coronation, 800 of
Kirkby Lonsdale's townspeople went in a procession to Underley. After songs
and toasts, Alexander Nowell climbed into his carriage and led the townsfolk
back to the Market Square to share a lunch of beef, 'plumb-pudding'
and ale.[141] A year later, Oddfellows passed through Underley as part of a
Whitsunday procession and toasted and cheered Nowell and his wife.[142]

Montagu Ainslie also distributed meat to his estate workmen and the poor
of Grizedale and Satterthwaite at Christmas and the New Year:

> Montagu Ainslie, Esq., Ford Lodge, Grizedale has, during this week, distributed
> to his workmen and the poor families of Satterthwaite and Grizedale, ten fine
> fat sheep, which, we understand, was most thankfully received by the donees.
> Such acts of charity, at this inclement season of the year, deserve to be made
> public. We would say to others that have means 'Go and do likewise'.[143]

There were a host of other, similar examples in which the houses of East
Indies returners provided the settings for these public expressions of benevolence. The mingling at those events was carefully staged to balance the fragile
integration of social distinction, benevolence and sociability. Achieving that
balance was by no means straightforward. Some failed. Nowell's extravagant
building works appeared to have been in excess of what was required to express
middling or even minor gentry success. His acquisitiveness embroiled him in
litigation and criminal charges.[144] He adopted practices usually restricted to
major gentry and aristocrats such as Lord Lonsdale or the Flemings of Rydal
Hall. When Nowell sent his servants out to challenge walkers in Underley's
park, his inability to maintain social distance while sustaining sociability
exposed him to ridicule. Gibson Maud reported the incident with glee:[145]

> A gentleman who... during his stay in Kirkby Lonsdale, took a walk down to see
> Underley. He had not been long in the grounds before servant in livery stepped

---

[139] 'Christmas Cheer', *Westmorland Gazette*, 31 December 1831.
[140] 'Underley Coursing Meeting', *Westmorland Gazette*, 26 December 1835.
[141] 'Kirkby Lonsdale', *Westmorland Gazette*, 30 June 1838.
[142] 'Kirkby Lonsdale – Whit-Tuesday', *Kendal Mercury*, 25 May 1839.
[143] 'Seasonable Benevolence', *Westmorland Gazette*, 26 December 1846; 'Entertainment', *Westmorland Gazette*, 22 January 1842.
[144] 'Criminal Information – The King against Alexander Nowell', *Leeds Intelligencer*, 24 July 1823.
[145] Battle, *Underley Hall*, p. 26.

up to him, demanded his name, and informed him that no-one was allowed to walk in the grounds... and that he was ordered to request him to leave. The gentleman gave his name as Sir... when the servant informed his mistress or master, he was sent back to inform the gentleman that Mr. Nowell would be glad if he would step back, view the grounds etc., and take breakfast, but the gentleman was gone.

Benevolence could, of course, be pursued with or without a sociable disposition. There were a multitude of charities to which middling and gentry could subscribe or donate, with contributions published in local newspapers. As landowners and employers their benevolence was of interest. Hugh Parkin, for instance, was reported by the conservative *Westmorland Gazette* as a generous landlord for allowing a tenant to break an unaffordable tenancy.[146] Andrew Hudleston was reported in similar terms:

> As a landlord, Mr Hudleston, was held in the highest estimation by his tenants; whatever was required to be done for the improvement of the property, he did it. In him the poor of the neighbourhood of Hutton John have lost their best friend. He would not allow any labourers to be idle; he found them work, and paid them for their labour, whether that labour was productive of any benefit to the estate or otherwise. In summer, if they could make more money elsewhere, they were at liberty to go; but in winter they were always sure of employment at Hutton John.[147]

East Indies returners were prominent on lists of benefactors and subscribers to charitable ventures. For instance, the twelve appointees in 1821 to the committee of the Whitehaven Dispensary included a ship-owner with a fleet servicing the East Indies, a father with a son in the Company's service, a past East Indiaman mariner and the brother-in-law of an East Indiaman commander.[148] Close connections with the East Indies could also be found among women members of the Whitehaven's Ladies Charity.[149] In 1848, Carlisle's House of Recovery attracted donations from a raft of families associated with India: Addison, Cust, Dobinson, Losh, Thurnam, Steel and Warwick.[150]

Three of the six stewards of the Westmorland Society's fifty-second anniversary dinner in London had East Indies connections, including the creditor of the Nabob of Arcot, contractor and parliamentarian, Richard Atkinson.[151] In 1806, the stewards of the Cumberland Society were similarly

---

[146] 'Generous Action', *Westmorland Gazette*, 9 November 1822.
[147] 'Death of Mr Hudleston of Hutton John', *Carlisle Journal*, 6 September 1861.
[148] 'Whitehaven Dispensary', *Cumberland Pacquet, and Ware's Whitehaven Advertiser*, 4 June 1821.
[149] 'Ladies Charity', *Cumberland Pacquet, and Ware's Whitehaven Advertiser*, 12 March 1805.
[150] 'House of Recovery', *Carlisle Patriot*, 9 December 1848.
[151] 'Westmorland Society', *Cumberland Pacquet, and Ware's Whitehaven Advertiser*, 27 February 1798.

infused with East Indies interests, with Henry Fletcher, John Dent, William Borradaile and James Wilkinson.[152] The stewards of the Westmorland Society in 1846 boasted a strong representation of East India returners and among the 115 subscribers were nine Cumbrian returners from the East Indies.[153]

The Cumberland and Westmorland societies combined pleasure with purpose, combining county patriotism, sociability and charitable works directed to the needs of Cumbrian children resident in London. But even pleasure alone expressed and reinforced social standing. East Indies sojourners ensured that they were seen in pursuit of fashionable but respectable watering holes. In 1817, for example, James Graham was reported as having visited Allonby. He was not the only East Indies returner. There was too Thomas Salkeld, who retired from the East India Company military in 1810, and a number of families (Fawcetts, Mounseys and Dobinsons) with close East Indies connections.[154] Also at that 'agreeable and fashionable water place' for sea bathing, was a bevy of gentry and respectable middling families including the Hasells of Dalemain, the Milbourns of Armathwaite Castle and the Speddings.[155] Being associated with the consumption of fashion and pleasure was not the only domain in which East Indies returners' success was noted.

The standing of East Indies returners, both as gentlemen and as men of applied learning, prompted their inclusion in advertising of a range of infra-structure schemes, especially canal and railway proposals. They were also incorporated into a host of advertisements for schools and schoolmasters. For instance, on Christmas Day 1819, the perpetual curate of Martindale invited parents to seek references from the East Indies returners Hugh Parkin and John de Whelpdale as to the quality of his teaching of 'every branch of a Classical and Commercial Education'.[156] The master of Barton school near Penrith, Henry Robinson, gave out a similar invitation three years later to those wishing their sons to be qualified for university, trade or professions.[157] These advertisements were not simply a benefit to the advertiser, although that is how advertisements such as these have generally been interpreted.[158] This advertising practice also acted to reinforce the social status of men like Parkin.

The translation of East Indies success into local recognition and authority was expressed in leading innovation and economic improvement. East Indies wealth was probably implicated in the burgeoning tourism industry around Keswick.

---

[152] 'Cumberland Society', *Cumberland Pacquet, and Ware's Whitehaven Advertiser*, 15 April 1806.

[153] 'Westmorland Society', *Kendal Mercury*, 16 May 1846.

[154] 'Allonby, July 24', *Carlisle Patriot*, 26 July 1817.

[155] See J. C. D. Spedding, *The Spedding Family with Short Accounts of a Few Other Families Allied by Marriage* (Dublin, Alex. Thom and Company, 1909).

[156] 'Education', *Carlisle Patriot*, 25 December 1819.

[157] 'Barton School', *Westmorland Gazette*, 28 December 1822.

[158] J. Stobart, *Sugar and Spice: Grocers and Groceries in Provincial England, 1650–1830* (Oxford, Oxford University Press, 2013), pp. 181–182.

Edward Stephenson built the Royal Oak Hotel.[159] The Low Door Hotel and the development associated with it of nearby waterfalls were established as a tourist attraction by the banker Rowland Stephenson (1728–1807).[160] Rowland Stephenson and his son Edward were promoters of the Keswick regattas.[161] The Knott's investments in, and eventual dominance of, charcoal iron smelting in the British Isles was through a combination of strategic marriages and, almost certainly, an injection of capital acquired in the East Indies. East Indies sojourners invested in Cumbrian mining and industry. Shipbuilding attracted considerable capital and there were technical innovations. William Berry was already involved in manufacturing ivory combs in Kendal when he sent his son off to Madras in 1806, but he brought the first steam engine to Kendal in the early 1820s for the purpose of ivory cutting.[162] James Graham's second son was involved in technical innovation in agricultural machinery.[163] James Graham, Andrew Hudleston and Montagu Ainslie were involved in land improvement. Similarly, Hugh Parkin encouraged his sons to acquire and improve agricultural land.[164] The next generations of Parkins were avid and successful participants in Penrith Horticultural Society events.[165] Nowell made Underley the centre of a successful horse-breeding venture, attracting not merely aristocratic expenditure but also a fashionable social set to Westmorland.[166]

East Indies wealth was used to provide credit. The nabob Edward Stephenson of Keswick, for example, was one of two significant lenders in Cumberland over the middle years of the eighteenth century. Sir James Lowther of Whitehaven was the other.[167] The Stephensons continued to act as creditors. Rowland Stephenson, Edward's cousin and a Lombard Street banker heavily involved in the East Indies, was providing credit to Sir Michael le Fleming in the mid-1780s.[168] James Graham established the Carlisle New Bank in 1804.

[159] J. J. Fisher Crosthwaite, 'Some of the Old Families in the Parish of Crosthwaite', *Transactions Cumberland and Westmorland Association Advancement of Literature and Science*, 10 (1884–85), p. 21.
[160] D. Denman, 'Materialising Cultural Value in the English Lakes, 1735–1845: A Study of the Responses of New Landowners to Representations of Place and People' (PhD dissertation, Lancaster University, 2011), p. 198f.
[161] A. Hankinson, *The Regatta Men* (Milnthorpe, Cicerone Press, 1988).
[162] Nicholson, *The Annals of Kendal*, p. 247.
[163] Godwin, 'Rickerby: An Estate and its Owners', pp. 234, 240, 244.
[164] See for instance, William Hunter Parkin's success with sheep and cattle at shows. 'Penrith Agricultural Society', *Carlisle Journal*, 1 October 1836.
[165] 'Penrith Horticultural Society', *Kendal Mercury*, 3 September 1836.
[166] Meline, Cans & Co., *The General Stud Book: Containing pedigrees Race Horses &c. &c. From the Earliest Accounts to the Year 1835 Inclusive in Four Volumes*, vol. iv (Brussels, Meline, Cans & Co., 1839), multiple entries of Nowell stallions and brood mares. See J. Pinfold, 'Horse Racing and the Upper Classes in the Nineteenth Century', *Sport in History*, 28, 3 (September 2008), pp. 414–430 for the developing elite associations with horse racing.
[167] J. V. Beckett, *Coal and Tobacco: The Lowthers and the Economic Development of West Cumberland 1660–1760* (Cambridge University Press, Cambridge), pp. 206–208.
[168] Three bonds from Sir Michael le Fleming to Rowland Stephenson 1785/86, CAS WDRY 1/4/62.

Conclusion

The Cumbrians who went to the East Indies were able to do so because they had some advantages. Kin, family and friends invested in sojourners' East Indies careers in the hope of future payoffs, not in India but in Cumbria. Returners sometimes realised their own and the ambitions of their families and friends, and others were disappointed. Some remitted wealth, others debt. For some the East Indies venture was full of life and success, for others it was death marked by the return of memorial keepsakes and trinkets and a death notice inserted in one of Cumbria's many newspapers. But in general, those who returned home did so with at least the ambition of an 'easy competence' fulfilled and, in some cases, much more. The evidence suggests that opportunities in the East Indies resulted in significant material returns among sojourners who survived to work their way through a reasonably long career cycle. East Indies sojourners were able to pursue those opportunities because they had advantageous access to both financial resources and social capital. The East Indies augmented and reinforced those advantages.

The East Indies infiltrated Cumbrian provincial life. The connections between East Indies sojourners and Cumbria were promoted and sustained through remittances, even where there was no bodily return, and through memorials and gravestones. For those monuments were directed not to the dead but to the living.[169] A substantial proportion of Cumbrians who returned to the British Isles, returned to Cumbria. Many Cumbrian men who returned married Cumbrian women and some returned to wives living in Cumbria. These were both a manifestation of attachments and served to cement those attachments to Cumbria. Others brought non-Cumbrian wives back to Cumbria with them and in doing so invigorated and expanded Cumbrian connections with other provincial centres in the British Isles, as well as with London, the East India Company and with the emerging British state in India.

East Indies returners were simultaneously disruptive and settling. East Indies wealth inhibited the dominance the Lowthers sought in the political arena. East Indies wealth supported the reconstitution of social elites combining gentry, leading urban families, professionals and merchants through their purchase of estates and housebuilding. When they returned, East Indies sojourners were part of the exercise of local authority. They injected life into the economy and civil society. They were anxious to express their success. They did it in ways they believed would present themselves not as nabobs but, whether in town or country, as polite, sociable people of refinement, taste and benevolence.

---

[169] S. Tarlow, 'Wormie Clay and Blessed Sleep: Death and Disgust in Later Historic Britain', in S. Tarlow and S. West (eds), *The Familiar Past*, p. 189.

Six

CONCLUSION: 'USE OF GLOBES'

Education – Eaglesfield. D. Saul respectfully informs the Public that he intends opening School at Eaglesfield on MONDAY the 7th Day of November, 1814, for the Purpose of instructing YOUTH in the subjoined Branches of Education… Use of Globes, Navigation, Spherics, Astronomy, Algebra, Euclid – *Cumberland Pacquet, and Ware's Whitehaven Advertiser*, 25 October 1814

The global emerges as a repeated motif in the advertising by Cumbria's many schools, academies and tutors in the long eighteenth century. The 'use of globes', navigation and something commonly referred to as 'preparation for a mercantile life', were typical disciplines in the educational finishing of Cumbrian young men. Those educational preoccupations were a manifestation of a realm of Cumbrian life which has been largely neglected. This book fills that profound empirical gap around Cumbria's involvement in the East Indies. It has uncovered the size and characteristics of the Cumbrians who went to the East Indies over the long eighteenth century and explored the drivers and sensibilities associated with that encounter. But it does more than retrieve the East Indies ventures of Cumbrian middling and gentry folk from the shadows.

What is revealed here is a profound connection between the eighteenth century provincial worlds of the British Isles and a global world connected through trade and increasingly subject to colonial expansion and territorial acquisition. It was not national preoccupations that prompted middling and gentry Cumbrians to investment quantities of financial, human and social capital in the East Indies. Those investments were directed to success as Cumbrians. In that context, the 'use of globes' can be read not merely as printed orb, twirled by tutors and in classrooms of schools and academies. It represents a deeper phenomenon: the accessing and utilisation of global resources by provincials for provincial purposes.

The early and comparative intensity of those investments were manifestations of the particular conditions of provincial life in Cumbria and shaped its regional social and economic development. But does the Cumbrian encounter with the East Indies only matter for Cumbria, or does it have implications beyond its own provincial world? There is no doubt that other provincial encounters with the East Indies will differ in intensity and be prompted by different domestic dynamics. What the Cumbrian case does is demonstrate that exploring those provincial dynamics and the interface between different provincial worlds and the global is worthwhile. It illuminates the nature of provincial life and regional development in the British Isles. It clarifies, too, the dynamics of imperialism as a more complex articulation of local, global and national than typically allowed.

Notably, while the concerns expressed in the loose collective of approaches represented in new imperial history and subaltern studies have accepted the idea of local conditions in colonised territories as critical, the recognition of the local as a driver of colonisers or imperial interests has remained muted. Despite undoubted shifts in recent years, the imperial and global narrative for the British Isles has remained one focused on the nation and London as the metropole of the nation. Still there tends to be a narrative in which through global trade, colonial expansion and territorial acquisition a fragile union of nations located on the British Isles was transformed into Great Britain. It is a narrative of territorial administration and rule being a crucible for the development of the phlegmatic British character and national attachments and loyalties supported British entrepreneurship and lubricated lucrative British global investment. The impact of empire at home has been associated with industrial expansion in the British Isles. More recently, the cultural impacts of the imperial world on domestic life and consumption have been foregrounded. Nevertheless, the metropole continues to be conceived of as the 'nation' and Britain's global reach and imperialism driven by the articulated interests of London merchants and national political elites, the dynamics of Union, and the forging of a British national identity.

Whether observed through the lens of the company state or nation-building, these portrayals tend to decouple empire and the global world from critical social and economic transformations evident in the British Isles during the eighteenth century. The potential articulations between the global world and domestic transformations such as the eighteenth-century renaissance of English provincial towns and the rise of middling folk remain largely neglected. Yet the patterns of the East Indies appointments and licences to the East Indies during the long eighteenth century show that the origins of many sojourners lay in provincial towns and regions far from the London metropolis. The Cumbrian provincial commitment to the East Indies presents a prospect that global encounters that eventually solidified into empire were not simply, or even primarily, driven by national imperatives.

Retrieving and piecing together the flotsam of Cumbria's encounter with the East Indies over the long eighteenth century provides a very different view of Cumbria, as well as the dynamics around Company rule in India and Britain's pursuit of economic and political imperialism. To weigh up the implications of what has been demonstrated to be a substantial Cumbrian encounter with the East Indies, this concluding chapter is divided into three parts. The first simply reflects on the overall characteristics of the Cumbrian encounter. The second part assesses long-standing lines of argument around East Indies encounters. One of those lines of argument is Hughes's suggestion that East Indies involvement was prompted by a retreat from political marginalisation, and consequently was specific to Cumbria's specific conditions.[1]

Other propositions are embedded in the historiographies of British India and empire. The first of those is that Company rule generated and then was propelled by dynastic families with a distinct Anglo-Indian identity and social milieu.[2] That proposition is supported by arguments that Britain's imperial activities in the East Indies, and those who were engaged in them, were driven by the welded interests of London merchants and the imperatives of nation-building.[3] The discussion in this part of the chapter ends by briefly addressing the proposition most effectively argued by the contributors to *At Home with the Empire*, that participation in empire became an integral part of everyday life and was largely unmediated by individual or collective reflexivity.[4]

The third part of this chapter considers the implications of the Cumbrian case and the lens of Cumbrian ventures in the East Indies for our understanding of, not only Cumbrian regional history, but also a broader range of problematics. It remarks on the areas which have been hinted at but left largely unexplored here. It considers directions for research into provincial life and the importance of giving closer attention to multi-layered networks articulated around local and global places, kinship, friendship and business.

At its simplest, this book reveals a neglected aspect of Cumbrian history. It started with a simple observation: that a succession of Cumbrian histories made sporadic references to the East Indies and, likewise, the historiography of the East Indies, British imperialism and the East India Company were redolent with references to men who had their origins in the Cumbrian counties. Together those raised the prospect of a significant but largely hidden encounter between Cumbrians and the East Indies over the long eighteenth century. If the traces of the past accessible to historians are 'tiny flotsam' of

---

1 E. Hughes, *North Country Life in the Eighteenth Century Vol II Cumberland & Westmorland 1700–1830* (London, Oxford University Press, 1965), p. 105.

2 S. Ghosh, *The Social Condition of the British Community in Bengal 1757–1800* (Leiden, E. J. Brill, 1970), pp. 33–56.

3 L. Colley, *Britons: Forging the Nation 1707–1837* (3rd revised edition, New Haven, CT, Yale University Press, 2009), pp. 79, 127–130; G. McGilvray, *East India Patronage and the British State: The Scottish Elite and Politics in the Eighteenth Century* (London, Tauris Academic Studies, 2008).

4 C. Hall and S. Rose (eds), *At Home with the Empire: Metropolitan Culture and the Imperial World* (Cambridge, Cambridge University Press, 2009).

'the great, brown, slow-moving, strandless river of Everything',[5] what this book has attempted to do is retrieve the flotsam floating past the historiographies of both Cumbria and the East Indies.

This book brings out of the shadows over 400 Cumbrian women and men directly involved in the East Indies. It has demonstrated that there was a substantial and persistent commitment to the East Indies evidenced by: the over-representation of Cumbrians as appointees and licensees to the East Indies compared to other counties; the mobilisation of Cumbrian networks and Cumbria's particular competitive advantages in education and Atlantic trading experience to promote their opportunities in the East India Company and the East Indies; Cumbrian sojourners' sustained attachments to Cumbria; and the way in which they were actively re-embraced by the provincial worlds of the Cumbrian counties if and when they returned.

The Cumbrian encounter was driven by hopes of success and shaped by fears of death, detachment and debt. The balancing of risk and reward preoccupied Cumbrian families as they prepared their sons, brothers, fathers and, less frequently but no less importantly, sisters and daughters for an East Indies sojourn. And it was a sojourn. The purpose lay in Cumbria, not the East Indies. The purpose was a financial return, preferably with an augmented personal reputation that would reflect well on kin, family and friends. There were mutual expectations of reciprocity among fellow country/county men and women. The twisted threads that wove their way through the cycle of preparation, passage and return were kin and friends embedded in place. Cumbrian attachment and identity sustained East Indies ventures and implicated Cumbrians at home in the global world, irrespective of whether they had personal or intimate connections with East Indies sojourners.

There is little doubt that a substantial proportion of returners had a profound impact on the Cumbrian counties. As investors in tourism, extractive industries, infrastructure development and agricultural improvement, East Indies returners and East Indies money helped to shape the Cumbrian landscape. That landscape was formed too by East Indies-funded house-building, renovation and restoration. East Indies returners, whether gentry or from middling ranks, took on the responsibilities of local authority. They became patrons, contributed to charities and participated in a raft of benevolent activities. In those roles they represented regulation, stability and continuity. At the same time, East Indies wealth was an unpredictable, and sometimes disruptive, force in the politics of parliamentary representation.

The long eighteenth century saw a succession of East Indies returners who were regarded as both successful and powerful. They cemented themselves within provincial elites. For some, that positioning was an extension of the

---

5   C. Steedman, *Dust: The Archive and Cultural History* (New Brunswick, NJ, Rutgers University, 2002), p. 18.

influential positions their families of origin already had. For others, East Indies success meant restoring and stabilising declining family fortunes. The liminal should not be forgotten, however. The mixed-race children found it difficult to find a place. Those problems were, as a previous chapter notes, evident in the trajectories of Thomas Cust's children and Richard Ecroyd. But there were others, such as the daughters of Sir Simon Heward, whose illegitimacy and race combined led to litigation late in the nineteenth century. While Ceta and Jessie were both dead at the time, that litigation exposed the fragility of their circumstances when they were alive, despite their father's wealth and careful provisions for them.[6]

For some families there were substantial shifts in rank arising from East Indies wealth combined with a determination to be active in their native country. Nowhere was that more evident than in 1754 when William Bellers released a set of engravings on to the London market. Bellers's six engravings of Cumberland and Westmorland presented views destined to become lionised in the emergence of the Lake District as a unique landscape and tourist destination. Five of the prints were dedicated to aristocratic and leading gentry landowners: The Marquis of Rockingham, Charles Howard of Greystoke, Sir James Lowther and Sir William Fleming of Rydal. The sixth of Beller's prints was dedicated to the Cumbrian returner from the East Indies, Edward Stephenson, a man born into a quite different order.[7]

The East Indies transmuted the Stephensons from merchants and minor yeoman landowners to a powerful extended kin network of Stephensons, Winders and Fawcetts. They had commercial and banking interests in London, Europe and India with extensive landholdings and commercial ventures in Cumbria. For more than a century, members of these families were influential social and economic actors, both within and outside of Cumbria as merchants and bankers. They married into gentry families including the Williams of Johnby Hall and the Stricklands of Sizergh.[8] That the East Indies became synonymous with wealth and influence in Cumbria is evidenced by the rather curious case of William Richardson.[9]

---

6   'The Queen's Proctor vs Fry', *Morning Post*, 16 May 1879; Untitled, *London Daily News*, 17 May 1879. Because much of their lives were lived outside, and the broader ramifications of their illegitimacy emerged outside the period on which this book is focused, the trajectories of Ceta and Jessie have not been explored here.

7   C. Powell and S. Hebron, *Savage Grandeur and Noblest Thoughts: Discovering the Lake District 1750–1820* (Grasmere, The Wordsworth Trust, 2010), pp. 39–42.

8   The marriage failed and its descendants became caught up in the collapse of the Stephenson's bank, Remington, Stephenson & Co. in 1828 through embezzlement and theft by Rowland Stephenson (1782–1856). This bank was connected to a number of established agency and merchant houses in India. See P. Bungay, *The Dapper Little Banker: The Life of Rowland Stephenson* (Kindle edition, Lancaster, Scotforth Books, 2011), Chapter 2.

9   J. Godwin, 'Rickerby: An Estate and its Owners – Part 1', *Transactions CWAAS*, New Series, 92 (1992), p. 233.

William Richardson spent most of his merchant career in London, having been sent there by his father, a yeoman farmer of Rickerby. By the late 1760s, however, he was accumulating land around Rickerby and, at a cost of £200, purchased the Lordship of the Manor of Rickerby. Over the next two decades he spent over £5,000 of land acquisitions around Rickerby and Bleatarn[10] and Bleatarn locals applied the appellation of nabob to him.[11] There is no clear evidence of William Richardson's direct involvement in the East Indies. He does not appear to have sojourned there. It was his nephew,[12] not he, who was sent out to India.

Explanations De-centring the Provincial World

Four propositions have threaded their way through Cumbrian and East Indies historiography over a number of years. These are the arguments: that Cumbrians retreated to the East Indies; that Company appointments were primarily through a closed set of dynastic, Anglo-Indian identified families; that East Indies encounters were driven out of the welded interests of London merchants and governmental desire to stabilise the Union and protect itself from European threats; and that participation in empire became a taken-for-granted, integral part of everyday life materially and ideologically.

Retreat

Despite occasional and fragmented references to East Indies careers, Cumbrian historiography has been largely silent on Cumbrian ventures to the East Indies and the implications of Company careers among Cumbrians. It was Edward Hughes in his history of North Country life that concluded, almost in an aside, that it was Jacobites and Non-Jurors who went into Company service.[13] Essentially, Hughes asserts that the East Indies Company was a retreat for those relegated and detached from Cumbria by political events. There is no evidence, direct or indirect, that would lead to that conclusion. Indeed, Hughes appears to be mistaken in fact as well as interpretation.

Hughes cites the passionate Jacobite Henry 'Galloper' Curwen (d.1725) of Workington in relation to the East India Company, but it was his kin, Patricius Curwen of Sella Park, who died on an East Indiaman in 1702. 'Galloper' Curwen himself died in Cumbria and his time exiled overseas was almost

---

10 Godwin, 'Rickerby: An Estate and its Owners', pp. 229, 233.
11 F. Haverfield, 'Report of the Cumberland Excavation Committee', *Transactions CWAAS*, Old Series, XIV (1897), p. 193.
12 IOR J/1/9 f.226.
13 Hughes, *North Country Life*, p. 105.

certainly in Europe.[14] Similarly, while the Catholic Musgraves were connected to East Indies, the Stricklands were not. The Musgraves' involvement in the East India Company was very long-standing. There seems little evidence that their limited involvement in the East Indies during the eighteenth century was determined by their Jacobite sympathies. Similarly, while James Grahme of Levens liquidated James II's East India Company stock after the latter's exile in France, there is no evidence of a close East India Company connection.[15] James Radcliffe lost both his life and his Derwentwater lands, and James Layburne lost his estates because of Jacobite loyalties. Neither of those families were obvious in the East Indies encounter subsequent to the 1745 Jacobite rebellion.

The idea that political and economic marginalisation associated with political and religious loyalties drove Cumbrian men to the East Indies fits with both the portrayal of a Cumbria with little hope and a gentry under stress. However, while individuals who needed assistance might be directed towards an East Indies career, they had an array of kin and friends behind them drawn from pre-existing and interlocking Cumbrian networks of gentry and middling kin, friends and business interests. That so many Cumbrian families invested their financial and human capital into East Indies ventures is evidence both of how important the East Indies was to Cumbrians and the importance of Cumbrians to the East India Company.

It is undoubtedly the case that some Cumbrians were sent to the East Indies because they irritated their family, kin and circle of friends at home. But even under those conditions, the pursuit of East Indies ventures and sojourns were not necessarily measures of retreat, failure, defeat or marginalisation by middling or gentry families. Mobilising the financial, human and social capital and patronage necessary to East India Company appointments depended on being integrated into influential Cumbrian kin and business networks. In short, those who sojourned in the East Indies were a minority of middling and gentry Cumbrians, but they were not on the periphery of the Cumbrian provincial world.

The East Indies was an integral part of Cumbria's social, political and economic life. Indeed, the anxiety around the possible detachment of sojourners from Cumbria was indicative of the central place the East Indies had in diversifying income- and wealth-generating opportunities for Cumbrian families. Fears of death, financial loss and of the potential seduction of sons, brothers, nephews and cousins by the luxury of the East were persistent themes in the correspondence of Cumbrians involved in the

---

14 W. Jackson, 'The Curwens of Workington Hall and Kindred Families', *Transactions CWAAS*, Old Series, V (1888), p. 213.

15 J. V. Beckett, 'The Finances of a Former Jacobite: James Grahme of Levens Hall', *Transactions CWAAS*, New Series, LXXXV (1985), pp. 135, 139.

East Indies. Those fears prompted a range of mitigative strategies. Letters of introduction, the provision of hospitality by Cumbrians in the way-station of London and in the East Indies, the provision of credit and financial support among Cumbrians, and the avid, gossipy correspondence which remains in the archives are all evidence of energetic attempts to simultaneously promote the opportunities of sojourners while sustaining ties to Cumbria.

Those efforts were not always effective. There were Cumbrian sojourners who became detached from Cumbria. Some simply died, although the disjuncture created by death alone should not be overstated. Even in death many remitted legacies back to Cumbria and their connections to Cumbria are carved in memorials in India, Cumbria and elsewhere in the British Isles. The connections to Cumbria of some sojourners, attracted by a lifestyle of opulence and, perhaps, independence offered by the East Indies, were clearly tenuous. Thomas Cust, Montagu Ainslie and John Bellasis were all examples. Despite claims to the contrary and despite sending his mixed-race children back to his mother and brother, there is little evidence that Thomas Cust ever had serious intentions of returning to Cumbria.

Similarly, Montagu Ainslie never showed a strong predilection for return. Nevertheless, when he did, his subsequent life in Cumbria was long and marked by his integration into and prominence in provincial life. He, like other East Indies returners, became implicated in the public life of the Cumbrian counties. Those men prominent in philanthropic causes, the expansion of Cumbria's road and rail, and clubs and societies throughout the Cumbrian counties, had been involved in the East Indies.

John Bellasis presents a variation to Ainslie's trajectory of eventual, if reluctant, return and Thomas Cust's neglect of his obligations in Cumbria. Bellasis repeatedly promised to return permanently but died in Bombay forty-five years after leaving Cumbria. He was arguably a man as much concerned with recognition as he was with wealth. Bombay offered both. But unlike Thomas Cust, Bellasis saw himself as a man with deep roots in Cumbria: he remitted monies to Cumbria; promoted marital alliances with Westmorland's urban elite; and perhaps most importantly he vociferously pursued the recognition of his family, usually referred to as Bellas, as an ancient Cumbrian family of Bellasis. He succeeded in getting the College of Arms to recognise his claims to arms in 1792. Unlike Thomas Cust, there is no evidence that John Bellasis was sucking resources out of his Cumbrian kin. He expressed disappointment when opportunities to retain family land or acquire small estates were missed, and he was vitally concerned with his and his family's reputation in Cumbria. In 1802, he requested that he be memorialised in his natal parish church.

Even those who yearned for Cumbria such as Andrew Hudleston delayed their return and John Brownrigg Bellasis admitted to what he saw as an inexplicable desire to stay in India:

It is very odd, I have a secret aversion to going home [from India] which I cannot account for.[16]

Overall, it must be concluded that East Indies ventures were not typically 'care-for-nobody' gambles undertaken by the desperate and marginal. They were measured and collective ventures. It was expected that everyone would work to minimise risks and optimise the chances of success. They required energy and a zealous commitment both in Cumbria and the East Indies. Cumbrian sojourners expressed a pronounced awareness of their provincial origins. For them, balancing risk and reward in the East Indies meant actively sustaining Cumbrian connections. Cumbrians in the East Indies were desperate not to be forgotten at home. Cumbrian sojourners exchanged information about, provided hospitality to, supported and occasionally remonstrated with fellow Cumbrians in the East Indies, even where the acquaintance was limited.

Dynastic Families

Chapter 2 set out a number of points around the long-standing and influential idea of dynastic families. It concludes that Cumbria's high rates of engagement in the East Indies were unlikely to be driven by a dynastic dynamic. That is not to suggest that none of the Cumbrian families were involved in a dynastic strategy. It is clear that a number were. However, three important findings suggest that dynastic dynamics were on the margins of the Cumbrian encounter. First, most of the kinship links between families involved in the East Indies were formed in Cumbria rather than the East Indies. Second, Cumbrian sojourners promoted their connections with their native counties. Third, if dynastic dynamics were the primary driver of the Cumbrian encounter with the East Indies, spatial pattern of natal origins would be less dispersed, concentrated both in the East Indies itself or in a small number of Cumbrian localities.

With regard to the latter, it is notable that the Dent and Wilkinson families, who intermarried and ensured their East Indies businesses were operated by a very close-knit kin group, retained a very strong Westmorland identity and presence. Rather than an Anglo-Indian dynasty, they are better seen as a Cumbrian entrepreneurial family operating in the East Indies. Entrepreneurial families operating in India included the Scottish Johnstone family and the Midlands Shaw family. Both those families have attracted attention recently as the subjects of micro-histories.[17] Both are characterised by a deep identification with home and their familial connections, rather than

---

16   John Brownrigg Bellasis's letterbook and diary, 1825, IOR Mss Eur Photo Eur 035, p. 134.

17   See respectively E. Rothschild, *The Inner Life of Empires: An Eighteenth-Century History* (Princeton, NJ, Princeton University Press, 2012) and A. Popp, *Entrepreneurial Families: Business, Marriage and Life in the Early Nineteenth Century* (London, Pickering & Chatto, 2012).

an adoption of an Anglo-Indian persona. The Cumbrian embeddedness of the Dents and Wilkinsons' East Indies ventures is indicated by their similarity to Cumbrian ventures elsewhere. The Dents and Wilkinsons undertook business management and familial practices reminiscent of the networks set up among Quakers pursuing business in North America during the eighteenth century.[18]

Primacy of London

The argument that London merchants were at the centre of the East India Company and the shape of emerging economic and political imperialism in the East Indies has already been subject to considerable criticism. Those have been set out in Chapter 1 and will not be rehearsed here. The major points in relation to Cumbria are these. Cumbrians did have influence in the Company. The Company directorate had a persistent Cumbrian presence throughout the long eighteenth century and Cumbrians were key participants in the establishment of factories and the presidencies early in the long eighteenth century. There were, too, Cumbrian parliamentarians influential in East Indies affairs who staunchly maintained their Cumbrian identity, the most important being John Robinson, Richard Atkinson and Henry Fletcher. That many resided in London should not take attention away from the way they used their influence to promote the interests of Cumbrian kin and friends.

There is an accumulating historiography suggesting an intricate interface between the provincial world, the East India Company and the East Indies. That interface was played out in Cumbrian politics as well as in social and economic life. The Cumbrian case suggests that while London was the setting for critical moments in the passage to the East Indies, it was not the dynamo of the Cumbrian encounter. Certainly, it was in London that individuals aspiring to cadetships and appointments as writers appeared for interview at the East India Company. Many Cumbrian sojourners left for the East Indies from London docks. Yet even at those moments, Cumbrians destined for the East Indies were embraced by Cumbrians. Marshall has shown that Cumbrian county societies were long-standing and active means by which London-based provincials maintained their identities and connections at home.[19] Their agency on the part of Cumbrian families sending their children to India was another mechanism for expressing and sustaining those provincial attachments.

It could be argued that some Cumbrians in London were as much sojourners in a 'foreign' world as Cumbrians in the East Indies. London

---

[18] A. J. L. Winchester, 'Ministers, Merchants and Migrants: Cumberland Friends and North America in the Eighteenth Century', *Quaker History*, 80, 2 (Fall 1991), pp. 85–99.

[19] J. D. Marshall, 'Cumberland and Westmorland Societies in London, 1734–1914', *Transactions CWAAS*, New Series, 84 (1984), pp. 239–254.

for many Cumbrians was merely a pathway to financial success and many returned to Cumbria. Examples among Cumbrians based in London but also with East Indies links include the Stephensons, the Winders, the Fawcetts, the Custs, the Dents, the Borradailes and Routledges. For many Cumbrians, London was a way-station between the provincial world and the East Indies, rather than at the centre of the East Indies encounter. In short, the Cumbrian case suggests that there were provincial drivers of imperialism in the provincial aspirations of the middling and gentry families. It reinforces the historiographical move away from treating London as the all-determining metropole, whether in the domestic, provincial or global worlds.[20]

Nationhood and Empire

There seems little evidence that Cumbrians in their engagements with the East Indies were driven, any more than the provincial world in general, by national sentiments around imperial expansion. While the government might, as McGilvary suggests, have seen East Indies patronage as a convenient way to sustain the Union, [21] there is no substantial evidence of either that desire or a nationalistic British sensibility or identity in the correspondence between East Indies-involved Cumbrians. It is not that they were disinterested in the security of the British Isles, it is simply that those anxieties were not linked to the East Indies or the notion of a Britannia. Indeed, compared to exhortations to provide hospitality, or assurances that hospitality had been provided, to Cumbrians arriving in the East Indies, references to geopolitics were few. There is no doubt that Cumbrians took opportunities presented by the East India Company's territorial acquisitions and its subsequent demand for manpower after the Battle of Plassey. But there is little indication that Cumbrians, either in Cumbria or sojourning in the East Indies, were primarily, or consciously, driven by a sense of national service.

Again, it was not because any notion of service was absent from Cumbrians' correspondence with each other. Rather, service was positioned differently. In their negotiations around emoluments and conditions around resignation and return, some Cumbrians referred to loyal service, but that was typically in

---

[20] See in particular H. V. Bowen, 'James H. Thomas, "The East India Company and the Provinces in the Eighteenth Century, vol. II: Captains, Agents, and Servants: A Gallery of East India Company Portraits"', *Economic History Review*, 61, 4 (2008), p. 1005; K. Wilson, *The Sense of the People: Politics, Culture and Imperialism in England, 1715–1785* (Cambridge, Cambridge University Press, 1998); K. Wilson (ed.), *A New Imperial History: Culture, Identity, Modernity, 1660–1840* (Cambridge, Cambridge University Press, 2004); J. H. Thomas, *The East India Company and the Provinces in the Eighteenth Century: Volume 1 Portsmouth and the East India Company 1700–1815* (Lewiston, NY, Edwin Mellen Press, 1999); J. H. Thomas, 'East India Company Agency Work in the British Isles, 1700–1800', in H. V. Bowen, M. Lincoln and N. Rigby (eds), *The Worlds of the East India Company* (Woodbridge, The Boydell Press, 2004), pp. 33–48.

[21] McGilvray, *East India Patronage and the British State*, pp. 17–20, 203–208.

relation to the Company rather than the nation. A notable exception was in Douglas's appeal for national support to deal with debts he claims arose from serving national interests at the beginning of the Opium Wars. Generally, expressions of service tended to be couched in terms of responsibilities to Cumbrian friends, kin, family and business partners. East Indies ventures were part of, rather than a disjuncture with or national overlay on, Cumbrian life.

Those who went to the East Indies, as well as their family, kin and friends, intended that there would be a return. Involvement in the East Indies and the sojourns of a substantial number of Cumbrians in the East Indies were not seen as constituting a decisive break from the provincial life. The point of the passage to India was success in Cumbria. There is little evidence in their letters that these Cumbrian middling and gentry families subordinated the risks of death, loss and disaster to some emerging imperial or national impulse.

Does that mean that Cumbrians did not recognise that they were becoming involved in an accelerating exercise of national power? The retrospective view shows us that the opportunities opening up to Cumbrians in the East Indies during the long eighteenth century were supported by, and implicated in, the development of a military fiscal state.[22] The accelerating expansion of British interests in the East and the formation of the second empire during the eighteenth century were undoubtedly fuelled by the threats presented by European powers and anxieties to cement the Union. But taking the opportunities in the East Indies generated by those dynamics does not mean that Cumbrians themselves were primarily driven by national or imperial imperatives. The motivations of Cumbrians were more prosaic, less exalted and rarely tinged by expressions of imperial zeal.

This is not to suggest that Cumbrians engaged in commercial imperialism or imperial territorial rule unconsciously. Many Cumbrians were involved in formal positions of power in the East India Company and the apparatus by which the East India Company imposed rule: the army, the civilian administration and the judiciary in the East Indies. That involvement may have since become obscured, but at the time the activities of Cumbrian sojourners in the East Indies were part of the everyday life of middling and gentry families in Cumbria. This was not a case of Seeley's or, later, Porter's notion of the acquisition of empire as a sort of 'Boy's Own' accidental accumulation of territory. Nor does the evidence suggest that Cumbrians in the long eighteenth century became implicated in empire 'at home' primarily

---

[22] For a discussion of the East India Company as a military-fiscal state, see T. Roy, 'Rethinking the Origins of British India: State Formation and Military-Fiscal Undertakings in an Eighteenth Century World Region', *London School of Economics Working Papers*, No. 142/10 (2010), pp. 3, 8–11.

as a 'taken-for-granted', mundane or unquestioned part of, as Hall and Rose characterise empire, a 'familiar and pragmatic' world.[23] On the contrary, Cumbrian ventures in the East Indies were conscious affairs, the tensions and ambivalences around which were resolved by recourse to a variety of explicitly articulated logics and considerations around the balancing of risk and reward.

For Cumbrians those logics resided primarily in their provincial world. East Indies ventures were part of a battery of adaptive strategies which included Atlantic and Mediterranean trade as well as London-based commercial activities. Those adaptive strategies emerged out of the Cumbrian gentry and middling families search for ways to break through the constraints imposed by Cumbria's biophysical limitations and the persistence of customary tenure. They reflected long-standing practices of forming intense marital and business networks between, as well as within, Cumbria's middling and gentry ranks and Cumbria's human capital advantages.

A Different Lens with New Views

Cumbria's encounter with the East Indies provides a new lens on both Cumbria's regional history and on a set of intersecting historiographies in which the eighteenth century has been pivotal in debates around change and continuity. In addition to Cumbria's regional history, those historiographies range across the mobilities and interactions of middling ranks and gentry respectively, provincial life and the evolving relations between the British Isles and the East Indies. Identifying and foregrounding the characteristics and dynamics around the close to 450 enumerated Cumbrian women and men involved in the East Indies, has illuminated various aspects of each of those historiographies.

In the context of regional history, seeing Cumbria through the lens of its encounter with the East Indies generates a very different understanding of the legacy of the long eighteenth century. It contributes to and amplifies the emerging re-visioning of Cumbria, which is leaving behind a preoccupation with Cumbria's transition from a feudal to an industrial society. That new historiography of Cumbrian development gives attention to a wider range of concerns including eighteenth-century trade, both domestic and global, innovation, education, vernacular building, the implications of customary tenure on the landscape and land distribution, the growth of tourism and resort towns. This book adds to that paradigmatic and empirical diversification.

---

23 B. Porter, *The Absent Minded Imperialists: What the British Really Thought About Empire* (Oxford, Oxford University Press, 2004), pp. 321f; J. R. Seeley, *The Expansion of England: Two Courses of Lectures* (London, MacMillan, 1914), p. 10; Hall and Rose (eds), *At Home with Empire*, p. 22.

Cumbria seen through the lens of its middling and gentry encounters with the East Indies shows a Cumbria marked by diversity and entrepreneurial drive.

Far from stultified, Cumbria was characterised by new industrial technologies and extractive industries, as well as by innovative approaches to trade. It was typified by new ways of using human capital and the development of early indicators of a nascent service sector. The comparatively high literacy evident in eighteenth-century Cumbria manifested itself in a surplus of individuals in the occupations associated with a growing service sector. Indeed, Cumbria should be seen as, not so much on the margins of the British Isles, but as a connective edge between the British Isles and its variegated global expansion.

There is no doubt of the importance of Cumbria's particular characteristics, the relative absence of aristocratic families, a gentry pressured by constraints on their returns from land, a tradition of town corporations with middling elites, significant merchant interests in overseas trade, and, despite gradual decline, the persistence of yeoman farmers. However, the very constraints often cited as the inhibiters of Cumbria's economic development arguably promoted business partnerships between middling and gentry families. The earlier 'shelling out' of some gentry families and the expansion of Cumbria's urban fabric during the eighteenth century provided emerging middling families with opportunities to formulate themselves into provincial elites in tandem with remaining gentry families. East Indies wealth provided a mechanism for those mobilities and reconstitutions.

There was a strong tendency for Cumbria's for middling and gentry families to be interlocked through kinship, their mutual attachments to place, and a willingness to partner with each other to diversify their economic opportunities. That tendency facilitated the East Indies encounter and built on experiences in Mediterranean, North American, Atlantic and Baltic trade. From the early years of the eighteenth century, Cumbrian middling and gentry families were sojourners within and outside the British Isles. They operated within a sojourning community in London, in Europe, in North America and then in the East Indies. Familiarity with sojourning as a pathway to success and early entry in the East India Company was the combination that drove the Cumbrian counties' comparatively high rates of Company appointment and licensing.

East Indies ventures were supported by the melding of middling and gentry interests. This raises one of the key issues of eighteenth- and nineteenth-century social and economic change and stability. That is, the permeability between gentry and middling ranks and the extent to which they sought to maintain distinction or pursued emulation as a ladder up the social hierarchy. The Cumbria network of kin nodes involved in the East Indies showed two seemingly contradictory tendencies. First, a tendency towards rank endogamy; and second, some significant clusters which drew together merchants and gentry. What is perhaps more important in the context of the debate around social mobility, rank permeability, distinction and emulation, was the way in which middling and gentry families were engaging in similar activities including consumption.

Even if the multiplicity of business and marital connections between Cumbrian middling and gentry families is set aside, the experience of operating in similar economic environments and conditions could be expected to generate at least some overlap in values and forms of consumption. In general, those similarities should be treated as convergence. With some rather socially unsuccessful exceptions, such as Alexander Nowell, they were not emulative. At the same time, nor were they strictly forms of distinction, although Mrs Pattinson's joy at compliments from the Fawcetts show that distinction was an important part of social interaction.[24] Those practices and values were not used to divide, but to allow the functional engagement of people from different ranks within the social hierarchy, although with similar material means and interests who were operating in shared domains – the provincial town, the county, the rural parish or the subscribed world of sojourners in the East Indies.

That interpretation is consistent with French's analysis of middle rank consumption and Vickery's claim that a higher degree of sociability, even intimacy, was evident in provincial contexts. It was an intimacy of shared experience which she and others have suggested marked the relations between lesser gentry and leading middling families.[25] This is not a view that suggests distinction was irrelevant. Rather that ideas and practices around refinement, taste and the exercise of politeness were acted on within a structured arena where respectable and respected members of separate ranks could operate together. It was a lubricant in a provincial world marked by social differentiation, but also enforced intimacy and where success was tied to the success of others. Those conditions pertained in provincial Cumbria, but they were also evident in the East Indies. They underpinned, for instance, John Bellasis's willingness and ability to place a young Thomas Cooper into the business of a fellow Cumbrian in Bombay.[26] In the notoriously precedent-bound world of the Company in its Indian settlements,[27] Bellasis was promoting the success of someone whose rank was significantly below his own in Bombay. The explanation for that largesse lies in Bellasis's and Cooper's Cumbrian connection.

---

24 Letter Mary Pattinson, Kirklinton, to Thomas Pattinson, Bombay, 31 August 1810, CAS DX 249/14iR.
25 H. R. French, *The Middle Sort of People in Provincial England, 1600–1750* (Oxford, Oxford University Press, 2007), pp. 144–145, 150–151, 174–175, 265; A. Vickery, *The Gentleman's Daughter: Women's Lives in Georgian England* (London, Yale University Press, 2003), pp. 1–30.
26 Letter John Bellasis, Bombay, to his brother Hugh Bellasis, Long Marton, 21 December 1788, CAS WDX 1641/1/1/29a.
27 P. Spear, *The Nabobs: A Study of the Social Life of the English in Eighteenth Century India* (London, Curzon Press, 1980), pp. 57–65.

As Halliday points out, there is no average or representative county or counties.[28] Nevertheless, Cumbria does appear to present a case that suggests provincial imperatives could directly drive and shape global and imperial encounters. Within the realm of provincial life and its interface with empire, the differential county rates of appointment and licensing to the East Indies evident in Figure 2.2 offers a framing for comparative studies at the provincial scale. Those rates signal some intriguing questions around the variability of county engagement. Proximity to London, the putative centre of imperial impulse, is clearly not the only, or even most, important factor. Not all the counties with apparently higher than national rates of county appointment and licences by the East India Company were coastal counties. Does that variability reflect differences in the human capital? Does it reflect differences in the way in which local gentry and middling families interact? How do those rates relate to the rates and nature of industrialisation and urban transitions?

Those questions all refocus attention on counties rather than national or British dynamics. In that regard, this book suggests, as Berry and Gregory do, that a revival of the historiographical mining of county and regional experience and identity evident four to five decades ago might be enriching.[29] In that context, this book has simultaneously filled a gap in Cumbrian historiography while opening up some tantalising prospects for future research. For those concerned with Cumbria's regional development, there are some immediately obvious and potentially fruitful strands that could be explored through the extensive and often rich in detail traces of Cumbrians' East Indies encounters.

The first is a close tracking of the flow of East Indies wealth into Cumbrian business enterprises, both in the industrial and service sectors. This would contribute to the re-visioning of Cumbria's economic change and expansion during the eighteenth century and the legacy for Cumbria's subsequent regional development. Another is comparing the drivers, dynamics and expressions of Cumbria's global engagement in the western hemisphere compared to that of the eastern hemisphere.

The existing historiography of Cumbrian involvement in the West Indies and the North American colonies suggests some commonalities as well as some contrasts between the western and eastern hemispheres. The importance of family and friends in establishing trade and influence appears to be similar in both hemispheres, although the use of religious affiliated networks seems less apparent in the East than the West. Colonial activities in both hemispheres were characterised by a tendency to establish family members

---

28 S. Halliday, 'Social Mobility, Demographic Change and the Landed Elite of County Durham, 1610–1819: An Open or Shut Case?', *Northern History*, 30 (1994), pp. 49–63.
29 H. Berry and J. Gregory (eds), *Creating and Consuming Culture in North-East England, 1660–1830* (Aldershot, Ashgate, 2004), pp. 1–4.

within colonial settlements to operate family business interests. At the same time, in comparison to the western hemisphere in which monopoly companies did not survive, the operation of the East India Company, both as commercial enterprise and as a territorial and administrative 'state', almost undoubtedly modified the expression of Cumbrian ambitions and operations in the East.

The impression from exploring the East Indies encounter and the current Cumbrian historiography around the Atlantic trade and North American ventures suggests that those encounters often engaged a similar network of families. There are, too, fragments that suggest that the Baltic trade through into Russia may have been part of the global reach of Cumbrian merchants. These, and the extent to which different circuits and the capital that flowed around them, were attached to or became disengaged from the Cumbrian provincial world would contribute to the historiographical agenda articulated by Bowen and others of exploring the 'transoceanic imperial presence', the dynamics of global movement and the development of a global world.[30]

There are also many dimensions that have been only alluded to within the limits of this book. For instance, attention has been drawn to the differing dynamics and experiences of Cumbrian women in their encounter with the East Indies, both as sojourners and as agents in Cumbria supporting sojourners in the East Indies. Those matters have been touched on but lightly, in part because tracing and categorising women implicated in Cumbrian encounters is complex empirically and conceptually. Indicative of the differences of the dynamics for women and men is the relatively small numbers of women who met the criteria for enumeration. Only twenty-three women have been enumerated compared to 421 men. This should not be interpreted as meaning that Cumbrian women were outside the Cumbrian encounter with the East Indies. They were critical actors. But their association with East Indies ventures lay less in the sojourn, although that became more frequent towards the end of the long eighteenth century, and more through providing a social as well as a personal anchor in the British Isles.

Women's experiences raise issues around the interface between place and proximity, marriage and kinship, as well as the challenge of capturing the nature of influence when women's voices are frequently absent from the record. In the Cumbrian case, many women, like the gentry Isabella Hudleston and Kitty Senhouse and the middling Dorothy Knott, Susannah Knott and Elizabeth Cust, invested in East Indies ventures by funding, promoting the interests of and mobilising resources for men sent to the East Indies. These were the women who supported nephews, sons, grandsons and great nephews. For them the importance of return lay in their husbands,

[30] H. V. Bowen, E. Mancke and J. G. Reid, 'Introduction', in H. V. Bowen, E. Mancke and J. G. Reid (eds), *Britain's Oceanic Empire: Atlantic and India Ocean Worlds, c. 1550–1850* (Cambridge, Cambridge University Press, 2015), pp. 1–11.

fathers, sons and brothers coming home. In addition to these women, a variety of other patterns of return can be discerned. There were Cumbrian women implicated in the East Indies by marriage to a sojourner actively involved in global travel but who themselves remained in the British Isles. Ann Gale, Elizabeth Hicks and Dorothy Knott were examples. Other Cumbrian women married Cumbrians when they returned from the East Indies, such as Margaret Braddyll, Elizabeth Lowry and Mary Aglionby.

Early in the eighteenth century, there were Cumbrian women, like Sarah Dodding, the wife of John Braddyll, who travelled to the East Indies with, or to meet, their husbands or fathers.[31] There were daughters born in India to Cumbrian fathers who remained in the East Indies until their adulthood or returned to the East Indies after schooling in England. Susan Cust, the mixed-race daughter of Thomas Cust was an example. Some women made multiple journeys back and forth between the East Indies and Cumbria. Some ended their lives at sea, others died in India. Some of the women involved with Cumbrian men who returned to Cumbria were not born, but died there. Maria Hardwick and Dorothy Rumbold are examples. Finally, of course, there were women connected to Cumbrian men who probably had no direct contact with Cumbria at all. The non-European women in the East Indies almost certainly fall into that category, but so too does the wife of Thomas Pearson, Sara Irwin, who was born and died in Calcutta. If tracing the trajectories of men present a challenge, evidence of women's trajectories is even more fragmentary. Despite their diversity, what is clear is that women bore many of the costs of East Indies ventures and had an interest in the pay-offs of imperial ventures.

Tracing Cumbria's mixed-race children is even more challenging than tracing women. Yet their experiences offer opportunities to explore the Cumbrian experience and broader dynamics around the interface between race, class and sex in domestic and imperial contexts. How mixed-race children were detached from their mothers, how their existence was embraced or resisted by their Cumbrian relatives, how they were treated under law, what the implications for them were when the protections, if any, of their fathers, relatives and friends had fallen away, are all significant questions. Those dynamics read to the emerging concern with the 'edges' of familial institutions: legitimacy and illegitimacy, the construction of the orphan as a social category, and relations between siblings as important nodes of continuity and change in the late eighteenth-century and into nineteenth-century Britain.[32]

---

[31] 1725–26 List of Free Merchants, Seafaring Men etc Constant and not Constant at Bombay and Factories Subordinate, IOR O/5/31 pt. 1.

[32] L. Davidoff, *Thicker than Water: Siblings and their Relations, 1780–1920* (Oxford, Oxford University Press, 2011); M. Finn, M. Lobban and J. Bourne Taylor (eds), *Legitimacy and Illegitimacy in Nineteenth Century Law, Literature and History* (Basingstoke, Palgrave Macmillan, 2010); M. Finn, 'The Barlow Bastards: Romance Comes Home from the Empire', in Finn,

There is another facet of provinciality of the East Indies encounter that has not been explored in this book but is worth noting. That is, the persistent but rarely commented upon portrayal of the Company's European settlements in India being 'provincial'. Indeed, one of the great criticisms of expatriate life in the East Indies, even in the great cities of the East India Company, Calcutta, Madras and Bombay, was its inexorable provinciality. This has often been interpreted as indicating that the sojourning communities were unsophisticated, out of step and out of touch with the fashionable London metropole and a rather boring, closed society.[33] But perhaps claims of provinciality should be taken more literally. As Mansfield shows, the structures of governance established by the East India Company closely resembled the structures established by charter among the provincial towns of England. Madras, Calcutta and Bombay, seen simultaneously by those in London as exotic and emulative of London itself, were managed in ways that would have been very familiar to the residents of eighteenth-century provincial towns.

The East India Company held to itself, like town guilds, the power to determine who might or might not operate commercially. The Company imposed conditions of trade on its own servants and on European residents in general. The mechanisms of governance favoured the elite in India just as they did in provincial towns in England. Just as powerful aristocratic figures frequently sought to dominate mayors, aldermen and council business, so too did the councils of the Company's presidencies influence appointments of mayors and aldermen in Madras, Calcutta and Bombay.[34]

As there was in English provincial towns, the population sojourning in the East Indies as well as the Company were persistently short of 'ready money' in the East Indies. Members of their small elites bickered and jealously protected their social status precedence. Just like eighteenth-century provincial towns, Madras, Calcutta and Bombay were marked by local elites indulging in the consumption and display of consumer goods.[35] Like provincial life in the British Isles, including in Cumberland, Westmorland and

Lobban and Bourne Taylor (eds), *Legitimacy and Illegitimacy in Nineteenth Century Law, Literature and History*, pp. 23–47; J. Bailey, *Parenting in England 1760–1830: Emotion, Identity and Generation* (Oxford, Oxford University Press, 2012); C. L. Nixon, *The Orphan in Eighteenth Century Law and Literature: Estate, Blood and Body* (Farnham, Ashgate, 2011).

[33] D. Kincaid, *British Social Life in India, 1608–1937* (London, Routledge & Kegan Paul, 1973), pp. 148f.

[34] T. A. Mansfield, 'Calcutta, from Fort to City: A Study of a Colonial Settlement, 1690–1750' (PhD thesis, University of Leicester, 2012), pp. 105–111.

[35] P. J. Marshall, 'The White Town of Calcutta under the Rule of the East India Company', *Modern Asian Studies*, 34, 2 (May 2000), pp. 307–331; P. J. Marshall, 'The Whites of British India, 1780–1830: A Failed Colonial Society?', *The International History Review*, 12, 1 (February 1990), pp. 26–44; N. Eaton, 'EXCESS IN THE CITY? The Consumption of Imported Prints in Colonial Calcutta, c.1780–c.1795', *Journal of Material Culture*, 8, 1 (2003), pp. 45–74.

Furness, social life in Calcutta, Madras and Bombay was organised around visiting, assembly rooms, newspapers, theatres and convivial societies, and consumption. But perhaps most importantly, many sojourners, as this book shows, were themselves provincials.

The Cumbrian experience in the East Indies reinforces, too, the importance of family and kinship to understanding economic and business behaviours. This is consistent with a range of research, perhaps most explicitly rendered in Popp's micro-history of John and Elizabeth Shaw, showing that imperatives embedded in familial relations, emotional life and interests went beyond narrowly conceived economic factors and business logics in shaping the exercise of entrepreneurship and business practice.[36] Those histories and this book highlight one of the most productive and potentially illuminating seams of empirical material; that which lies in the intersection of the global and imperial with the familial and provincial.

The experiences and dynamics highlighted in this book reinforce Tadmor's and others' renditions of the protean nature and multi-layered, amorphously bounded and fluid concepts of household, family, kin and friends.[37] The flexibility of access to what Steedman describes as the 'flotsam' of the past[38] provided in the digital world allows us to explore those layers and the connections between individuals, families, place, nation and global interactions in ways that leverage and integrate the power of three methodological approaches: quantitative and structural analysis; thematic analysis around experience, sensibility and identity; and biographical narratives that trace the contingent and complex trajectories of people's lives.

---

[36] Popp, *Entrepreneurial Families*, and R. J. Morris, *Men, Women and Property in England, 1780–1870: A Social and Economic History of Family Strategies Amongst the Leeds Middle Classes* (Cambridge, Cambridge University Press, 2005).

[37] N. Tadmor, *Family and Friends in Eighteenth Century England: Household, Kinship and Patronage* (Cambridge, Cambridge University Press, 2001).

[38] Steedman, *Dust*, p. 18.

APPENDIX A: EAST INDIES ENUMERATED CUMBRIAN MEN

Surname	1st Names	Appointed	Position	Place of Service	Dates	Natal Origins	Death or Burial	Father	Mother
Adderton	Henry	1772	Mariner Army	Bombay	1750–	Cumb.		Jeremiah Adderton	Helena Curwen
Adderton	Jeremiah	1775	Army	Madras	1754–c. 1794	Cumb.	India	Jeremiah Adderton	Helena Curwen
Adderton	Richard	1778	Army	Madras	1756–c.1781	Cumb.	Abroad	Jeremiah Adderton	Helena Curwen
Addison	Edmund	1782	Army	Bengal	1750–1784	Cumb.	India	Richard Addison	Lucy Tattersall
Addison	Eldred	1772	Writer	Calcutta	1753–1787	Cumb.	Eng.	William Thomas Addison	Isabella Curwen
Addison	Gulston	1694	Governor	Madras	1673–1709	Westm.	India	Lancelot Addison	Jane Gulston
Addison	Lancelot	1700s		Madras	c.1680–1710	Westm.	India	Lancelot Addison	Jane Gulston
Addison	Robert	1790s	Coffee grower	Java	1775–1862	Westm.	Westm.	Christopher Addison	Elizabeth
Addison	Robert	1800s	Coffee grower	Java	1790–1880	Westm.	Westm.	Robert Addison	Elizabeth Dent
Aglionby	John	1763	Mariner	East Indiaman	1748–1763	Cumb.	At sea	Henry Aglionby	Ann Musgrave
Aikenby	John	1795	Army		1777–	Cumb.		John Aikenby	
Ainslie	Montagu	1807	Writer	Bengal	1792–1884	Westm.	Lancs.	Henry Ainslie	Agnes Ford

Surname	1st Names	Appointed	Position	Place of Service	Dates	Natal Origins	Death or Burial	Father	Mother
Ainslie	William	1806	Writer	Did not go to India	1791–1810	Westm.		Henry Ainslie	Agnes Ford
Airey	Henry Cookson	1828	Army	Bengal	1810–1866	Westm.		Thomas Airey	Julia Atkinson
Allason	Charles	1798	Writer	Bengal	1779–	Cumb.		Thomas Allason	Barbara
Arm-strong	John	1799	Army	Madras	1785–	Cumb.		William Arm-strong	Bridget
Ashburner	James	1767	Factor	Bengal	1744–1774	Lancs.	India	William Ashburner	Dorothy Taylor
Ashburner	John	1757	Writer	Bombay	1741–1772	Lancs.	East Indies	William Ashburner	Dorothy Taylor
Ashburner	Luke	1803	Planter	Bombay	1772–1844	India	USA	Bombay Ashburner	Mary Sparks
Ashburner	William Bombay	1753	Factor	Poonah	1737–1793	Lancs.	India	William Ashburner	Dorothy Taylor
Ashburner	William	1794	Attorney Planter	Bombay	1769–1798	India	India	William	Mary Sparks
Ashburner	William Page	1810s	Free Merchant	Bombay	1791–1862	India	Eng.	William Ashburner	Elizabeth Cotgrave
Atkinson	Edward	1783	Writer		1766–	Westm.			
Atkinson	Michael	1782	Writer	Bengal	1763–1821	Westm.	Eng.	George Atkinson	Bridget Maughan

Surname	1st Names	Appointed	Position	Place of Service	Dates	Natal Origins	Death or Burial	Father	Mother
Atkinson	Richard	1803	Army	Bengal	1786–1830	Westm.		Mathew Atkinson	Mary Gilbanks
Atkinson	Richard	N/A	Contractor Agent Director	N/A	1738–1785	Westm.	Eng.	Matthew Atkinson	Margaret Sutton
Ballantine	Fretcheville Dykes	1799	Army	Bombay	1782–1849	Cumb.	Eng.	Lawson Dykes Ballantine	Jane
Barnett	John	1804	Mariner	East Indiaman	1785–1814	Westm.		William Barnett	Elizabeth
Barnett	William	1799	Army		1783–	Westm.		Michael Barnett	Elizabeth
Barwise	William	1760s	Army	Bengal	–c.1765	Cumb.			
Bateman	Jonathan	1807	Army	Bengal	1790–1809	Cumb.	India	William Bateman	Ann Dawson
Beck	John		Army	Bombay	–1829	Cumb.	India		
Bell	James Thomas	1829	Assistant Surgeon	East Indiaman	1804–1880	Cumb.	Eng.	James Bell	Mary Robinson
Bellasis	Daniel Hutchins	1801	Army	Bombay	1784–1836	Westm.	Eng.	John Bellasis	Ann Martha Hutchins
Bellasis	Edward	1800	Army	Bombay	1782–1842	Westm.	Eng.	John Bellasis	Ann Martha Hutchins
Bellasis	George Bridges	1804	Army	Bombay	1767–1825	Westm.	India	George Bellas	Margaret Harvey
Bellasis	George Hutchins	1801	Army	Bombay	1778–1822	Westm.	Westm.	John Bellasis	Ann Martha Hutchins

Surname	1st Names	Appointed	Position	Place of Service	Dates	Natal Origins	Death or Burial	Father	Mother
Bellasis	George Hutchins	1820s	Army	Bombay	1807–1862	Berkshire	Westm.	George Hutchins Bellasis	Charlotte Maude Ward
Bellasis	John	1763	Army	Bombay	1743–1808	Westm.	India	Joseph Bellas	Margeret Hill
Bellasis	John	1810	Army	Bombay	1792–1837		India	John Bellasis	Ann Martha Hutchins
Bellasis	John Brownrigg	1821	Army	Bombay	1806–1890	Westm.	Eng.	George Hutchins Bellasis	Charlotte Maude Ward
Bellasis	Joseph	1801	Writer	Bombay	1781–1816	Westm.	India	John Bellasis	Ann Martha Hutchins
Bellasis	Joseph Harvey	1785	Army	Bengal	1759–1799	Berkshire	India	George Bellas	Margaret Harvey
Bellasis	William	1797	Mariner	East Indiaman	–1789	Westm.	India	Hugh Bellasis	
Benn	Henry Clavering	1815	Army	Madras	1797–1817	Cumb.	India	John Benn	Elizabeth Thornton
Benn	William		Army		1767–	Cumb.	India	Anthony Benn	Margaret Spedding
Benn Walsh	John	1776	Writer	Bengal	1759–1825	Cumb.	Eng.	William Benn	Mary Nicolson
Benson	Richard	1805	Army	Bengal	1785–1858	Cumb.	Cumb.	Thomas Benson	
Benson	William	1821	Army	Bengal	1804–1848	Cumb.	India	Joseph Moffat	

Surname	1st Names	Appointed	Position	Place of Service	Dates	Natal Origins	Death or Burial	Father	Mother
Berry	John Braithwaite	1806	Army	Madras	1788–1811	Westm.	India	William Berry	Margaret
Best	John		Army	Madras	1765–1821	Cumb.	India		
Bird	Henry	1771	Writer	Bengal	1756–1771	Westm.	India	Rev James Bird	Mary Dennison
Bird	Luke	1800	Army	Bengal	1783–1802	Cumb.	India	Isaac Bird	
Birkett	Thomas	1808	Army	Bengal	1788–1836	Cumb.	India		
Blackett	Curtis	1758	Army						
Boak	William	1758	Maritime	East Indiaman	1740–1764	Cumb.		Thomas Boak	
Borradaile	Alfred	1820s	Army	Madras	1804–1861		India	William Borradaile	Ann Delapierre
Borradaile	Harry	1819	Writer	Bombay	1800–1876		Eng.	Henry Borradaile	Ann Fletcher
Borradaile	Richardson	1780s	Maritime	East Indiaman	1795–1811	Cumb.	China	Richardson Borradaile	Elizabeth Cotton
Borradaile	Richardson	N/A	Ship owner Insurer, Director of East India Dock Co.	N/A	1762–1835	Cumb.	Eng.	John Borradaile	Mary Richardson
Borradaile	Thomas	1808	Mariner	East Indiaman	1793–1822	London	At sea	William Borradaile	Ann Delapierre
Borradaile	William	N/A	East India ship owner	N/A	1750–1830	Cumb.		John Borradaile	Mary Richardson

Surname	1st Names	Appointed	Position	Place of Service	Dates	Natal Origins	Death or Burial	Father	Mother
Borradaile	John	1767	Mariner	East Indiaman	1754–1782	Cumb.	India	John Borradaile	Mary Richard-son
Borradaile	Joseph	1780s	Mariner	East Indiaman	1767–1783	Cumb.	India	John Borradaile	Mary Richard-son
Boustead	John	1810	Army	Ceylon	1784–1861	Cumb.	Eng.	Thomas Boustead	Mary Pears
Bowness	George	1784	Army	Madras	1762–1833	Westm.	Eng.		
Bowser	Thomas	1771	Army	Madras	1749–1833	Westm.	Eng.	John Bowser	Margaret Hutton
Braddyll	Dodding	1728	Merchant		1689–1748	Lancs.	Eng.	John Braddyll	Sarah Dodding
Braddyll	John	1699	Mariner	East Indiaman	1657–1727	Lancs.	Lancs.	Thomas Braddyll	Jane Rishton
Braddyll	John	1720s	Merchant	Possibly Surat Bombay	1695–1753	Lancs.	Eng.	John Braddyll	Sarah Dodding
Braddyll	Roger	1684	Factor Agent	Bengal Madras	–1723	Lancs.		Edward Braddyll	Mary Smith
Braddyll	Thomas	1710s	Writer	Calcutta	1691–1747	Lancs.	Eng.	John Braddyll	Sarah Dodding
Briscoe	C or E	1780	Army	Bengal	1780		India	Horton Brisco	Millicent Jane Banks
Briscoe	Horton	1763	Army	Bengal	1741–1802	Cumb.	India	Rev John Briscoe	Catherine Hylton
Briscoe	John	1778	Army	Bengal	1761–1779	Cumb.	India	Musgrave Brisco	Mary Dyne

Surname	1st Names	Appointed	Position	Place of Service	Dates	Natal Origins	Death or Burial	Father	Mother
Briscoe	John	1768	Writer	Bengal	1739–1805	Cumb.		Rev John Briscoe	Catherine Hylton
Briscoe	John Jessop	1780s	Army	Bengal	1765–1792	Bengal	India	Horton Brisco	Mary Howett
Briscoe	William Musgrave	1764	Army	Bengal	1745–1765	Cumb.	India	Rev John Briscoe	Catherine Hylton
Bristow	John Charles	1800s	Writer	Bengal	1784–1856	Westm.	Westm.	John Bristow	Emilia Wrang-ham
Brougham	Peter	1750s	Army		1733–	Cumb.		Thomas Brougham	
Brougham	Thomas	1780	Army	Bengal	1762–1819	Cumb.	Scotland	Peter Brougham	Matilda Wybergh
Brown	Abraham	1754	Writer		1735–	Cumb.		William Brown	Mary
Browne	William	1770s	Army	Bombay	1756–1805	Cumb.	Cumb.	Henry Browne	
Buchanan	G W		Army						
Burnyeat	Philip	1770s	Mariner	East Indiaman	1759–1796	Cumb.	At sea	Thomas Burnyeat	Mary
Calvert	Robert	1806	Army	Madras	1785–1824	Cumb.	India	Thomas Calvert	Jane Nixon
Christian	Edward	1806	Haileybury	N/A	1758–1823	Cumb.	Eng.	Charles Christian	Anne Dixon
Christian	Edward	1746	Army	Madras	1725–1758	Cumb.	Eng.	John Christian	Bridget Senhouse

Surname	1st Names	Appointed	Position	Place of Service	Dates	Natal Origins	Death or Burial	Father	Mother
Church	Charles	1816	Chaplain	Madras	1785–1822	Cumb.	At sea	Charles Church	
Clerk	Frederick Joseph	1823	Army	Madras	1805–1873	Somerset	Eng.	Thomas Clerk	Dorothy Taylor
Clerk	Henry	1819	Army	Bengal	1803–1838	Somerset	India	Thomas Clerk	Dorothy Taylor
Clerk	Robert	1816	Writer	Madras	1798–1873	Bucks.	Eng.	Thomas Clerk	Dorothy Taylor
Clerk	Thomas	1813	Writer	Bengal	1796–1820	Bucks.	At sea	Thomas Clerk	Dorothy Taylor
Cobbe	William Lowther	1800s	Army	Madras	1783–	Cumb.	India	Rev Charles Cobbe	
Cookson	Thomas	1773	Writer		1757–1775	Cumb.		John Cookson	Elizabeth Lutwidge
Cooper	James Lowther	1790s	Mariner	East Indiaman	1774–1796	Cumb.	At sea	Major Cooper	
Cooper	Myles	1790s	Mariner	East Indiaman	1778–1802	Cumb.	India	Major Cooper	
Cooper	Thomas	1788	Army Surgeon	Bombay		Cumb.			
Cragg	Thomas	1823	Army	Madras	1800–1849	Westm.	India	John Cragg	
Crosby	James Ainsley	181Cs	Army	Bombay	1798–1831	Westm.	India	Joseph Crosby	Ann
Crosthwaite	Peter	1758	Mariner	Bombay	1735–1808	Westm.	Cumb.	Robert Crosthwaite	

Surname	1st Names	Appointed	Position	Place of Service	Dates	Natal Origins	Death or Burial	Father	Mother
Crozier	Robert				–1836	Cumb.	India		
Cumming	John	1775	Mariner	East Indiaman	1759–	Westm.			
Curwen	Patricius	1702	Mariner	East Indiaman	1688–1702	Cumb.	At sea	Darcy Curwen	Isabel Lawson
Cust	Charles	1800s	Mariner Army		c.1783–	India		Thomas Cust	Noor Begum Bibby
Cust	Richard	1800s	Army		1784–1830	India	Lancs.	Thomas Cust	Maria
Cust	Thomas	1813	Army		1793–	India	Australia	Thomas Cust	Baharrie Connum
Cust	William	N/A	N/A		c.1788–1797	India	Cumb.	Thomas Cust	Baharrie Connum
Cust	Thomas	1765	Army		1752–1795	Cumb.	India	Thomas Cust	Elizabeth Cooke
Dacre	Charles	1803	Army	Bengal	1786–1823	Cumb.	India	William Dacre	Elizabeth Wilkinson
Dacre	Joseph	1802	Writer	Madras	1785–1828	Cumb.	India	William Dacre	Elizabeth Wilkinson
Dalston	Fletcher	1783	Army	Bengal	1768–1834	Cumb.	France	George Dalston	Hannah
Dalston	John		Marine	Madras	1724–c. 1787	Westm.	Ceylon	William Dalston	Bridget Fetherston-haugh
de Vitre	James Denis	1808	Writer	Bombay	1782–1875	Cumb.	Eng.	John Baptiste de Vitre	Bridget Fawcett

Surname	1st Names	Appointed	Position	Place of Service	Dates	Natal Origins	Death or Burial	Father	Mother
de Vitre	Matthew Theodosius		Free merchant	Bombay	1794–1870	Cumb.	Eng.	John Baptiste de Vitre	Bridget Fawcett
de Whelpdale	John		Army		1760–1844	Cumb.	Cumb.	John Richardson	Elizabeth Whelpdale
Deane	Charles	1754	Mariner	East Indiaman	1732–1787	Westm.	Westm.	Joseph Deane	
Dent	John	1810s	Writer	Madras	1795–1815	Westm.		William Dent	Jane Wilkinson
Dent	Lancelot	1820s	Free merchant	Canton	1799–1853	Westm.	Westm.	William Dent	Jane Wilkinson
Dent	Robert	1810s	Super-cargo	Bombay	1793–1835	Westm.	Eng.	William Dent	Jane Wilkinson
Dent	Robert	N/A	Ship owner Banker	N/A	1731–1805	Westm.	Eng.	John Dent	Eleanor Teasdale
Dent	Thomas	1810s	Merchant		1796–1872	Westm.	Eng.	William Dent	Jane Wilkinson
Dent	Wilkinson	1820s	Merchant		1800–1886	Westm.	Westm.	William Dent	Jane Wilkinson
Dent	William	1815	Writer		1798–1877	Westm.	Eng.	William Dent	Jane Wilkinson
Dent	William	1780s	Free merchant		1762–1801	Westm.	Westm.		
Dent	William	N/A	Ship owner	N/A	1740–1823	Westm.	Eng.	John Dent	Eleanor Teasdale

Surname	1st Names	Appointed	Position	Place of Service	Dates	Natal Origins	Death or Burial	Father	Mother
Denton	Charles	1820s	Army	Bombay	1802–1844	Cumb.	India	Isaac Denton	
Dixon	Henry	1824	Army	Madras	1803–1825	Cumb.		Henry Dixon	Diana Whelpdale
Dixon	Joseph	1770	Writer		1745–	Cumb.		Joseph Dixon	
Dobinson	Thomas		Mariner	Bombay	–1802	Cumb.	India	William Dobinson	Julian Curwen
Dobinson	William	1783	Army	Bombay	1766–1789	Cumb.	India	William Dobinson	Julian Curwen
Docker	Joseph	1829	Surgeon		1802–1884	London	Australia	Robert Docker	Eliza Perry
Douglas	Joseph Abraham	1810s	Mariner	East Indiaman	1797–1866	Cumb.	Surrey	Joseph Douglas	Ann Leggat
Douglas	William Douglas	1770	Writer	Bengal	1749–1902	Cumb.		Archibald Douglas	Elizabeth Burchard
Dowell	William	1780s	Mariner	East Indiaman	1774–1828	Cumb.	Eng.		
Drinkel	Francis	1765	Writer	Bengal	1741–1772	Westm.	India	Francis Drinkel	Frances Wilson
Ecroyd	Richard	1761	Surgeon	Bengal	1730–1765	Westm.	India	John Ecroyd	Martha Smith
Ecroyd	Richard		Merchant. Possibly a planter.	Bengal	1766–1797	India	India	Richard Ecroyd	Maria Saunier

Surname	1st Names	Appointed	Position	Place of Service	Dates	Natal Origins	Death or Burial	Father	Mother
Edmunds	Thomas	1827	Army	Bombay	1809–1840	Lancs.	India	John Edmunds	Mary
Ewart	David	1818	Army	Bengal	1803–1880	Cumb.	Scotland	John Ewart	Isabella Hodgson
Ewart	William	1816	Army	Bengal	1800–1842	Cumb.	India	John Ewart	Isabella Hodgson
Falcon	Michael	1790s	Mariner	East Indiaman	1784–1858	Cumb.	Cumb.	Michael Falcon	Ann Fawcett
Fallowfield	Jonathan	1800s	Surgeon	Bengal	1780–1860	Cumb.	Cumb.	John Fallowfield	Ann Dawson
Fallowfield	Thomas	1780	Mariner	East Indiaman	1755–1796	Cumb.	India		
Farish	James	1806	Writer	Bombay	1791–1873	Cambridge	Eng.	James Farrish	Dorothy Fawcett
Farrer	Henry	1810s	Mariner	East Indiaman	1798–1853	Cumb.	Cumb.	Henry Farrer	Jane Bennell
Farrer	Frederick	1768	Writer	Bengal				James Farrer	Mary Lyddal
Farrer	Joseph Liddell	1768	Army		1749–			James Farrer	Mary Lyddal
Farrer	Thomas	1760s			–1777		India	James Farrer	Mary Lyddal
Farrer	Henry	1760s	Mariner	East Indiaman	1747–1800	Yorkshire	St Helena	James Farrer	Mary Lyddal

Surname	1st Names	Appointed	Position	Place of Service	Dates	Natal Origins	Death or Burial	Father	Mother
Fawcett	Edward Gordon	1823	Writer	Bombay	1807–1871	Eng.	Cumb.	Henry Fawcett	Helen Hutchins Bellasis
Fawcett	Henry	1782	Writer Merchant Accountant-general	Bombay	1762–1816	Cumb.	Eng.	James Fawcett	Agnes Stephenson
Fawcett	Henry	1822	Army	Bombay	1798–1845	India	Cumb.	Henry Fawcett	Helen Hutchins Bellasis
Fawcett	James	1820s	Writer	Bombay	1800–1831	London	Eng.	Henry Fawcett	Helen Hutchins Bellasis
Fayrer	Robert	1816	Free mariner	India	1788–1869	Lancs.	France	Jospeh Fayrer	Bridget Dickinson
Fell	James	1806	Army		1789–1809	Lancs.	At sea	William Fell	Martha Irton
Fell	William	1820s	Army India Navy Clerk	Bombay	1813–1856	Cumb.	Cumb.	William Fell	Mary Bowes
Fetherston-haugh	Charles	1823	Warehouse-man	N/A	1762–1839	Cumb.	Cumb.	Charles Smalwood	Joyce Fetherston-haugh
Fisher	Thomas	1765	Mariner	East Indies Marine	c. 1743–1820		Cumb.		
Fleming	Michael	1815	Private Trader	Madras	–1816	Cumb.	India	Roger Fleming	Marian Isabella Hicks

Surname	1st Names	Appointed	Position	Place of Service	Dates	Natal Origins	Death or Burial	Father	Mother
Fleming	Peter Joseph	1819	Army	Bengal	1802–1833	Westm.	India	Rev John Fleming	Jane Taylor
Fletcher	Henry	1740s	Mariner	East Indiaman	1727–1807	Cumb.	Eng.	John Fletcher	Isabella Senhouse
Fletcher	John	1740s			–1748	Cumb.	India	John Fletcher	Isabella Senhouse
Fletcher	Lowther	1740w	Mariner		1726–1756	Cumb.	At sea	John Fletcher	Isabella Senhouse
French	Patrick Theodore	1821	Army	Bombay	1804–1890	Cumb.	Eng.	Anthony French	
Frith	Edward	1754	Army	Madras	1704–1769	Cumb.	Eng.		
Gaitskell	James Gandy	1829	Army	Bengal	1813–1885	Surrey	Eng.	Henry Gaitskell	Elizabeth Gandy
Gaitskell	John Frederick	1828	Army Writer	Bengal	1811–1833	Surrey	India	Henry Gaitskell	Elizabeth Gandy
Gale	Curwen	1829	Army	Bengal	1800–1849	Surrey	India	John Gale	Eleanor Ethelstone
Gale	Humphrey Senhouse	1808	Army	Madras	1793–1818	Cumb.	India	Gustavus Gale	Elizabeth Bas
Gale	John Littledale	1803	Army	Bengal	1783–1832	London	India	John Gale	Catherine Littledale
Gale	Thomas	1770s	Mariner	East Indiaman	1753–1778	Cumb.	India	John Gale	Ann Hartley
Gale	William Senhouse	1817	Free mariner	Bengal	1796–1837	Cumb.	Cumb.	Gustavus Gale	Elizabeth Bas

Surname	1st Names	Appointed	Position	Place of Service	Dates	Natal Origins	Death or Burial	Father	Mother
Gawith	William	1760s	Army	Bengal	1744–1798	Lancs.	Lancs.		
Gibson	Thomas	1820s	Army	East Indiaman	1793–1843	Cumb.	India		
Gilpin	Richard	1814	Surgeon						
Gilpin	Martin	1760s	Army	Bengal	1743–1824	Cumb.	Cumb.		
Goodenough	Robert Henry	1824	Army	Bombay	1805–1847	Oxfordshire	Cumb.		
Golding	John	1783	Mariner	East Indiaman	1763–	Cumb.			
Graham	John Brisco			Bengal	1766–	Cumb.		William Graham	Dorothy
Graham	George	1824	Maritime Assist Surgeon	East Indiaman	1801–1838	Westm.	Cumb.	William Graham	Frances Graham
Graham	Charles Henry	1818	Army	Madras	1802–1824	Cumb.	India	James Graham	Harriet Simpson
Graham	Graham James	1820s	Army	Bombay	1805–1831	Westm.	India	James Graham	Harriet Simpson
Graham	James	1780	Writer	Bengal	1747–1820	Cumb.	Cumb.	William Graham	Sarah
Graham	James Richard	1817	Army	Bengal	1800–1830	Westm.	India	James Graham	Harriet Simpson
Graham	William	1808	Army	Madras	1790–1823	Westm.	India	William Graham	Mary
Graves	Richard			Madras	–c. 1780		India		

Surname	1st Names	Appointed	Position	Place of Service	Dates	Natal Origins	Death or Burial	Father	Mother
Haistwell	Edward	1700s	Ship owner	N/A	1658–1709	Westm.	Eng.	Thomas Haistwell	
Hall	Grayson	1802	Assistant Surgeon	Bengal	1780–1811	Cumb.	India	Joseph Hall	Jane
Hall	Henry Humphrey Senhouse	1790s	Writer	Madras	1769–1820	Cumb.	Cumb.	Joseph Hall	Anne Drury
Hall	William	1810s	Army	Madras	1787–1827	Cumb.	India	Matthew Hall	Jane Singleton
Hall		1770s	Army	Bombay	1756–1791	Cumb.	India	Joseph Hall	Anne Drury
Hamilton	Anthony	1778	Army	Bengal	1752–1830	Cumb.	Cumb.	Isaah Hamilton	Frances Langton
Hammond	John	1815	Army Surgeon		1787–1822	Cumb.	St Helena	Alexander Johnston	
Hardisty	William		Army	Ceylon	1804–1846	Cumb.	India	Jonas Blakey Hardisty	Sarah Dover
Harriman	Edward	1770s	Mariner	East Indiaman	1756–1828	Cumb.	Eng.	Edward Harriman	
Harris	Michael Thomas	1799	Writer	Madras	1783–1824	Cumb.	India	George Harris	Ann Carteret Dixon
Harrison	Henry	1790s	Mariner	East Indiaman	1769–	Cumb.			
Harrison	Joseph	1820s	Mariner	East Indiaman	1811–1829	Cumb.	India	John Harrison	Betty
Harrison	Matthew	1810s	Merchant Agent	Bengal	1790–1827	Cumb.	India		

Surname	1st Names	Appointed	Position	Place of Service	Dates	Natal Origins	Death or Burial	Father	Mother
Harrison	Robert Orfeur	1799	Army	Bengal	1782–1804	Westm.	India	Thomas Harrison	Mary
Hartley	John Charles	1828	Army	Bombay	1808–1863	Cumb.	Eng.	Samuel Richard Hartley	Dorothy Fleming
Hasell	John	1750s	Mariner	Bombay	1740–1781	Cumb.	India	Edward Hasell	Julia Musgrave
Hender-son	Robert	1770s	Mariner	East Indiaman	1756–1783	Cumb.		Thomas Henderson	
Heward	Simon	1796	Army	Madras	1768–1846	Cumb.	Cumb.	Robert Heward	Elizabeth Scaife
Hewatson	John Wilson	1796	Army		1777–	Cumb.		Joseph Hewatson	Margeret
Hindson	John	1820s	Army	Bengal	1802–1826	Cumb.	India	John Hindson	
Hodgson	George	1780	Writer	Bengal	1751–1780	Cumb.	India	Richard Hodgson	Mary Clark
Hodgson	James	1781	Army	Bengal	1764–1825	Cumb.	Cumb.	Richard Hodgson	Mary Clark
Hodgson	James Denis	1783	Writer	Bombay	1760–1804	Cumb.	India	Thomas Hodgson	Ann
Hodgson	John	1808	Army Surgeon	Bengal	1786–1814	Cumb.	Java	John Hodgson	Esther Simpson
Hodgson	Richard	1781	Army	Bengal	1760–1833	Cumb.	Cumb.	Thomas Hodgson	

Surname	1st Names	Appointed	Position	Place of Service	Dates	Natal Origins	Death or Burial	Father	Mother
Hodgson	Samuel Irton	1802	Army	Madras	1784–1836	Lancs.	Lancs.	Matthew Hodgson	Frances Irton
Hodgson	William	1770s			1745–1775	Cumb.	India	Richard Hodgson	Mary Clark
Holme	John	1731	Merchant	Bengal	1702–1769	Cumb.	India	John Holme	Catherine Brisco
Holme	John	1759 and 1762	Writer	Bengal	1738–1779	Cumb.	India	John Holme	
Holmes	John		Army	Bombay				George Holmes	Sophia Hamilton
Holmes	George	1779	Army	Bombay	1764–1816	Cumb.	Eng.		
Huddart	Johnson	1786	Mariner	East Indiaman	1770–1795	Cumb.	Italy	Joseph Huddart	Elizabeth Johnston
Huddart	Joseph	1771	Mariner	East Indiaman	1741–1816	Cumb.	Eng.	Huddart	
Huddart	William	1780s	Mariner	East Indiaman	1762–1787	Cumb.	China	Joseph Huddart	Elizabeth Johnston
Hudleston	William	180Cs	Writer		1793–1855	Cumb.	Eng.	John Hudleston	Honoria Marshall
Hudleston	Andrew Fleming	1812	Writer		1795–1861	Cumb.	Eng.	Andrew Hudleston	Elizabeth Fleming
Hudleston	John	1760s	Writer Director	Madras	1749–1835	Cumb.	Cumb.	William Hudleston	Mary Burland
Hudleston	John	1800s	Writer	Madras	1789–1823	Bucks.		John Hudleston	Honoria Marshall

Surname	1st Names	Appointed	Position	Place of Service	Dates	Natal Origins	Death or Burial	Father	Mother
Hudleston	Josiah Andrew	1818	Writer	Madras	1799–1865	Berkshire		John Hudleston	Honoria Marshall
Hudleston	Robert Burland	1819	Writer	China	1801–1877	Berkshire	Eng.	John Hudleston	Honoria Marshall
Hudson	William			Bombay					
Hughes	George Cumb.	1807	Army	Madras	1807–1877	Cumb.	Westm.	John Cumberland Hughes	Elizabeth Stanley
Hutton	George	1828	Army	Madras	1808–1837	Westm.	India	William Hutton	Catherine Pedder
Ireland	Joseph		Army	Bombay	1743–	Cumb.			
Irton	Samuel	1778	Army	Madras	1763–1813	Cumb.	Lancs.	Samuel Irton	Frances Tubman
Irwin	John		Army		–1824	Cumb.		Thomas Irwin	
Jackson	Thomas	1810s	Army	Madras	1788–1822	Westm.	India	Thomas Jackson	Hannah
James	John Irving	1807	Army	Madras	1793–1826	Cumb.	East Indies	John James	Mary Bate
James	Peter	1822	Mariner	East Indiaman	1798–1829	Cumb.	Cumb.	John James	Mary Bate
Janson	John	1807	Army	Bengal	1792–1819	Cumb.	Cumb.	John Janson	Mary
Johnson	John	1750s	Writer		1742–1800	Cumb.	Cumb.	William Johnson	
Johnson	John				1781–	India		John Johnson	Native woman

Surname	1st Names	Appointed	Position	Place of Service	Dates	Natal Origins	Death or Burial	Father	Mother
Johnston	Joseph		Mariner	East Indiaman	1784–1826	Cumb.	India	Andrew Johnston	
Johnston	Robert	1828	Army Veterinary Surgeon			Ireland	Cumb.	Alexander Johnston	Ann Hunter
Jones (Skelton)	Arnoldus Jones	1767	Army	Bengal	1751–1793		Cumb.	James Jones	Jemima Tullekens
Kendall	Harry	1778	Mariner	East Indiaman	1759–	Lancs.			
Kendall	William	1801	Army	Bombay	1785–	Westm.		Richard Kendall	Elizabeth
Kenmal	William	1805	Mariner	East Indiaman	1785–	Lancs.			
Kinsey	Thomas	1799	Army	Madras	1783–1805	Westm.		Charles Kinsey	Elizabeth Rudd
Knott	George	1762	Army	Bengal	1744–1783	Westm.	Lancs.	Michael Knott	Susannah Fleming
Knott	John	1770s	Writer	Bengal	–1779		India		
Langhorne	Joshua	1780s	Mariner	Easr Indiaman	1768–c.1798	Westm.	At sea	William Lang-horne	Elizabeth
Laverock	John	1753	Army	Madras	1726–1780	Cumb.	Cumb.	John Laverock	Frances Eaglesfield
Law	Ewan	1763	Writer	Bengal	1747–1829	Cumb.	Eng.	Edmund Law	Mary Christian

Surname	1st Names	Appointed	Position	Place of Service	Dates	Natal Origins	Death or Burial	Father	Mother
Law	Ewan		Writer	Bengal		India	India	Ewan Law	Henrietta Sarah Markham
Law	George Ewan	1812	Writer	Bengal	1796–1820	London	India	Ewan Law	Henrietta Sarah Markham
Law	Thomas	1773	Writer	Bengal	1756–1834	Cumb.	USA	Edmund Law	Mary Christian
Leeson	William Frederick		Army	Bombay		Cumb.		Robert Leeson	
Lightfoot	William	1788	Mariner	East Indiaman	1761–1800	Cumb.		George Lightfoot (Probably)	
Lonsdale	John	1764	Army	Bombay	1737–1802	Westm.		John Lonsdale	Ann Bird
Lonsdale	Mark	1808	Army		1792–1823	Cumb.	Westm.		
Losh	John Joseph	1824	Army	Madras	1806–1862	Nor-thumber-land	Cumb.	James Losh	Cecelia Baldwin
Lowry	Richard	1828	Army	Bengal	1808–1842	Cumb.	East Indies	Richard Lowry	Jane Wilson
Lowther	James	1802	Army Writer	Madras then Bengal	1783–1815	London	India	James Lowther	Mary Codrington
Lowther	Robert	1808	Writer	Bengal	1790–1879	London	Eng.	James Lowther	Mary Codrington

Surname	1st Names	Appointed	Position	Place of Service	Dates	Natal Origins	Death or Burial	Father	Mother
Lowther	William	1803	Writer	Bengal	1782–1833	London	India	James Lowther	Mary Codring-ton
Lushing-ton	James Law	1796	Army	Madras	c.1780–1859	Kent	Eng.	James Stephen Lushington	Mary Christian
Lutwidge	Skivington	1790s	Army	Madras	1779–1854	Lancs.	Eng.	Henry Lutwidge	Jane Molyneax
Moorhouse	Jonathan	1799	Army	Madras	1782–1823	Westm.	India	Jonathan Moor-house	Barbara Stockdale
Morland	Brisco	1790s	Army	Bombay	1774–1804	Westm.	At sea	Jacob Morland	Dorothy Brisco
Morland	Jacob	1790s	Army	Bombay	1770–1800	Westm.	India	Jacob Morland	Dorothy Brisco
Mounsey	George Stephenson	1781	Cadet	Bengal	1757–1838	Cumb.	Cumb.	George Mounsey	Margaret Stephen-son
Musgrave	Thomas	1787	Army	Bengal	1738–1812	Cumb.	Eng.	Richard Musgrave	Ann Hylton
Myers	Thomas	1781	Army Writer	Bengal	1764–1835	Westm.	Eng.	Thomas Myers	Anne Wordsworth
Nicolson	Edward	1820s	Planter	Bengal	1808–1832	Cumb.	India	William Nicolson	
Nicolson	Isaac	1807	Army	Madras	1787–	Cumb.		William Nicolson	
Nicolson	John				1808–1826	Cumb.	At sea		

Surname	1st Names	Appointed	Position	Place of Service	Dates	Natal Origins	Death or Burial	Father	Mother
Nowell	Alexander	1783	Army	Bengal	1761–1842	Lancs.	Westm.	Ralph Nowell	Sarah Whitaker
Olive	George	1820	Army	Bombay	1798–1826	Westm.	Wales	John Olive	Sarah Hollin Grove
Parkin	Hugh	1770s	Mariner	East Indiaman	1753–1838	Westm.	Westm.	James Parkin	Philis Robinson
Parkins	Joseph Wilfred	1787	Merchant	Calcutta	1770–1840	Cumb.	USA	Chris Parkins	Ann Barnfather
Pattenson	Charles	1826	Army	Bengal	1805–1868	India	India	Charles Pattenson	Eliza Harris
Pattenson	Charles	1798	Writer	Bengal	1776–1831	Cumb.	India	Thomas Pattenson	Barbara Grainger
Pattenson	John Edward	1795	Writer	Bengal	1774–1817	Cumb.	india	Thomas Pattenson	Barbara Grainger
Pattenson	Thomas	1770	Army	Bengal	1747–1811	Cumb.	Cumb.	Lancelot Pattenson	Margaret Orfeur
Pattenson	Thomas Francis	1827	Army	Bengal	1811–1842	Dorset	India	Charles Pattenson	Eliza Harris
Pattinson	Thomas George	1806	Army	Bombay	1788–1818	Cumb.	India	Thomas Pattinson	Mary Story
Pearson	Edward	1801	Army	Bombay	1783–1833	Cumb.	India	John Pearson	Mary
Pearson	John	1799	Army		1781–	Westm.		Thomas Pearson	Nancy
Pearson	Richard	1750	Mariner	East Indiaman	1731–1806	Westm.	London	Richard Pearson	Hannah

Surname	1st Names	Appointed	Position	Place of Service	Dates	Natal Origins	Death or Burial	Father	Mother
Pearson	Henry Shepherd		Civil	Bombay	1775–1840	Kent	France	Richard Pearson	Margaret Harrison
Pearson	Richard Harrison	1780s	Mariner	East Indiaman	1765–1838	Westm.	Eng.	Richard Pearson	Margaret Harrison
Pearson	Thomas	1761	Army	Bengal	1740–1781	Westm.	India	Henry Pearson	Mary
Peill	William	1795	Mariner Free merchant	East Indiaman	1770–1825	Cumb.	India	Peter Piell	Elizabeth
Pennington	Edward	1772	Army	Bengal	1750–1804	Westm.	Lancs.	Edward Pennington	Isabel
Pennington	Henry	1778	Army	Bengal	1761–1831	Westm.	India	Edward Pennington	Ellinor Stephenson
Pennington	James	1778	Army	Bengal	1760–1798	Westm.	Java	Edward Pennington	Ellinor Stephenson
Pennington	James Masterson		Army		1786–1862	Westm.	Eng.	James Pennington	
Pennington	John		Army		1793–1833	Westm.	India	James Pennington	
Ponsonby	Willliam Browne	c. 1828	Army	Bombay	1811–1855	Cumb.	France	John Ponsonby	Elizabeth Browne
Pratt	John Backhouse	1803	Army	Bengal	1784–1837	Durham	Eng.	John Pratt	Mary Backhouse
Preston	George	1805	Army	Bengal	1789–1822	Westm.	India	William Stephenson Preston	Sarah Todd

Surname	1st Names	Appointed	Position	Place of Service	Dates	Natal Origins	Death or Burial	Father	Mother
Preston	William	1806	Army		1787–	Cumb.		John Stephen-son Preston	Bella Garnett
Richardson	John Lowry	1800s	Army		1789–	Cumb.		William Richardson	Elizabeth Lowry
Richardson	William	1776	Writer		1758–1840	Cumb.	Cumb.	John Richardson	Jane
Richardson	William		Tailor	East Indiaman	–1753	Cumb.			
Richardson	William		Army	Bengal	–c.1812			William Richard-son	
Rigg	Jonathan	1820s	Planter	Java	1809–	Yorkshire		Hugh Rigg	Maria Addison
Rigg	Jonathan	1820s	Planter	Java	1810–	Westm.		Thomas Rigg	Anne Thwaites
Ritson	John	1815	Army		1792–1826	Cumb.	East Indies	Thomas Ritson	Elizabeth Ismay
Ritson	Edward	1765	Writer		1747–	Cumb.		Joseph Ritson	Mary Jefferson
Robinson	Anthony	1780	Army	Bengal	1761–	Westm.		Daniel Robinson	Mary Hilton
Robinson	Christopher	1776	Army	Bengal	1757–1809	Westm.	Cumb.	Daniel Robinson	Mary Hilton
Robinson	John		Deputy Secretary Treasury						
Robinson	John	N/A		N/A	1727–1802	Westm.	Eng.	Charles Robinson	Hannah Deane

Surname	1st Names	Appointed	Position	Place of Service	Dates	Natal Origins	Death or Burial	Father	Mother
Robson	Robert	1796	Mariner	East Indiaman	1768–	Cumb.		John Robson	Jane Heward
Romney	James	1770s	Army	Bombay	c.1749–1807	Lancs.	Eng.	John Romney	Ann Wordsworth
Roper	William	1807	Army		1791–	Lancs.		William Roper	
Routledge	John	1783	Writer	Bengal	1763–1811	Cumb.	Cumb.	Henry Routledge	
Routledge	John	1751	Surgeon	East Indiaman	1722–1798	Cumb.	Eng.	John Routledge	
Routledge	John		Army		–1805	Cumb.	East Indies	Andrew Routledge	
Salkeld	Joseph Carleton	1825	Army	Bengal	1810–1886	Cumb.	Eng.	Joseph Salkeld	Margaret Wiseman
Salkeld	Thomas	1780	Army	Bengal	1760–1820	Cumb.	Westm.	Joseph Salkeld	
Salmond	Francis	1790s	Madras Marine	Madras	1770–1823	Cumb.	Westm.	William Salmond	Jane Hasell
Salmond	Francis Charles	1826	Writer	Penang	1809–1827	Sumatra	East Indies	Francis Salmond	Anne Salmond
Salmond	James Hanson	1782	Army	Bengal	1766–1837	Westm.	Eng.	William Salmond	Jane Hasell
Salmond	James William	1823	Writer	Penang	1807–1848	Sumatra	East Indies	James Hanson Salmond	Louisa Scott

Surname	1st Names	Appointed	Position	Place of Service	Dates	Natal Origins	Death or Burial	Father	Mother
Sandys	Thomas	1800s	Mariner	East Indiaman	1792–1856	Lancs.	Eng.	Myles Sandys	Elizabeth
Scott	William	1799	Army	Madras	1784–	Westm.			
Senhouse	Joseph	1759	Mariner	East Indiaman	1743–1829	Cumb.	Cumb.	Humphrey Senhouse	Mary Fleming
Senhouse	Joseph Ashley	1800s	Mariner	East Indiaman	1791–1867	Cumb.	Eng.	Joseph Senhouse	Mary Ashley
Seward	Richard	1806	Army	Madras	1786–1816	Westm.	India	Abraham Seward	Mary
Sharpe	Anthony				1757–	Cumb.			
Sill	Henry	1828	Assistant Surgeon	Bengal	1806–1852	Westm.	India	Henry Sill	Elizabeth Towers
Simonds	William	1807	Army	Bengal	1786–1865	Cumb.	Eng.	James Simonds	Belinda Robinson
Skelton	Charles Cornwallis	1829	Army	Bengal	1778–1836	Cumb.	India	Daniel Jones Skelton	Mary Theed
Skelton	Henry Jones	1799	Army		1769–1836	Cumb.	Cumb.	Arnoldus Jones (Skelton) MP	Elizabeth Hicks
Slater	Thomas		Army		–c.1765	Cumb.			
Smith	John Stanley	1807	Army	Madras	1792–1811	Lancs.	India	John Smith	Mary Wordsworth
Smith	Richard Wordsworth	1810	Mariner	East Indiaman	1793–1832	Lancs.	Lancs.	John Smith	Mary Wordsworth
Sowerby	John	N/A	East Indiaman insurer	N/A	1745–1823	Cumb.	Eng.	William Sowerby	

Surname	1st Names	Appointed	Position	Place of Service	Dates	Natal Origins	Death or Burial	Father	Mother
Sowerby	John	1808	Army	Bengal	1791–1887	Cumb.		Wasdale Sowerby	Ann Scott
Sowerby	John	1810s	Army		1793–1839				
Spedding	William	1798	Writer	Bengal	1777–1806	Cumb.	Eng.		Margaret Benn
Stables	John	1759	Army	Madras	1740–1795	Westm.	Eng.	John Stables	Christabella Bainbridge
Stalker	Foster	1818	Army	Bombay	1798–1857	Cumb.	Iran	Joshua Stalker	Esther Penrice
Stalker	Thomas	1819	Army	Bombay	1800–1861	Cumb.	Cumb.	Joshua Stalker	Esther Penrice
Stamper	Henry	1795	Army	Bengal	1775–1805	Cumb.	India	Jacob Stamper	Isabella Lowes
Stamper	William Benson				1784–1827	Cumb.	Cumb.	Jacob Stamper	Isabella Lowes
Stamper	Richard	1804	Army	Bombay	1788–1825	Cumb.	India	Jacob Stamper	Isabella Lowes
Stanley	Edward	1801	Chaplin	Did not proceed	1776–	Cumb.	Cumb.	Edward Stanley	Julia Christian
Stanley	Richard	1797	Army		1782–	Cumb.		Edward Stanley	Julia Christian
Steel	Anthony	1800s	Mariner	East Indiaman	1796–1842	Cumb.	At sea	Joseph Steel	Dorothy Ponsonby
Steel	James	1806	Army	Bengal	1792–1859	Cumb.	Eng.	Joseph Steel	Dorothy Ponsonby

Surname	1st Names	Appointed	Position	Place of Service	Dates	Natal Origins	Death or Burial	Father	Mother
Stephenson	Edward	1708	Merchant	Bengal	1691–1768	Cumb.	Cumb.	Edward Stephenson	Rebecca Winder
Stephenson	Edward		Army	Bombay	1739–1784			Robert Stephenson	Elizabeth
Stephenson	John	1700s	Merchant	Bengal	1700–1771	Cumb.		Edward Stephenson	Rebecca Winder
Stephenson	John	1765	Director	N/A	1710–1794	Cumb.	Eng.	Thomas Stephenson	Margaret
Strickland	Jarrad Edward	1801	Army	Bombay	1782–1844	Westm.		Jarrad Strickland	Cecia Townley
Stubbs	Richmond Robert	1807	Army Assistant Surgeon		1782–1804	Cumb.		Rev Robert Stubbs	Isabella Baynes
Swin-burne	R				1779–1862	Cumb.			
Taylor	John	1818	Army	Bengal	1802–1822	Lancs.	India	Henry Taylor	Charlotte Andrews
Taylor	John	1740s	Surgeon	Bengal	1722–1784	Lancs.	Westm.	Harry Taylor	Sarah Symson
Taylor	John	1770	Army		1754–	Cumb.		William Taylor	Grace Fletcher
Taylor	John Bladen	1778	Army	Madras	1764–1820	India	Westm.	John Taylor	Dorothy Rumbold
Taylor	Peter	1798	Army		1778–1827	Cumb.	Westm.	Peter Taylor	Isabella Fleming
Taylor	Robert	1816	Bengal		1800–1843	Lancs.	India	Henry Taylor	Charlotte Andrews

Surname	1st Names	Appointed	Position	Place of Service	Dates	Natal Origins	Death or Burial	Father	Mother
Taylor	Thomas Rumbold	1790s	Mariner	East Indiaman	1776–1804	Westm.	India	John Taylor	Dorothy Rumbold
Taylor	William	1814	Mariner	East Indiaman	1803–	Lancs.		Henry Taylor	Charlotte Andrews
Taylor	Henry	1780s	Writer	Madras	1763–1806	Bengal		John Taylor	Dorothy Rumbold
Teasdale	John	1772	Army	Bengal	–1796	Westm.		Thomas Teasdale	
Thompson	John	1765	Mariner	East Indiaman	–1784	Cumb.	India		
Thompson	Lancelot	1778	Army	Bengal	1760–	Westm.		John Thompson	
Thompson	William		Mariner		1778–1834	Cumb.	India		
Thurnam	William Graham	1807	Army	Bombay	1792–1823	Westm.	India	Timothy Thurnam	Dorothy Graham
Tiffin	John	1780s	Mariner		1760–	Cumb.		Nathaniel Tiffin	
Tomkinson	Thomas	1811	Army Surgeon	Madras	1789–	Cumb.		John Tomkinson	Elizabeth
Troughton	Edward	N/A	Instrument maker	N/A	1753–1835	Cumb.	Eng.	Framcis Toughton	Mary Stable
Troughton	John	N/A	Instrument maker	N/A	1739–	Cumb.		Framcis Toughton	Mary Stable
Tullie	Isaac			Bengal	–1775		India	Timothy Tullie	Eleanor How

Surname	1st Names	Appointed	Position	Place of Service	Dates	Natal Origins	Death or Burial	Father	Mother
Tullie	George		Merchant	Madras	–1724	Cumb.		Timothy Tullie	
Tullie	Philip	1721	Mariner	East Indiaman			India	Timothy Tullie	
Tullie	Timothy	1711	Mariner Free Merchant	Madras		Cumb.	Eng.	Timothy Tullie	
Tullie	Timothy	1749	Merchant	Madras	1732–1751	India	India	Timothy Tullie	Eleanor How
Udale	Charles	1824	Mariner	Madras	1804–1836	Cumb.	Lancs.	John Udale	Agnes
Varty	William	1802	Army	Madras	1784–1815	Lancs.	India	Joseph Varty	
Vaughan	Thomas		Army		1769–	Westm.			
Wake	Charles Hamilton Charles	1827	Army	Bengal	1808–1871	Cumb.	Cumb.	Baldwin Wake	Sarah Spedding
Wake	Spedding Arden	1828	Army	Madras	1808–1833	Cumb.	India	Charles Wake	Ann Spedding
Wane	Wilfred	1769	Army	Bengal	1741–1770	Cumb.	India	Joseph Wane	Mary Irton
Ward	John	1763	Mariner	East Indiaman	–1769		India		
Warwick	Francis	1819	Army	Bombay	1802–1857	Cumb.	India	Robert Bonner	Sarah Andersen
Watts	Henry	1820s	Army	Madras	1810–1838	Cumb.	India	John Nicolsen Watts	Ann Pitt Dodson

Surname	1st Names	Appointed	Position	Place of Service	Dates	Natal Origins	Death or Burial	Father	Mother
Watts	John James	N/A		N/A	1803–1883	India	Eng.	John Nicolson Watts	Ann Pitt Dodson
Watts	John Nicholson	1796	Writer	Madras	1780–1815	Cumb.	India	Clement Watts	Mary Benn
Watts	Montagu	1821	Army	Madras	1808–1867	India	Eng.	John Nicolson Watts	Ann Pitt Dodson
Watts	Thomas	1800s	Writer	Madras	1789–1811	Cumb.	India	Clement Watts	Mary Benn
White	Charles Herbert	1819	Army	Bengal	1801–1850	Devon	Westm.	Charles White	Sophia James
White	Francis Howard	1820s	Writer	Bengal	1809–183–	Westm.	India	Charles White	Sophia James
White	William	1783	Attorney	Bombay	1753–1811	Cumb.	Cumb.	Isaiah White	Ann Key
Wilkinson	James	1820s	Army	Bombay	1801–1838	Westm.	Westm.	James Wilkinson	Nanny Eggleston
Wilkinson	Joseph	1827	Army	Madras	1803–1854	Lancs.	Lancs.	William Wilkinson	Elinor
Wilkinson	Lancelot	1821	Writer	Bombay	1805–1841	Westm.	Westm.	James Wilkinson	Nanny Eggleston
Wilkinson	Peter	1797	Army		1778–	Cumb.		John Wilkinson	Mary
Wilkinson	Robert	1824	Free Merchant	Bombay	1807–1887	Westm.	Eng.	James Wilkinson	Nanny Eggleston

Surname	1st Names	Appointed	Position	Place of Service	Dates	Natal Origins	Death or Burial	Father	Mother
Wilkinson	Thomas	1810	Army	Bengal	1795–1867	Westm.	Eng.	James Wilkinson	Nanny Eggleston
Wilkinson	Thomas	1770s	Writer	Bombay	1759–1840	Westm.	Eng.	Lancelot Wilkinson	Mary Dent
Wilkinson	William	1812	Writer	Bengal	1797–1859	Westm.	Eng.	James Wilkinson	Nanny Eggleston
Wilson	Christopher	1726	Army	N/A	1689–1773	Lancs.	Lancs.		
Wilson	Richard	1733	Contractor	N/A	1702–1766	Westm.	Eng.	Richard Wilson	Hester
Wilson	Thomas		Ship's Carpenter	East Indiaman	1782–1817	Cumb.	India		
Wilson	William	1829	Writer	Madras	1810–1880	Westm.	Westm.	Christopher Wilson	Catherine
Wilson	William	N/A	Contractor	N/A	1765–1832	London	Eng.	Richard Wilson	Martha Barwell
Wilson	William	N/A	Contractor	N/A	1732–1808	London	Eng.	William Wilson	Mary Munn
Winder	Jonathan	1699	Merchant		1669–1718	Cumb.	Eng.	John Winder	Mary
Winder	Jonathan	1700s	Merchant		–1735	Cumb.		Samuel Winder	Elizabeth Beak
Winter	Thomas Washington	1757	Writer		1740–	Westm.		Thomas Winter	Mary Washington
Wordsworth	Flavell	1777	Writer	Madras	1760–1783	Yorkshire	India	Richard Words-worth	Elizabeth Favell
Wordsworth	James	1770s	Writer	Bengal	1757–1840	Yorkshire	Eng.	Richard Words-worth	Elizabeth Favell

Surname	1st Names	Appointed	Position	Place of Service	Dates	Natal Origins	Death or Burial	Father	Mother
Wordsworth	John	1780s	Mariner	East Indiaman	1772–1805	Cumb.	At sea	John Wordsworth	Ann Cookson
Wordsworth	John	1770s	Mariner	East Indiaman	1754–1819	Cumb.	Cumb.	Richard Wordsworth	Elizabeth Favell
Wordsworth	Joseph	1798	Mariner	East Indiaman	1782–1847	Cumb.	Cumb.	Richard Wordsworth	Mary Scott
Yates	John Orfeur	1759	Merchant	Bombay	1744–1818	Cumb.	Cumb.	Francis Yates	Anne Orfeur
Zouch	Charles Samuel	1820	Army	Madras	1803–1823	Cumb.	India	Richard Zouch	Charlotte

APPENDIX B: EAST INDIES ENUMERATED CUMBRIAN WOMEN

Name	Parents	Birth Place and Date	Death Place and Date	Married	Spouse	Status of Spouse
Elizabeth Ashburner	William Ashburner and Dorothy Taylor	1763 Dalton in Furness, Lancashire	1791 Bombay	1779 Bombay	William Page	HEIC – Not Cumbrian
Charlotte Bellasis (Bellas)	Rev. George Bellas and Margaret Harvey	1761 Berkshire	1784 Bombay	1784 Bombay	Daniel Beat Christie	HEIC – Not Cumbrian
Helen Hutchins Bellasis	John Bellasis and Ann Martha Hutchins	1777 Bombay	1840 London	1794 Bombay	Henry Fawcett	Enumerated Cumbrian
				1819 London	Barrington Tristram	Not Cumbrian
Elizabeth Brisco	Horton Brisco and Milicent Jane Banks	1778 Calcutta	1831 Leicester	1796 Calcutta	George Arbuthnot	HEIC – Not Cumbrian
Maria Brisco	Horton Brisco and Milicent Jane Banks	1776 Calcutta	1796 Calcutta	N/A	Unmarried	N/A
Susan Cust	Thomas Cust and Maria	1781 Barrackpore	1797 At Sea	N/A	Unmarried	N/A
Elizabeth Warden Dent	John Dent and Emily Jane Ricketts	1818 Madras	1840 China	1838 London	Robert Wilkinson	Enumerated Cumbrian
Sarah Dodding	Miles Dodding and Margaret Kirby	1665 Ulverston, Lancashire	1744 Ulverston, Lancashire	1683 Ulverston, Lancashire	John Braddyll	Enumerated Cumbrian
Maria Dundas	George Dundas	1785 Papcastle, Cumberland	1842 London	1809 Bombay	Peter Graham	HEIC – Not Cumbrian

Name	Parents	Birth Place and Date	Death Place and Date	Married	Spouse	Status of Spouse
Mary Douglas	William Douglas and Jane Bell	1794 Calcutta	1884 Newton Abbott	1821 London	Edward Stanley	Ponsonby Hall, Cumberland
Elizabeth Jane Fawcett	James Fawcett and Agnes Stephenson	1776 Scaleby, Cumberland	1826 At sea	1799 Scaleby, Cumberland	Thomas T Thomason	HEIC – Not Cumbrian
Elizabeth M Fawcett	Rowland Fawcett and Frances Mercy Farish	1776 Scaleby, Cumberland	1825 Poona	1817 Bombay	James Farish	Enumerated Cumbrian
Frances Fawcett	Rowland Fawcett and Frances Mercy Farish	1801 Scaleby, Cumberland	1886 Carlisle	1822 Scaleby, Cumberland	Henry Farrer	Enumerated Cumbrian
Frances Ann Fell	William Atkis Fell and Frances Harrison	1811 Ulverston, Lancashire	1854 London	1828 Calcutta	Arthur Pittar	Free merchant – Not Cumbrian
Mary Fell	William Atkis Fell and Frances Harrison	1808 Ulverston, Lancashire	Before 1844		James Johnston	Enumerated Cumbrian
Margaret Sarah Gale-Braddyll	Wilson Gale-Braddyll and Jane Gale	1780 Conishead, Lancashire	1807 Conishead, Lancashire		Gordon Elliot Forbes	Free merchant – Not Cumbrian
Catherine Holme	John Holme and Catherine Brisco	1736 Carlisle, Cumberland	1771 Surrey	Abt 1858 possibly Calcutta	William B. Sumner	HEIC – Not Cumbrian
Charlotte Lutwidge	Henry Lutwidge and Jane Molyneaux	1770 Lancashire	Possibly 1791	1789 Moresby	William Benn	Enumerated Cumbrian

Name	Parents	Birth Place and Date	Death Place and Date	Married	Spouse	Status of Spouse
Catherine Paxton	Paxton of Whitehaven	1796 Whitehaven, Cumberland	1856 Whitehaven, Cumberland	1815 Whitehaven, Cumberland	Charles Church	Enumerated Cumbrian
Dorothy Taylor	John Taylor and Dorothy Rumbold	1774 Kendal, Westmorland	1847 Somerset	About 1793 Madras 1796 Surrey	Jeremiah Adderton Thomas Clerk	Enumerated Cumbrian HEIC – Not Cumbrian
Helen Cramer Watts	John Nicholson Watts and Ann Pitt Dodson	1805 Tanjore	1831 Ootacamund	1827 Trichinopoly	Henry Dickinson	HEIC – Not Cumbrian
Mary-Anne Watts	John Nicholson Watts and Ann Pitt Dodson	Born 1811. Baptised 1815 Carlisle, Cumberland	1830 Mangalore		Henry Briggs	HEIC – Not Cumbrian
Ellen Wilkinson	James Wilkinson and Nanny Eggleston	1813 Flass, Westmorland	1879 London	1829 Masulipatam	James Noble	HEIC – Not Cumbrian

APPENDIX C: EAST INDIES WOMEN, ASSOCIATED CUMBRIAN MEN AND THEIR CHILDREN

East Indies Woman	Cumbrian Sojourner	The Children			
Jewee Bhoo[1]	Charles Denton	Charles	Mary		
Saheb Bibee[2]	Eldred Addison	John			
Chindanah[3]	Humphrey Senhouse Gale				
Unnamed	James Pennington[4]	James Masterson	Rowland	John	Thomas
Mary Smith[5]	John Charles Bristow	May Charlotte	Emelia Sophia	John Purling	
Meda[6]	John Hodgson	William			
Unnamed	John Johnson[7]	John			
Unnamed	John Knott[8]	John	Thomas Robert		
Bet[9]	John Teasdale	Nancy			
Chebow[10]	John Ashburner				
Fattemah[11]	Jonathan Moorhouse				
Manoo	Richard Ecroyd	Unnamed			
Maria Saunier	Richard Ecroyd	Richard			
Unnamed	Simon Heward	Ceta Ellen Jane	Jessie Maria		
Begum Bibby Noor	Thomas Cust	Charles	William	Elizabeth	Charlotte
Connum Baharrie	Thomas Cust	Thomas			
Maria	Thomas Cust	Susan	Richard		
Unnamed	Thomas Cust	Jane			
Unnamed	Thomas Cust	William			
Goolab Bibby	Thomas Dobinson[12]	Julia	Thomas		
Jane Anmah	Thomas Jackson[13]	Eliza			
Unnamed	Thomas Law[14]	John	Edmund	George	Thomas
Unnamed	Thomas Myers[15]	Unnamed	Francisca		
Possibly Parsee[16]	William 'Bombay' Ashburner	Kavasji Mankeji			

Notes

1 IOR L/AG/34/29/349 f.184
2 National Archives, PCC, *PROB 11 Piece 1158.*
3 IOR L/AG/34/29/219 f.1.
4 IOR L/AG/34/29/11 f.40.
5 *Church of England Parish Registers, 1538–1812*: London – Saint Marylebone, Day book of baptisms, Feb. 1811–Mar. 1812. P89/MRY1/013. Accessed http://home.ancestry.co.uk.
6 IOR L/AG/34/29/29 f.301.
7 National Archives, PCC, *PROB 11 Piece 1345.*
8 IOR N/1/2 f.115; IOR N/1/2 f.183.
9 IOR L/AG/34/29/10 f.175.
10 National Archives, PCC, *PROB 11 Piece 979.*
11 IOR L/AG/4/27/256 f.24 and IOR L/AG/34/29-222 f.55.
12 IOR L/AG/34/19/343 f.9.
13 IOR L/AG/34/29/222 f.44.
14 IOR N/1/4 f.52; New Monthly Magazine, vol. 42 (1834), pp. 258–259; G. A. *Townsend, 'Thomas Law, Washington's First Rich Man',* Records of the Columbia His*torical Society,* 14 (1901), pp. 222–245.
15 E. de Selincourt (ed.), The *Letters of William and Dorothy Wordsworth: The Early Years, 1787–1805 (2nd edition revised by C. Shaver, Oxford, Clarendon Press, 1967), pp. 147n. IOR N/2/2 f. 267.*
16 See www.geni.com/people/Luke-Ashburner/6000000014733316665. There is no direct evidence. There was a close business relationship between his son Luke Ashburner and Kavasji Mankeji Ashburner. See Anon., Gazetteer of the Bombay Presidency: Tha'na: places of inter*est,* vol. 14 (Bombay, Government Central Press, 1882), p. 44.

APPENDIX D: HUDLESTON, KIN CONNECTIONS AND THE EAST INDIES*

A →

B →

C →

Andrew HUDLESTON

Andrew HUDLESTON = Catherine LAWSON
(see E)

John SENHOUSE = Mary HUDLESTON
d.1667

John SENHOUSE = Jane LAMPLUGH
of Netherhall   1663 – 1720
1660 – 1694

John FLETCHER = Isabella SENHOUSE
of Clea Hall   1693 – 1774
1717 – 1756

William TAYLOR = Grace FLETCHER

John TAYLOR

John FLETCHER
d.1748
Pondicherry

Lowther FLETCHER

Henry FLETCHER = Catherine LINTOT
1729 – 1807   1731 – 1816

John CHRISTIAN = Bridget SENHOUSE
d.1749

John CHRISTIAN = Jane CURWEN   Humphrey CHRISTIAN = Elizabeth BRETT
1719 – 1767   d.1762   1720 – 1773

(See D)

Isabella CURWEN = John CHRISTIAN
CURWEN

Edward STANLEY = Julia CHRISTIAN
1762 – 1816   1746 – 1793

Edward STANLEY
1776 – 1834

Richard STANLEY
b.1782

George BROWN = Clara
HEIC   STANLEY
1784 – 1869   1785 – 1852

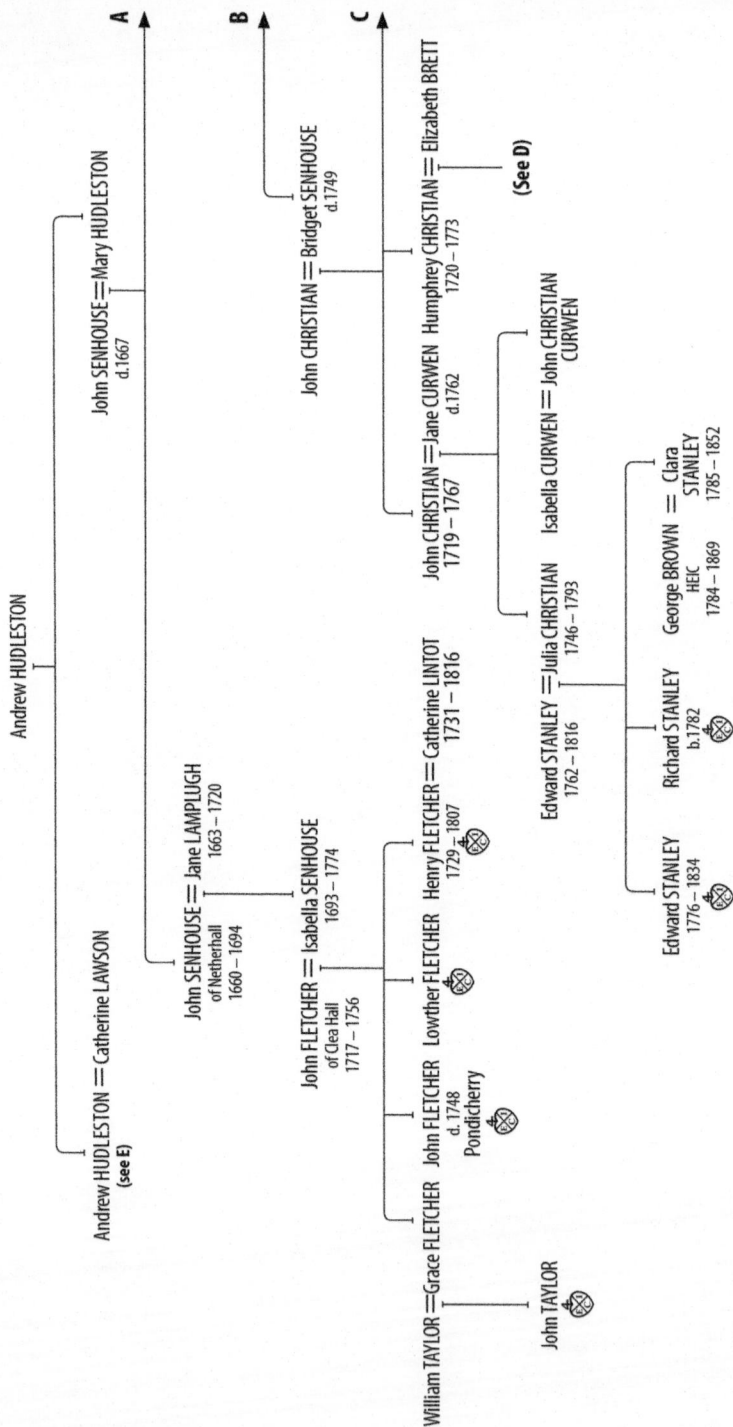

* Only key individuals are included

◈ Enumerated Cumbrian   HEIC Non-enumerated East India Company appointee or licensee

◈ Non-enumerated East India Company appointee or licensee

A

Humphrey SENHOUSE = Eleanor KIRBY
1679 –1738   d.1790

B

Humphrey SENHOUSE = Mary FLEMING
1706 – 1770   d.1749

Mary SENHOUSE = Robert GALE   William SENHOUSE   Humphrey SENHOUSE = Kitty WOOD   Joseph SENHOUSE = Mary ASHLEY
d.1778   1721 – d.1773   1741 – 1800   d.1814   1743 – 1829

Gustavus GALE
1766 – 1799

Humphrey GALE   William GALE = Ann HOLIDAY
1793 – 1818   non-HEIC Mariner
                              1758 – 1823

Joseph SENHOUSE
1743 – 1829

C

Edmund LAW = Mary CHRISTIAN   Charles CHRISTIAN = Anne DIXON
Bishop of Carlisle   1722 –1762   1729 – 1768
1703 – 1787

(See D)

Fletcher CHRISTIAN   Edward CHRISTIAN
Mutineer   1758 – 1823

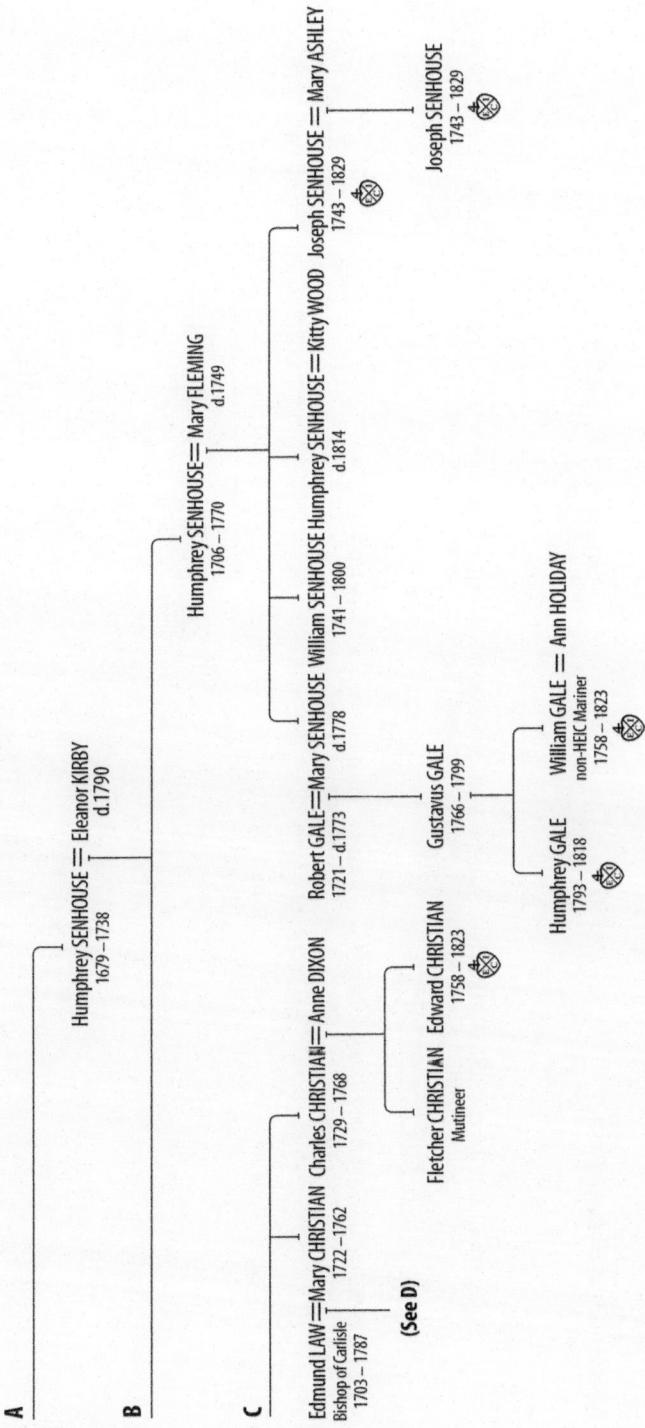

⊛ Enumerated Cumbrian   **HEIC** Non-enumerated East India Company appointee or licensee

* Only key individuals are included

D (See above)

Humphrey CHRISTIAN = Elizabeth BRETT
1720 – 1773

(See C above)

Edmund LAW = Mary CHRISTIAN
Bishop of Carlisle   1722 –1762
1703 – 1787

Mary CHRISTIAN = James LUSHINGTON
b.1749   d.1801

Mary LAW
1744 – 1768

Ewan LAW = Henrietta MARKHAM
1747 – 1829   d.1844

Joanna LAW = Thomas RUMBOLD
1753 – 1823   1836 – 1791

Thomas LAW = Henrietta MARKHAM
1759 –1834   d.1844

Indian Woman = Thomas LAW

Stephen LUSHINGTON
HEIC
1776 – 1868

James LUSHINGTON
1780 – 1859

Charles LUSHINGTON
HEIC
1784 – 1844

George LAW
1796 – 1820

Ewan LAW = Mary-Ann HUNGERFORD
d.1818

George LAW
1784 – 1822

George LAW   Edmond LAW   Thomas LAW   Elizabeth LAW
b.1790

Enumerated Cumbrian   HEIC Non-enumerated East India Company appointee or licensee

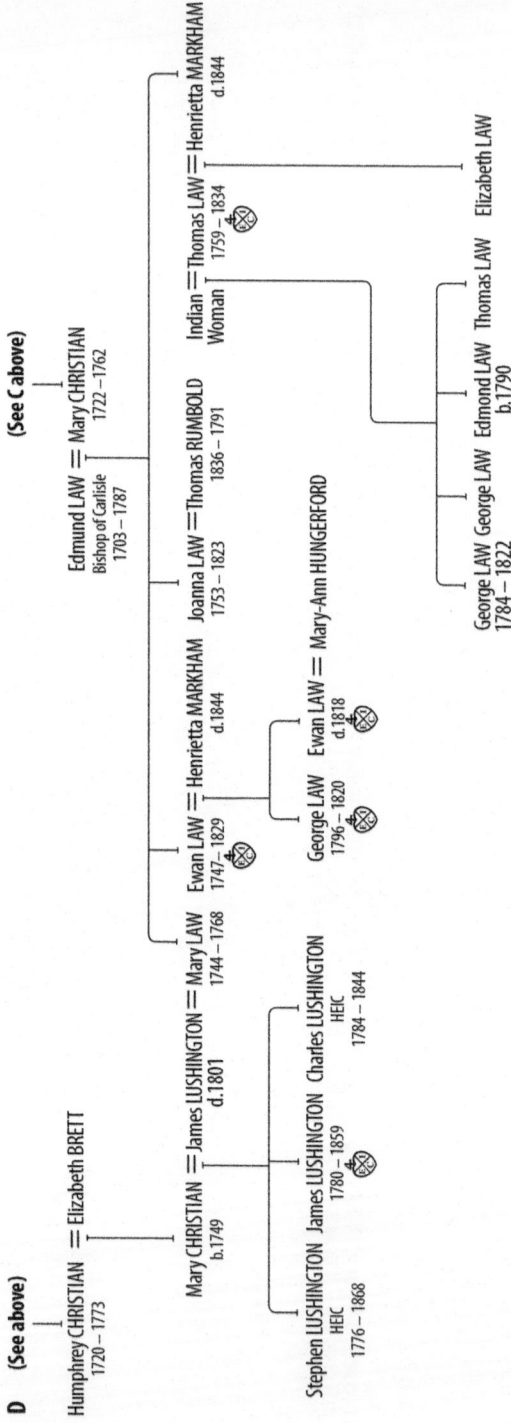

* Only key individuals are included

E

Wilfred LAWSON = Jane MUSGRAVE
of Isell, Cumberland
d.1689

Catherine LAWSON

Darcy CURWEN = Isabel LAWSON

Patricius CURWEN 1688–1702

Elizabeth WALKER = Eldred CURWEN 1692–1746 = Julian CLENMOE d.1759

(See F)

Andrew HUDLESTON = Catherine LAWSON
(see above)

Wilfred HUDLESTON d.1728 = Joyce CURWEN

Lawson HUDLESTON Archdeacon of Bath 1677–1743 = Hellena HARRINGTON of Kelston

Peter HOW = Jane HUDLESTON 1699–1772

William HUDLESTON 1716–1766 = Mary BURLAND of Wells, Somerset

John HUDLESTON 1749–1835 = Honoria MARSHALL d.1807

Andrew HUDLESTON = Mary FENTON of Plumbton Hall d.1780

Andrew HUDLESTON = Elizabeth FLEMING d.1830
of Hutton John

Isabella HUDLESTON

(See G)

Andrew Fleming HUDLESTON 1796–1861

(See G)

John HUDLESTON 1789–1823

William HUDLESTON 1793–1855

Frederic HUDLESTON 1794–1865

Josiah HUDLESTON 1799–1865

Robert HUDLESTON 1801–1877

* Only key individuals are included

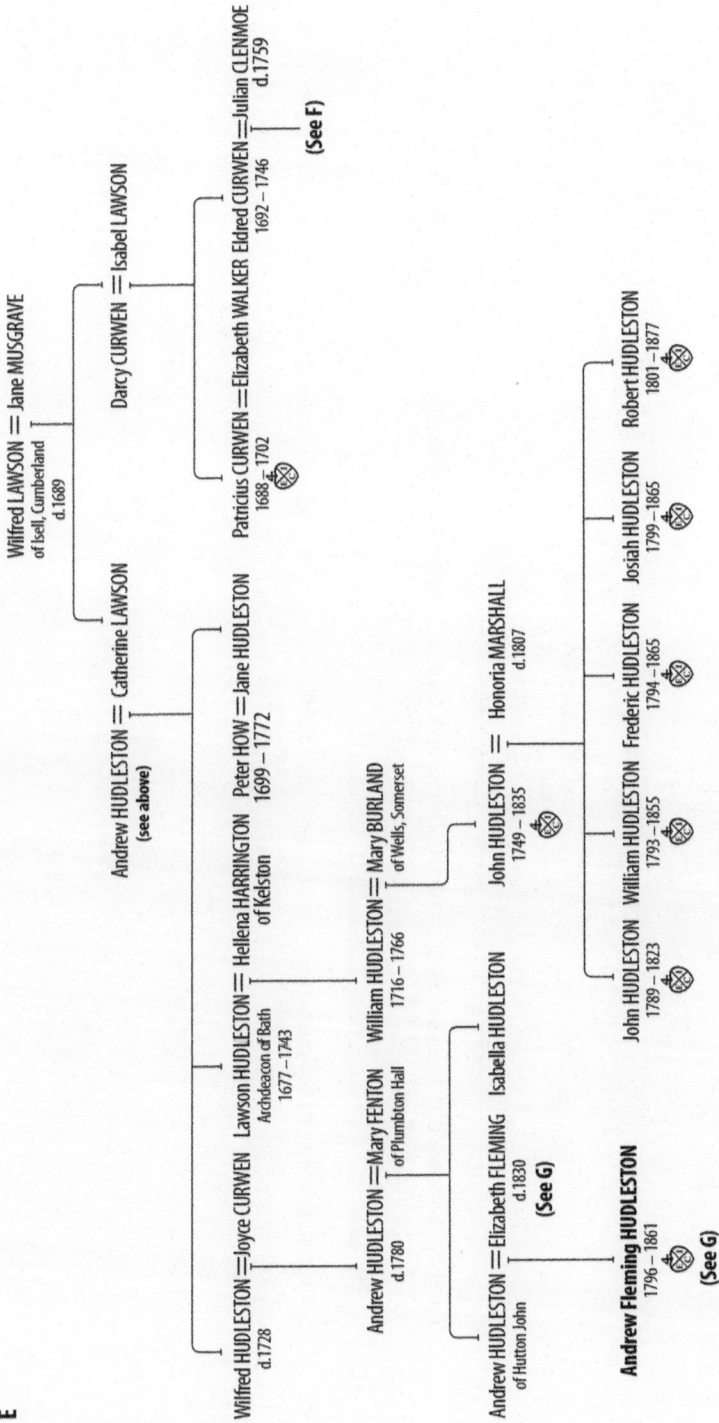

Enumerated Cumbrian   **HEIC** Non-enumerated East India Company appointee or licensee

F

(See above)

Eldred CURWEN = Julian CLENMOE
1692 – 1746   d.1759

Henry CURWEN = Isabella GALE   Jeremiah ADDERTON = Helena CURWEN   William ADDISON = Isabella CURWEN   William DOBINSON = Julian CURWEN
d.1778   d.1776   1718 – 1770   d.1792   d.1755   1734 – 1778   1734 – 1779

Henry ADDERTON   Jeremiah ADDERTON = Dorothy TAYLOR = Thomas CLERK   Richard ADDERTON   Eldred ADDISON = Bibee SAHEB   Thomas DOBINSON = Goolab   William DOBINSON
                  1774 – 1847   HEIC   d.1780 India   1753 – 1787   d.1807   d.1789

John ADDISON
1782 – 1859

Julia DOBINSON   Thomas DOBINSON

* Only key individuals are included

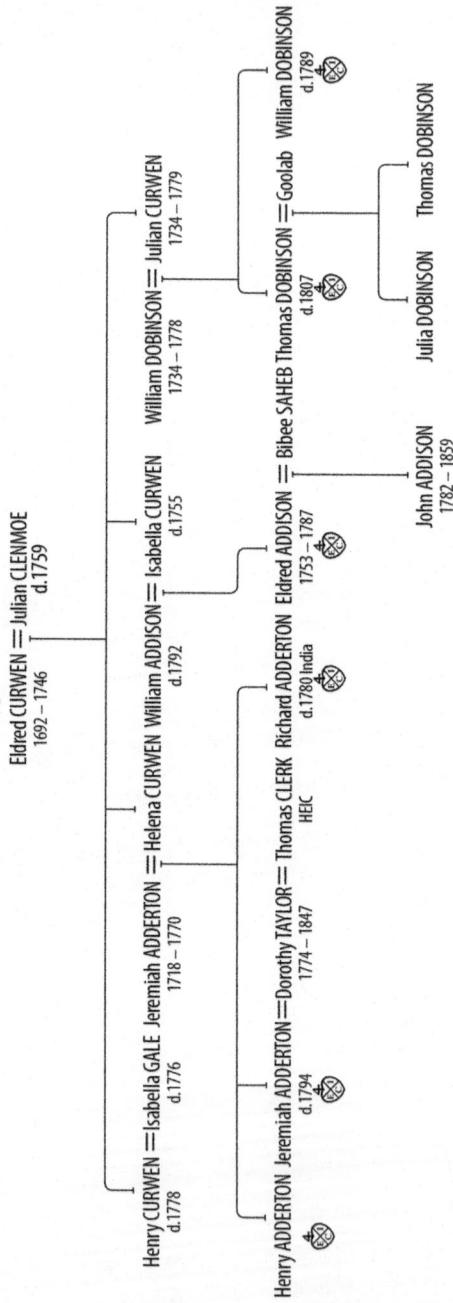

⊕ Enumerated Cumbrian   HEIC Non-enumerated East India Company appointee or licensee

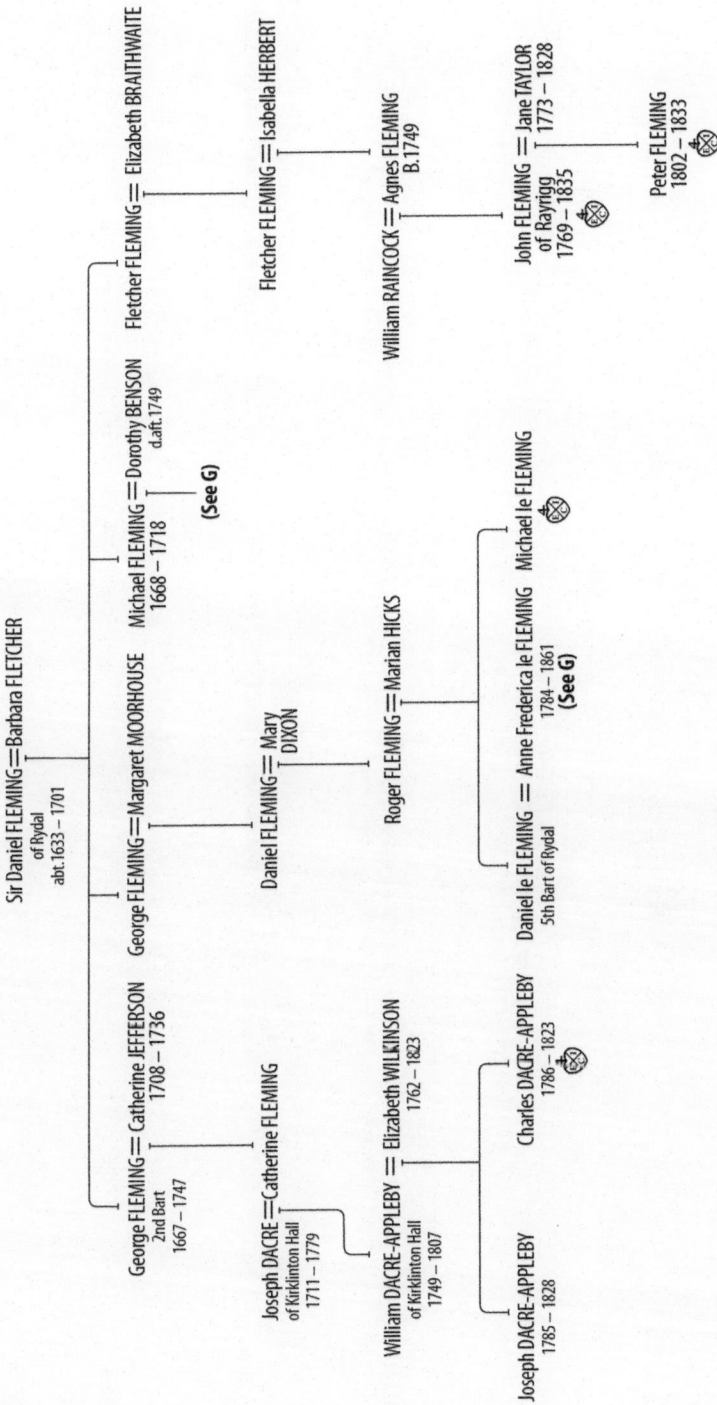

Sir Daniel FLEMING
of Rydal
abt.1633 – 1701 = Barbara FLETCHER

George FLEMING
2nd Bart
1667 – 1747

Michael FLEMING
1668 – 1718 = Dorothy BENSON
d.aft.1749
(See G)

Fletcher FLEMING = Elizabeth BRAITHWAITE

George FLEMING = Catherine JEFFERSON
1708 – 1736

Joseph DACRE
of Kirklinton Hall
1711 – 1779 = Catherine FLEMING

George FLEMING = Margaret MOORHOUSE

Daniel FLEMING = Mary DIXON

Fletcher FLEMING = Isabella HERBERT

Roger FLEMING = Marian HICKS

William RAINCOCK = Agnes FLEMING
B.1749

Daniel le FLEMING
5th Bart of Rydal = Anne Frederica le FLEMING
1784 – 1861
(See G)

Michael le FLEMING

John FLEMING
of Rayrigg
1769 – 1835 = Jane TAYLOR
1773 – 1828

Peter FLEMING
1802 – 1833

William DACRE-APPLEBY = Elizabeth WILKINSON
of Kirklinton Hall   1762 – 1823
1749 – 1807

Joseph DACRE-APPLEBY
1785 – 1828

Charles DACRE-APPLEBY
1786 – 1823

* Only key individuals are included

Enumerated Cumbrian   **HEIC** Non-enumerated East India Company appointee or licensee

G

(See above)

Michael FLEMING = Dorothy BENSON
1668 – 1718   d.aft.1749

Michael KNOTT = Susannah le FLEMING   William le FLEMING = Elizabeth PETYT
1696 – 1772   1712 – 1767   3rd Bart of Rydal   d.1788
                                        d.1757

George KNOTT = Catherine FORD   Indian = John KNOTT = Dorothy KNOTT   Andrew HUDLESTON = Elizabeth FLEMING
1743 – 1784   1753 – 1785   Unnamed d.1779   d.1795   of Hutton John   d.1830

John   Thomas

Andrew Fleming HUDLESTON
1796 – 1861

(See E)

(See above)

Michael le FLEMING = Diana HOWARD
4th Bart of Rydal 1748   d.1816
– 1806

George STANLEY = Dorothy FLEMING
1748 – 1806   d.1786

John HUGHES = Elizabeth STANLEY
                1775 – 1856

George Cumberland HUGHES
1807 – 1877

Daniel le = Anne Frederica le FLEMING
FLEMING   1784 – 1861
5th Bart of Rydal   (See above)

* Only key individuals are included

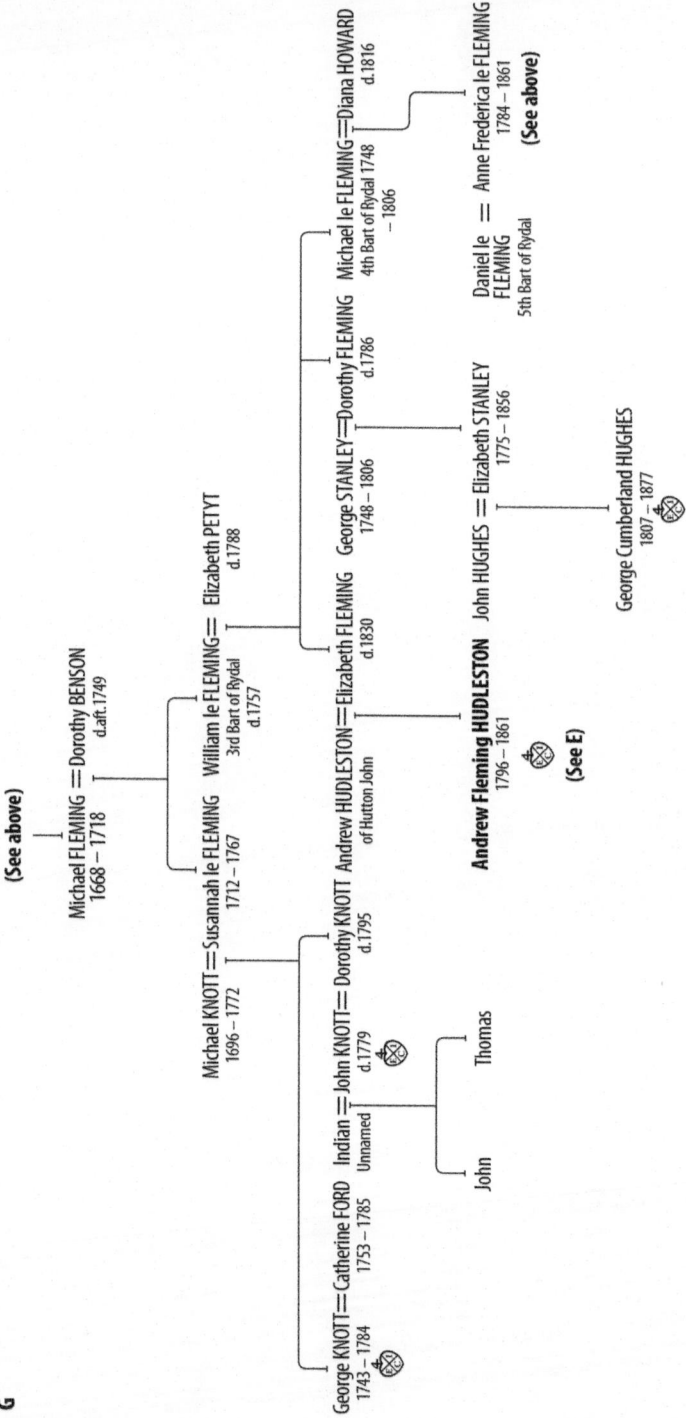

Enumerated Cumbrian   **HEIC**   Non-enumerated East India Company appointee or licensee

APPENDIX E: EAST INDIES CONNECTIONS OF THE WINDERS, STEPHENSON AND FAWCETTS*

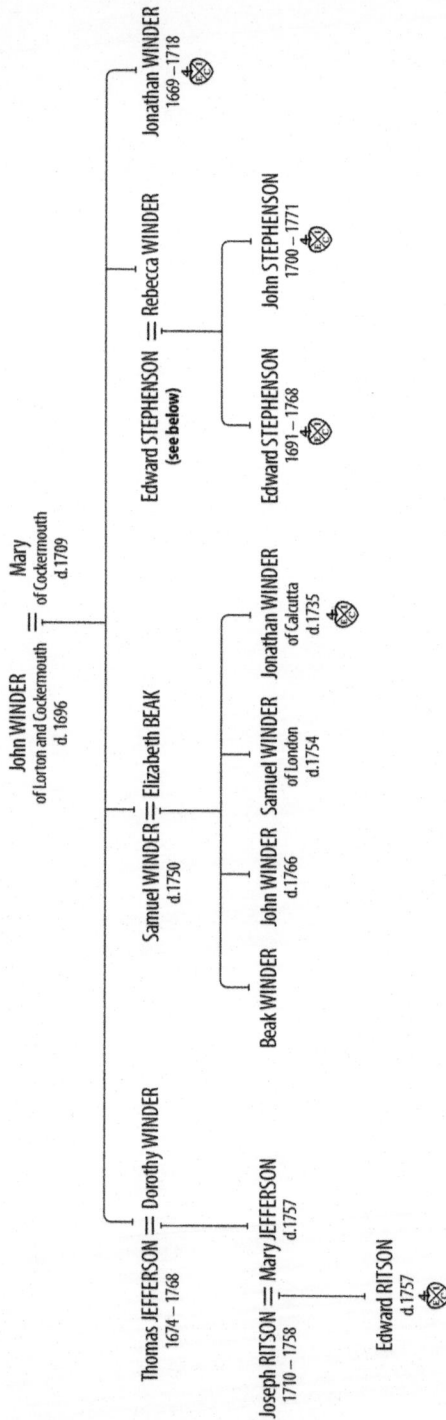

John WINDER
of Lorton and Cockermouth
d.1696
== Mary
of Cockermouth
d.1709

Thomas JEFFERSON
1674 – 1768
== Dorothy WINDER

Samuel WINDER
d.1750
== Elizabeth BEAK

Edward STEPHENSON
(see below)
== Rebecca WINDER

Jonathan WINDER
1669 – 1718

Joseph RITSON
1710 – 1758
== Mary JEFFERSON
d.1757

Beak WINDER

John WINDER
d.1766

Samuel WINDER
of London
d.1754

Jonathan WINDER
of Calcutta
d.1735

Edward STEPHENSON
1691 – 1768

John STEPHENSON
1700 – 1771

Edward RITSON
d.1757

* Only key individuals are included

Enumerated Cumbrian   **HEIC** Non-enumerated East India Company appointee or licensee

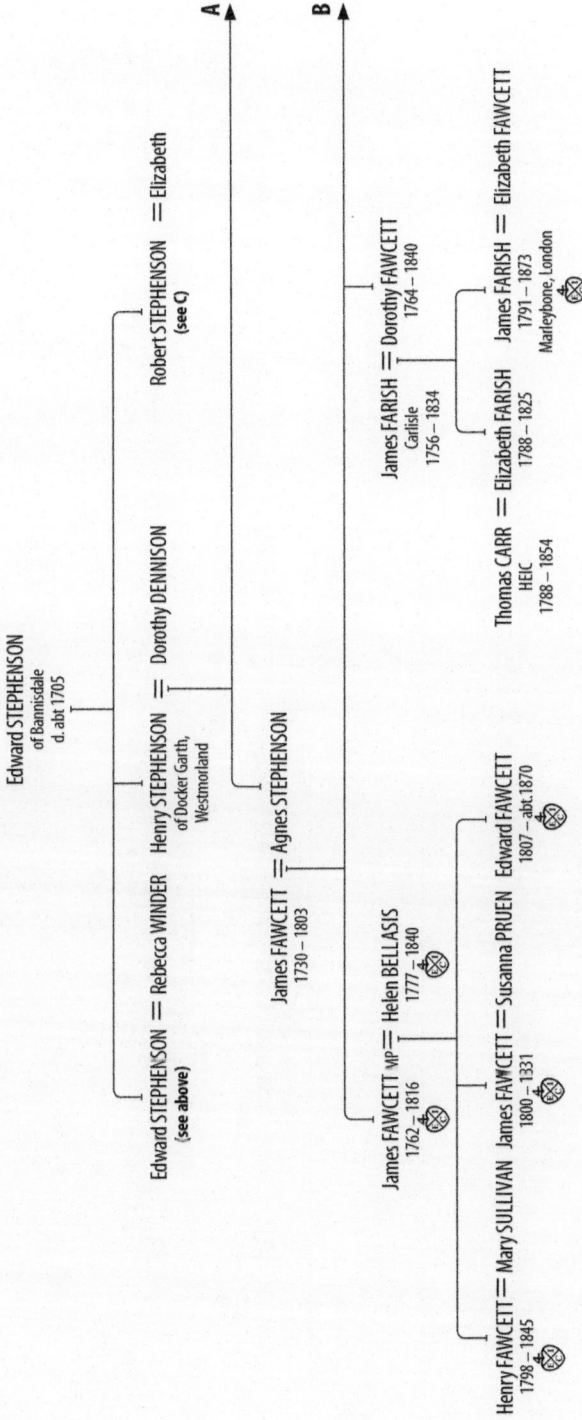

Edward STEPHENSON
of Bannisdale
d. abt 1705

Edward STEPHENSON = Rebecca WINDER
(see above)

Henry STEPHENSON = Dorothy DENNISON
of Docker Garth,
Westmorland

Robert STEPHENSON = Elizabeth
(see C)

A

B

James FAWCETT = Agnes STEPHENSON
1730 – 1803

James FARISH = Dorothy FAWCETT
Carlisle   1764 – 1840
1756 – 1834

Thomas CARR = Elizabeth FARISH
HEIC   1788 – 1825
1788 – 1854

James FARISH = Elizabeth FAWCETT
1791 – 1873
Marylebone, London

James FAWCETT MP = Helen BELLASIS
1762 – 1816   1777 – 1840

James FAWCETT = Susanna PRUEN
1800 – 1331

Edward FAWCETT
1807 – abt.1870

Henry FAWCETT = Mary SULLIVAN
1798 – 1845

* Only key individuals are included

Enumerated Cumbrian   HEIC Non-enumerated East India Company appointee or licensee

A

B

Rowland STEPHENSON = Elizabeth DRINKEL
of Lombard St   1734–
1728 – 1807   **(see D)**

Edward STEPHENSON = Mary STRICKLAND
1759 – 1833   1766 – 1817

Rowland STANDISH
a.k.a. Rowland Stephenson
d.1843

Rowland STEPHENSON = Mary STEPHENSON
d.1856   (see B)   d.1821

Rowland FAWCETT = Frances FARISH
Scaleby Castle   d.1840
1768 – 1831

John DE VITRE = Bridget FAWCETT
1757 – 1847   d.1826

Elizabeth FAWCETT = Thomas Thomason
d.1826

James DE VITRE   Matthew DE VITRE
1792 – 1875   1792 – 1875

Henry FARRER = Frances FAWCETT
1798 – 1853   1801 – 1886

* Only key individuals are included

Enumerated Cumbrian   **HEIC** Non-enumerated East India Company appointee or licensee

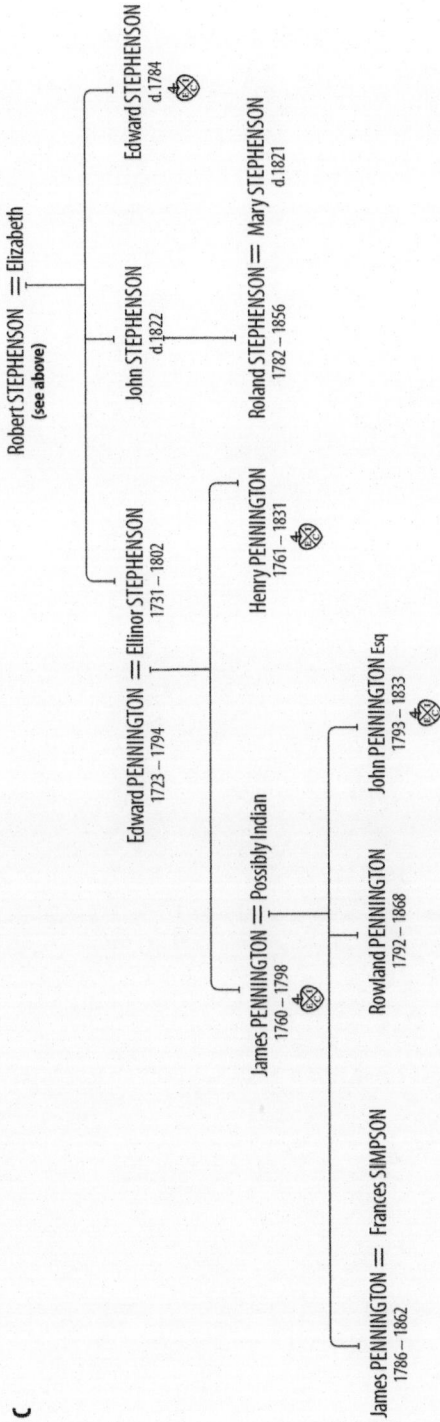

C

Robert STEPHENSON = Elizabeth
(see above)

Edward STEPHENSON
d.1784

John STEPHENSON
d.1822

Roland STEPHENSON = Mary STEPHENSON
1782 – 1856   d.1821

Edward PENNINGTON = Ellinor STEPHENSON
1723 – 1794   1731 – 1802

Henry PENNINGTON
1761 – 1831

James PENNINGTON = Possibly Indian
1760 – 1798

John PENNINGTON Esq
1793 – 1833

Rowland PENNINGTON
1792 – 1868

James PENNINGTON = Frances SIMPSON
1786 – 1862

D

Francis DRINKEL = Frances WILSON
Mayor of Kendal   of Black Hall
1711 – 1787

Francis DRINKEL
d.bef 1773

James FARRER = Ann DRINKEL
1734 – 1826   d.abt 1820

Rowland STEPHENSON = Elizabeth DRINKEL
of Lombard St   1734 –
1728 – 1807   (see above)

* Only key individuals are included

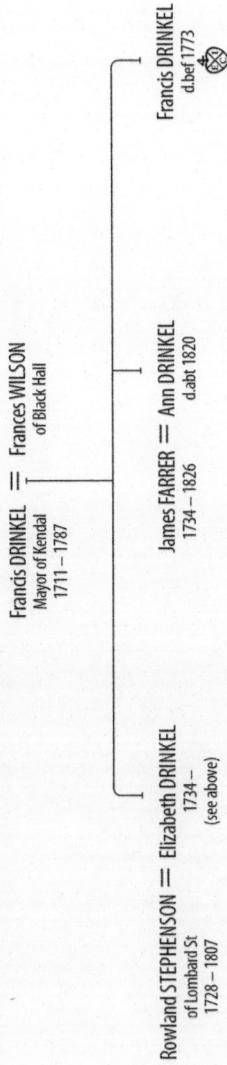

Enumerated Cumbrian

HEIC Non-enumerated East India Company appointee or licensee

Non-enumerated East India Company appointee or licensee

APPENDIX F: EAST INDIES CONNECTIONS OF THE BRADDYLLS, WILSONS AND GALES*

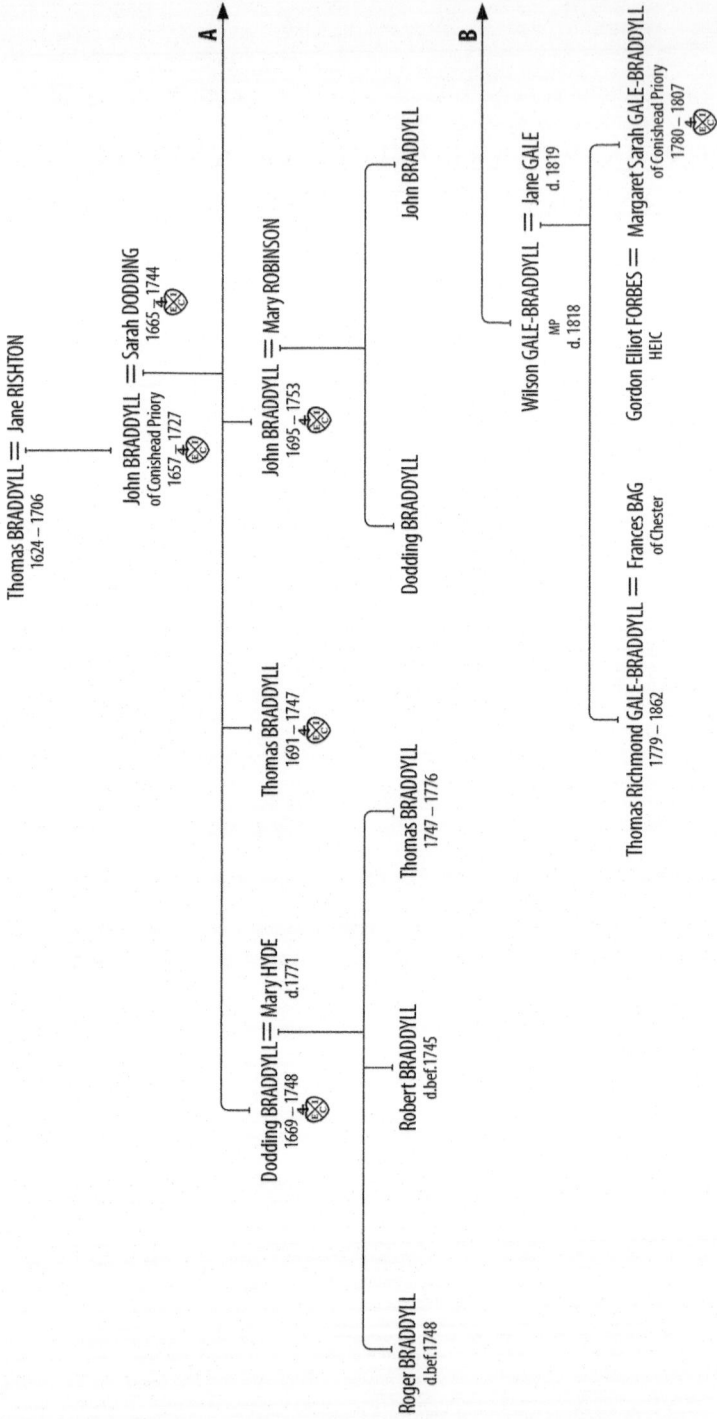

Thomas BRADDYLL = Jane RISHTON
1624 – 1706

John BRADDYLL = Sarah DODDING
of Conishead Priory   1665 – 1744
1657 – 1727

John BRADDYLL = Mary ROBINSON
1695 – 1753

John BRADDYLL

Dodding BRADDYLL

Dodding BRADDYLL = Mary HYDE
1669 – 1748   d.1771

Thomas BRADDYLL
1691 – 1747

Thomas BRADDYLL
1747 – 1776

Robert BRADDYLL
d.bef.1745

Roger BRADDYLL
d.bef.1748

A

B

Wilson GALE-BRADDYLL = Jane GALE
MP   d. 1819
d.1818

Thomas Richmond GALE-BRADDYLL = Frances BAG
1779 – 1862   of Chester

Gordon Elliot FORBES = Margaret Sarah GALE-BRADDYLL
HEIC   of Conishead Priory
1780 – 1807

⊗ Enumerated Cumbrian   **HEIC** Non-enumerated East India Company appointee or licensee

A

Margaret BRADDYLL
of Conishead Priory
1696 – 1781

= Christopher WILSON
1689 – 1727

Margaret
WILSON

John GALE = Sarah WILSON
of Whitehaven   d. 1774
1730 – 1814

B

Henry Richmond GALE = Sarah BALDWIN
of Bardsea Hall   1741 – 1802
d. 1814

William GALE = Cecilia LOSH
1788 – 1865   1801 – 1856

James LOSH = Cecilia BALDWIN

Joseph LOSH
1806 – 1862

* Only key individuals are included

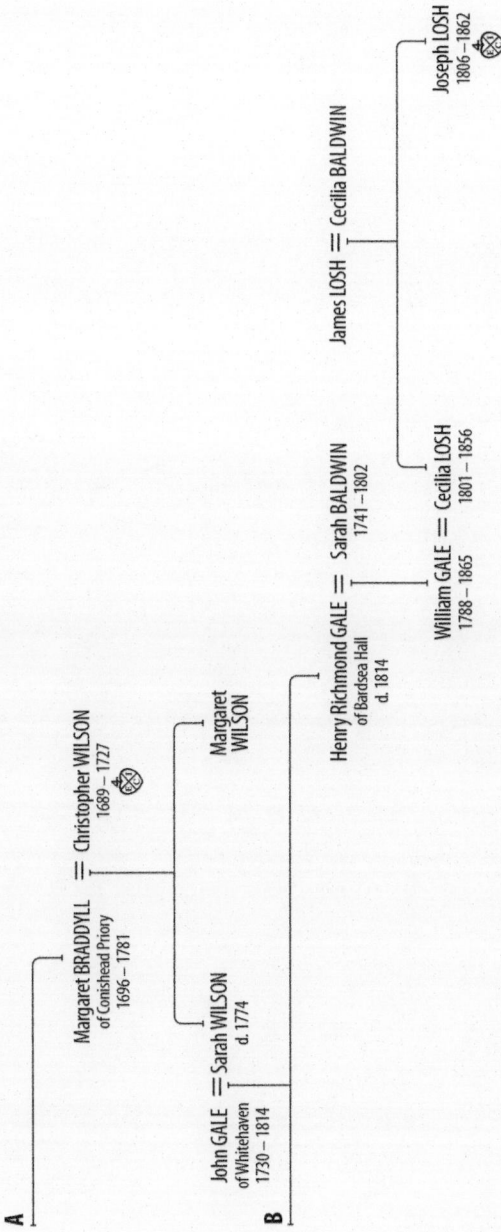

Enumerated Cumbrian   **HEIC** Non-enumerated East India Company appointee or licensee

APPENDIX G: KIN CONNECTIONS OF CATHERINE HOLME*

Richard MUSGRAVE 2nd Bart, Hayton Castle 1650 – abt 1718 == 1670 Dorothy JAMES

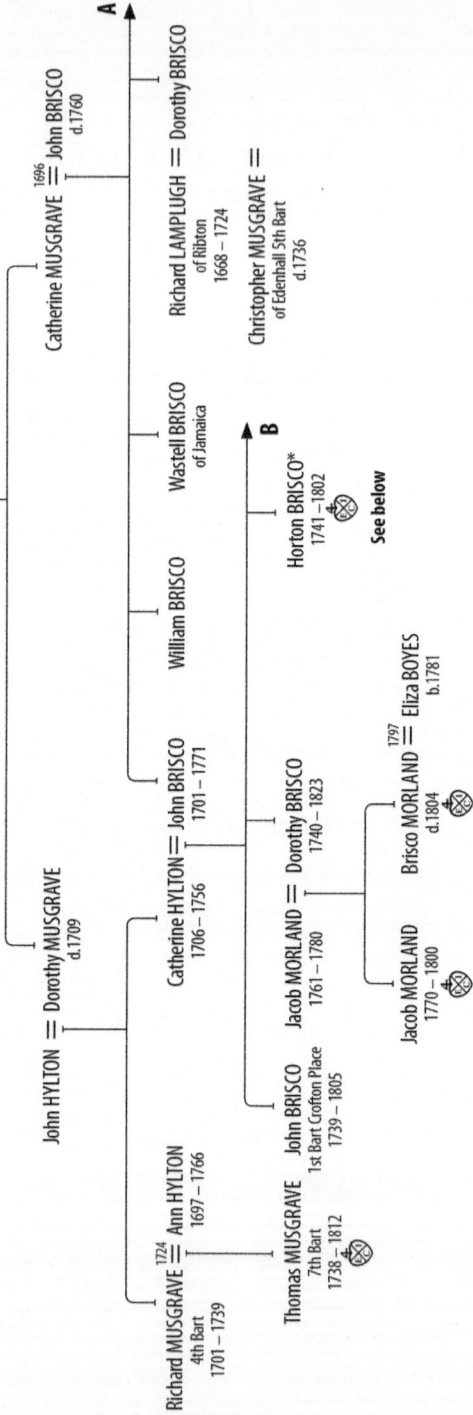

Catherine MUSGRAVE == 1696 John BRISCO d.1760

Richard LAMPLUGH of Ribton 1668 – 1724 == Dorothy BRISCO

Christopher MUSGRAVE of Edenhall 5th Bart d.1736 ==

John HYLTON == Dorothy MUSGRAVE d.1709

Catherine HYLTON 1706 – 1756 == John BRISCO 1701 – 1771

Wastell BRISCO of Jamaica

William BRISCO

Horton BRISCO* 1741 – 1802 — **See below** — B

Richard MUSGRAVE 4th Bart 1701 – 1739 == 1724 Ann HYLTON 1697 – 1766

John BRISCO 1st Bart Crofton Place 1739 – 1805

Jacob MORLAND 1761 – 1780 == Dorothy BRISCO 1740 – 1823

Brisco MORLAND d.1804 == 1797 Eliza BOYES b.1781

Jacob MORLAND 1770 – 1800

Thomas MUSGRAVE 7th Bart 1738 – 1812

A

B

Enumerated Cumbrian   HEIC Non-enumerated East India Company appointee or licensee

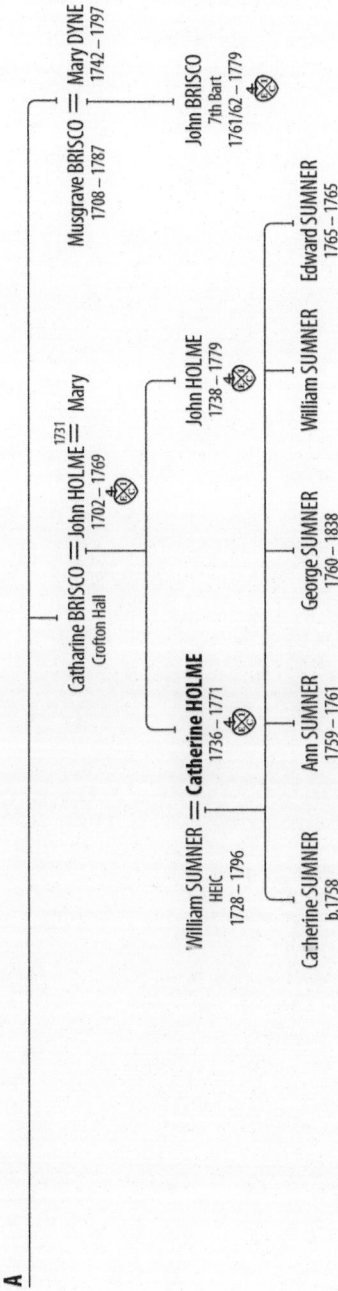

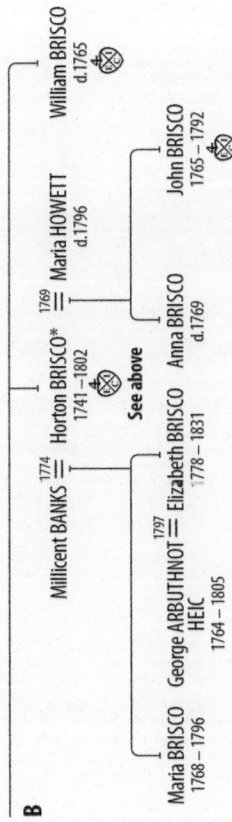

* Only key individuals are included

Enumerated Cumbrian   HEIC Non-enumerated East India Company appointee or licensee

Non-enumerated East India Company appointee or licensee

APPENDIX H: KIN CONNECTIONS OF THOMAS CUST*

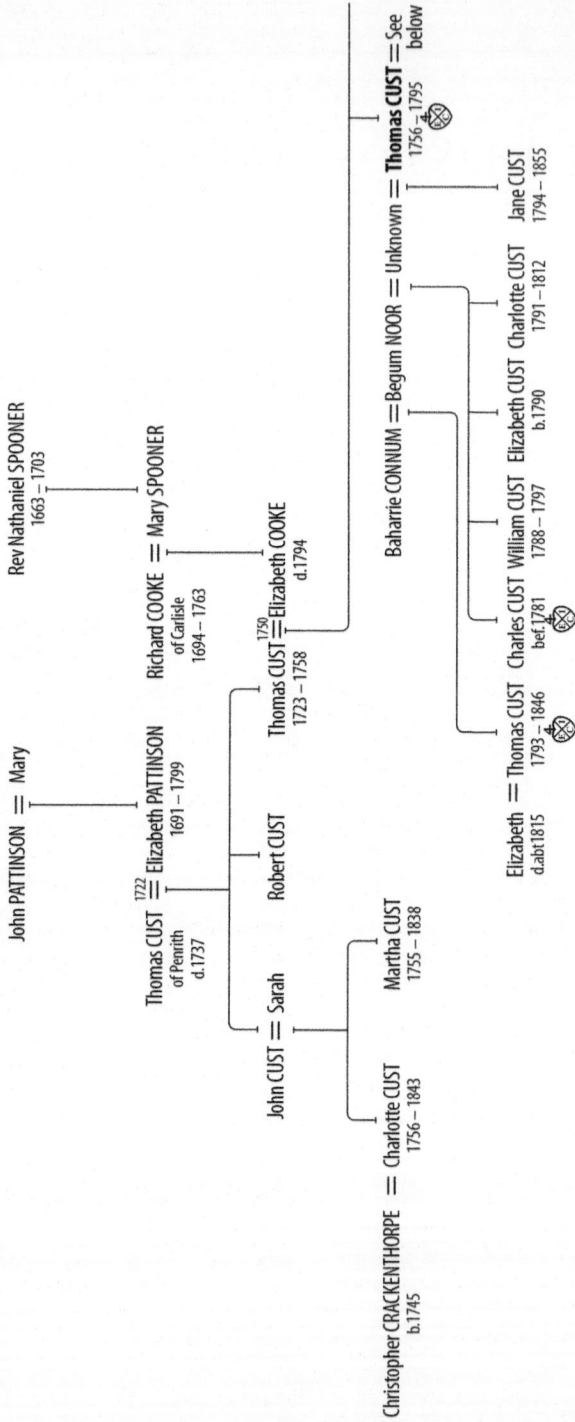

Rev Nathaniel SPOONER
1663 – 1703

Mary SPOONER

Richard COOKE
of Carlisle
1694 – 1763
= Mary SPOONER

John PATTINSON = Mary

Elizabeth PATTINSON
1691 – 1799

Thomas CUST
of Penrith
d.1737
= 1722
Elizabeth PATTINSON

Thomas CUST
1723 – 1758
= 1750
Elizabeth COOKE
d.1794

Robert CUST

John CUST = Sarah

Christopher CRACKENTHORPE
b.1745
= Charlotte CUST
1756 – 1843

Martha CUST
1755 – 1838

Baharrie CONNUM = Begum NOOR = Unknown = **Thomas CUST**
1756 – 1795
= See
below

Elizabeth
d.abt1815
= Thomas CUST
1793 – 1846

Charles CUST
bef.1781

William CUST
1788 – 1797

Elizabeth CUST
b.1790

Charlotte CUST
1791 – 1812

Jane CUST
1794 – 1855

Enumerated Cumbrian   **HEIC**   Non-enumerated East India Company appointee or licensee

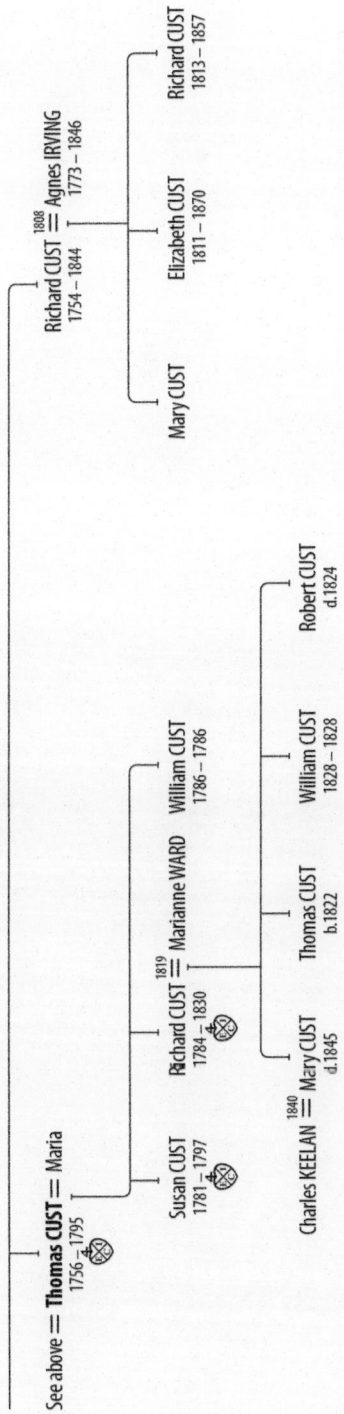

See above = **Thomas CUST** = Maria
1756 – 1795

Richard CUST [1808] = Agnes IRVING
1754 – 1844   1773 – 1846

Mary CUST   Elizabeth CUST   Richard CUST
1811 – 1870   1813 – 1857

Susan CUST
1781 – 1797

Richard CUST [1819] = Marianne WARD   William CUST
1784 – 1830   1786 – 1786

Charles KEELAN [1840] = Mary CUST   Thomas CUST   William CUST   Robert CUST
d.1845   b.1822   1828 – 1828   d.1824

* Only key individuals are included

⊗ Enumerated Cumbrian   **HEIC** Non-enumerated East India Company appointee or licensee

BIBLIOGRAPHY

Primary Sources

Archives and Manuscript Sources

A. Cumbria Archives Service (CAS)
BDBROUGHTON 19/39 Manor of Broughton-in-Furness
BDL/P3/63 Iain Maci. Livingston & Co., Solicitors, Ulverston: James Pennington, solicitors, Broughton-in-Furness
BPR 29/I/2 Satterthwaite All Saints
DAY 6/4/3 Aglionby Family of the Nunnery, Armathwaite
DBEN Benson Solicitors of Cockermouth
DCART C11/11, C11/32, C11/40, C11/42, C11/54, C11/61, C11/62 Cartmells, Solicitors of Cartmell: Deeds and Papers Relating to the Cust Family
DCC 2/51 Carleton Cowper Family, Carleton Hall, Penrith
DCU 1, 3/7 Curwen Family of Workington Hall
DHUD 5/12, 8, 10/2, 11, 12, 13/2, 13/3, 13/4, 13/11, 13/12, 14/1, 14/2 Hudleston Family of Hutton John, Greystoke
DSEN 5/5/1/4, 5/5/1/9 Senhouse Family of Netherhall, Maryport
DSHEFF 1 Sheffield family of Broadfield, Southwaite
DX 38/38 Brockbank Family, Quakers of Stanwix and Carlisle
DX 249/14, 294/16 Fergusson and Pattinson Families of Kirklinton
PROB Wills and Administrations: Diocese of Carlisle probate records, 1548–1858; Carlisle Probate Registry records, 1858–1941
WDFA 2/1, 2/4 Farrer Family of Witherslack
WDPP 8/1 Pearson and Pearson, Solicitors of Kirkby Lonsdale: Papers relating to the Underley Estate
WDRY ¼, 3/3 Le Fleming Family of Rydal Hall
WDX 1641/1 Miscellaneous documents for Long Marton and the Bellasis Family
YDLEW 10/49 Lewthwaite family of Broadgate, Thwaites, Millom

B. India Office Records and Private Papers (IOR) British Library
E: East India Company: General Correspondence 1602–1859
F: Board of Control Records 1784–1858
J: East India College, Haileybury
L/AG: Accountant General's Records c. 1601–1974
L/MAR: India Office: Marine Records c. 1600–1879
L/MIL: India Office: Military Department Records 1708–1959

Mss Eur G37: The Clive Collection
Mss Eur Photo Eur 035: John Brownrigg Bellasis papers 1821–1841
N: Returns of Baptisms, Marriages and Burials 1698–1969
O: Biographical Series 1702–1948
Z: Original Registers and Indexes to Records Series c. 1700–1950

C. Lancashire Archives Service (LAS)
ARR 11 Archdeaconry of Richmond Marriage Bonds
W/RW/C Probate Records Archdeaconry of Richmond Copeland Deanery

D. Nottingham University Manuscripts (NUM)
Pw F Portland (Welbeck) Collection 1571–1896

E. British Library (BL)
Add MS 29172: 1790–1792 Correspondence of Warren Hastings: Vol. xli. 1790–1792

F. Durham University Special Collections
GB 033 HUD Hudleston Papers

G. Carlisle Library Special Collections
Heward, J., Diary of Jessie Heward, 1847

Online Databases

Bank of England Wills Extracts 1717–1845. www.findmypast.co.uk.
Cambridge University Alumni, 1261–1900 [online database]. Provo, UT, USA: Ancestry.com
    Operations Inc, 1999. http://home.ancestry.co.uk/
Church of England Parish Registers, 1538–1812: London – Saint Marylebone, Day book of
    baptisms, Feb. 1811–Mar. 1812 [online database]. Provo, UT, USA: Ancestry.com
    Operations, Inc., 2010. http://home.ancestry.co.uk/
Clergy of the Church of England Database 1540–1835. http://theclergydatabase.org.uk/
Collected Letters of Robert Southey, L. Pratt, T. Fulford and I. Packer (eds), www.rc.umd.edu/
    editions/southey_letters/
*The Cullen Project: The Consultation Letters of Dr William Cullen (1710–1790) at the Royal College
    of Physicians of Edinburgh.* http://cullenproject.ac.uk/.
England and Wales, Criminal Registers, 1791–1892 [online database]. Provo, UT, USA:
    Ancestry.com Operations Inc, 2009. http://home.ancestry.co.uk/
England Deaths and Burials, 1813–1980 [online database]. Provo, UT, USA: Ancestry.com
    Operations, Inc., 2010. http://home.ancestry.co.uk/
England Marriages 1538–1973 Transcriptions [online database]. Provo, UT, USA: Ancestry.
    com Operations, Inc., 2010. http://home.ancestry.co.uk/
England, Return of Owners of Land, 1873 [online database]. Provo, UT, USA: Ancestry.com
    Operations, Inc., 2010. http://home.ancestry.co.uk/
Familysearch: England Births and Christenings, 1538–1975, database. https://familysearch.org/
Plarr's Lives of the Fellows Online. http://livesonline.rcseng.ac.uk.
UK and Ireland, Find A Grave Index, 1300s–Current [online database]. Provo, UT, USA:
    Ancestry.com Operations, Inc., 2012. http://home.ancestry.co.uk/

India Office Family Search Index. http://indiafamily.bl.uk/ui/home.aspx

Oxford University Alumni, 1500–1886 [online database]. Ancestry.com Operations Inc, 2007. http://home.ancestry.co.uk/

National Archives, *Prerogative Court of Canterbury and Related Probate Jurisdictions: Will Registers (PCC)* http://discovery.nationalarchives.gov.uk/ and http://home.ancestry.co.uk/ Ancestry.com

Prerogative & Exchequer Courts of York, Probate Index, 1688–1858. http://search.findmypast.co.uk

Principal Probate Registry, *England & Wales, National Probate Calendar (Index of Wills and Administrations) 1858–1966* [online database]. Provo, UT, USA: Ancestry.com Operations Inc, 2010. http://home.ancestry.co.uk/

New South Wales Convicts Indents 1788–1842, State Archives New South Wales. Ancestry.com. *New South Wales, Australia, Convict Indents, 1788–1842* [online database]. Provo, UT, USA: Ancestry.com Operations, Inc., 2011. http://home.ancestry.co.uk/

U.K. and U.S. Directories, 1680–1830 [online database]. Provo, UT, USA: Ancestry.com Operations Inc, 2003. http://home.ancestry.co.uk/

Contemporary Printed Sources

A. Newspapers and Periodicals

Allen's Indian Mail
The Annual Register
Asiatic Journal and Monthly Miscellany
Asiatic Journal
The Asiatic Register
Berkshire Chronicle
Bombay Courier
Bombay Times
Bombay Times and Journal of Commerce
Carlisle Journal
Carlisle Patriot
Cumberland and Westmorland Advertiser, and Penrith Literary Chronicle
Cumberland Pacquet, and Ware's Whitehaven Advertiser
East India Register and Directory
East India Register & Army List
The European Magazine and London Review
Gentleman's Magazine
Inverness Courier
Kendal Mercury
Lancaster Gazette
Leeds Intelligencer
London Daily News
Manchester Courier and Lancashire General Advertiser
Missionary Register
The Monthly Magazine: Or, British Register
Morning Chronicle
Morning Post

Newcastle Courant
Newcastle Journal
New Monthly Magazine
Oriental Journal
Oxford Journal
The Patrician
Preston Chronicle
Sussex Advertiser
Western Times
Westmorland Gazette
Worcester Journal

Official Publications

Brougham, H., Education of the Poor, House of Commons Debate 28 June 1820, vol. 2., *Hansard*, cc. 49–91
Government of Tamil Nadu, Records of Fort St. George: Public Despatches from England 1756~1757, vol. 60 (Madras, Government of Tamil Nadu, 1971)
The London Gazette, www.thegazette.co.uk
Parliamentary Papers, *House of Commons and Command*, Volume 6 HM Stationery 1821 by Great Britain. Parliament. House of Commons

Diaries, Letters, Memoirs, Books, and Pamphlets of Contemporary Material

Anon., *A Picture of Carlisle and Directory; Containing an Historical and Topographical Account of that City, its Public Buildings and Institutions; also a View of the Progress of Commerce and Manufactures; Arts, Literature &c., With a short description of the most remarkable seats and curiosities in the adjoining parts of Cumberland* (Carlisle, A. Henderson, 1810)
Atkinson, G., *The Worthies of Westmorland: Or Notable Persons Born in that County since the Reformation* (London, J. Robinson, 1850)
Bailey, P., *South Park Street Cemetery, Calcutta: MIs Up to 1851* (CALCUTTA, HOLMES & CO., 2009)
Baines, E., *A Companion to the Lakes of Cumberland, Westmorland, and Lancashire: In a Descriptive Account of a Family Tour and Excursions on Horseback and on Foot: With a New, Copious, and Correct Itinerary* (London, Simpkins and Marshall, 1834)
Bellasis, E. (ed.), *Westmorland Church Notes: Being the Heraldry, Epitaphs and other Inscriptions in the Thirty-two Ancient Parish Churches and Churchyards of that County*, vols 1 and 2 (Kendal, Titus Wilson, 1889)
Betham, W., *The Baronetage of England: Or The History of the English Baronets, and Such Baronets of Scotland, as are of English Families; with Genealogical Tables, and Engravings of Their Coats of Arms*, vol. 4 (London, E. Lloyd, 1804)
Burke, E., *Mr. Burke's speech, on the 1st December 1783, upon the question for the Speaker's leaving the chair, in order for the House to resolve itself into a committee on Mr. Fox's East India Bill* (London, J. Dodsley, 1784)
Burke, J., *A Genealogical and Heraldic History of the Commoners of Great Britain and Ireland Enjoying Territorial Possessions Or High Official Rank: But Uninvested with Heritable Honours*, vol. 2 (London, Henry Colburn, 1836)

Burke, J., *A Genealogical and Heraldic History of the Commoners of Great Britain and Ireland Enjoying Territorial Possessions Or High Official Rank: But Uninvested with Heritable Honours*, vol. 3 (London, Henry Colburn, 1836)

Burke, J., *A Genealogical and Heraldic History of the Landed Gentry; Or, Commoners of Great Britain and Ireland Etc*, vol. 3 (London, Henry Colburn, 1838)

Cooke, G. A., *Topography of Great Britain Being an Accurate and Comprehensive Topographical and Statistical Description of all the Counties in England, Scotland and Wales, with the Adjacent Islands: Illustrated with Maps of the Counties, Which Form a Complete British Atlas*, vol. 22 (London, Sherwood, Neeley and Jones, 1820)

de Selincourt, E. (ed.), *The Letters of William and Dorothy Wordsworth: The Early Years, 1787–1805* (2nd edition revised by C. Shaver, Oxford, Clarendon Press, 1967)

Ferguson, R. S. and W. Nanson (eds), *Some Municipal Records of the City of Carlisle : viz., the Elizabethan Constitutions, Orders, Provisions, Articles, and Rules from the Dormont Book, and the Rules and Orders of the Eight Trading Guilds, Prefaced by Chapters on the Corporation Charters and Guilds :Illustrated by Extracts from the Courtleet Rolls and From the Minutes of the Corporation and Guilds Extra Series (Cumberland and Westmorland Antiquarian and Archaeological Society)*, no. 4 (Carlisle, C. Thurnam & Sons, 1887)

Hardy, H. C., *A Register of Ships, Employed in the Service of the Honorable the United East India Company, from the Year 1760 to 1810: With an Appendix, Containing a Variety of Particulars, and Useful Information Interesting to Those Concerned with East India Commerce* (London, Black, Parry, and Kingsbury, 1811)

Heysham, J., *An Account of the Jail Fever, or Typhus Carcerum: As it Appeared at Carlisle in the Year 1781* (London, T. Cadell, J. Murray, R. Faulder, 1782)

Heysham, J., *Observations on the Bills of Mortality in Carlisle for the year M DCC LXXXVII* (London, Gale ECCO, Print Editions, 2010)

Hibbert, S., Palmer, J., Whatton, W., and J. Greswell, *History of the Foundations in Manchester of Christ's College, Chetham's Hospital, and the Free Grammar School*, vol. 2 (London, William Pickering, 1834)

Hill, M. A. (ed.), *An Independent Woman's Lake District Writings: Harriet Martineau* (New York, Humanity Books, 2004)

Holmes & Co., *The Bengal Obituary: Or, a Record to Perpetuate the Memory of Departed Worth, Being a Compilation of Tablets and Monumental Inscriptions from Various Parts of the Bengal and Agra Presidencies. To which is Added Biographical Sketches and Memoirs of Such as Have Preeminently Distinquished Themselves in History of British India, Since the Formation of the European Settlement to the Present Time* (London, Thacker & Co., 1851)

Huddart, J., *Memoir of the late Captain Joseph Huddart, F. R. S. & C* (London, W. Phillips, 1821)

Hull, E, *The European in India, or, an Anglo-Indian's Vade-Mecum* (New Delhi, Asian Educational Services, 2004)

Hutchinson, W., *The History and Antiquities of the City of Carlisle: and its Vicinity* (Carlisle, F. Jollies, 1796)

Jollie, F., *Jollie's Cumberland Guide & Directory* (Carlisle, F. Jollie & Sons, 1811)

Jollie, F. (ed.), *A Political History of the City of Carlisle from the Year 1700 to the Present Time* (Carlisle, F. Jollie jun. and J. Jollie, 1820)

Ketcham, C. (ed.), *The Letters of John Wordsworth* (Ithaca, NY, Cornell University Press, 1969)

Le Pichon, A., *China Trade and Empire: Jardine, Matheson & Co. and the Origins of British Rule in Hong Kong, 1827–1843* (Reprint, Oxford, Oxford University Press, 2007)

Lewis, T. H. (ed.), *The Lewin Letters: A Selection from the Correspondence & Diaries of an English Family 1756–1884*, vol. 1 (London, Archibald Constable & Co., 1909)

Lysons, D., *The Environs of London: Volume 4, Counties of Herts, Essex and Kent* (London, T. Cadell and W. Davies, 1796)

Lysons, D. and S. Lysons, *Magna Britannia; being a Concise Topographical Account of the Several Counties of Great Britain – Volume the Fourth: Cumberland* (London, T. Cadell and W. Davies, 1816)

Love, H. D., *Vestiges of Old Madras, 1640–1800: traced from the East India Company's records preserved at Fort St. George and the India Office and from other sources*, vols 1–3 (London, John Murray, 1913)

McGrath, J. R. (ed.), *The Flemings in Oxford: Being documents selected from the Rydal papers in Illustration of the Lives and Ways of Oxford Men* (Oxford, Oxford Historical Society, 1913)

Medland, W. and C. Weobly, *A Collection of Remarkable and Interesting Criminal Trials, Actions at Law, &c: To which is Prefixed, an Essay on Reprieve and Pardon, and Biographical Sketches of John Lord Eldon, and Mr. Mingay*, vol., 2 (London, J. D Dewick, 1804)

Meline, Cans & Co., *The General Stud Book: Containing pedigrees Race Horses &c. &c. From the Earliest Accounts to the Year 1835 Inclusive in Four Volumes*, vol. iv (Brussels, Meline, Cans & Co., 1839)

Neale, J. P., *Views of the Seats of Noblemen and Gentlemen*, vol. 3 (Second Series, London, Sherwood, Gilbert and Piper, 1826)

Nicholson, C., *The Annals of Kendal: Being a Historical and Descriptive Account of Kendal and the Neighbourhood: With Biographical Sketches of Many Eminent Personages Connected with the Town* (2nd edition, London, Whitaker & Co., 1861)

Nowell, A., Copy of the petition of Alexander Nowell, esq. to the Honourable the Court of Directors of the East India Company, dated the 15th April 1811, with enclosures nos. 1. & 2., on the subject of advances by the Bengal Government to the indigo planters – together with copy of the reply of the Court of Directors to the said petition, dated the 14th June 1811, *Papers Relating to East India Affairs: Advances by the Bengal Government to Indigo Planters: Financial Letter from Bengal and One from the Court of Directors in Answer Thereto; Supplies Furnished from India to China; Merchandize and Bullion* (London, House of Commons, 10 July 1813)

O'Malley, L. S. S., *Bihar and Orissa District Gazetteers: Monghyr* (New Delhi, Concept Publishing, 2007)

Otley, J., *A Concise Description of the English Lakes and Adjacent Mountains: With General Directions to Tourists; Notices of the Botany, Minerology, and Geology of the Distinct; Observations on Meteorology; The Floating Island in Derwent Lake; And the Black-Lead Mine in Borrowdale* (5th edition, Keswick, J. Otley, 1835)

Penney, N. (ed.), *The Household Account Book of Sarah Fell of Swarthmoor Hall* (Cambridge, Cambridge University Press, 2014)

Pigot and Co., *National Commercial Directory for 1828–9: Cumberland Lancashire Westmorland* (facsimile edition, Norwich, Michael Winton, 1995)

Prinsep, C. G. (ed.), *Record of Services of the Honourable East India Company's Civil Servants in the Madras Presidency, from 1741 to 1858 …: Including Chronological Lists of Governors, Commanders-in-Chief, Chief Justices and Judges, of the Madras Presidency, Between 1652 and 1858 As well as Lists of the Directors of the East India Company; Chairmen and Deputy Chairmen of the Direction; and Presidents of the Board of Control* (Reprint, BiblioLife, no date)

Romney, J., *Memoirs of the Life and Works of George Romney Including Various Letters and Testimonies to his Genius &c., Also, Some Particulars of the Life of Peter Romney, His Brother, A Young Artist of Great Genius and Promising Talents but of Short Life* (London, Baldwin and Cradock, 1830)

Smith, S. D. (ed.), *'An Exact and Industrious Tradesman': The Letter Book of Joseph Symson of Kendal 1711–1720* (Oxford, Oxford University Press, 2002)

Sopwith, T., *An Account of the Mining Districts of Alston Moor, Weardale and Teesdale in Cumberland and Durham: Comprising Descriptive Sketches of the Scenery, Antiquities, Geology and Mining Operations in the Upper Dales of the Rivers Tyne, Wear and Tees* (Alnwick, W. Davison, 1833)

Theall, G., *Records of the Cape Colony 1793–1831 Copied for the Cape government, From the Manuscript Documents in the Public Record Office* (London, Cape Colony Government, 1897)

Tyson, B. (ed.), *The Estate and Household Accounts of Sir Daniel Fleming of Rydal Hall, Westmorland from 1688–1701* (Kendal, CWAAS Record Series Volume XIII, 2001)

West, T. and W. Close, *The Antiquities of Furness: Illustrated with Engravings* (Ulverston, George Ashburner, 1805)

Whellan, W., *The History and Topography of the Counties of Cumberland and Westmorland, Comprising their Ancient and Modern History, A General View of their Physical Character, Trade, Commerce, Manufactures. Agricultural Condition, Statistics, Etc.* (Pontefract, W. Whellan and Co., 1850)

Williamson, T., *The East India Vade Mecum or the Complete Guide to Gentlemen Intended for the Civil, Military or Naval Service of the Hon. East India Company vol. 1* (London, Black, Parry and Kingsbury, 1810)

Williamson, T., *The European in India: From a Collection of Drawings by Charles D'Oyley* (New Delhi, Asian Educational Services, 1995)

Wilson, C. R. (ed.), *The Early Annals of the English in Bengal: The Bengal Public Consultations for the First Half of the Eighteenth Century* (London, Thacker, 1900)

Wilson, C. R. (ed.), *Indian Records Series Old Fort William in Bengal: A Selection of Official Documents Dealing with its History, Vol. 1* (London, John Murray, 1906)

Wilson, C. R., *The Early Annals of the English in Bengal. Being the Bengal Public Consultations for the First Half of the Eighteenth Century. Vol. II, Part II: The Surman Embassy* (Calcutta, The Bengal Secretariat Book Deposit, 1911)

Winchester, A. J. L. (ed.), *The Diary of Isaac Fletcher of Underwood, Cumberland 1756–1781* (Kendal, CWAAS, Extra Series XXVII, 1994)

Wordsworth, W., *Guide to the Lakes* (London, Frances Lincoln, 2004)

Secondary Sources

Books

Anon., *Gazetteer of the Bombay Presidency: Tha'na: places of interest*, vol. 14 (Bombay, Government Central Press, 1882)

Anderson, C., *Subaltern Lives: Biographies of Colonialism in the Indian Ocean World, 1790–1920* (Cambridge, Cambridge University Press, 2012)

Anderson, J. W., 'TAYLOR, John Bladen (1764–1820)', in R. Thorne (ed.), *The History of Parliament: The House of Commons 1790–1820* (1986): www.historyofparliamentonline.org/volume/1790-1820/member/taylor-john-bladen-1764-1820.

Anderson, J. W. and R. G. Thorne, 'FAWCETT, Henry (1762–1816) of Scaleby Castle, nr. Carlisle, Cumb.', in R. Thorne (ed.), *The History of Parliament: The House of Commons 1790–1820* (1986): www.historyofparliamentonline.org/volume/1790-1820/member/fawcett-henry-1762-1816.

Anderson, J. W. and R. G. Thorne, 'HUDLESTON, John (1749–1835) of Bathwick, Som.', in R. Thorne (ed.), *The History of Parliament: The House of Commons 1790–1820*

(1986): www.historyofparliamentonline.org/volume/1790-1820/member/hudleston-john-1749-1835.

Arbuthnot, A., *Memories of the Arbuthnots of Kincardineshire and Aberdeenshire*, (London, G. Allen & Unwin, 1920)

Arkell, T., N. Evans and N. Goose (eds), *When Death Do Us Part: Understanding and Interpreting the Probate Records of Early Modern England* (Oxford, Leopard's Head Press, 2004)

Armitt, M. L., *Rydal* (Kendal, Titus Wilson & Son, 1916)

Baggs, A. P., D. K. Bolton and P. Croot, 'Islington: Growth: Highbury', in T. Baker and C. R. Elrington (eds), *A History of the County of Middlesex: Volume 8: Islington and Stoke Newington Parishes* (London, Victoria County History, 1985)

Baker, T. and C. R. Elrington (eds), *A History of the County of Middlesex: Volume 8: Islington and Stoke Newington Parishes* (London, Victoria County History, 1985)

Bardsley, C. W., *Chronicles of the Town and Church of Ulverston* (Ulverston, James Atkinson, 1885)

Barczewski, S., *Country Houses and the British Empire, 1700–1930* (Manchester, Manchester University Press, 2014)

Battle, J. (ed.), *Underley Hall Kirkby Lonsdale – Westmorland: A History of House and Occupants* (no publisher, 1969)

Beattie, J., 'Health Panics, Migration and Ecological Exchange in the Aftermath of the 1857 Uprising: India, New Zealand and Australia', in R. Peckham (ed.), *Empires of Panic: Epidemics and Colonial Anxieties* (Hong Kong, Hong Kong University, 2015)

Becket, J. V., *Coal and Tobacco: The Lowthers and the Economic Development of West Cumberland 1660–1760* (Cambridge, Cambridge University Press, 1981)

Bellasis, M., *Honourable Company* (London, Hollis & Carter, 1952)

Berg, M., 'Consumption in Eighteenth Century and Early Nineteenth Century Britain', in R. Floud and P. Johnson (eds), *The Cambridge Economic History of Modern Britain: Volume 1 Industrialisation, 1700–1860* (Cambridge, Cambridge University Press, 2004)

Berry, H. and J. Gregory (eds), *Creating and Consuming Culture in North-East England, 1660–1830* (Aldershot, Ashgate, 2004)

Bingham, R., *Kendal: A Social History* (Milnthorpe, Cicerone Press, 1995)

Black, J., *Eighteenth-Century Britain, 1688–1783* (2nd edition, London, Palgrave Macmillan, 2008)

Bleackley, H., *Some Distinguished Victims of the Scaffold* (London, Kegan Paul, Trench, Trubner, & Co., 1905)

Bonsall, B., *Sir James Lowther and Cumberland and Westmorland Elections 1754–1775* (Manchester, Manchester University Press, 1960)

Borradaile, A., *Sketch of the Borradailes of Cumberland* (London, MacClure and MacDonald, 1881)

Borsay, P. (ed.), *The Eighteenth Century Town, 1688–1820* (London, Longman, 1990)

Borsay, P., *The English Urban Renaissance: Culture and Society in the Provincial Town 1660–1770* (Oxford, Clarendon Press, 1991)

Bouch, C. L. and G. P. Jones, *A Short Economic and Social History of the Lake Counties 1500–1830* (Manchester, Manchester University Press, 1961)

Boumphrey, R. S., C. R. Hudleston and J. Hughes, *An Armorial for Westmorland and Lonsdale* (Kendal, Lake District Museum Trust and CWAAS, 1975)

Bourdelais, P., *Epidemics Laid Low: A History of What Happened in Rich Countries* (Baltimore, MD, Johns Hopkins University Press, 2006)

Bourdieu, P., 'The Forms of Capital', in J. Richardson (ed.), *Handbook of Theory and Research for the Sociology of Education* (New York, Greenwood, 1986)

Bourdieu, P., *The Logic of Practice* (Cambridge, Polity Press, 1990)

Bourdieu, P., *Distinction: A Social Critique of the Judgement of Taste* (London, Routledge & Kegan Paul, 1994)

Bowen, H. V., 'Cotton, Joseph (1745–1825)', *Oxford Dictionary of National Biography* (Oxford, Oxford University Press, 2004; online edition, Jan. 2008): www.oxforddnb.com/view/article/6421, accessed 31 October 2015.

Bowen, H. V., *The Business of Empire: The East India Company and Imperial Britain, 1756–1833* (Cambridge, Cambridge University Press, 2008)

Bowen, H. V., M. Lincoln and N. Rigby (eds), *The Worlds of the East India Company* (Woodbridge, The Boydell Press, 2004)

Bowen, H. V., J. McAleer, and R. J. Blyth, *Monsoon Traders: The Maritime World of the East India Company* (London, Scala, 2011)

Bowen, H. V., E. Mancke and J. G. Reid (eds), *Britain's Oceanic Empire: Atlantic and India Ocean Worlds, c. 1550–1850* (Cambridge, Cambridge University Press, 2015)

Brant, C., *Eighteenth-Century Letters and British Culture* (Basingstoke, Palgrave Macmillan, 2010)

Brewer, J. and R. Porter (eds), *Consumption and the World of Goods* (London, Routledge, 1994)

Brooke, J., 'FLETCHER, Henry (c.1727–1807) of Clea Hall, Cumb.', in L. Namier (ed.), *The History of Parliament: The House of Commons 1754–1790* (1964): www.historyofparliamentonline.org/volume/1754-1790/member/fletcher-henry-1727-1807.

Buckham, S., '"The men that worked for England they have their graves at home": Consumerist issues within the production and purchases of gravestones in Victorian York', in S. Tarlow and S. West (eds), *The Familiar Past: Archaeologies Britain, 1550–1950* (London, Routledge, 1999)

Bulley, A., *The Bombay Country Ships, 1790–1833* (Richmond, Curzon Press, 2000)

Bungay, P., *The Dapper Little Banker: The Life of Rowland Stephenson* (Kindle edition, Lancaster, Scotforth Books, 2011)

Burke, B., *Genealogical and Heraldic History of the Landed Gentry of Great Britain & Ireland*, vol. 1 (London, Harrison, 1879)

Burton, A. (ed.), *Archive Stories: Facts, Fictions, and the Writing of History* (Durham, NC, Duke University Press, 2006)

Campbell, C., *The Romantic Ethic and the Spirit of Modern Consumerism* (Oxford, Blackwell, 1987)

Campbell, C., 'Understanding Traditional and Modern Patterns of Consumption in Eighteenth Century England: A Character-Action Approach', in J. Brewer and R. Porter (eds), *Consumption and the World of Goods* (London, Routledge, 1994)

Campbell, D. M., *Java: Past & Present A Description of the Most Beautiful Country in the World, its Ancient History, People, Antiquities and its Products*, vol. 1 (London, William Heinemann, 1915)

Cannon, J., *Aristocratic Century: The Peerage of Eighteenth-Century England* (Cambridge, Cambridge University Press, 1987)

Chatterton, E. Keble, *A World for the Taking: The Ships of the Honourable East India Company* (Tucson, AZ, Fireship Press, 2008)

Chattopadhyay, S., 'The Other Face of Primitive Accumulation: The Garden House in British Colonial Bengal', in P. Scriver and V. Prakash (eds), *Colonial Modernities: Building, Dwelling and Architecture in British India and Ceylon* (London, Routledge, 2007)

Chaudhuri, N., S. J. Katz and M. E. Perry (eds), *Contesting Archives: Finding Women in the Sources* (Urbana, University of Illinois Press, 2010)

Christie, C., *The British Country House in the Eighteenth Century* (Manchester, Manchester University Press, 2002)

Christie, I. C., 'ATKINSON, Richard (1738–85) of Fenchurch St., London', in J. Brooke (ed.), *The History of Parliament: The House of Commons 1754–1790* (1964): www.historyof-parliamentonline.org/volume/1754-1790/member/atkinson-richard-1738-85.

Churches, C., 'Putting Women in Their Place: Female Litigants at Whitehaven, 1660–1760', in N. E. Wright, M. W. Ferguson and A. R. Buck (eds), *Women, Property and the Letters of the Law in Early Modern England* (Toronto, University of Toronto Press, 2004)

Colley, L., *Britons: Forging the Nation 1707–1837* (3rd revised edition, New Haven, CT, Yale University Press, 2009)

Corfield, P. J., *Power and the Professions in Britain 1700–1850* (London, Routledge, 2000)

Cox, J. and N. Cox, 'Probate 1500–1800: System in Transition', in T. Arkell, N. Evans and N. Goose (eds), *When Death Do Us Part: Understanding and Interpreting the Probate Records of Early Modern England* (Oxford, Leopard's Head Press, 2004)

Crosbie, B., *Irish Imperial Networks: Migration, Social Communication and Exchange in Nineteenth-Century India* (Cambridge, Cambridge University Press, 2012)

Cruickshanks, F. and R. Harrison, 'MUSGRAVE, Sir Christopher, 4th Bt. (c.1631–1704) of Edenhall, Cumberland', in D Hayton, E. Cruickshanks and S. Handley (eds), *History of Parliament* (1802): www.historyofparliamentonline.org/volume/1690-1715/member/musgrave-sir-christopher-1688-1736.

Curtin, P., *Death by Migration: Europe's Encounter with the Tropical World in the Nineteenth Century* (Cambridge, Cambridge University Press, 1989)

Danvers, F. C., M. Monier-Williams, S. C. Bayley, P. Wigram and B. Sapte (eds), *Memorials of Old Haileybury* (Westminster, A. Constable, 1894)

Davidoff, L., *Thicker than Water: Siblings and their Relations, 1780–1920* (Oxford, Oxford University Press, 2011)

Davidoff, L. and Leonore Davidoff (Author)› Visit Amazon's Leonore Davidoff Page Find all the books, read about the author, and more. See search results for this author name Are you an Author? Learn about Author Central

Hall, C., *Family Fortunes: Men and Women of the English Middle Class 1780–1850* (revised edition, Abingdon, Routledge, 2003)

Dickson, D., J. Parmentier and J. Ohlmeyer (eds), *Irish and Scottish Mercantile Networks in Europe and Overseas in the Seventeenth and Eighteenth Centuries* (Gent, Academia Press, 2007)

Docker, F., 'Docker, Joseph (1802–1884)', *Australian Dictionary of Biography*, National Centre of Biography, Australian National University: http://adb.anu.edu.au/biography/docker-joseph-3420/text5093, accessed 13 January 2016.

Dodwell, H., *The Nabobs of Madras* (New Delhi, Asian Educational Services, 1986)

Dresser, M. and A. Hann (eds), *Slavery and the British Country House* (Swindon, English Heritage, 2013)

Drummond, M., 'STEPHENSON, Rowland (?1728–1807) of Scaleby Castle, nr. Carlisle, Cumb.', in L. Namier and J. Brooke (eds), *The History of Parliament: The House of Commons 1754–1790* (1964): www.historyofparliamentonline.org/volume/1754-1790/member/stephenson-rowland-1728-1807.

Drummond, 'STEPHENSON, John (?1709–94) of Brentford, Mdx.', in L. Namier and J. Brooke (eds), *The History of Parliament: The House of Commons 1754–1790* (1964): www.histo-ryofparliamentonline.org/volume/1754-1790/member/stephenson-john-1709-94.

Dyer, C. (ed.), *The Self-Contained Village? The Social History of Rural Communities 1250–1900* (Hatfield, University of Hertfordshire Press, 2007)

Eddershaw, M., *Grand Fashionable Nights: Kendal Theatre 1575–1985* (Lancaster, Centre for North West Regional Studies, University of Lancaster, 1989)

Eden District Council, *Dufton Conservation Area Character Appraisal* (Eden District Council, December 2007)

Edwardes, M., *The Nabobs at Home* (London, Constable, 1993)

Escott, M., 'LUSHINGTON, James Law (1780–1859) of 14 Portman Square, Mdx.', in D. R. Fisher (ed.), *The History of Parliament: The House of Commons 1820–1832* (2009): www.historyofparliamentonline.org/volume/1820-1832/member/lushington-james-1780-1859.

Escott, M., 'NOWELL, Alexander (1761–1842) of Underley Park, Kirkby Lonsdale, Westmld. and Wimpole Street, Mdx.', in D. R. Fisher (ed.), *The History of Parliament: The House of Commons 1820–1832* (2009): www.historyofparliamentonline.org/volume/1820-1832/member/nowell-alexander-1761-1842.

Farrington, A., *A Biographical Index of East India Company Maritime Officers 1600–1834* (London, British Library, 1999)

Fell, A, *The Early Iron Industry of Furness and District* (London, Frank Cass & Co., 1968)

Finn, M., *The Character of Credit: Personal Debt in English Culture, 1740–1914* (Cambridge, Cambridge University Press, 2007)

Finn, M., 'The Barlow Bastards: Romance Comes Home from the Empire', in M. Finn, M. Lobban and J. Bourne Taylor (eds), *Legitimacy and Illegitimacy in Nineteenth Century Law, Literature and History* (Basingstoke, Palgrave Macmillan, 2010)

Finn, M., M. Lobban and J. Bourne Taylor (eds), *Legitimacy and Illegitimacy in Nineteenth Century Law, Literature and History* (Basingstoke, Palgrave Macmillan, 2010)

Fisher, S., 'Huddart, Joseph (1741–1816)', *Oxford Dictionary of National Biography*, (Oxford, Oxford University Press, 2004; online edition, Jan. 2008): www.oxforddnb.com/view/article/14023, accessed 31 October 2015.

Floud, R. and P. Johnson (eds), *The Cambridge Economic History of Modern Britain: Volume 1 Industrialisation, 1700–1860* (Cambridge, Cambridge University Press, 2004)

Forrest, G., *Life of Lord Clive* (London, Gassell and Company, 1918)

Forsyth, A., *Highway to the World: The People and Their Little Wooden Ships, Brigs, Brigantines, and Snows of Cumberland in the 18th and 19th Centuries* (Carlisle, Bookcase, 2011)

Foster, J., *The Pedigree of Wilson of High Wray and Kendal and the Families Connected with Them* (Printed for private circulation, 1871)

French, H. R., *The Middle Sort of People in Provincial England, 1600–1750* (Oxford, Oxford University Press, 2007)

Furber, H., *Bombay Presidency in the Mid-eighteenth Century* (London, Asia Publishing House, 1965)

Furber, H., *John Company at Work: A Study of European Expansion in India in the Late Eighteenth Century* (New York, Octagon Books, 1970)

Furber, H., *Private Fortunes and Company Profits in the India Trade in the 18th Century* (Aldershot, Variorum, 1997)

Galbraith, A., *The Fleming Family of Rydal Hall* (London, Shoes With Rockets, 2006)

Gater, G. H. and W. H. Godfrey (eds), *Survey of London: Volume 15, All Hallows, Barking-By-The-Tower (Part II)* (London, London County Council, 1934)

Ghosh, D., 'Decoding the Nameless: Gender, Subjectivity, and Historical Methodologies in Reading the Archives of Colonial India', in K. Wilson (ed.), *A New Imperial History: Culture, Identity, Modernity, 1660–1840* (Cambridge, Cambridge University Press, 2004)

Ghosh, D., *Sex and the Family in Colonial India: The Making of Empire* (Cambridge, Cambridge University Press, 2006)

Ghosh, D., 'National Narratives and the Politics of Miscegenation: Britain and India', in A. Burton (ed.), *Archive Stories: Facts, Fictions, and the Writing of History* (Durham, NC, Duke University Press, 2006)

Ghosh, S., *The Social Condition of the British Community in Bengal 1757–1800* (Leiden, E. J. Brill, 1970)

Gibson, W., 'Fleming, Sir George, second baronet (1667–1747)', *Oxford Dictionary of National Biography* (Oxford, Oxford University Press, 2004; online edition, Oct. 2007): www.oxforddnb.com.ezproxy.lancs.ac.uk/view/article/9698, accessed 29 June 2014.

Goose, N. and N. Evans, 'Wills as a Historical Source', in T. Arkell, N. Evans and N. Goose (eds), *When Death Do Us Part: Understanding and Interpreting the Probate Records of Early Modern England* (Oxford, Leopard's Head Press, 2004)

Grassby, R., *Kinship and Capitalism: Marriage, Family, and Business in the English-Speaking World, 1580–1740* (Cambridge, Cambridge University Press, 2006)

Groseclose, B., *British Sculpture and the Company Raj: Church Monuments and Public Statutory in Madras, Calcutta, and Bombay to 1858* (Newark, DE, University of Delaware Press, 1995)

Hall, C., N. Draper, K. McClelland, C. Donington and R. Lamb, *Legacies of British Slave-Ownership: Colonial Slavery and the Formation of Victorian Britain* (Cambridge, Cambridge University Press, 2014)

Hall, C. and S. Rose (eds), *At Home with the Empire: Metropolitan Culture and the Imperial World* (Cambridge, Cambridge University Press, 2009)

Hankinson, A., *The Regatta Men* (Milnthorpe, Cicerone Press, 1988)

Hans, N., *New Trends in Education in the Eighteenth Century* (London, Routledge & Kegan Paul, 1951)

Harrison, M., *Climates and Constitutions: Health, Race, Environment and British Imperialism in India, 1600–1850* (New York, Oxford University Press, 2000)

Harrison, M., 'Networks of Knowledge: Science and Medicine in Early Colonial India, c.1750–1820', in D. M. Peers and N. Gooptu (eds), *India and the British Empire* (Oxford, Oxford University Press, 2012)

Hawes, C., *Poor Relations: The Making of a Eurasian Community in British India 1773–1833* (Richmond, Curzon Press, 1996)

Hayton, D., 'J. Evans (*c.*1652–1724)', *Oxford Dictionary of National Biography* (Oxford, Oxford University Press, 2004, online edition, Jan. 2008): www.oxforddnb.com /view/ article/8961, accessed 6 July 2013.

Hedley, W. P. and C. R. Hudleston, *Cookson of Penrith, Cumberland and Newcastle upon Tyne* (Kendal, T. Wilson, 1964)

Hindle, P., *Roads and Tracks of the Lake District* (Milnthorpe, Cicerone Press, 1998)

Hodson, V., *List of the Officers of the Bengal Army 1758–1834 Volumes 1–4* (Reprint, Eastbourne, A Naval and Military Press, 1927)

Hoffheimer, M. H., 'Christian, Edward (*bap.* 1758, *d.* 1823)', *Oxford Dictionary of National Biography* (Oxford, Oxford University Press, 2004, online edition): www.oxforddnb.com. ezproxy.lancs.ac.uk/view/article/5355.

Holmes, R., *Sahib: The British Soldier in India 1750–1914* (London, Harper Perennial, 2005)

Holmes, S. E., *The Paradise of Furness: The Story of Conishead Priory & Its People* (Sedbergh, Handstand Press, 2012)

Howard, H. H., *Miscellanea Genealogica Et Heraldica, vol. 1* (London, Hamilton, Adams & Co., 1874)

Howe, A. C., 'Cotton, William (1786–1866)', *Oxford Dictionary of National Biography* (Oxford, Oxford University Press, 2004; online edition, Oct. 2006): www.oxforddnb.com/view/article/6432, accessed 31 October 2015.

Hudleston, C. R. and R. Boumphrey, *Cumberland Families and Heraldry: With a Supplement to an Armorial for Westmorland and Lonsdale* (Kendal, CWAAS, 1978)

Hudson, P. (ed.), *Regions and Industries: A Perspective on the Industrial Revolution in Britain* (Cambridge, Cambridge University Press, 1989)

Hughes, E, *North Country Life in the Eighteenth Century Vol 11 Cumberland & Westmorland 1700–1830* (London, Oxford University Press, 1965)

Hunt, M. R., *The Middling Sort: Commerce, Gender and the Family in England 1680–1780* (Berkeley, University of California Press, 1996)

Hyde, M. and N. Pevsner, *Cumbria: Cumberland, Westmorland and Furness* (London, Yale University Press, 2010)

Jones, M. G., *The Charity School Movement: A Study of Eighteenth Century Puritanism in Action* (Cambridge, Cambridge University Press, 2013)

Kidson, A., *George Romney, 1734–1802* (Princeton, NJ, Princeton University Press, 2002)

Kincaid, D., *British Social Life in India 1608–1937* (London, Routledge & Kegan Paul, 1973)

King, M., 'Working With/In the Archives', in S. Gunn and L. Faire (eds), *Research Methods for History* (Edinburgh, Edinburgh University Press, 2011)

King, S. and G. Timmins, *Making Sense of the Industrial Revolution: English Economy and Society 1700–1850* (Manchester, Manchester University Press, 2001)

Labaree, B. W., *Catalyst for Revolution: The Boston Tea Party* (Boston, MA, Massachusetts Bicentennial Commission Publication, 1973)

Langford, P., *A Polite and Commercial People: England 1727–1783* (Oxford, Oxford University Press, 1992)

Laughton, J. K., 'Pearson, Sir Richard (1731–1806) A. W. H. Pearsall', *Oxford Dictionary of National Biography* (Oxford, Oxford University Press, 2004; online edition, Jan. 2008): www.oxforddnb.com.ezproxy.lancs.ac.uk/view/article/21722.

Law, P. K., 'Dent Family (*per. c.*1820–1927)', *Oxford Dictionary of National Biography* (Oxford, Oxford University Press, 2004; online edition, Jan. 2015): www.oxforddnb.com/view/article/53862, accessed 31 October 2015.

Lawlor, C., *Consumption and Literature: The Making of the Romantic Disease* (Basingstoke, Palgrave, 2006)

Lawson, P., *The East India Company: A History* (London, Longman, 1987)

Lindley, B. C. and J. A. Heyworth, *Penrith Through Time* (Stroud, Amberley Publishing, 2013)

Lindsay, L. and J. Wood Sweet (eds), *Biography and the Black Atlantic* (Kindle edition, Philadelphia, University of Pennsylvania, 2014)

McCabe, I., *A History of Global Consumption: 1500–1800* (Abingdon, Routledge, 2015)

McConnell, A., 'Troughton, Edward (1753–1835)', *Oxford Dictionary of National Biography* (Oxford, Oxford University Press, 2004; online edition, Oct. 2007): www.oxforddnb.com.ezproxy.lancs.ac.uk/view/article/27767.

McGilvray, G. K., *East India Patronage and the British State: The Scottish Elite and Politics in the Eighteenth Century* (London, Tauris Academic Studies, 2008)

McVicker, M. F., *Women Adventurers, 1750–1900: A Biographical Dictionary, with Excerpts from Selected Travel Writings* (Jefferson, NC, McFarland Publishing, 2008)

Marr, J. E., *Westmorland* (New York, Cambridge University Press, 2013)

Marshall, J. D., *Kendal 1661–1801: The Growth of a Modern Town* (Kendal, Titus Wilson & Son, no date)

Marshall, J. D., *Furness and the Industrial Revolution* (Beckernet, Barrow in Furness Library, 1958)

Marshall, J. D., 'Stages of industrialisation in Cumbria', in P. Hudson (ed.), *Regions and Industries: A Perspective on the Industrial Revolution in Britain* (Cambridge, Cambridge University Press, 1989)

Marshall, J. D. and J. K. Walton, *The Lake Counties from 1830 to the Mid-Twentieth Century: A Study of Regional Change* (Manchester, Manchester University Press, 1981)

Marshall, P. J., *East Indian Fortunes: British in Bengal in the Eighteenth Century* (Oxford, Oxford University Press, 1976)

Marshall, P. J., *The Making and Unmaking of Empires: Britain, India and America, c.1750–1783* (Oxford, Oxford University Press, 2005)

Massie, A. W., 'Musgrave, Sir Thomas, seventh baronet (1738–1812)', *Oxford Dictionary of National Biography* (Oxford, Oxford University Press, 2004, online edition, Jan. 2008): www.oxforddnb.com.ezproxy.lancs.ac.uk/view/article/19666.

Mentz, S., *The English Gentleman Merchant at Work: Madras and the City of London 1660–1740* (Copenhagen, Museum Tusculanum Press, University of Copenhagen, 2005)

Menuge, A., '"Inhabited by Strangers": Tourism and the Lake District Villa', in J. K. Walton and J. Wood (eds), *The Making of a Cultural Landscape: The English Lake District as Tourist Destination, 1750–2010* (Farnham, Ashgate, 2013)

Miller, J., 'A Historical Appreciation of the Biographical Turn', in L. Lindsay and J. Wood Sweet (eds), *Biography and the Black Atlantic* (Kindle edition, Philadelphia, University of Pennsylvania, 2014)

Mingay, G. E., *English Landed Society in the Eighteenth Century* (London, Routledge, 2007)

Mitchell, B., *British Historical Statistics* (Cambridge, Cambridge University Press, 2011)

Morgan, K., *Slavery, Atlantic Trade and the British Economy, 1660–1800* (Cambridge, Cambridge University Press, 2000)

Morris, R. J., *Men, Women and Property in England, 1780–1870: A Social and Economic History of Family Strategies Amongst the Leeds Middle Classes* (Cambridge, Cambridge University Press, 2005)

Murdoch, A., *British History 1660–1832: National Identity and Local Culture* (Basingstoke, Macmillan Press, 1998)

Murphy, B. and R. G. Thorne, 'BENN WALSH, John (1759–1825) of Warfield Park, Berks.', in R. Thorne, *The History of Parliament: The House of Commons 1790–1820* (1986): www.historyofparliamentonline.org/volume/1790-1820/member/benn-walsh-john-1759-1825.

National Museums Liverpool, Maritime Archives & Library Information Sheet 18: Thomas & John Brocklebank, www.liverpoolmuseums.org.uk/maritime/archive/sheet/18.

Nechtman, T., *Nabobs: Empire and Identity in Eighteenth-Century Britain* (Cambridge, Cambridge University Press, 2010)

Nixon, C. L., *The Orphan in Eighteenth Century Law and Literature: Estate, Blood and Body* (Farnham, Ashgate, 2011)

Norcliffe, C. B., *Some Account of the Family of Robinson of the White House, Appleby, Westmorland* (Westminster, Nichols & Son, 1874)

Ogborn, M., *Global Lives: Britain and the World 1550–1800* (Cambridge, Cambridge University Press, 2008)

Page, W. (ed.), 'Parishes: Ewhurst', in *A History of the County of Hampshire: Volume 4* (London, Victoria County History, 1911)

Parkinson, C. N., *Trade in the Eastern Seas 1793–1813* (Cambridge, Cambridge University Press, 2010)

Pearsall, S., *Atlantic Families: Lives and Letters in the Later Eighteenth Century* (Oxford, Oxford University Press, 2011)

Peckham, R. (ed.), *Empires of Panic: Epidemics and Colonial Anxieties* (Hong Kong, Hong Kong University, 2015)

Peers, D. M., *India under Colonial Rule 1700–1885* (Harlow, Pearson Longman, 2006)

Peers, D. M. and N. Gooptu, *India and the British Empire* (Oxford, Oxford University Press, 2012)

Philips, C. H., *The East India Company 1784–1834* (2nd edition, London, Hesperides Press, 2006)

Popp, A., *Entrepreneurial Families: Business, Marriage and Life in the Early Nineteenth Century* (London, Pickering & Chatto, 2012)

Porter, B., *The Absent Minded Imperialists: What the British Really Thought About Empire* (Oxford, Oxford University Press, 2004)

Porter, P., 'Science, Provincial Culture and Public Opinion in Enlightenment England', in P. Borsay (ed.), *The Eighteenth Century Town, 1688–1820* (London, Longman, 1990)

Powell, C. and S. Hebron, *Savage, Grandeur and Noblest Thoughts: Discovering the Lake District 1750–1820* (Grasmere, Wordsworth Trust, 2010)

Price, J. M., 'Haistwell, Edward (*c*.1658–1709)', *Oxford Dictionary of National Biography* (Oxford, Oxford University Press, 2004; online edition, Jan. 2008): www.oxforddnb.com.ezproxy.lancs.ac.uk/view/article/49857.

Raistrick, A., *Two Centuries of Industrial Welfare: London (Quaker) Lead Company, 1692–1905* (3rd revised edition, Littleborough, George Kelsall, 1988)

Richardson, J., *Furness, Past and Present: Its Histories and Antiquities*, vol. 1 (Barrow-in-Furness, J. Richardson London, Simpkin, Marshall, and Co., 1880)

Riddick, J. F., *The History of British India: A Chronology* (Westport, CT, Praeger, 2006)

Robins, N., *The Corporation That Changed the World: How the East India Company Shaped the Modern Multinational* (London, Pluto Press, 2006)

Rollinson, W., *A History of Cumberland and Westmorland* (Chichester, Phillimore Publishing, 1996)

Rothschild, E., *The Inner Life of Empires: An Eighteenth-Century History* (Princeton, NJ, Princeton University Press, 2012)

Routledge, A. W., *History & Guide Whitehaven* (Stroud, Tempus, 2002)

Routledge, G. B. (ed.), *Carlisle Grammar School Memorial Register 1264–1924* (Carlisle, Charles Thurnam and Sons, 1924)

Rubenstein, W. D., *Capitalism, Culture and Decline in Britain 1750–1990* (London, Routledge, 1994)

Rubenstein, W. D., *Men of Property: The Very Wealthy in Britain Since the Industrial Revolution* (2nd edition, London, Social Affairs Unit, 2006)

Rubenstein, W. D., *Who Were the Rich? A Biographical Directory of British Wealth-holders Volume One 1809–1839* (London, Social Affairs Unit, 2009)

Salmon, P., 'BORRADAILE, Richardson (1762–1835) of All Hallows Lane, London; 14 Duke Street, Westminster, Mdx. and Balham, Surr.', in D. R. Fisher, *The History of Parliament: The House of Commons 1820–1832* (2009): www.historyofparliamentonline.org/volume/1820-1832/member/borradaile-richardson-1762-1835.

Satchell, J. and O. Wilson, *Christopher Wilson of Kendal: An Eighteenth Century Hosier and Banker* (Kendal, Kendal Civic Society & Frank Peters Publishing, 1988)

Scriver, P. and V. Prakash (eds), *Colonial Modernities: Building, Dwelling and Architecture in British India and Ceylon* (London, Routledge, 2007)

Seeley, J. R., *The Expansion of England: Two Courses of Lectures* (London, Macmillan, 1914)

Smith, L., *A South Lakeland Nautical Dynasty: Captain Joseph Fayrer of Milnthorpe* (Arnside, Cumbria, Lensden Publishing, 2012)

Smith, S., *Slavery, Family and Gentry Capitalism in the British Atlantic: The World of the Lascelles 1648–1834* (Cambridge, Cambridge University Press, 2006)

Snell, K. D. M., *Parish and Belonging: Community, Identity and Welfare in England and Wales, 1700–1950* (Cambridge, Cambridge University Press, 2006)

Spear, P., *The Nabobs: A Study of the Social Life of the English in Eighteenth Century India* (London, Curzon Press, 1980)

Spedding, J. C. D., *The Spedding Family with Short Accounts of a Few Other Families Allied by Marriage* (Dublin, Alex. Thom and Company, 1909)

Starck, N., *Life after Death: The Art of Obituary* (Melbourne, Melbourne University Press, 2006)

Steedman, C., *Dust: The Archive and Cultural History* (New Brunswick, NJ, Rutgers University, 2002)

Stern, P. J., *The Company-State: Corporate Sovereignty and the Early Modern Foundations of the British Empire in India* (Oxford, Oxford University Press, 2011)

Stobart, J., *Sugar and Spice: Grocers and Groceries in Provincial England, 1650–1830* (Oxford, Oxford University Press, 2013)

Stone, L. and J. C. Fawtier-Stone, *An Open Elite? England 1540–1880* (Oxford, Clarendon Press, 1984)

Summerson, H., *'An Ancient Squires Family' The History of the Aglionbys c. 1130–2002* (Carlisle, Bookcase, 2007)

Sutherland, L., *The East India Company in 18th Century Politics* (Oxford, Clarendon Press, 1952)

Sweet, R., *The Writing of Urban Histories in Eighteenth-Century England* (Oxford, Clarendon Press, 1997)

Sweet, R., *The English Town, 1680–1840: Government, Society and Culture* (London, Routledge, 2014)

Tadmor, N., *Family and Friends in Eighteenth Century England: Household, Kinship and Patronage* (Cambridge, Cambridge University Press, 2001)

Tarlow, S., 'Wormie Clay and Blessed Sleep: Death and Disgust in Later Historic Britain', in S. Tarlow and S. West (eds), *The Familiar Past: Archaeologies Britain, 1550–1950* (London, Routledge, 1999)

Tarlow, S. and S. West (eds), *The Familiar Past: Archaeologies Britain, 1550–1950* (London, Routledge, 1999)

Tattersfield, N., *The Forgotten Trade: Comprising the Log of the Daniel and Henry of 1700 and Accounts of the Slave Trade from the Minor Ports of England 1698–1725* (Kindle edition, Pimlico, Random House, 1998)

Taylor, A., *The Websters of Kendal: A North-Western Architectural Dynasty* (CWAAS Record Series 17, edited Janet Martin, Kendal, CWAAS, 2004)

Thomas, J. H., *The East India Company and the Provinces in the Eighteenth Century: Volume 1 Portsmouth and the East India Company 1700–1815* (Lewiston, NY, Edwin Mellen Press, 1999)

Thomas, J. H., *The East India Company and the Provinces in the Eighteenth Century: Volume II Captains, Agents and Servants: A Gallery of East India Company Portraits* (Lewiston, NY, Edwin Mellen Press, 2007)

Thomas, J. H., 'East India Company Agency Work in the British Isles, 1700–1800', in H. V. Bowen, M. Lincoln and N. Rigby (eds), *The Worlds of the East India Company* (Woodbridge, Boydell Press, 2004)

Thompson, F. M. L., *Gentrification and the Enterprise Culture: Britain 1780–1980* (Oxford, Oxford University Press, 2001)

Thompson, I., *The English Lakes: A History* (London, Bloomsbury, 2010)

Thompson, T. W., *Wordsworth's Hawkshead* (Oxford, Oxford University Press, 1970)

Thorne, R. G., 'LAW, Ewan (1747–1829) of Lower Brook Street, Mdx. and Horsted Place, Little Horsted, Suss.', in R. G. Thorne (ed.), *The History of Parliament: The House of Commons 1790–1820* (1986): www.historyofparliamentonline.org/volume/1790-1820/member/law-ewan-1747-1829.

Thorne, R. G., 'Mackreth, Sir Robert (*bap.* 1727, *d.* 1819)', *Oxford Dictionary of National Biography* (Oxford, Oxford University Press, 2004; online edition, Jan. 2008): www.oxforddnb.com/view/article/17629.

Thorne, R. G., 'MYERS, Thomas (1764–1835) of 4 Tilney Street, Mdx. and Greys, Sible Hedingham, Essex', in R. Thorne (ed.), *The History of Parliament: The House of Commons 1790–1820* (1986): www.historyofparliamentonline.org/volume/1790-1820/member/myers-thomas-1764-1835.

Uglow, J., *The Pinecone: The Story of Sarah Losh, Forgotten Romantic Heroine – Antiquarian, Architect and Visionary* (London, Faber and Faber, 2012)

Veblen, T., *The Theory of the Leisure Class* (reissued edition, Oxford, Oxford University Press, 2009)

Vickery, A., 'Women and the World of Goods: a Lancashire Consumer and Her Possessions 1751–1781', in J. Brewer and R. Porter (eds), *Consumption and the World of Goods* (London, Routledge, 1994)

Vickery, A., *The Gentleman's Daughter: Women's Lives in Georgian England* (London, Yale University Press, 2003)

Vickery, A., *Behind Closed Doors: At Home in Georgian England* (London, Yale University Press, 2009)

von Lünen, A. and C. Travers (eds), *History and GIS: Epistemologies, Considerations and Reflections* (New York, Springer, 2013)

Wahrman, D., *Imagining the Middle Class: The Political Representation of Class in Britain, c.1780–1840* (Cambridge, Cambridge University Press, 1995)

Wahrman, D., *The Making of the Modern Self: Identity and Culture in Eighteenth Century England* (New Haven, CT, Yale University Press, 2006)

Walton, J. K., 'Landscape and Society: The Industrial Revolution and Beyond', in J. K. Walton and J. Wood (eds), *The Making of a Cultural Landscape: The English Lake District as Tourist Destination, 1750–2010* (Farnham, Ashgate, 2013)

Walton, J. K. and P. Borsay (eds), *Resorts and Ports: European Seaside Towns since 1700* (Kindle edition, Bristol, Channel View Publications, 2011)

Walton, J. K. and J. Wood (eds), *The Making of a Cultural Landscape: The English Lake District as Tourist Destination, 1750–2010* (Farnham, Ashgate, 2013)

Ward, H., and W. Roberts, *Romney: A Biographical and Critical Essay, With a Catalogue Raisonné of His Works*, vol. 1 (London, Thomas Agnew & Sons, 1904)

Watson, P., 'STEPHENSON, Edward (1691–1768) of Dawley, Mdx.', in R. Sedwick, (ed.), *The History of Parliament: The House of Commons 1715–1754* (1970): www.historyofparliamentonline.org/volume/1715-1754/member/stephenson-edward-1691-1768.

Weatherill, L., 'The Meaning of Consumer Behaviour in Late Seventeenth and Early

Eighteenth Century England', in J. Brewer and R. Porter (eds), *Consumption and the World of Goods* (London, Routledge, 1994)

Weatherill, L., *Consumer Behaviour & Material Culture in Britain 1660–1760* (2nd edition, London, Routledge, 1996)

Webster, A., *The Richest East India Merchant: The Life and Business of John Palmer of Calcutta, 1767–1836* (Woodbridge, Boydell Press, 2007)

White, A., *A History of Kendal* (Lancaster, Carnegie, 2013)

Whyte, I., 'Cumbrian Village Communities: Continuity and Change, c.1750–c.1850', in C. Dyer (ed.), *The Self-Contained Village? The Social History of Rural Communities 1250–1900* (Hatfield, University of Hertfordshire Press, 2007)

Wiener, M., *English Culture and the Decline of the Industrial Spirit 1870–1980* (2nd edition, Cambridge, Cambridge University Press, 2004)

Wilkins, F., *Hasells of Dalemain: A Cumberland Family: 1736–1794* (Kidderminster, Wyre Forest Press, 2003)

Wilson, K., *The Sense of the People: Politics, Culture and Imperialism in England, 1715–1785* (Cambridge, Cambridge University Press, 1998)

Wilson, K., 'Introduction: Histories, Empires, Modernities', in K. Wilson (ed.), *A New Imperial History: Culture, Identity, Modernity, 1660–1840* (Cambridge, Cambridge University Press, 2004)

Wilson, K. (ed.), *A New Imperial History: Culture, Identity, Modernity, 1660–1840* (Cambridge, Cambridge University Press, 2004)

Wilson, R. and A. Mackley, *Creating Paradise: The Building of the English Country House, 1660–1880* (London, Hambledon, 2000)

Winchester, A. J. L., 'The Landscape Encountered by the First Tourists', in J. K. Walton and J. Wood (eds), *The Making of a Cultural Landscape: The English Lake District as Tourist Destination, 1750–2010* (Farnham, Ashgate, 2013)

Wolff, J. and J. Seed (eds), *The Culture of Capital: Art, Power and the Nineteenth-Century Middle Class* (Manchester, Manchester University Press, 1988)

Wright, N. E., M. W. Ferguson and A. R. Buck (eds), *Women, Property and the Letters of the Law in Early Modern England* (Toronto, University of Toronto Press, 2004)

Wright, S., 'Brougham, Henry (*bap.* 1665, *d.* 1696)', *Oxford Dictionary of National Biography* (Oxford, Oxford University Press, online edition, Jan. 2008): www.oxforddnb.com/view/article/3580, accessed 17 December 2012.

Wrightson, K., *Earthly Necessities: Economic Lives in Early Modern Britain* (New Haven, CT, Yale University Press, 2000)

Zahedieh, N., 'An Open Elite? Colonial Commerce, the Country House and the Case of Sir Gilbert Heathcote and Normanton Hall', in M. Dresser and A. Hann (eds), *Slavery and the British Country House* (Swindon, English Heritage, 2013)

Articles

Armstrong, W. A., 'The Trend of Mortality in Carlisle between the 1780s and 1840s: A Demographic Contribution to the Standard of Living Debate', *Economic History Review*, New Series, 34, 1 (February 1981), pp. 94–114.

Bailey, L., 'Consumption and Status: Shopping for Clothes in a Nineteenth-Century Bedfordshire Gentry Household Midland History Prize Essay 2010', *Midland History*, 36, 1 (2011), pp. 89–114.

Barry, E., 'From Epitaph to Obituary: Death and Celebrity in Eighteenth-Century British Culture', *International Journal of Cultural Studies*, 11 (2008), pp. 259–275.

Beckett, J. V., 'English Landownership in the Later Seventeenth and Eighteenth Centuries: The Debate and the Problems', *Economic History Review*, New Series, 30, 4 (November 1977), pp. 567–581.

Beckett, J. V., 'The Eighteenth-Century Origins of the Factory System: A Case Study from the 1740s', *Business History*, 19, 1 (1977), pp. 55–67.

Beckett, J. V., 'The Making of a Pocket Borough: Cockermouth 1722–1756', *Journal of British Studies*, 20, 1 (Autumn 1980), pp. 140–157.

Beckett, J. V., 'Regional Variation and the Agricultural Depression, 1730–1750', *Economic History Review*, New Series, 35, 1 (February 1982), pp. 35–51.

Beckett, J. V., 'The Decline of the Small Landowner in Eighteenth- and Nineteenth-Century England: Some Regional Considerations', *Agricultural History Review*, 30 (1982), pp. 97–111.

Beckett, J. V., 'Absentee Land Ownership in the Later Seventeenth and Early Eighteenth Centuries: The Case of Cumbria', *Northern History*, 19 (1983), pp. 87–107.

Beckett, J. V., 'The Pattern of Landownership in England and Wales, 1660–1880', *Economic History Review*, New Series, 37, 1 (February 1984), pp. 1–22.

Beckett, J. V., 'The Finances of a Former Jacobite: James Grahme of Levens Hall', *Transactions CWAAS*, New Series, LXXXV (1985), pp. 131–142.

Bohun, J., 'Protecting Prerogative: William III and the East India Trade Debate, 1689–1698', *Past Imperfect*, 2 (1993), pp. 63–86.

Boot, H., 'Real Incomes of the British Middle Class, 1760–1850: the Experience of the Clerks at the East India Company', *Economic History Review*, LII, 4 (1999), pp. 639–640.

Bowen, H. V., 'The "Little Parliament": The General Court of the East India Company, 1750–1784', *The Historical Journal*, 34, 4 (1991), pp. 857–872.

Bowen, H. V., 'Sinews of Trade and Empire: The Supply of Commodity Exports to the East India Company during the Late Eighteenth Century', *Economic History Review*, New Series, 55, 3 (2002), pp. 466–486.

Bowen, H. V., 'James H. Thomas, "The East India Company and the Provinces in the Eighteenth Century, Vol. II: Captains, Agents, and Servants: A Gallery of East India Company Portraits"', *Economic History Review*, 61, 4 (2008), p. 1005.

Buchan, P. B., 'The East India Company 1749–1800: The Evolution of a Territorial Strategy and the Changing Role of the Directors', *Business and Economic History*, 23, 1 (Fall 1994), pp. 52–61.

Chadha, A., 'Ambivalent Heritage: Between Affect and Ideology in a Colonial Cemetery', *Journal of Material Culture*, 11 (2006), pp. 339–363.

Chakrabarti, P., '"Neither of meate nor drinke, but what the Doctor alloweth": Medicine amidst War and Commerce in Eighteenth-Century Madras', *Bulletin of the History of Medicine*, 80 (2006), pp. 1–38.

Cockerill, T., 'Myles Cooper, President of King's College, New York', *Transactions CWAAS*, New Series, LXIV (1964), pp. 336–348.

Connell, A., 'Appleby in Westminster: John Robinson, MP (1727–1802)', *Transactions CWAAS*, Third Series, X (2010), pp. 217–236.

Connell, A., 'John Robinson 1727–1802 – Clarification and Lines for Further Enquiry', *Transactions CWAAS*, Third Series, XI (2011), pp. 248–251.

Crocker, A. and P. Sandbach, 'A Harrison Ainslie Gunpowder Stock Book of 1871–1876', *Transactions CWAAS*, Third Series, XX (2010), pp. 13–34.

Crosbie, B., 'Ireland, Colonial Science, and the Geographical Construction of British Rule in India, c. 1820–1870', *The Historical Journal*, 52, 4 (2009), pp. 963–987.

Curwen, J. F., 'Scaleby Castle', *Transactions CWAAS*, New Series, XXVI (1926), pp. 398–414.

Downs, C., 'The Business Letters of Daniel Eccleston of Lancaster (1745–1821): Trade, Commerce, and Marine Insurance in Late-Eighteenth-Century Liverpool, Lancaster, and Whitehaven', *Northern History*, XLI, 1 (March 2004), pp. 129–148.

Eaton, N., 'EXCESS IN THE CITY? The Consumption of Imported Prints in Colonial Calcutta, c.1780–c.1795', *Journal of Material Culture*, 8, 1 (2003), pp. 45–74.

Ellis, R., 'William Calvert (1770–1829)', *CeNtreWoRdS*, 10 (2011), pp. 14–23.

Finn, M., 'Men's Things: Masculine Possession in the Consumer Revolution', *Social History*, 25, 2 (2000), pp. 133–155.

Finn, M., 'Law's Empire: English Legal Cultures at Home and Abroad', *The Historical Journal*, 48, 1 (2005), pp. 295–303.

Finn, M., 'Colonial Gifts: Family Politics and the Exchange of Goods in British India, c. 1780–1820', *Modern Asian Studies*, 40, 1 (2006), pp. 203–231.

Finn, M, 'Anglo-Indian Lives in the Later Eighteenth and Early Nineteenth Centuries', *Journal for Eighteenth-Century Studies*, 33, 1 (2010), pp. 49–65.

Fisher Crosthwaite, J. J., 'Some of the Old Families in the Parish of Crosthwaite', *Transactions Cumberland and Westmorland Association Advancement of Literature and Science*, 10 (1884–85), pp. 11–28.

George, A. D., 'The Early Iron Industry in Furness – A Revolution in the 18th Century', *Cumbria Industrial History Occasional Papers*, 5 (2005), pp. 49–59.

Glaisyer, N., 'Networking: Trade and Exchange in The Eighteenth Century British Empire', *The Historical Journal*, 47, 2 (June 2004), pp. 451–476.

Godwin, J., 'Rickerby: An Estate and its Owners – Part 1', *Transactions CWAAS*, New Series, 92 (1992), pp. 229–250.

Green, D. and A. Owens, 'Gentlewomanly Capitalism? Spinsters, Widows and Wealth Holding in England and Wales, c. 1800–1860', *Economic History Review*, LVI, 3 (2003), pp. 510–536.

Gregson, N., 'Tawney Revisited: Custom and the Emergence of Capitalist Class Relations in North-East Cumbria, 1600–1830', *Economic History Review*, New Series, 42, 1 (February 1989), pp. 18–42.

Haggerty, S., 'Trade and Trust in the Eighteenth-Century Atlantic World', *Business History*, 52, 7 (2010), pp. 1188–1190.

Hainsworth, D. R., 'The Lowther Younger Sons: A 17th-Century Case Study', *Transactions CWAAS*, New Series, 88 (1988), pp. 149–160.

Halliday, S., 'Social Mobility, Demographic Change and the Landed Elite of County Durham, 1610–1819: An Open or Shut Case?', *Northern History*, 30 (1994), pp. 49–63.

Harrison, J. V., 'The Routledges of Cumcrook', *Transactions CWAAS*, New Series, LXV (1965), pp. 320–370.

Haverfield, F., 'Report of the Cumberland Excavation Committee', *Transactions CWAAS*, Old Series, XIV (1897), pp. 185–197.

Hay, W. A., 'Henry Brougham and the 1818 Westmorland Election: A Study in Provincial Opinion and the Opening of Constituency Politics', *Albion: A Quarterly Journal Concerned with British Studies*, 36, 1 (Spring 2004), pp. 28–51.

Healey, J., 'Agrarian Social Structure in the Central Lake District, c. 1574–1830: The Fall of the "Mountain Republic"?', *Northern History*, 1, 2 (September 2007), pp. 73–91.

Heldman, J., 'How Wealthy is Mr. Darcy Really?', *Persuasions*, 12 (1990), pp. 38–49.

Hindle, P., 'The First Large Scale County Maps of Cumberland and Westmorland in the 1770s', *Transactions CWAAS*, Third Series, I (2001), pp. 139–154.

Houston, R., 'The Development of Literacy: Northern England, 1640–1750', *Economic History Review*, 35, 2 (May 1982), pp. 199–216.

Hudleston, C. R., 'The Dalstons of Acornbank', *Transactions CWAAS*, New Series, CVIII (1958), pp. 140–179.

Hudleston, C. R., 'The Wane Family', *Transactions CWAAS*, New Series, 67 (1967), pp. 232–233.

Jackson, W., 'The Curwens of Workington Hall and Kindred Families', *Transactions CWAAS*, Old Series, V (1888), pp. 181–232, 311–342.

Jackson, W., 'The Hudlestons of Hutton John, the Hudlestons of Kelston, now of Hutton John, and the Hudlestons of Whitehaven', *Transactions CWAAS*, Old Series, XI (1891), pp. 435–466.

James, J. A., 'Personal Wealth Distribution in Late Eighteenth-Century Britain', *Economic History Review*, New Series, 41, 4 (November 1988), pp. 543–565.

Jarvis, R. C., 'Cumberland Shipping in the Eighteenth Century', *Transactions CWAAS*, New Series, LIV (1955), pp. 212–235.

Jones, G. P., 'Some Sources of Loans and Credit in Cumbria before the Use of Banks', *Transactions CWAAS*, New Series, 75 (1975), pp. 275–292.

Kaye, J. W., 'Governor's House Keswick', *Transactions CWAAS*, New Series, LXVI (1966), pp. 339–346.

Kitson, P. J., 'The Wordsworths, Opium, and China', *Wordsworth Circle*, 43, 1 (2012), pp. 2–12.

Knight, G. R., 'East of the Cape in 1832: The Old Indies World, Empire Families and "Colonial Women" in Nineteenth-century Java', *Itinerario*, 36 (2012), pp. 22–48.

Lancichinetti, A. and S. Fortunato, 'Community Detection Algorithms: A Comparative Analysis', *Physical Review E*, 80, 1 (2009), pp. 056117-1- 056117-11.

Lawson, P. and J. Phillips, '"Our Execrable Banditti": Perceptions of Nabobs in Mid-Eighteenth Century Britain', *Albion: A Quarterly Journal Concerned with British Studies*, 16, 3 (Autumn 1984), pp. 225–241.

Leach, R. E., 'Benefactors to the Library, Appleby Grammar School', *Transactions CWAAS*, Old Series, VIII (1894), pp. 20–36.

Leffel, J. C., '"Her diamond cross was . . . at the bottom of it all": Colonial Wealth and Cultural Difference in Maria Edgeworth's Castle Rackrent (1800)', *European Romantic Review*, 23, 5 (2012), pp. 613–634.

Lester, A., 'Imperial Circuits and Networks: Geographies of the British Empire', *History Compass*, 4, 1 (2006), pp. 124–141.

Lindert, P. H., 'Unequal English Wealth since 1670', *Journal Political Economy*, 94, 1 (1966), pp. 1127–1162.

Lindert, P. and J. Williamson, 'Revising England's Social Tables 1688–1812', *Explorations in Economic History*, 19 (1982), pp. 385–408.

Loudon, I., 'The Nature of Provincial Medical Practice in Eighteenth-Century England', *Medical History*, 29 (1985), pp. 1–32.

McQuiston, J. R., 'The Lonsdale Connection and its Defender, William, Viscount Lowther 1818–1830', *Northern History*, 11, 1 (1979), pp. 143–179.

Marshall, J. D., 'Agrarian Wealth and Social Structure in Pre-Industrial Cumbria', *Economic History Review*, New Series, 33, 4 (1980), pp. 503–521.

Marshall, J. D., 'Cumberland and Westmorland Societies in London, 1734–1914', *Transactions CWAAS*, New Series, 84 (1984), pp. 239–254.

Marshall, J. D. and C. A. Dyhouse, 'Social Transition in Kendal and Westmorland c.1760–1860', *Northern History*, 12 (1976), pp. 127–157.

Marshall, P. J., 'The Personal Fortune of Warren Hastings', *Economic History Review*, 17, 2 (1964), pp. 284–300.

Marshall, P. J., 'The Bengal Commercial Society of 1775: Private British Trade in the Warren Hastings Period', *Historical Research*, 421, 6 (1969), pp. 173–187.

Marshall, P. J., 'The Whites of British India, 1780–1830: A Failed Colonial Society?', *The International History Review*, 12, 1 (February 1990), pp. 26–44.

Marshall P. J., 'The White Town of Calcutta under the Rule of the East India Company', *Modern Asian Studies*, 34, 2 (May 2000), pp. 307–331.

Nechtman, T. W., 'Nabobinas: Luxury, Gender, and the Sexual Politics of British Imperialism in India in the Late Eighteenth Century', Journal of Women's History, 18, 4 (Winter 2006), pp. 8–30.

Nechtman, T. W., 'A Jewel in the Crown? Indian Wealth in Domestic Britain in the Late Eighteenth Century', *Eighteenth-Century Studies*, 41, 1 (2007), pp. 71–86.

Newman, R., 'Port Development and Town Planning in North West England', *Journal of Maritime Archaeology*, 8, 2 (2013), pp. 283–309.

Pearson, R. and D. Richardson, 'Social Capital, Institutional Innovation and Atlantic Trade before 1800', *Business History*, 50, 6 (2008), pp. 765–780.

Philips, C. H. and D. Philips, 'Alphabetical List of Directors of the East India Company from 1758 to 1858', *Journal of the Royal Asiatic Society of Great Britain and Ireland*, 4 (October 1941), pp. 325–336.

Pinfold, J., 'Horse Racing and the Upper Classes in the Nineteenth Century', *Sport in History*, 28, 3 (September 2008), pp. 414–430.

Pratt, H. T., 'Peter Crosthwaite: John Dalton's "Friend and Colleague"', *Ambix*, 38, 1 (March 1991), pp. 11–28.

Razzell, P., 'The Social Origins of the Indian and British Home Army: 1758–1962', *The British Journal of Sociology*, 14, 3 (1963), pp. 248–260.

Richardson, D. and M. M. Schofield, 'Whitehaven and the Eighteenth-century British Slave Trade', *Transactions CWAAS*, Second Series, XCII (1992), pp. 183–204.

Robinson, F., 'The Education of an Eighteenth Century Gentleman: George Edward Stanley of Dalegarth and Ponsonby', *Transactions CWAAS*, New Series, 70 (1970), pp. 181–191.

Robinson, F. and P. Wallis, 'Early Mathematical Schools in Whitehaven', *Transactions CWAAS*, New Series, 75 (1975), pp. 262–274.

Robinson, M., 'The Port of Carlisle: Trade and Shipping in Cumberland, 1675–1735', *Transactions CWAAS*, Third Series, VIII (2008), pp. 147–157.

Roy, T., 'Rethinking the Origins of British India: State Formation and Military-Fiscal Undertakings in an Eighteenth Century World Region', London School of Economics Working Papers, No. 142/10 (2010).

Rushworth, D., 'Tom Ellen: A Malayan in Cumberland and the Caribbean in the Later 18th Century', *Transactions CWAAS*, Third Series, VIII (2008), pp. 169–175.

Scarre, C. and J. Roberts, 'The English Cemetery at Surat: Pre-colonial Cultural Encounters in Western India', *Antiquaries Journal*, 85 (2005), pp. 250–291.

Schellenberg, B. A., 'Coterie Culture, the Print Trade, and the Emergence of the Lakes Tour, 1724–1787', *Eighteenth-Century Studies*, 44, 2 (Winter 2011), pp. 203–221.

Searle, C. E., 'Custom, Class Conflict and Agrarian Capitalism: the Cumbrian Customary Economy in the Eighteenth Century', *Past & Present*, 110, 1 (1986), pp. 106–133.

Searle, C. E., 'Customary Tenants and the Enclosure of the Cumbrian Commons', *Northern History*, 29 (1993), pp. 126–153.

Skidmore, P., 'Vessels and Networks: Shipowning in North-west England's Coasting Trade in the Late Eighteenth and Early Nineteenth Centuries', *The Mariner's Mirror*, 99, 2 (2013), pp. 153–170.

Smith, S., 'The Provenance of Joseph Symson's Letter Book (1711–20)', *Transactions CWAAS*, Third Series, III (2003), pp. 157–168.

Smylitopoulos, C., 'Rewritten and Reused: Imaging the Nabob Through "Upstart Iconography"', *Eighteenth-Century Life*, 32, 2 (Spring 2008), pp. 39–59.

Squire, S. J., 'Wordsworth and Lake District Tourism: Romantic Reshaping of Landscape', *The Canadian Geographer/ Le Géographe canadien*, 32, 3 (1988), pp. 237–247.

Steedman, C., 'Something She Called a Fever: Michelet, Derrida, and Dust', *The American Historical Review*, 106, 4 (October 2001), pp. 1159–1180.

Stern, P. J., 'History and Historiography of the English East India Company: Past, Present, and Future!', *History Compass*, 7, 4 (2009), pp. 1146–1180.

Stobart, J. and A. Hann, 'Retailing Revolution in the Eighteenth Century? Evidence from North-West England', *Business History*, 462 (2004), pp. 171–194.

Sweet, R., 'The Production of Urban Histories in Eighteenth-century England', *Urban History*, 23, 2 (1996), pp. 171–188.

Swift, F. 'The Oldest Parish Registers of Bassenthwaite', *Transactions CWAAS*, New Series, 66 (1966), pp. 276–292.

Taylor, S., 'The Irtons of Irton Hall', *Transactions CWAAS*, New Series, 41 (1941), pp. 72–122.

Thomas, J. H., 'County, Commerce and Contacts: Hampshire and the East India Company in the Eighteenth Century', *Hampshire Studies*, 68 (2013), pp. 169–177.

Tomkins, A., 'Who Were His Peers? The Social and Professional Milieu of the Provincial Surgeon-Apothecary in the Late-Eighteenth Century', *Journal of Social History*, 44, 3 (Spring 2011), pp. 915–935.

Townsend, G. A., 'Thomas Law, Washington's First Rich Man', *Records of the Columbia Historical Society*, 14 (1901), pp. 222–245.

Travers, R., 'Death and the Nabob: Imperialism and Commemoration in Eighteenth Century India', *Past and Present*, 196 (August 2007), pp. 83–124.

Tyson, B., 'Attempts to Smelt Metal with Coal Near Whitehaven before 1700', *Cumbria Industrial History Occasional Papers*, 2 (1999), pp. 3–22.

Tyson, B., 'Heavy Transport in Cumbria before 1800: Methods, Problems and Costs', *Cumbria Industrial History Occasional Papers*, 4 (2002), pp. 13–33.

Warren, J., 'Harriet Martineau and the Concept of Community: *Deerbrook* and Ambleside', *Journal of Victorian Culture*, 13, 2 (2008), pp. 223–246.

Whyte, I., '"Wild, Barren and Frightful" – Parliamentary Enclosure in an Upland County: Westmorland 1767–1890', *Rural History*, 14, 1 (2003), pp. 21–38.

Whyte, I., 'Owners and Occupiers: Subtenancy and Subtenants in Watermillock, Cumberland, c. 1760–c.1840: A Case Study', *Northern History*, L, 1 (March 2013), pp. 77–92.

Williams, J. E., 'Whitehaven in the Eighteenth Century', *Economic History Review*, 8, 3 (1956), pp. 393–404.

Wilson, R. and A. Mackley, 'How Much did the English Country House Cost to Build, 1660–1880?', *Economic History Review*, New Series, 52, 3 (1999), pp. 436–468.

Winchester, A. J. L., 'Ministers, Merchants and Migrants: Cumberland Friends and North America in the Eighteenth Century', *Quaker History*, 80, 2 (Fall 1991), pp. 85–99.

Winchester, A. J. L., 'Wordsworth's "Pure Commonwealth"? Yeoman Dynasties in the English Lake District', *Armitt Library Journal* (1998), pp. 86–113.

Winchester, A. J. L., 'Regional Identity in the Lake Counties: Land Tenure and The Cumbrian Landscape', *Northern History*, 42, 1 (March 2005), pp. 29–58.

Winchester, A. J. L., 'Personal Names and Local Identities in Early Modern Cumbria', *Transactions CWAAS*, Third Series, XI (2011), pp. 29–49.

Winder, F. A., 'The Winders of Lorton', *Transactions CWAAS*, Old Series, XII (1893), pp. 439–457.

Winder, F. A., 'Further Notes on the Winders of Lorton', *Transactions CWAAS*, Old Series, XV (1898), pp. 229–238.

Wiseman, W. G., 'Caleb Rotheram, Ecroyde Claxton and their Involvement in the Movement for the Abolition of the Trans-Atlantic Slave Trade', *Transactions CWAAS*, New Series, IX (2009), pp. 153–160.

Withey, A., '"Persons that Live Remote from London": Apothecaries and the Medical Marketplace in Seventeenth- and Eighteenth-Century Wales', *Bulletin of the History of Medicine*, 85, 2 (Summer 2011), pp. 222–247.

Wright, A., 'Loyalty and Tradition: Jacobitism Amongst the Gentry of North-West England, 1640-1720', *Transactions CWAAS*, New Series, X (2010), pp. 147–162.

Wright, A., 'Loyalty and Tradition, Part II: Networking Among the North-Western Catholic Gentry in England and Abroad, 1640–1720: The Case of the Layburnes', *Transactions CWAAS*, New Series, XIV (2014), pp. 103–124.

Theses and Dissertations

Denman, D., 'Materialising Cultural Value in the English Lakes, 1735–1845: A Study of the Responses of New Landowners to Representations of Place and People' (PhD dissertation, Lancaster University, 2011)

Holzman, J., 'The Nabobs in England: A Study of the Returned Anglo-Indian, 1760–1785' (PhD dissertation, Columbia University, New York, 1926)

McCartor, R. L., 'The John Company's College: Haileybury and the British Government's Attempt to Control the Indian Civil Service' (PhD thesis, Texas Tech University, 1981)

Mansfield, T. A., 'Calcutta, from Fort to City: A Study of a Colonial Settlement, 1690–1750' (PhD thesis, University of Leicester, 2012)

Parker, J. G., 'The Directors of the East India Company 1754–1790' (PhD thesis, University of Edinburgh, 1977)

Robinson, F., 'Trends in Education in Northern England during the Eighteenth Century: A Biographical Study' (PhD thesis, University of Newcastle, 1972)

Internet Publications and Websites

Appleby-in-Westmorland, *Mayors of Appleby*, www.applebytown.org.uk/uploads/Town%20Council/Info/Mayor/MAYORS%20OF%20APPLEBY.pdf, accessed October 2015.

Sandbach, P, Harrison Ainslie's Shipping Interests, http://lindal-in-furness.co.uk/History/harrisonainslie.htm, accessed October 2012.

Sharma, Y. and P. Davies, '"A jaghire without a crime": East India Company and the Indian Ocean Material World at Osterley 1700–1800', http://blogs.ucl.ac.uk/eicah/files/2013/02/Osterley-Park-PDF-Final-19.08.14.pdf.

Smith, K., 'Warfield Park, Berkshire Longing, Belonging and the Country House', *East India Company at Home* (August 2014): http://blogs.ucl.ac.uk/eicah/files/2013/02/Warfield-Park-Final-PDF-19.08.14.pdf.

Unpublished and Other Online Genealogical Material

Ainslie, A., 'Ainslie: History of the Ainslies of Dolphinston, Jedburgh, Grizedale, Hall Garth & Their Descendants' (Unpublished, Bradford Peverell, Dorset, A. Ainslie, 2008)

Anon., www.geni.com/people/Luke-Ashburner/6000000014733316665.

Church of St Thomas of Canterbury, Monumental Inscriptions, www.eastclandon.org.uk/PDF-Files/Monumental%20inscriptions_EC%20website.pdf.

Hardisty, A., 'The Hardisty Family Tree', accessed www.hardistyfamilytree.com.

Lorton & Derwent Fells Local History Society Archive Reference ldf/pr2/3 St. Bartholomew's Churchyard, Loweswater, Cumbria.

Lundy, D., 'The Peerage: A Genealogical Survey of the Peerage of Britain as Well as the Royal Families of Europe', accessed www.thepeerage.co.

Lyon, J. and A. Gough, 'Some Cumberland Churchyard Inscriptions: Visits to Bolton Gate (All Saints) Summer 1983 (AG) & 6th June 1994 (JL)', accessed http://freepages.genealogy.rootsweb.ancestry.com/~andrewgough/Cumberland/cumbmi.htm.

Mandell, G., 'The Gale-Gayle Families', accessed http://gale-gaylefamilies.com.

INDEX

Abbott Hall, Kendal 114, 143, 152
abolition of slavery 5, 51, 136, 217
Adderton family
   Helena (nee Curwen) 116–7
   Henry, East Indies mariner 103
   Jeremiah 82-83, 118, 120
Addison family 37, 40, 89, 118, 163
   Eldred, prepared for an HEIC career
      104, 140
   Gulston, president of Madras 47, 71
   John of Whitehaven 84–5, 97, 107,
      108, 141
   Robert, java coffee grower and
      merchant 84, 127, 137, 142,
      143, 144, 152
   Robert the younger 138
   William, Rev. 104
Aglionby family of Nunnery 43, 83
   Henry, mayor of Carlisle, Lowther
      supporter 143
   John, East Indies mariner 103, 124,
      145, 163
   Mary, wife of John Orfeur Yates 184
Ainslie family of Kendal 116,
   Harrison, Ainslie & Co 60
   Henry, physician and ironmaster 61,
      116,
   ironmasters 59, 116
   James, father of Henry portrayed by
      Romney 157
   Montagu, HEIC and Grizedale 45,
      56–62, 84, 116, 138, 152, 157,
      162, 165, 174
   William 116
Airey, Henry Cookson, Westmerian,
      Bengal army 137
Allonby 37, 103, 164
Alston Moor, lead mines 6, 17
American colonies 1, 4, 5, 8, 34–5, 90,
      182
American War of Independence 1, 6, 13,
      34–5

Anglo-Indian
   definition xiii, xiv
   dynastic families 1, 2, 38, 169, 172,
      175–6
   identities and networks 29, 38–9, 65,
      169
Appleby, county town of Westmorland 103,
      119, 143, 144, 150, 151, 152
archives, records, and method 19–28, 35,
      135
Ashburner family of Dalton-in-Furness
      and Bombay 37, 39, 71, 137
Atkinson of Temple Sowerby 37
Atkinson, Richard of Temple Sowerby
   contractor and merchant based in
      London 105, 163
   creditor of the Nabob of Arcot 163
   East India Company director 20, 114,
   member of parliament 163-4
Atlantic trade and world 2, 6, 7–8, 35,
      118, 119, 170, 179, 180, 183

Baltic trade 4, 90, 180, 183
Bardsea 31, 37, 71, 94, 148
Barrock Lodge 144, 151
Bateman of Newbiggin Hall 41
Battle of Plassey 34, 45, 177
Bell, James of Cumberland, East
      Indiaman surgeon 138
Bellasis family of Long Marton
   financial problems 139, 144, 151
   George, Doctor of Divinity 73,
      101fn15, 139
   George Hutchins, Holly Hill,
      Windermere 137, 140, 143, 154
   John Brownrigg 114, 138, 174
   Joseph Harvey, mercenary in India 57
Bellasis, John, General in Bombay, and
   advice from brother on an HEIC
      career 73
   advice on nephew's East Indies career
      104–5, 108, 112–3

advice on opportunities in India 74
allowance to son, George Hutchins, 'Holly Hill' Windermere 140
antiquarian and genealogical interests 156, 174
appointment as HEIC military cadet 116
desire to acquire a Cumbrian estate 151
financial ambitions and success in India 139
financial assistance to family 73
good health in India 93
John Hasell of Dalemain's 1781 death in Bombay 81
makes claim for arms with the College of Arms 174
memorials at Long Marton and Bombay Cathedral 134
networks with Cumbrians in India 126, 128, 181–2
patronage 112–3, 116
Randall Lodge, Malabar Hill, Bombay 154–5
wealth 139–140
Benn family
    John, later Benn Walsh, resident of Benares 117, 142
    networks in the East Indies 42, 43, 142
    opium dealing 142
Benson, Richard of Cockermouth, Bengal army 142
Berry, William, Kendal mayor sends son to Madras 143, 165
Birkett, Thomas of Moresby dies intestate Barrackpore 140
Boak, William, East Indies mariner educated Carlisle 103
Borradaile, Cumbrian shipowners based in London 119, 177
    Alfred 137
    William 164
Bourdieu, P., concepts of capital, consumption, taste and biography 11, 28, 77, 97–8, 112
Boustead, John of Cumberland, Ceylon army 137
Bowser, Sir Thomas, Westmerian, portrait by Thomas Hickey 156
Braddyll family 32, 71, 89, 111, 119
    Dodding, HEIC director 71, 114, 132, 142, 145, 148

John, Conishead and Bardsea, India merchant, 89, 184
John the younger, HEIC merchant, memorial at Carshalton 131, 133, 142
Margaret, wife of Christopher Wilson, HEIC 94, 184
Roger of Conishead, merchant 47, 110
Thomas, governor of Bengal 71, 132, 141–2
Thomas, sheriff of Lancashire, son of Dodding 145, 148
Wilson 128, 146
Brisco family of Crofton Hill 50–1
    Catherine, mother of Catherine Holme 49
    connected middling and gentry families involved in the East Indies 43, 50–1
    West Indies slaves 51
Bristow, John, returned sojourner 153
British India and dynastic families 175–6
British India and imperialism 1, 2, 14–9, 20, 29, 32, 38–9, 90 104, 168–70, 172, –1759
Brougham, Henry, cousin of George Fleming 70
Brougham, Henry, of Brougham Hall Westmorland, journalist 64, 100, 145,
Brown, Abraham prepared for an HEIC career 104
Browne, William of Tallantire Hall 42
Burke, Edmund 67, 68

Carlisle
    bishops of 50, 115
    East Indies connections 37, 43–4, 49, 65, 90
    health, mortality and life expectancy 90, 92
    houses of East Indies returners 153
    mayors with East Indies connections 143–4
    middling families 43, 49, 70, 90,
    population 7
    provincial development 6, 7, 65
    returning East Indies sojourners to 53, 54–5,
    schools and vocational education in 49, 102, 103
Carlisle House of Recovery 163
Carlisle New Bank 151

Christian family of Ewanrigg Hall 41, 50, 89, 114, 125, 146–7
Clerk family
  Robert, HEIC Cumbrian director 114
  Robert's HEIC nephews, sons of Dorothy Taylor, Abbot Hall 137
climate and health 90–95
Clive, Robert of India 34, 49–51, 85, 116, 117
Conishead 47, 71, 89, 94, 132, 148
consumer goods and consumption
  and the provincial renaissance 12
  by Cumbrians in the East Indies 47, 53, 61, 81, 124–5, 140, 154–5, 156
  by East Indies returners 71, 146–8, 155–6
  opportunities for middling ranks to express success and distinction 10–1, 77, 155 fn120
Cooper, Thomas of Long Marton, appointed to Cumbrian business in Bombay 118
country and town houses 50, 60, 148–155
Crosby Ravensworth 37
cultural capital 12, 98, 99, 105
Cumbrians acclimatisation to India 91
Cumbrian counties
  aristocracy and aristocrats 9, 40, 59, 61, 90, 116, 118, 126, 145, 151, 162, 171
  banking 8, 101
  coastal ports 4–5
  constituent counties xiii
  county societies 125–6, 163–4
  customary tenure xiii, 4, 9, 179
  debt in middling and gentry families 71, 72, 108, 139, 149–50, 151
  differing portrayals of economic development 4–9
  extractive industries and mining 6, 9, 165, 170, 180
  gentry and middling ranks shared education 99–106
  global reach 182–3
  high rates of literacy 99, 100, 180
  historiography neglects East India Company connections 2–3, 168–70
  manufactory of clerks 101, 105
  networks between middling and gentry families 41–4
  networks in the East Indies 126

population increase 6–7, 164, 170, 179
rates of East India Company
  appointments and licensing 35–37, 65, 175, 180, 182
similarities with the East Indies 65, 185
slave trade and slave ownership 2, 4, 5, 51, 57
superior, affordable education 53–4, 98–106, 128–9, 167, 170
tourism 5, 6, 8,
trade products 4–5, 7–8, 44
Cumbrian East Indies ventures and sojourns, and
  balancing risk and reward 69, 88–96, 170
  banking and credit 84, 109
  businesses connecting Cumbrian counties, London and the East Indies 40
  contrasting fortunes of Cumbrian men dying in East Indies 139–141
  costs 106–9, 121
  debt 52, 60, 61, 68, 77–83, 94–5, 115, 125, 140–1, 166, 178
  dynastic tendencies 39, 63, 90
  houses and accommodation in India 60, 61, 63, 154–5
  intestate deaths 140
  letter of credit 126
  letters of introduction 126, 127, 174
  local grammar schools, academies and tutors 53, 101–4, 105–6, 167
  networks in India 126, 157
  shaped by provincial preoccupations 19, 167, 170–2
  spatial pattern of enumerated men's origins 37, 38, 65, 175
  venture capital and private trade 35, 47, 97, 100, 108, 109, 110–2, 140
  vocational education for East Indies careers 49, 101, 102, 104–6
Cumbrian iron industry 6, 8–9, 16, 42, 59–60, 61, 165
  Harrison, Ainslie & Co 59, 60
Curwen family
  alliances and East Indies connections 145–6
  appointments and patronage 116-8
  connected to Addison family, 140
  connected to Gale family 40
  Eldred, of Sella Park 140
  'Galloper' incorrectly associated with HEIC 32, 172–3

Helena, mother of Adderton sons in
    HEIC 116–7
Henry, of Workington Hall 40,42,
    82–3, 109, 120, 145
Isabella, mother of Eldred Addison 104
John Christian 42, 126, 146
merchant families, intermarriage with
    40, 140
Patricius of Sella Park, East Indies
    mariner 103, 172
Cust family of Penrith and Carlisle
    Charles, mixed race son of Thomas,
        52, 54, 82, 103
    Charlotte, mixed race daughter of
        Thomas 52, 54
    Elizabeth, mixed race daughter of
        Thomas, 52, 54
    Elizabeth, mother of Thomas, 52–3,
        54, 72, 78–80, 87, 108–9
    extensive correspondence 26
    financial losses and debt 72
    Jane, mixed race daughter of Thomas
        52, 54
    middling family 72
    Richard, brother of Thomas and
        guardian of his children 52,
        53–6, 82
    Richard, mixed race son of Thomas
        52, 82
    Susan, mixed race daughter of
        Thomas 52, 54, 93, 107–8, 184
    tensions around mixed race children
        and their care 53, 54–6, 82,
        107–8
    Thomas, mixed race son of Thomas
        deported to Australia 81–2
Cust, Thomas, Bengal army officer
    agent in Cumbria, Mounseys 103,
        107–8
    agent in India, John Palling, 83
    appointment HEIC cadet 51, 72
    borrows from brother and other
        relatives 53
    borrows from Cumbrians in India 52,
        78, 151
    children sent to England 54
    demands his mother honours his bills
        52–3
    dies at Barrackpore 51, 93
    illegal disposition of property in his
        will 52
    limited provision for his children 52,
        54, 174

    liquidates assets in Cumberland and
        Westmorland 53, 78
    opulent consumption in India 53–4
    relations with Indian women 52, 103

Dalston Hall purchased by East Indiaman
    investor 149
Dalton-in-Furness 37, 71, 156
Deane, Charles, John Robinson's cousin
    116, 119
death and health, comparative risks 83–8,
    90–5
Dent of Crosby Ravensworth and Maulds
    Meaburn, and businesses in
    China, Hong Kong and India
    90, 111, 118
    familial network used in East Indies
        businesses 90
    James of Flass, agent, banking and
        opium 144
    John, steward of Cumberland Society
        164
    kinship and intermarriage with
        Wilkinson family 43, 118
    Lancelot, opium trader, of Skirsgill and
        Flass 150
    local middling families involved in the
        East Indies 37
    London presence 105, 132, 177
    mayors and sheriffs in Cumbrian
        counties 143, 144
    opium dealers 90, 118
    shipping 106, 119
    Thomas 137, 142
    Westmorland identity and presence
        175–6
    Wilkinson 138, 142, 143
    William, managing owner of *Earl of
        Abergavenny* 106, 119, 143
    William the younger, George Millet's
        nominee 115, 144
Denton, Charles died in India
    memorialised at Crosthwaite, Keswick
        134
    mixed race children 228
de Vitre, James Denis 115, 137
Dobinson, Thomas, East Indies mariner
    103
Docker, Joseph, letter of introduction to
    Jardine 127
Dodding family of Conishead 89, 184
Douglas, Joseph, debt and Opium War
    141, 178

Douglas, William tuition for East Indies
     career 104
Drinkel family of Kendal 43, 50, 117, 143,
     157

East India Company (HEIC)
     appointments and patronage 17, 25,
          67, 97, 99, 104, 107, 113–120,
          128–9, 145–6, 173, 177
     commercial monopoly to fiscal military
          state 34, 178
     Court of Directors 17, 47, 84, 99, 136
     Cumbrian chairmen 17, 18, 71, 99,
          114, 125
     Cumbrian directors 18, 71, 89, 99,
          136, 145
     diminished prospects of fortunes 74,
     education and appointments 104
     historiography neglects impact of
          Cumbrian interests 20
     importance of friends 51, 59, 88–90,
          97, 107
     importance of the provincial world
          neglected in historiography 14–9
     inducements to directors 107
     non-Cumbrian directors support
          Cumbrian appointments 114–5,
          116, 118, 183
     population of Europeans in HEIC
          settlements 34
     provincial agents 16
     provincial rates of appointment 35–7,
          65, 175, 180, 182
     provincial sources of goods 16–7
East Indiaman xiv
     behaviour of commanders on board
          84, 97–8
     Bengal 121
     commanders' power and patronage
          118, 146
     Cumbrian commanders 50, 71, 81,
          103, 119, 140, 150
     Duke of Portland 110
     Earl of Abergavenny 106, 112, 119
     Earl of Sandwich 119
     Godolphin 84
     Lynn 118
     Osterley 119 fn113
     purchase of command 106
     Royal George 57
     Scaleby Castle 109
     ships husbands and owners 107, 114,
          118

     slaving 57
     Stormont 118
East Indies returners, and
     acquisition of land and estates 152
     advertisements 164
     agricultural and estate improvement 6,
          165, 170
     agriculture, horticulture, livestock
          societies 60, 65, 165
     aldermen and mayors 143–4, 150,
     banking and money-lending 48, 105,
          126, 135, 143, 151, 156, 165,
          171
     benevolence 132, 148, 161–3, 166
     business enterprises 135, 143, 144, 171
     charitable institutions in Cumbria 163
     county societies 125–6, 163–4
     development of railways 60, 65, 164
     house acquisition, building and
          renovations 25, 48, 50, 60, 61,
          71, 148–156, 161, 162–3, 166,
          170
     industrial and technical innovation 151,
          165, 182
     justice of the peace, magistrates, grand
          juries and assizes 60, 144
     local parliamentary elections and seats
          13, 61, 99, 114, 136, 143–7
     parliamentary seats elsewhere 13–14,
          136
     political threat to dominant elites
          143–7
     sheriffs and lieutenants 60, 65, 144–5
     social profile 39–40
     wealth 50, 135–142
Ecroyd, Richard
     ambitions for East India Company
          appointment 56
     desire for a Quaker wife 56, 58
     educated in England 58
     indigo manufactory 58
     mixed race siblings 57
     posthumous son of ship's surgeon 45,
          56–9, 78
     probably mixed race 57–8, 171
     under care of Richard Barwell, wealthy
          nabob 57
Edmunds, Thomas of Ambleside prepared
     for HEIC 104
emulation thesis and
     consumption, its interpretive limits
          10–11, 77, 148, 153, 155 fn120,
          161, 180–1

explanations of Britain's alleged decline
in industrial innovation 11–2
enumerating Cumbrians in East Indies
ventures
enumerated men 187–221
enumerated women 223-36
method 22–4
natal locations of enumerated men
37–8
network of families sharing East Indies
sojourner kin 40–3
numbers of women and men 22
social characteristics of enumerated
men 39–42
Ewart, David, of Cumberland, Bengal
army 138

Falcon, Michael, Cumberland East Indies
mariner 137
Fallowfield, Jonathan, HEIC surgeon,
Watermillock house 137, 153
Farish, James, of Kendal, writer of
Bombay 43–4, 137
Farrer family and
Henry, East Indiaman commander and
of Scaleby Hall 150
network of Cumbrian middling
families with shared East Indies
sojourners 43–4
Fawcett family of Scaleby Castle and
Bombay 239–43
Cumbrian social elite 76, 88, 164, 181
diverse business interests in the East
Indies 111, 171
Edward Gordon, wealth 137
James, memorial in Bombay cathedral
134
London business presence 132, 177
network of Cumbrian middling
families with shared East Indies
sojourners 43–4, 90
Fawcett, Henry of Scaleby Castle, London
and Bombay
Bombay Council 109
influence and patronage, East India
Company directors 76, 88, 105,
115
member of parliament for Carlisle 20,
146–7
modernises Scaleby Castle 150
shipping interests 48, 109
son-in-law of John Bellasis 126
Fetherstonhaugh of Kirkoswald 41, 144

financial capital 2, 35, 112, 138, 166, 167,
173, 174
Fleming (le) family of Rydal 40–44
George Cumberland Hughes 137
kin to gentry and middling families 75,
116
Lady Anne Frederica 64
Lady Diana 64
Sir Daniel 40, 69–70, 95, 111
Sir George, son of Sir Daniel, Bishop
of Carlisle 69, 102, 111, 127
Sir Michael 117, 165
Sir William 171
Fletcher, Henry of Clea Hall
advantaged by the expansion of global
trade 111
anti-Lowther alliance with Curwens
145–6
appointments of local gentry sons to
East Indiaman 118–9, 143, 146
East Indiaman commander 50, 71, 121
HEIC chairman and director 17, 99,
176
London residence and Cumbrian
attachment 176
member, Cumberland Society 125–6,
164
Member of Parliament for
Cumberland 145
opposition to Lowther interests 145, 146
recipient and dispenser of patronage
113, 118–9, 143, 146, 176
Fletcher, Isaac of Underwood,
Cumberland exporting to
American colonies 5
French, Patrick Theodore 138
friends
Bourdieu's definition, association with
social capital 112
credit and venture capital 52, 78, 80,
81, 97, 99, 113, 166
Cumbrian and non-Cumbrian HEIC
directors 114–116
Cumbrian networks, care and
hospitality 96, 107, 112, 174,
175, 176, 177
East Indies friends 126–128
embedded in place 166, 173
friendlessness 184
importance in the eighteenth century
73, 78, 80, 85, 88–90, 186
influencing HEIC careers 51, 59, 80,
97, 99, 112–3, 169

logics of East Indiamen ship-owners
and shareholders 106
London friends 120–6
Furness 6–7, 42, 60, 186,

Gaitskell, James Gandy, son, Elizabeth
Gandy, Kendal 138
Gale family, merchants of Whitehaven
245–7
Ann, wife of East Indiaman
commander, John Wordsworth
184
Gustavus, leaves family dependent on
Senhouses 127
John, supports John Wordsworth's
career, 119
marital alliances with gentry families 40
pervasive networks with families
involved in the East Indies 43–4
Thomas, 1st mate of the East
Indiaman, *Osterley* 119
trading North America, London, St
Petersburg 40
William, son of Gustavus, East Indies
free mariner 75
Gale, Humphrey Senhouse, son of
Gustavus
anxieties expressed, to his great aunt
Kitty Senhouse 113, 127–8
bequest to his 'girl', Chindanah 139
debts 80–1, 125
dies in India 139
letters of introduction 127
nominated by non-Cumbrian director
Joseph Cotton 114–5
recipient of Joseph Huddart's
friendship 122
seeking to relieve relatives of his
dependence 139
wealth at death in India 139–40
Gale-Braddyll, Wilson of Conishead
Priory, 156
'garden houses' in India 154–5
Gilpin family of Carlisle and Scaleby
financial problems and debt 82,
149–50
Richard, sells Eccleriggs estate for
India career 82, 107
William, distinguished Cumbrian
master of Cheam School 101–2
Gilcrux 38, 128
Graham, James of Carlisle Writer and
merchant Calcutta 90

agricultural and estate improvement
152
established Carlisle New Bank 165
house renovations 152
portrait by Zoffany 156
private money-lender to Cumbrians in
Calcutta 53, 78
Rickerby estate and Barrock Lodge 41,
144, 151–2
socially ambitious son of a Carlisle
surgeon 151–2, 164
Hall, Humphrey of Gilcrux, HEIC
Madras army, 128
Hasell, John of gentry family seated at
Dalemain
alcoholism and repudiation by family
81, 83, 111
death in Bombay 124
East India Company appointment,
dismissal and reinstatement 110,
145
educated at Appleby Grammar School
103
family's East Indies connections 41,
43, 153
friendship with John Bellasis 123–4
portrait by Zoffany 156
private trade 110, 111
Heward, Sir Simon, army surgeon in
Madras presidency
gift to Carlisle museum 131
house in Carlisle for two mixed race
daughters 153
mixed race daughters and litigation
over will 171
historiography and method
'archival traces' 19–20, 22, 24–5, 27,
28
biography and the 'biographical turn'
20, 21–2, 24, 27–8, 45, 186
Cumbria, window on cross-cutting
historiographies 3, 28–9, 179–86
Cumbria's regional history 4–9, 20,
169–70, 172–5, 176–7
East India Company (HEIC), British
India and imperialism 14–19,
20, 38, 104, 169–70, 175–9
kin nodes and kinship 42–44, 170,
180–1
letters and their interpretations 26–7
method and the impacts of digitisation
20–2, 29
middling ranks and the gentry, mobility,

sociability and consumption
9–12, 148, 155
'piecing together', Clare Anderson's
method in *Subaltern Lives* 19,
21–2, 27
place attachment 24, 131, 170
problems in establishing wealth and
its attribution to the East Indies
135–6
provincial towns, life and attachments
12–14, 172–9, 185
memorials as an evidential source 20,
25, 134–5
tracing individuals in global spaces
21–2
Hodgson, James Denis of Strand Carlisle
apprenticed to London oilman
prior to HEIC 105
Hodgson, Richard of Moorhouse Hall,
Carlisle 153,
Hodgson, Richard, mercer and alderman
of Carlisle, and
George, son, Bengal revenue
department 143–4
James, son, alderman of Carlisle,
Bengal army 144
Sir Richard, second son, brewer mayor
of Carlisle 143
Holme, Catherine of Holme Hill, Dalston
49–52, 249–251
children painted by Zoffany 156
husband's wealth and allegations of
corruption 49–50
irritates Robert Clive 49
loses child 49
marries William Brightwell Sumner
49, 71
memorial at East Clandon 133
resides and dies at Hatchlands, Surrey
50
Holme family of Holme Hill, Dalston
249–251
John, brother of Catherine, dies in
Calcutta 49, 103–4, 134
John, father of Catherine, Mayor's
Court registrar, Calcutta 49, 71,
107
Musgraves, Morlands and Hiltons 51
probably assisted Thomas Cust 52
Holme Hill, Dalston purchased by East
Indies returner 149
How, Peter, merchant, financial collapse
5, 8

Howard, Charles, of Greystoke 171
Huddart, Joseph of Allonby and
Greenwich
advises on Humphrey Senhouse Gale
India debt 77, 80–1
cordage manufacturing company,
Limehouse 115
director of the East India Dock
Company 115
East Indiaman commander and
interests 80–81, 132–3
education 103
Elder Brothers of Trinity 115
friendship, Humphrey Senhouse Gale
122, 125
friendship, with gentry Senhouse family
80–1, 125
influence with HEIC directors 114–5,
Hudleston, Andrew Fleming 62–5
active interest in Cumbria while in
India 64–5
advises Anna Frederica le Fleming
against evicting William
Wordsworth from Rydal Mount
64
and Lady Diana le Fleming's (nee
Howard) will 64
appointment and career in Madras
presidency 62–63
assistance in India from family and
friends 126
assists in the planning of the new
church at Rydal 64
benevolence and sociability 65, 163
extensive correspondence to mother
and aunt 26
female relatives help fund travel to
India 62–3, 108, 122
financial ambitions and prudence 63–4,
79
health and India 86, 87, 91, 92, 93
Hutton John 41, 64, 149
inherits Rydal 64
preparing to travel to India 121, 122–3,
124
saw transformation of HEIC from
trade to rule 45
supports Duke of Norfolk interest 64
supports Henry Brougham 64
wealth 137
Hudleston family of Hutton John
Andrew, father of Andrew Fleming,
London lawyer 41

Elizabeth (nee Fleming of Rydal)
    mother of Andrew Fleming 40
financial difficulties over successive
    generations 76
Isabella of Whitehaven, aunt, avid
    correspondent with Andrew
    Fleming 63, 64, 76, 91–4,
    100–1, 183
Josiah Andrew, son of John 137
networked with gentry and middling
    Cumbrian families with East
    Indies involvement 43–4, 231–8
Robert Burland, son of John 137
William, son of John 93
Hudleston, John, descended from Hutton
    John branch 142
appointment as writer 113, 136
business interests in Whitehaven 133
East Indies wealth 136
HEIC director 89, 113, 136
member of parliament 136
patronage and assistance to Cumbrians
    63, 113, 122, 136
residence in Windsor 133
tendencies to Anglo-Indian dynastic
    family 63
human capital 2, 173, 179, 180, 182

identity, importance of provincial
    imperatives in East Indies
    ventures 1–2, 13–4,
Irton family of Irton Hall 41, 43–4,
Irwin family of Justice Town 41

Jacobite and non-juror loyalties not a
    driver of Cumbrian East Indies
    involvement 32, 172–3
Jacobite rebellions, impact on the
    Cumbrian counties 6, 173
Johnson, John of Whitehaven, nabob and
    appointment 149
builds Castlesteads near Carlisle 149
Cumbrian network in Calcutta 50
mixed race son appointed to HEIC
    206
son, William Ponsonby of Walton
    House 42, 145–6

Kendal and its
East Indies connected elite families 37,
    43, 51, 57, 59, 143
East Indies sojourners 50, 71, 116, 134,
    143, 152, 157

eighteenth century urban development
    6
ivory comb manufacture 165
mayors with East Indies connections
    143
non-conformist elite 56–7
population increase 7
schools and vocational education 102,
    104
Websters, architects and builders 152,
    154
Kirkby Lonsdale 23, 147, 152, 161–3
Knott family, statesman family
dominates the charcoal-based iron
    industry 42, 59, 165
East Indies wealth and the iron
    industry 165
John, secretary to Henry Verelst at
    Calcutta 42, 50, 156
marriage into gentry Fleming family of
    Rydal 40
Michael, steward of Rydal and
    ironmaster 40
Susannah Knott, wife of John, supports
    Andrew Fleming Hudleston's
    sojourn to India 62–3, 108, 122,
    183
upward social mobility 41
Knott, George
batta mutiny 109
connected to Ainslies by marriage and
    in business 59
connected to the Hudlestons of Hutton
    John 62, 64
cousin and brother-in-law to John
    Knott of Calcutta 50
East Indies wealth and emergence of
    'Lake Villas' 153
HEIC army career advanced by
    Cumbrian networks 85, 126
ironmaster and owner of George Knott
    & Co. 59
Monk Coniston 153
survived India but early death in
    Cumbria 133

'Lake Villas' 153–154
compared to 'Garden Houses' in India
    154–155
Langhorne, Joshua of Bampton 103
Law family of Cartmel, Greystoke and
    Carlisle
Edmund, Bishop of Carlisle 115

Ewan, son of Edmund and Mary,
      Bengal writer 50
Joanna, daughter of Edmund and
      Mary, marries nabob Thomas
      Rumbold 115
Mary (nee Christian) of Ewanrigg Hall
      50
Romney portrait of Edmund Law
      commissioned by Thomas
      Rumbold 157
libraries of sojourners in India and on
      return 156
London
   Cumbrian presence 105,120–6, 132,
      133–4, 176–7
   dominant city in the British Isles 12–3,
      14–5
   HEIC clerks in London 15
   over-emphasis on London interests
      in the HEIC 14-15, 168–9,
      176–177
London Lead Company 6, 17
Losh family East Indies connections 42,
      82, 137, 163
Lowthers, ambitious family, ennobled as
      Lonsdale 4, 8, 81, 99, 125, 133,
      143, 166
   James, significant money lender in
      Cumbria 31, 47, 116, 145–7,
      165, 171
   James, 'Wicked Jimmy' 13–4, 59
   Robert 137
   William, Lord Lonsdale 59, 111, 116,
      147–8
Lushington, James Law
   chain of patronage 116
   descended from Christian and
      Senhouse families 147
   HEIC director and chairman 113–4
   typified as 'Indian juggler' in election
      for Carlisle seat 147
   wealth 137
Lutwidge middling family 8, 41, 144

Mackreth, Robert, Westmerian, London
      bookmaker 115
   connections to East Indies interests
      115–6
Maulds Meaburn 37, 150
memorials and gravestones 20, 25, 45, 46,
      48, 88, 116, 132, 133–5, 141,
      157, 166, 174
middling ranks and gentry 9–12

business alliances between 8–9, 29,
      180–1
culture of benevolence, gentility,
      politeness, respectability,
      sociability 11, 26, 42, 51, 56, 57,
      65, 69, 75–83, 124, 125, 132,
      148, 157, 161–2, 164, 166, 181
distinction, emulation and rank
      endogamy 2, 11, 44, 77, 98,
      160–1, 162, 180–1
intermarriage of middling and gentry
      families 41, 181
mobilising networks for East Indies
      sojourns 97, 129, 173
shared experiences 44, 90, 95–6,
      100–106, 108, 179
Milbourn family of Armathwaite Castle
      41, 164
mixed race children 23, 45, 52, 54–5, 58,
      82, 87, 153, 171, 184, 227–9
Monk Coniston estate, villa 153
Moorhouse Hall, Carlisle, taken by
      returner Richard Hodgson 153
Moorhouse, Jonathan
   bequest to native woman 141
   Mysore burial, memorialised Clifton,
      Westmorland 134
   wealth 140–1
Morland family of Capplethwaite Hall
      50–1
Mounsey, ambitious middling family in
      Cumbria, London
   agents for Thomas Cust 52–3
   and East Indies 52, 53–8, 78, 164
   and Thomas Cust's children 54, 55,
      103, 106, 107–8
   George Stephenson, HEIC Bengal
      army 78
   moneylending 78
Musgrave family, Catholic gentry family
      40, 51, 81, 83, 111, 119, 149,
      153, 173

nation-building and imperialism 177–179
Forging the Nation challenged 168–9
natives of the East Indies buried in
      Cumbrian counties 3
Nevinson, Charles, Cumbrian apothecary
      Westminster 78–9
Nowell, Alexander, of Kirkby Lonsdale
   art collection 155
   East Indies career, army and indigo
      planter 147

elected to Westmorland as an
independent 147–8
emulation of aristocratic practices
162–3, 181
horse breeding and stud at Underley 165
pretentions and assertion of elite public
persona 161–3
Underley estate, extravagant building
and property 152

Parkin, Hugh
acts as referee for schoolmaster in
Martindale 164
annuity to wife 142
appointment to East Indiaman
promoted by kinsman John
Robinson 117
appointed to grand juries for assizes
144
benevolence as landlord 163
James, father, repeatedly mayor of
Appleby
promotes agricultural improvement 165
purchases Skirsgill from the Whelpdales
and rebuilds 150
share in East Indiaman *Earl of
Abergavenny* 106
son, William Hugh, mayor of Appleby
143
widow's personal wealth 142
Pattensons of Melmerby Hall 39, 41, 43
Pattinson family of Kirklinton
East Indies aspirations, fears for son
Thomas 73–4, 88–9, 91
costs of Thomas' fit out and travel to
Bombay 109
parental concerns about respectable
behaviour 76, 124
Thomas, death at Corry Guam 88
Thomas' letters of introduction 126
Pearson (Pierson), Thomas 50, 149, 156,
157, 160, 184
Pennington of Kendal 43–4
James, Bengal army, memorialised in
Kendal 134
James Masterson, mixed race son of
James, 137
Penrith
enumerated men 37
Penrith Horticultural Society 165
population 7
townhouse of John Wordsworth 153, 164
tuition and schools 102, 164

provincial life and its historiography
12–14, 185–6

opium 3, 73, 110, 111, 118, 141, 142, 143,
144, 150, 178

Quakers and global reach 5, 17, 56, 58,
90, 176

regattas, Keswick 48, 75, 165
Reynolds, Joshua, portraits for Wilson
Gale-Braddyll 156
Richardson, William, London-based
Cumbrian with East Indies
interests 151–2
Rickerby 42, 151–2,
Rigg family of Crosby Ravensworth and
Java 37, 111, 118, 137
Ritson, Edward prepared for an HEIC
career 104
Robinson, John of Appleby, secretary to
the Treasury
builds the White House, Appleby 152
Cumbrian attachments neglected
in East India Company
historiography 20
estate proximate to London 132
falling out with Lowther 13–14, 147
parliamentary career 13–14, 176
patronage and influence on HEIC
appointments 116, 117 118, 119,
150
Robinson, John of Kirkby Thore, Bombay
business 117
Robson, Robert, East Indies mariner 103
Romney, George, portraits 156–60
Romney, James of Dalton-in-Furness 37
Routledge, Cumbrian returners,
Cheapside 109, 132, 177
Royal Oak Hotel, Keswick
built by Edward Stephenson 47, 165
landlady's East Indies aspirations for
son 75
Rumbold, Thomas, notorious nabob
connected to Cumbrian counties
families 114–5, 116, 152, 157,
184

Salkeld, Joseph Carleton of Cumberland,
Bengal army 138
Salkeld, Thomas HEIC returner to
Holme Hill and Carlisle 144,
153, 163

Senhouse, gentry family of Cumberland, and
  attempts to diversify sources of income 5
  education 102, 103
  family networks with gentry and middling families involved in the East Indies 41, 43, 114
  Henry Fletcher, East Indiaman command 118–9, 143, 145
  Joseph Ashley 137
  Joseph, East Indiaman and later West Indies career 118–9, 121–2, 124, 144, 146
  orphaned Gale nephews in India 75, 77, 80, 81, 113, 127–8
Sharpe, Anthony, seeks loan for East Indies fitting out 109
Simonds, Williams of Cumberland, Bengal army 137
social capital 2, 29, 97–9, 112, 125, 129, 138, 166, 167, 173
Sowerby, John, investor in East Indiamen
  business and residence in London 132
  friendship with non-Cumbrian HEIC director 115
  influences nephew's appointment to HEIC 115
  insurer 215
  purchases Dalston Hall 149
  wealth 149
Spedding of Mirehouse 41, 164
Stables, John, Westmerian HEIC director
  appointment as director 114
  part of Cumbrian network in Calcutta 50
  patronage from John Robinson 116
  portraits by Romney 157, 158, 159
Stanley family of Ponsonby Hall 40, 41, 43–4, 89, 102
Steel, James of Carlisle, Bengal army 137, 163
Stephenson family, merchants and bankers 239–43
  connections to the Drinkels of Kendal 117, 143
  extensive and early East Indies ventures 32, 71, 89, 111
  familial and trade networks 43, 47, 71, 104
  John, HEIC director 114, 132, 142
  leveraged business through Indian wealth 111

London used as a way-station to India 105, 132
  political opposition to Lowther 146
  Rowland, recipient of East Indies wealth 48, 117, 146, 150, 157, 165
Scaleby Castle 149–50
Stephenson, Edward, of Keswick 45–8
  1714 delegation to Delhi 33, 45
  acquisition of property 47
  among aristocrats, William Bellers engravings 171
  appointed to the Bengal Council 47
  buried before the alter of Crosthwaite Parish Church 46
  encouraged middling families' East Indies ambitions 75
  governor of Bengal 47
  'Governor's House' Keswick 48, 146
  Howrahs, fields outside Keswick 48
  money-lender in Cumbria 31, 149–50, 164–5
  private trade and merchant networks 47
  sheriff of Cumberland 144
  social mobility 171
  threat to Lowther interests 48, 145
  wealth 48, 142
Sumner, William Brightwell, husband of Catherine Holme 49, 50, 51
Symons, William 137
Symson, Joseph of Kendal 5, 143

Taylor, John of Newby Bridge and Abbott Hall
  and Abbott Hall, Kendal 114, 143, 152
  and Cumbrian East Indies families and Kendal middling elites 143
  appointed as HEIC surgeon 90
  Dorothy, daughter, marries into Clerk family 114
  dynastic tendency 39, 90
  East Indies venture prompted by father's debts 71
  John Bladen, son of John, HEIC director 113
  marries Dorothy Rumbold, sister of governor of Madras 71, 115, 152
  retrieves Landing estate lost by his father 151
  Thomas Rumbold, son of John, East Indiaman commander 140, 143
  wealth 151–2

Teasdale, John and 'Garden House',
    Dinapore 154–5
The Friary, Appleby 144, 152
Tullie family of Carlisle
    early involvement in the East Indies
        103
    George, registrar of Calcutta Mayor's
        Court 71
    Philip, member of the Madras Council
        71
    succession of sheriffs in Cumberland
        144
    Timothy, HEIC 71

Varty, William, of Hawkshead 140
Verelst, Henry 50, 85, 126, 156–7

Wake, Charles Hamilton of Cumberland,
    Bengal army 137
Warwick family of Warwick Hall 42, 163
    Francis, Bombay army 137
Watts family of Hawkesdale Hall 137, 138
Whelpdale (de) family of Skirsgill 150
    John, HEIC army 144, 164
White, William, Bombay attorney, and
    Keswick 75, 153
Whitehaven
    charities with East Indies connections
        163
    East Indies sojourners 37, 45, 50, 64,
        75, 85, 97, 116, 133, 149
    global presence and port 7–8
    Lowther influence 81, 116, 165
    merchants 8, 40, 44, 45, 75, 119
    population 8
    schools and academies educating for
        the East Indies 102–3
White House, Appleby 152
Wilkinson of Flass
    East Indies wealth 111
    familial networks for East Indies
        business 90, 118
    James 144, 163–4
    marriage and business networks with
        Dents 175, 176
    opium trade 118
    Robert 138
    Thomas 137
    William 137, 143, 144
Wilson, Edward, seeks support to the East
    Indies 117
Wilson family of Conishead and Bardsea
    Hall

Christopher 32, 94, 135, 148, 156
Sarah (nee Dodding) wife of
    Christopher 71, 135
Wilson family of Kendal
    Christopher, hosier and mayor of
        Kendal 135
    William, Madras writer 135–6, 138,
        142
Winder family of Lorton 239–43
    extensive and early East Indies ventures
        32–3, 45–6, 89, 110, 111
    familial and trade networks 43, 104,
        171, 177
    Jonathan, brother-in-law of Edward
        Stephenson 32–3, 45–6, 133–4
    London presence 105, 132, 133–4
    memorial in All Hallows, Barking-by-
        the-Tower 133–4
    other global trade ventures 47, 71, 90,
        171, 177
    re-amalgamating 'new' and 'old' East
        India companies 32–3
    Samuel, sends domestic goods to India
        110, 133–4
women, Cumbrians 224-6
    advice to sojourners 68
    challenges in tracing and
        understanding women
        sojourning in the East Indies
        183
    charitable involvement in Cumbrian
        counties 163
    exclusions from enumeration 23
    financial support of East Indies
        ventures 68
    implication in East Indies ventures 68,
        184
    literacy and education 100–1
    marriage to Cumbrian and other East
        Indies sojourners 74 166, 184
    nabobina xiv, 48–9, 50, 68
    number sojourning in the East Indies
        183
    returning from the East Indies 132
    sustaining connections between home
        and East Indies sojourners
        183–4
women, native to the East Indies 23–4,
    52, 57,
Wordsworth, John senior, East Indiaman
    commander
    built sumptuous Penrith townhouse
        153

career supported by Charles Deane,
John Robinson, William Dent
and Gale family 119
East Indiaman investor 123
grand jury member 144
HEIC director 113
patronage dispensed to Cumbrians
106, 150
sixteenth share in the *Earl of Abergavenny*
106
Wordsworth, John of Cockermouth,
brother of the poet
appointed 4th mate of the *Osterley* 108
appoints cousin, Joseph, as mate of
Earl of Abergavenny 119
cost of fitting out 108
desire to support family through East
Indies venture 73
drowned with loss of his first command,
Earl of Abergavenny 112
East Indiaman command supported by
cousin John, Hugh Parkin and
William Dent 106

East Indies as a means to personal
wealth 73
educated at Hawkshead 103, 105
losses from private trade 73
private trade, including opium 110–1
venture capital from family 111–2
Workington 7, 37, 82, 104, 172

Yates, John Orfeur
appointment to East Indiaman 83–4,
119
builds Skirwith Abbey 42, 71, 84,
148–9, 151
East Indies career to rebuild family
fortunes 72–3, 151
East Indies wealth and financial
difficulties 71, 84
intermarriage with Aglionby family 83
resides in Hutton Hall 41
with other Cumbrians in Calcutta 50

Zoffany, John, painter of Cumbrian
nabobs, 49, 153

WORLDS OF THE EAST INDIA COMPANY

The Richest East India Merchant: The Life and Business of John Palmer of Calcutta, 1767–1836, Anthony Webster

The Great Uprising in India, 1857–58: Untold Stories, Indian and British, Rosie Llewellyn-Jones

The Twilight of the East India Company: The Evolution of Anglo-Asian Commerce and Politics, 1790–1860, Anthony Webster

Scottish Orientalists and India: The Muir Brothers, Religion, Education and Empire, Avril A. Powell

The East India Company's London Workers: Management of the Warehouse Labourers, 1800–1858, Margaret Makepeace

The East India Company's Maritime Service, 1746–1834: Masters of the Eastern Seas, Jean Sutton

The East India Company and Religion, 1698–1858, Penelope Carson

British Naval Power in the East, 1794–1805: The Command of Admiral Peter Rainier, Peter A. Ward

The Emergence of British Power in India, 1600–1784: A Grand Strategic Interpretation, G. J. Bryant

Naval Resistance to Britain's Growing Power in India, 1660–1800: The Saffron Banner and the Tiger of Mysore, Philip MacDougall

Trade and Empire in Early Nineteenth-Century Southeast Asia: Gillian Maclaine and his Business Network, G. Roger Knight

Lascars and Indian Ocean Seafaring, 1780–1860: Shipboard Life, Unrest and Mutiny, Aaron Jaffer

Defending British India against Napoleon: The Foreign Policy of Governor-General Lord Minto, 1807–13, Amita Das, edited and updated by Aditya Das